Mastering

MAXScript and the SDK for 3D Studio MAX

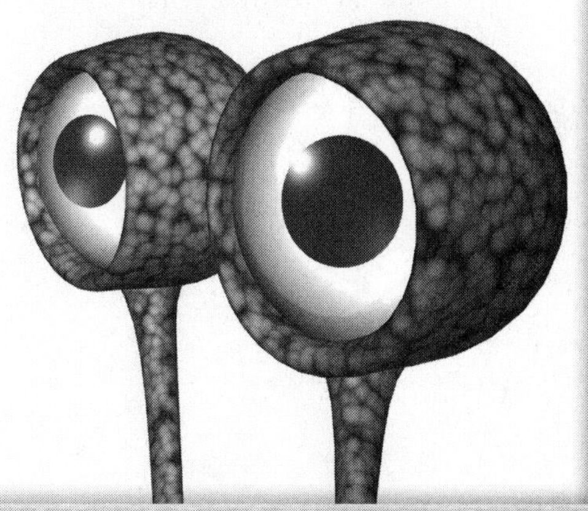

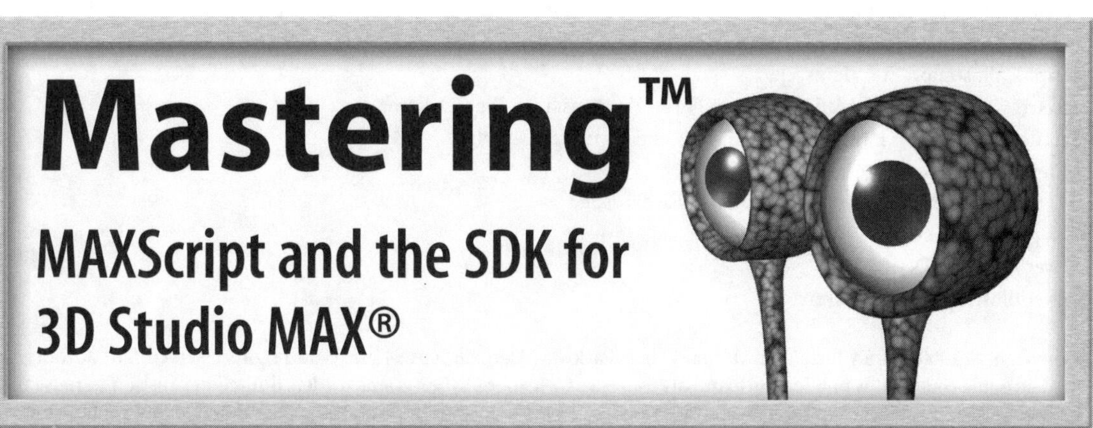

Mastering™ MAXScript and the SDK for 3D Studio MAX®

Alexander Bicalho

Simon Feltman

San Francisco • Paris • Düsseldorf • Soest • London

Associate Publisher: Cheryl Applewood
Contracts and Licensing Manager: Kristine O'Callaghan
Acquisitions & Developmental Editor: Mariann Barsolo
Editors: Raquel Baker, Pete Gaughan, Jim Gabbert
Production Editor: Dennis Fitzgerald
Technical Editor: Scott Onstott
Book Designer: Maureen Forys, Happenstance Type-O-Rama
Graphic Illustrator: Eric Houts, epic
Electronic Publishing Specialist: Maureen Forys, Happenstance Type-O-Rama
Proofreaders: Dennis Fitzgerald, Nathan Whiteside, Jennifer Campbell
Indexer: Ted Laux
CD Coordinators: Kara Eve Schwartz, Ceola Richardson
CD Technician: Keith McNeil
Cover Designer: Design Site
Cover Illustrator: Jack D. Myers

Copyright © 2000 SYBEX Inc., 1151 Marina Village Parkway, Alameda, CA 94501. World rights reserved. The authors created reusable code in this publication expressly for reuse by readers. Sybex grants readers limited permission to reuse the code found in this publication or its accompanying CD-ROM so long as the authors are attributed in any application containing the reusable code and the code itself is never distributed, posted online by electronic transmission, sold, or commercially exploited as a stand-alone product. Aside from this specific exception concerning reusable code, no part of this publication may be stored in a retrieval system, transmitted, or reproduced in any way, including but not limited to photocopy, photograph, magnetic, or other record, without the prior agreement and written permission of the publisher.

Library of Congress Card Number: 00-106118

ISBN: 0-7821-2794-0

SYBEX and the SYBEX logo are trademarks of SYBEX Inc. in the USA and other countries.

Mastering is a trademark of SYBEX Inc.

Screen reproductions produced with Collage Complete.

Collage Complete is a trademark of Inner Media Inc.

The CD interface was created using Macromedia Director, Copyright © 1994, 1997-1999 Macromedia Inc. For more information on Macromedia and Macromedia Director, visit http://www.macromedia.com.

TRADEMARKS: SYBEX has attempted throughout this book to distinguish proprietary trademarks from descriptive terms by following the capitalization style used by the manufacturer.

The author and publisher have made their best efforts to prepare this book, and the content is based upon final release software whenever possible. Portions of the manuscript may be based upon pre-release versions supplied by software manufacturer(s). The author and the publisher make no representation or warranties of any kind with regard to the completeness or accuracy of the contents herein and accept no liability of any kind, including but not limited to performance, merchantability, fitness for any particular purpose, or any losses or damages of any kind caused or alleged to be caused directly or indirectly from this book.

Manufactured in the United States of America

10 9 8 7 6 5 4 3 2 1

Software License Agreement

Terms and Conditions

The media and/or any online materials accompanying this book that are available now or in the future contain programs and/or text files (the "Software") to be used in connection with the book. SYBEX hereby grants to you a license to use the Software, subject to the terms that follow. Your purchase, acceptance, or use of the Software will constitute your acceptance of such terms.

The Software compilation is the property of SYBEX unless otherwise indicated and is protected by copyright to SYBEX or other copyright owner(s) as indicated in the media files (the "Owner(s)"). You are hereby granted a single-user license to use the Software for your personal, noncommercial use only. You may not reproduce, sell, distribute, publish, circulate, or commercially exploit the Software, or any portion thereof, without the written consent of SYBEX and the specific copyright owner(s) of any component software included on this media.

In the event that the Software or components include specific license requirements or end-user agreements, statements of condition, disclaimers, limitations or warranties ("End-User License"), those End-User Licenses supersede the terms and conditions herein as to that particular Software component. Your purchase, acceptance, or use of the Software will constitute your acceptance of such End-User Licenses.

By purchase, use or acceptance of the Software you further agree to comply with all export laws and regulations of the United States as such laws and regulations may exist from time to time.

Reusable Code in This Book

The authors created reusable code in this publication expressly for reuse for readers. Sybex grants readers permission to reuse for any purpose the code found in this publication or its accompanying CD-ROM so long as the authors are attributed in any application containing the reusable code, and the code itself is never sold or commercially exploited as a stand-alone product.

Software Support

Components of the supplemental Software and any offers associated with them may be supported by the specific Owner(s) of that material but they are not supported by SYBEX. Information regarding any available support may be obtained from the Owner(s) using the information provided in the appropriate read.me files or listed elsewhere on the media.

Should the manufacturer(s) or other Owner(s) cease to offer support or decline to honor any offer, SYBEX bears no responsibility. This notice concerning support for the Software is provided for your information only. SYBEX is not the agent or principal of the Owner(s), and SYBEX is in no way responsible for providing any support for the Software, nor is it liable or responsible for any support provided, or not provided, by the Owner(s).

Warranty

SYBEX warrants the enclosed media to be free of physical defects for a period of ninety (90) days after purchase. The Software is not available from SYBEX in any other form or media than that enclosed herein or posted to www.sybex.com. If you discover a defect in the media during this warranty period, you may obtain a replacement of identical format at no charge by sending the defective media, postage prepaid, with proof of purchase to:

SYBEX Inc.
Customer Service Department
1151 Marina Village Parkway
Alameda, CA 94501
(510) 523-8233
Fax: (510) 523-2373
e-mail: info@sybex.com
WEB: HTTP://WWW.SYBEX.COM

After the 90-day period, you can obtain replacement media of identical format by sending us the defective disk, proof of purchase, and a check or money order for $10, payable to SYBEX.

Disclaimer

SYBEX makes no warranty or representation, either expressed or implied, with respect to the Software or its contents, quality, performance, merchantability, or fitness for a particular purpose. In no event will SYBEX, its distributors, or dealers be liable to you or any other party for direct, indirect, special, incidental, consequential, or other damages arising out of the use of or inability to use the Software or its contents even if advised of the possibility of such damage. In the event that the Software includes an online update feature, SYBEX further disclaims any obligation to provide this feature for any specific duration other than the initial posting.

The exclusion of implied warranties is not permitted by some states. Therefore, the above exclusion may not apply to you. This warranty provides you with specific legal rights; there may be other rights that you may have that vary from state to state. The pricing of the book with the Software by SYBEX reflects the allocation of risk and limitations on liability contained in this agreement of Terms and Conditions.

Shareware Distribution

This Software may contain various programs that are distributed as shareware. Copyright laws apply to both shareware and ordinary commercial software, and the copyright Owner(s) retains all rights. If you try a shareware program and continue using it, you are expected to register it. Individual programs differ on details of trial periods, registration, and payment. Please observe the requirements stated in appropriate files.

Copy Protection

The Software in whole or in part may or may not be copy-protected or encrypted. However, in all cases, reselling or redistributing these files without authorization is expressly forbidden except as specifically provided for by the Owner(s) therein.

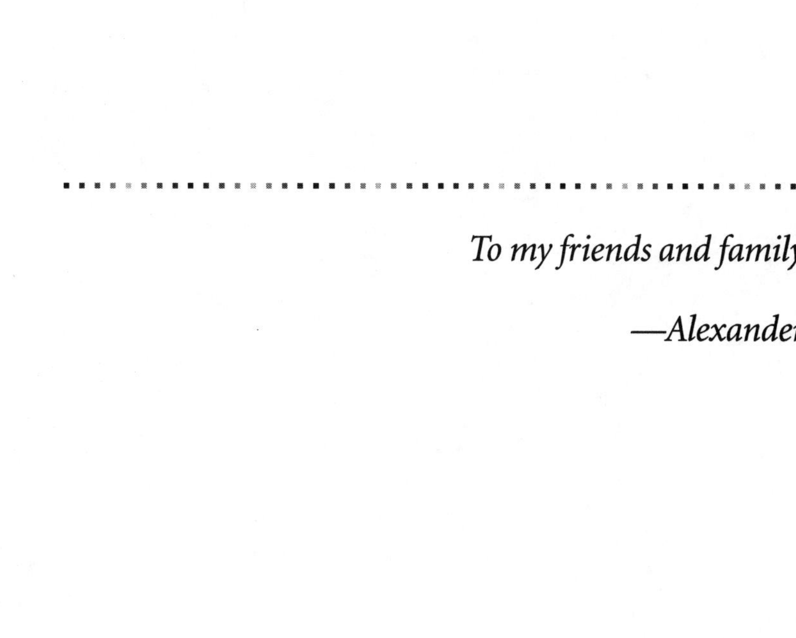

To my friends and family

—Alexander

Acknowledgments

I would like to thank Borislav Petrov and Larry Minton for all their support in helping me with my MAXScript doubts. They're my real teachers. I would also like to thank all the Sybex team: Mariann, Cheryl, Raquel, Dennis, Kara, and Dan for their help and effort. And also a great thanks for Scott's technical review. Without them, this book would be nothing more than a pile of words and images. They are the ones who shaped it and made it reality.

Special thanks to Simon Feltman who accepted and embraced this book's idea. Thanks also for the great sample plug-ins for the CD-ROM. They are really helpful.

Thanks for the folks at Discreet. MAX would not exist without you. Thanks to John Wainwright, Ravi Karra, Simon Feltman, and Larry Minton for MAXScript. Thanks to all the folks at Discreet Learning and Training and to all the Discreet Training Specialists. It's amazing how much one can learn from and share with these folks.

Thanks for all the developers who supplied plug-ins or scripts for the CD-ROM: Neil Blevins, Chris Dragon, David Humpherys, Larry Minton, Fred Moreau, François Mourlevat, Borislav Petrov, Fred Ruff, and John Wainwright. The MAX community would not be the same without your valuable help.

This book would not have been published if it weren't for Chris Murray. If he hadn't invited me to write *Mastering 3D Studio MAX R3* (Sybex, 2000) with him, Alex Monteiro, and Catalina Woods, I wouldn't have the opportunity to write this one.

Thanks to my family, my friends, and my girlfriend for all their love, support, and patience.

—Alexander

Thanks to all the programmers and artists that have inspired me throughout my career.

Special thanks to Alexander Bicalho for giving me the opportunity to write this book.

—Simon

Contents at a Glance

Contents

Introduction

This book is the result of several months of work and struggle. Its idea was born after we finished *Mastering 3D Studio MAX R3* (Sybex, 2000). The primary idea was to write a book exclusively on MAXScript. Then, a question emerged: Why not write about MAXScript *and* the SDK? So we did; we went a step further in MAXScript and wrote a whole part on MAX's SDK.

3D Studio MAX is written totally in C++ and is entirely based in modules or plug-ins that can be added to its core, thereby enhancing its feature set. The Software Development Kit, or SDK, offers a series of examples, as well as information, that allows developers to write their own plug-ins.

On the other hand, since MAX 2.0, MAX featured a new entry-level programming language: MAXScript. MAXScript is a simple programming language aimed at users who don't have any previous programming knowledge. It integrates seamlessly into MAX, allowing you to create your own user interface that will manipulate your MAX scene, as well as create, modify, and animate any parameter.

MAXScript also offers you the capability to manipulate file assets and manage MAX files, external files, and bitmaps. MAXScript became very popular and gained momentum in MAX R3, which implemented a Macro Recorder and even allows the user to create plug-ins.

Who Should Read This Book

This book is not designed for the beginning user but, instead, for the intermediate or advanced user who wants to move one step ahead into programming in MAX.

You will find two levels of programming: an entry-level programming language that is easy to learn and implement in MAXScript, and a more complex and comprehensive language, which is implemented by the SDK using Visual C++.

What's Covered in This Book

This book is divided in two parts. The first part covers MAXScript, and the second part covers the SDK. Both parts were written based on 3D Studio MAX R3, but since MAX carries a lot of compatibility, you will also be able to use this book in previous and future versions of MAX.

Part I: Mastering MAXScript

There's no prerequisite for reading the MAXScript part, except a good knowledge of MAX, creativity, and dedication. We do not explain the MAX features, but if you need any help learning MAX, a good starting point is the previously mentioned *Mastering 3D Studio MAX R3* (Sybex, 2000). Another suggestion is to run all tutorials that come with the software and also to read the literature available for MAX.

Chapter 1 gives you a nice introduction to MAXScript. It has a series of tutorials that teach you how to build simple scripts and how to create a user interface.

Chapter 2 introduces the Macro Recorder, as well as how to work with materials, maps, and material libraries. You will also learn how to work with functions to optimize your scripts.

Chapter 3 teaches you how to work with modifiers, transformations, and sub-objects. It also shows you how to work with editable meshes and editable splines.

Chapter 4 goes one step further, talking about render and environment effects and finishing the coverage of all objects: lights, helpers, compound objects, particles, and NURBS.

Chapter 5 familiarizes you with the different interface items that you can use in your scripts and teaches you how to manipulate bitmaps and render images, and even how to access extended channels.

Chapter 6 talks about file I/O, showing you how MAXScript can be useful to manipulate your file assets, as well as to import and export data.

Chapter 7 tells you everything about animation, from controllers to keyframes. It also covers keyframe manipulation methods, script controllers, and methods to create and access Track View nodes.

Chapter 8 introduces you to variables and also teaches you how to work with callbacks, which are event-driven scripts. Some other miscellaneous functions and concepts are covered, giving you scripting tips and tricks.

Chapters 9 and 10 talk about Plug-in scripts, which are plug-ins made of scripts. You will see how to create different types of plug-ins.

Chapter 11 integrates plug-ins and scripts, teaching you how to use MAXScript extensions, which are plug-ins written to add new MAXScript methods and functions to your scripts. In this chapter, you will use two plug-ins: MAXScript Control Library and Avguard Extensions, which are both available on the CD-ROM.

Part II: Mastering the SDK

To work with the SDK, besides knowing MAX, you also need to know C++ and Win32 programming.

Chapter 12 introduces the MAX SDK and the requirements for writing plug-ins, as well as some of the basic SDK concepts.

Chapter 13 teaches you how to create a Utility plug-in. This chapter also goes into detail about accessing MAX scene data and object properties, as well as how to retrieve mesh data from triangle-based geometry.

Chapter 14 digs deeper into the geometry pipeline and shows how to create Object plug-ins.

Chapter 15 describes the 2D side of the MAX SDK. This includes bitmaps, the G-Buffer, and Rendering Effects plug-ins.

Chapter 16 teaches you how to create Modifier plug-ins that have the ability to deform vertices or completely change the topology of a mesh.

Chapter 17 teaches how to create a Global Utility plug-in, which is a generic plug-in type that can be used to add functionality like custom Right-Click menus and event notification handlers.

Chapter 18 covers creating MAXScript extensions. This chapter teaches you how to add functions and system variables to the MAXScript language.

What's on the CD-ROM

The CD-ROM contains files that will be used for the tutorials and exercises in the book. There are several places that direct you to the CD-ROM, either to read a file at the beginning of an exercise, or to illustrate the final results of an exercise.

The CD-ROM also features a series of MAXScript extensions and scripts from various developers.

These are the developers that provided samples for our CD-ROM and a brief description of each of them. The CD-ROM contains a Director interface that will guide you through each plug-in or script that the developers supplied.

Simon Feltman

Simon Feltman provided the following plug-ins:

MAXScript Control Library 2.2 (`\Plugins\SimonFeltman\CtrlLib`) CtrlLib is a suite of UI controls and methods to make nice looking interfaces for MAXScript.

Binary File Stream MAXScript Extension (`\Plugins\SimonFeltman\BinStream`) Allows you to read and write binary data in 8-, 16-, and 32-bit formats along with strings.

Mulitple Mapping Channel MAXScript Extension (`\Plugins\SimonFeltman\MultiMap`) Accesses all 99 mapping channels available through the scripter!

Skeletal Animation Viewer and Export Plug-in for 3D Studio MAX Application and Plug-in (`\Plugins\SimonFeltman\DejaView`) Exports meshes and animations from MAX and views them in the real-time viewer. Supports Character Studio and the MAX Skin modifier. Thanks to Mike O'Rourke for the HHEV mesh and animation and to Kelcey Privett for the bones mesh and animation.

Check out Simon's Web site at `http://www.asylum-soft.com` for updates for his free scripts and plug-ins.

Neil Blevins

Neil Blevins is a full-time 3D artist who also does scripting in his free time. He specializes in sci-fi and fantasy artwork and is currently working at Blur studio. You can check out his Web site at `http://www.neilblevins.com`.

He included the following scripts:

- BigBrother
- GlobalMotionBlur
- MeshsmoothControl
- NoiseControllerRandomSeed
- ParticleBuddy
- SmokeThis

Chris Dragon

Chris is a programmer by profession. His artistic side inspires him to work in 3D as a hobby, sometimes creating his own plug-ins to aid in his efforts. You can check out his Web site at `http://max.draconic.com`.

He contributed the following plug-in:

- MAXScript Shortcuts Manager

David Humpherys

Animator and Technical Director at REZN8. REZN8 creates broadcast packaging, trailers and titles, visual effects for film and television, commercial production, corporate branding and design, and Internet design and programming. You can check out his Web site at `http://www.rezn8.com/gearhead`.

He contributed the following scripts:

- Layer Manager BETA
- Light Manager
- Random Colors MacroScript
- Rename MacroScript
- Safe Frame Render Effect
- Time Stamp Render Effect

Larry Minton

Larry Minton works at Discreet QE.

He contributed the following plug-in:

- Avguard MAXScript Extensions

Fred Moreau

Fred works for Discreet as a demo artist in Paris. You can check out his Web site at `http://perso.cybercable.fr/fredm`.

He provided the following scripts:

- Cel Shader Plug-in script
- MacroCollector Right-Click menu
- Max FreeHand Tools v2.0

François Mourlevat

François is an AutoCAD and 3D Studio MAX teacher in Paris. You can check out his Web site at `http://www.maxfrance.net/`.

He contributed the following scripts:

- 360 Render World 2.0
- WavePlans Generator 3.0
- Filter Script FX 2.0
- Matlib Catalogue 3.1
- UnderWater World "Poséidon" 2
- Vista Script Pro 2.0 "VULCANIA"

Borislav Petrov

A passionate 3D Studio user since 1993, Borislav Petrov has worked in the areas of architectural visualization and multimedia and is currently involved in a 3D game development project. He started scripting right after MAX R2 shipped in 1997 and still can't stop. You can check out his Web site at `http://gfxcentral.com/bobo`.

He contributed the following scripts:

- CUI Merge 0.4 Macro Script
- FilmAge 0.52 REffect
- Render Hidden Wire 1.0 Macro Script
- MAXscriber RenderEffect 1.6
- MissingTextures 3.1 MacroScript
- QuickRegionRenderer 0.65 Macro Script
- CustomRCMenu
- ScripToons 0.62 REffect
- ViewportsLayout 0.2 Macro Script

Frederick Ruff

Based in San Francisco, California, Fred focuses on graphics scripting and effects for film, video, the Web, multimedia applications, game development, and more. He works with many different clients across the globe. Knowing 3D Studio Max extremely well, he can also write custom tools via MaxScript. He works on jobs varying from character animation to Web page graphics. You can check out his Web site at `http://www.ruff-stuff.com`.

He contributed the following scripts:

- Hand Controller
- Morph Shape Creator
- Polygon Counter
- Crate Plug-in script
- Attributes Modifier

John Wainwright

John Wainwright is a software developer and consultant. He is the developer of MAXScript.

He contributed the following plug-in:

- Mousetrack Extension

How to Reach the Authors

Alexander can be reached at `aebicalho@origamy.com.br`. Additional scripts and information on this book can be found on his Web site at `http://www.origamy.com.br`.

Simon can be reached at `simon@asylum-soft.com` and updates for his free scripts and plug-ins can be found at `http://www.asylum-soft.com`.

Part I
Mastering MAXScript

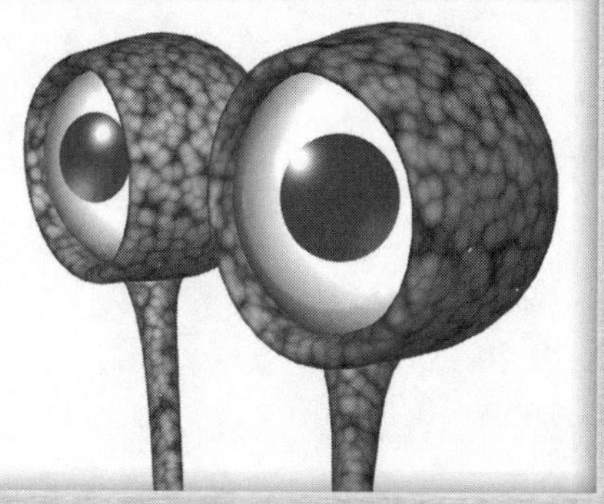

In This Part

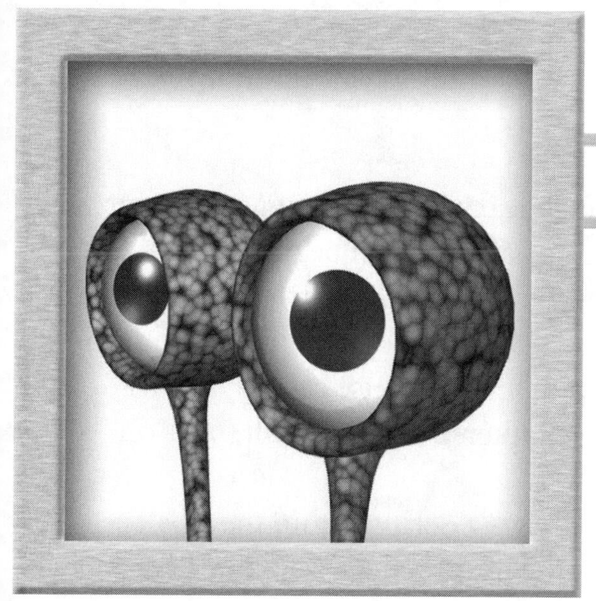

Basic MAXScript

MAXSCRIPT

Chapter 1

In this chapter, you are going to learn the basics of MAXScript through a series of simple tutorials. You will begin by creating a simple script that will show you how MAXScript works. Instead of explaining each feature to you, we will pack them inside the tutorials, giving you practical examples of how to use each. These features will be explained in future chapters, where we will focus on each of them.

If you are already familiar with MAXScript within the MAX interface, you may want to skim the next section or go directly to the section "Writing a Utility Script."

This chapter covers the following topics:

- Understanding the MAXScript user interface
- Writing utility scripts
- Creating user interface items
- Using the Script Editor
- Selecting objects
- Animating objects

Accessing the MAXScript Tools

The first step to understanding MAXScript is to know where to access its commands and functions. MAXScript resides in the MAX user interface (UI) in several places, as seen in Figure 1.1.

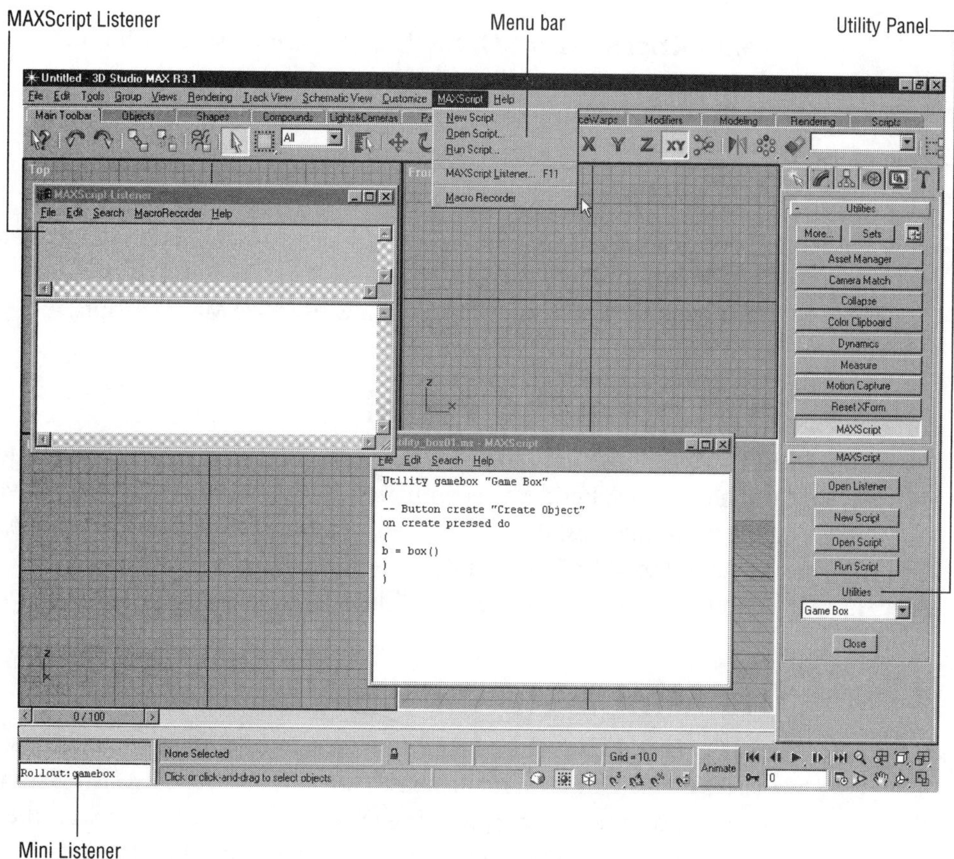

Figure 1.1 *TheMAXScript user interface*

Let's take a look at the MAX user interface in more detail.

The Menu Bar

The menu bar contains the basic MAXScript commands:

File New Opens a blank Script Editor.

File Open Opens a script file in the Script Editor.

Run Executes a script file.

MAXScript Listener Opens the MAXScript Listener window.

Macro Recorder Turns the Macro Recorder on or off.

Toolbars

The toolbars contain the Macro Scripts. Once a Macro Script is evaluated, you can assign it to a button on a toolbar.

See Chapter 4 for instructions on how to create Macro Scripts.

The Command Panel

MAXScript commands can be found in the Utility Panel, which can be found in the Command Panel. Besides the commands that allow you to open and save, you also have a drop-down list that will process utility scripts. These scripts appear as new rollouts below the MAXScript utility or as floaters in the main UI.

You will learn how to create utilities later in this chapter.

The Mini Listener

The *Mini Listener* is where can quickly type MAXScript commands or see script outputs. It's divided into two main areas: The upper part is the *Macro Recorder*, where you can see the commands that are being recorded; and the lower part is the *Listener window*, where you type the commands or view script output. By right-clicking the Mini Listener, you have the option to execute a previous command that was entered or recorded, or you can open the Listener (see Figure 1.2).

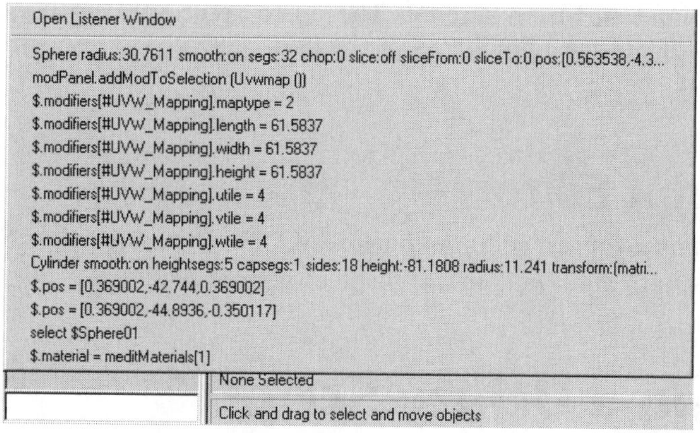

```
Open Listener Window
Sphere radius:30.7611 smooth:on segs:32 chop:0 slice:off sliceFrom:0 sliceTo:0 pos:[0.563538,-4.3...
modPanel.addModToSelection (Uvwmap ())
$.modifiers[#UVW_Mapping].maptype = 2
$.modifiers[#UVW_Mapping].length = 61.5837
$.modifiers[#UVW_Mapping].width = 61.5837
$.modifiers[#UVW_Mapping].height = 61.5837
$.modifiers[#UVW_Mapping].utile = 4
$.modifiers[#UVW_Mapping].vtile = 4
$.modifiers[#UVW_Mapping].wtile = 4
Cylinder smooth:on heightsegs:5 capsegs:1 sides:18 height:-81.1808 radius:11.241 transform:(matri...
$.pos = [0.369002,-42.744,0.369002]
$.pos = [0.369002,-44.8936,-0.350117]
select $Sphere01
$.material = meditMaterials[1]
None Selected
Click and drag to select and move objects
```

***Figure 1.2** Mini Listener options in the Open Listener window. (Your history will be different.)*

The Listener

The *Listener* is our command line area. It has the same divisions the Mini Listener has, with the ability to resize them. Besides opening the Listener as a floating window, you can also configure one viewport to be the Listener.

From the Listener, you have the same commands as on the menu bar, with some additional commands that allow you to configure how the Macro Recorder works.

There are several ways to open the Listener:

- Through the menu bar
- In MAXScript utility
- By right-clicking the Mini Listener
- By placing the Listener in one viewport
- Using a keyboard shortcut (F11 by default)

The Macro Recorder

Macro Recorder, as its name says, records actions in MAX as macros or scripts. You can select the recorded lines and drag them to any toolbar, automatically creating a script.

You can configure the Macro Recorder in the Listener. See Chapter 2 for more information about the Macro Recorder. The Macro Recorder is very useful because it provides a very handy tool for writing scripts so that you do not have to memorize all the commands.

The Script Editor

The *Script Editor* is the text editor used inside MAX to write our scripts. See the section "Using The Script Editor" later in this chapter for more details.

Writing a Utility Script

You will now start creating your first script. It's a script that creates a Box object and applies a little tapering on it. This script creates an object that can be used in a game engine as a box or a base. Since it is a utility script, it will reside in the Utility Panel.

You will write the script adding features step by step. By the end of this section, you will have the script ready, and you will know how to write simple code.

Let's start by opening MAXScript in the Utility Panel. To do so, follow these steps:

1. Click New Script and type the following code:

   ```
   Utility gamebox "Game Box"
   (
   )
   ```

2. In the Script Editor, select File ➜ Evaluate All, or press CTRL+E. Evaluate executes the script. Game Box will appear in the drop-down list.

3. Select Game Box, and you will notice that a new rollout opens below it containing a Close button, as in Figure 1.3. No code was created in step 1. We only created the rough skeleton of a utility script. All utility scripts have a rollout and a Close button.

4. To add a button that will create the object when pressed, type the following code inside the parenthesis that we left empty in step 1:

   ```
   Button create "Create Object"
   ```

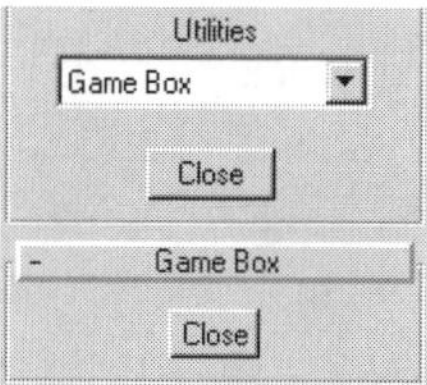

Figure 1.3 *The Game Box utility script*

5. A new button appears in your utility, as shown in Figure 1.4. Press it. Nothing happens, and nothing should happen because you did not specify any action or event in this script.

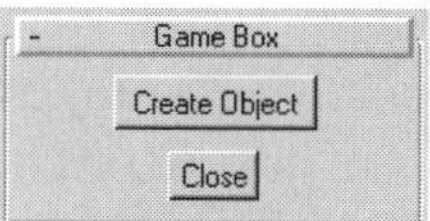

Figure 1.4 *The Game Box script with a Create Object button*

6. Continue writing the script as follows. Place this code below *button* and before the end of the script:

```
on create pressed do
(
box()
)
```

This code is the event that will be executed when the *Create* button is pressed. There's only one action in it, which is *box()*. *Box()* will create a default size box object.

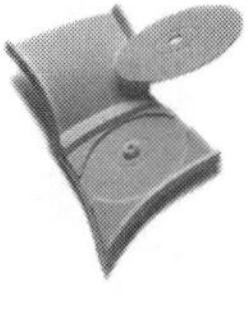

The final script can be found on the CD-ROM as `utility_box01.ms`.

Notice how straightforward the script is. The syntax `on create pressed` works as if you are just talking to the computer.

Now, evaluate the script and click the button. You will see a box created in the screen. If you click it again, a new box will be created, but you cannot adjust anything nor define its position and size. Let's move ahead, and you will see how these actions are done.

Adding Variables

You are now going to improve the script we just created, working with variables and allowing the user to adjust the object properties. First, you will change the way you created the object by assigning it to a variable.

Instead of using `box()`, you should use `b = box()`. This way, every time you want to manipulate this object in the future, you just use `b`. That's the main purpose of variables, to hold one value, object, or parameter, in a way that we can refer to it easily in the future.

Variables can hold any type of data. In this example, `b` is an object, but variables can also hold numbers, text, colors, xyz coordinates, and so on. We will see different types of variables in our exercises.

Edit the script you wrote and change `box()` to `b = box()`.

Manipulating Object Properties

One of the important uses of MAXScript is to manipulate object properties. Using the Game Box script, you will probably need different sizes of boxes or even different objects with different properties.

MAXScript gives you access to all the objects' properties. But first, how can you know which properties an object has? Of course, a box has height, width, and length, but a sphere would not have the same properties. To know an object's properties, you can use the *showproperties* function.

Let's see how it works:

1. Using the Game Box script, `utility_box01.ms`, create a box.
2. Open the Listener.
3. Type **showproperties b.**

You should now see the following:

```
    .height : float
    .length : float
    .lengthsegs : integer
    .width : float
    .widthsegs : integer
    .mapCoords : boolean
    .heightsegs : integer
OK
```

These are the properties that you can access in the Box object, which in our example is assigned to the variable b.

To access these properties, you use *obj.property* syntax, where *obj* is the object you want to access. In our Game Box example, to access the box's height, you would use the syntax `b.height`. All other properties work in exactly the same way.

Notice also that in the property list we have a colon and text. This is to identify the type of the property:

Float Means that it's a real number between 1.18E–38 and 3.40E38.

Integer Means that it needs to be an integer number between –2,147,483,648 and 2,147,483,648.

Boolean Means that it's *true* or *false*, *on* or *off*.

Using the Game Box example, the number of segments is always an integer number because we cannot have a box with 2.5 segments. Also, you can have the mapping coordinates turned on or off, which is a Boolean value.

Let's edit our Game Box example and set a couple of properties in the object. After `b = box()`, enter the following:

```
b.height = 30
b.width = b.length = 40
b.mapcoords = on
b.heightsegs = 5
```

The final script with these latest changes can be found on the CD-ROM and is named `utility_box02.ms`.

Using the Script Editor

Now that you have been introduced to the Script Editor, it's time to broaden your knowledge. Here, you will learn some techniques to make your scripts easier to use, such as tabbing to create blocks and color-coding.

Creating Blocks with Tabulation

The Script Editor allows you to create blocks in the script by using the Tab key. This makes it easier for you to read the script and to see where parenthesis, which define a block of commands, start and end, as in Figure 1.5.

utility_box03.ms - MAXScript

File Edit Search Help

```
Utility gamebox "Game Box"
(
    button create "Create Object"

    on create pressed do
    (
        b = box()
        b.height = 30
        b.width = b.length = 40
        b.mapcoords = on
        b.heightsegs = 5
    )
)
```

Figure 1.5 *An example of tabbed script*

For example, take a look at the file `utility_box03.ms` on the CD-ROM and notice how different it is when it's tabulated. It's a lot easier to see where the commands start and end.

Adding Comments

Comments are another nice feature you can add to your scripts. They contain information that will help you understand the script better, and also help other people know how the script works and understand the logic of your code.

To add a comment to a script, all you need to do is add two hyphen (--) symbols, like this:

```
-- this is a comment
```

You can add a comment in a blank line or in the same line as you have your code if you place the comment at the end of the code.

Take a look at file `utility_box04.ms` on the CD-ROM for a series of examples on how to use comments.

Using Color Codes

One of the nicest features of the MAXScript Editor is that it can use color codes that allow you to see your script more clearly.

Basically, it applies three colors:

Green For comments

Blue For special words such as *on*, *if*, or *while*

Dark red For texts (strings)

The rest of the text remains black.

To apply the color-coding, just press CTRL+D, and you will see the colors applied on your screen.

As an example, open the file `utility_box04.ms` and press CTRL+D to see it color-coded.

Navigating through Scripts

When you have large scripts, it's often easy to get lost. The Script Editor has a way to navigate through events and UI items very easily. Using CTRL+Right-click, you will see a navigation window that can take you to a specific event or to a UI item in the script.

Open the file `utility_box04.ms` and press the key combination CTRL+Right-click to display a menu similar to the one in Figure 1.6.

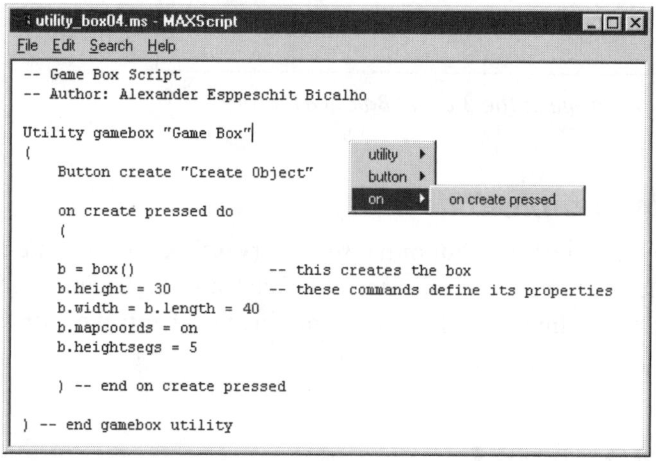

utility_box04.ms - MAXScript

File Edit Search Help

```
-- Game Box Script
-- Author: Alexander Esppeschit Bicalho

Utility gamebox "Game Box"
(
    Button create "Create Object"

    on create pressed do
    (

    b = box()                   -- this creates the box
    b.height = 30               -- these commands define its properties
    b.width = b.length = 40
    b.mapcoords = on
    b.heightsegs = 5

    ) -- end on create pressed

) -- end gamebox utility
```

utility

button

on

on create pressed

Figure 1.6 *The navigation menu*

Bracket Balance

In large scripts, sometimes you can lose track of where a block of code starts and ends, causing you to leave extra parenthesis or miss some in the script. To easily find these missing parenthesis, you can use CTRL+B, and MAXScript will highlight the block you've stopped your cursor on, showing you the start and end parenthesis.

Using the Game Box script, place your cursor before `b = box()` and press CTRL+B. You will see the block highlighted, as in Figure 1.7.

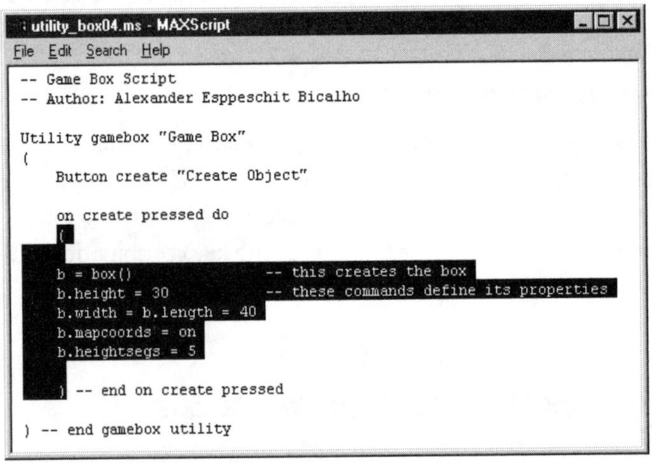

utility_box04.ms - MAXScript

File Edit Search Help

```
-- Game Box Script
-- Author: Alexander Esppeschit Bicalho

Utility gamebox "Game Box"
(
    Button create "Create Object"

    on create pressed do
    (
    b = box()               -- this creates the box
    b.height = 30           -- these commands define its properties
    b.width = b.length = 40
    b.mapcoords = on
    b.heightsegs = 5

    ) -- end on create pressed

) -- end gamebox utility
```

Figure 1.7 *An example of the Bracket Balance feature*

Text-Editing Commands

Like any text editor, the Script Editor has some very well-known features. These features cover File Open, Save, and Save As; Edit; Cut; Copy; Paste; Find; and Replace. These features work similarly to how they work in any other text editor, so we don't need to elaborate on them here.

Using Modifiers

You will now start tapering the object. This will teach you how to work with modifiers. This chapter has an introduction to modifiers, we will study them in depth in Chapter 3.

To add the Taper modifier, you will use the following code:

```
addmodifier b (taper())
```

This will add the Taper modifier to object b.

Each modifier has different properties. For instance, the Bend modifier has an *angle* property, while the Taper modifier has an *amount* property. How can you tell which properties a modifier has? Simple, use the *showproperties* function. Once you add a modifier to an object, you can access it using the syntax *object.modifier_name*, which, in our example, is `b.taper`. To see the properties of the Taper modifier, type the following:

```
showproperties b.taper
```

You will see this result:

```
.curve : float
.limit : boolean
.upperlimit : float
.lowerlimit : float
.amount : float
.primaryaxis : integer
.effectaxis : integer
.symmetry : boolean
.center : point3
.gizmo : transform
```

Here, you see listed all the properties that appear in the Modify Panel and also the two sub-objects that we have in Taper: Center and Gizmo. We will learn how to access Gizmo and more about modifiers in Chapter 3.

In our exercise, let's define that we want a taper with an amount of –0.2, which will make it smaller on top. You would use the following code:

```
b.taper.amount = -0.2
```

What if you did not want the Taper modifier but another one, and you cannot remember how MAXScript accesses it? That's where the Macro Recorder comes in. You simply turn it on and see how it applies the modifier. Then, you copy it to your script, making some changes if needed, and that's it. You have saved yourself from memorizing lots of commands. We will discuss this process in Chapter 2, where you will learn how to use the Macro Recorder to help you create scripts.

You can find the script file with the Taper modifier added in `utility_box05.ms` file on the CD-ROM.

Adding a Spinner to the User Interface

Now that you added the modifier, you can give the user flexibility on how much taper to add. You can add a spinner that allows the user to define the taper amount value, as in Figure 1.8. Let's do so.

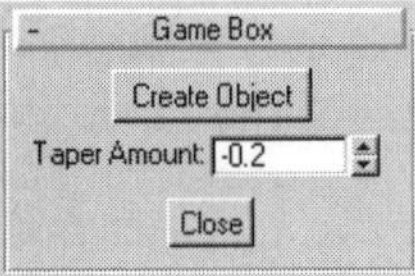

Figure 1.8 *The Game Box script with a spinner*

After the Create Object button in the script, add the following code:

```
spinner amount "Taper Amount:"
```

Evaluate the script and notice a spinner after the button in the UI.

Now, as with the button, we need to define the event that will occur when the user adjusts the spinner. Add another block of commands to the script:

```
on amount changed val do
   (
   b.taper.amount = val
   )
```

Here, you are telling the script that when the spinner changes its value, assign this value to the taper amount.

Now, evaluate and test the script, first creating the box and then adjusting the amount of the taper.

When you test the script, you will notice some problems. First, the amount cannot be negative because the spinner will not allow a negative number. Second, although the value is –0.2, when you touch the spinner, it jumps to 0.0. You need to create a spinner with the default value of –0.2 that can be set from –10 to 10. You can do this by adding the following syntax to the spinner: `range:` *[start,end,default value]*. Edit the script to add the following code:

```
spinner amount "Taper Amount" range:[-10,10,-0.2]
```

This will allow you to add the correct values to the spinner.

Notice also that the script will crash if you try to adjust the spinner before creating the object. You will learn how to fix this later in the text by adding some code that will check if the object was created or not, or by disabling the spinner and making it available only after the button is pressed.

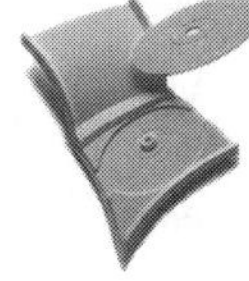

The file `utility_box06.ms` on the CD-ROM contains all these changes.

Positioning an Object

So far, your script creates boxes and always places them in the origin at 0,0,0. Now, you will allow the user to select the object's position using a mouse-click on-screen.

To do this, you will need to learn two things. First, you need to assign an object's position. This is done by using *object.position*, or *object.pos*. You can do this independently in each axis by using *object.position.axis*, where *axis* will be *x*, *y*, or *z*. If you use separate values for *x*, *y*, and *z*, these values are float or integer numbers. If you want to assign all three values at once, you need to use a point3 variable, which has the syntax [*a*,*b*,*c*], where *a*, *b*, *c* are floats or integers that represent the values in *x*, *y*, and *z*.

Now, you need to learn the second part: how to ask the user to input a position. This is done using the *pickpoint* function. *Pickpoint* will display a crosshair cursor and wait for the user input on-screen. After the user clicks, *pickpoint* returns the desired *xyz* position.

Let's edit the script and add the *pickpoint* function to it. Before `b = box()`, add the following:

```
pt = pickpoint prompt:"Select Object Position:"
```

After `b = box()`, add the following:

```
b.pos = pt
```

Now, try the script and notice how you can add the object wherever you want on-screen.

Check the file `utility_box07.ms` on the CD-ROM to see these changes.

Enhancing the User Interface

Now that you learned how to create this script, let's polish it a little bit, enhancing the UI and making it easier to use.

You can make a better script if you split the script into two parts. For instance, you can create the box on the first part and then assign the taper on the second part. Also, you can make the Taper button and the spinner unavailable, unless the box is created. Let's see some properties that a button has that will help us.

First of all, you can change the size of a button, specifying its width and height. For instance,

```
button create "Create Object" width:120 height:30
```

will create a button with a larger size (see Figure 1.9). This makes it easier for you to create the scripts with a better look, instead of MAXScript having to auto-resize them.

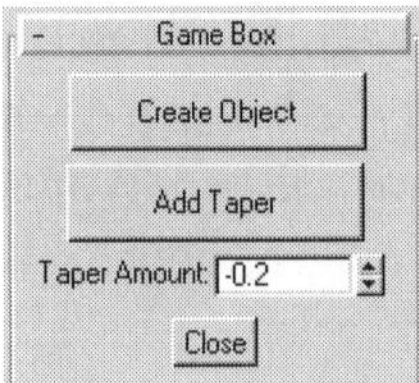

Figure 1.9 *Buttons with a larger size*

You can also define whether a button is enabled or not. This makes the script fluid because it allows you to give an option to the user only under certain conditions.

For instance, open script `utility_box07.ms` on the CD-ROM. This script has another button assigned for the taper. Let's disable this button and the spinner. Then, we'll enable the button as the user creates the box and enable the spinner when the user applies the taper. This way the script will not crash if you play with the spinner before creating the box because the spinner will be disabled.

To do so, first edit the Taper button and the spinner lines by adding `enabled:false` at the end of each.

Now, anywhere in the *On Create Pressed* event, add the following:

```
taper_it.enabled = true
```

This will enable the *Taper_it* button when the box is created.

Next, in the *On Taper_it Pressed* event, add the following:

```
amount.enabled = true
```

This code will enable the spinner as soon as the taper is applied.

The final script is located on the CD-ROM named `utility_box09.ms`. Try it and see the results.

Creating More Complex Scripts

Thus far, you have written a script that creates an object, modifies it, and gives you control to adjust it through a user interface. You will now move ahead and learn a little bit more about MAXScript, learning how to work with selections and a few other UI features that will ask you to select objects. You will also learn how to work with conditions and define the direction that a script will follow.

Using a Pickbutton

Let's start another script that will select two objects and show us the distance between them, as in Figure 1.10.

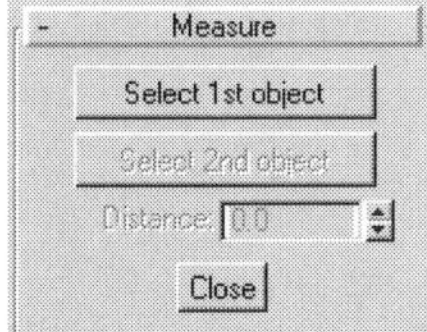

Figure 1.10 *The Measure script*

To do this, you will need to use a different button, called a *pickbutton*. The pickbutton selects an object already in the scene so that you can manipulate it. It is very similar to a button, but its event changes a little bit because a pickbutton does not work when pressed, instead, it works when it picks an object.

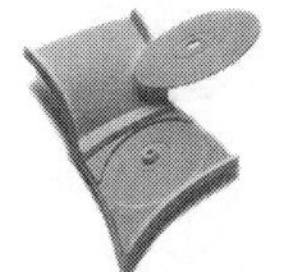

Take a look at the `utility_measure01.ms` file on the CD-ROM and notice how we used the pickbutton. The only events defined assign variables to each selected object and calculate the distance between both objects using the *distance* function.

There's also a new pickbutton property used called *pickbutton.text*. It is the text that appears in the pickbutton. Basically, the selected object's name appears in the pickbutton so you can know that something was selected.

You will continue using the Measure script for the next steps.

If Functions

Sometimes you will must make decisions within the script and use different options depending on the circumstances. This is done using *if...then...else* expressions.

In our script, we want to select only 3D objects. How can we know if an object is a 3D object? Every object has two properties that identify its type: a *class* and a *superclass*. An *object class* defines which object it is. For example, a sphere belongs to the Sphere class. An *object superclass* defines the type of object, where sphere and box belong to the *GeometryClass* superclass, while circle and helix belong to the *Shapes* superclass.

You must check to see if the objects belong to a specific superclass and then you can accept the object or not. To do this, you need to use *superclassof obj method*, which will return the superclass. You can compare the superclass that is returned to the superclass that you want and then accept or reject the object. You can create comparisons using six different operators, as shown in Table 1.1.

Table 1.1 Comparison Operators

SIGN	COMPARISON
== (two equal signs)	Equal
!=	Different
>	Greater than
<	Lower than
>=	Greater or equal
<=	Lower or equal

Now, you can create a condition and define which action to take if it is met and which action to take if it is not. You will use the *if*...(condition)...*then*...(action if condition is true)...*else*...(action if condition is false) expression.

Using the Measure script, let's add a condition to check if the object is a GeometryClass object:

After *on obj1 picked obj* do, enter the following lines of code:

```
if superclassof obj == GeometryClass then
(
```

After *obj2.enabled* = *true*, close the brackets.

When you evaluate the script, you'll notice that if you select an object that is not a 3D object, the script will not move ahead. If it is a 3D object, the script executes the actions.

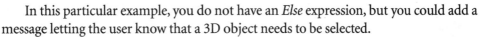

In this particular example, you do not have an *Else* expression, but you could add a message letting the user know that a 3D object needs to be selected.

The file `utility_measure02.ms` on the CD-ROM contains all these changes.

Booleans

Sometimes you need two conditions at the same time. For instance, you might want to have the ability to select 3D objects and particles, or you might want to select spheres that have a radius of more than 20, or something like this. There are two ways that you can create this two-condition dependency: by using an *if...then* expression and another nested *if...then* expression, or by using *booleans*, which allow you to test more then one condition at the same time.

There are three booleans, as shown in Table 1.2.

Table 1.2 Booleans

BOOLEAN	HOW THE CONDITION IS TESTED
And	Both conditions must be true
Or	At least one condition must be true
Not	Inverts the condition result

For example, if you test two conditions and both must be true, you can use the following syntax:

```
if...(condition1)...and...(condition2)...then
```

You are not limited to only two conditions. You can use as many booleans as you wish, and even mix them. It just depends on what you need.

In our example, you need to test the object and make sure that it's of the GeometryClass superclass. But there is a problem, a target object is also part of the GeometryClass superclass, but you do not want it. So, update the condition to look like this:

```
superclassof obj == GeometryClass and not classof obj ==
Targetobject
```

Notice that you could do it differently. Instead of using *`not classof obj ==`*, you could use `classof obj !=`. Both will have the same result.

The file `utility_measure03.ms` on the CD-ROM has all of these changes.

Adding Output Messages

We can make our scripts friendly by outputting error messages on the screen. For instance, in the `utility_measure03.ms` script, nothing happens if the user has not selected a 3D object, so the user will not know what to do. It would be nice if we could add a message saying that the selected object must be a 3D object.

Let's do so. After the end of the if...then block, add the following line of code:

```
else print "\nPlease select a 3D Object"
```

This will print the error message either on the Listener and Mini Listener, so you will be showing the user what to do. The `\n` character means that MAXScript will start writing on a new blank line.

Another option is to add an alert box, which will appear on-screen showing the error to the user. It's surely more visible, as you can see in Figure 1.11.

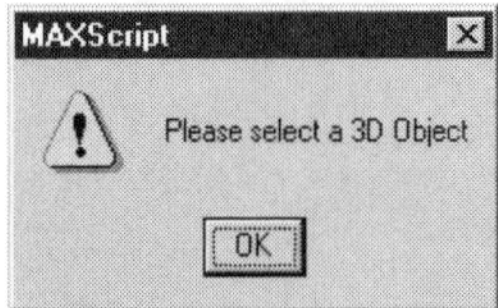

Figure 1.11 *An example of an alert box*

In this case, you would write the following code:

```
else messagebox "Please select a 3D Object"
```

The file `utility_measure04.ms` on the CD-ROM incorporates these changes, adding the Print method to the first pickbutton and the alert box to the second pickbutton.

Manipulating Objects: Selections and Animation

You will likely need to manipulate specific objects in a scene or objects in a selection. You can also use MAXScript for managing animation tasks. For instance, when you create a character or an object that requires specific and sometimes complex animation, you can automate this task using MAXScript. In the next sections, you will learn how to work with animation and selections.

Managing Simple and Multiple Selections

Selections are very important to MAXScript. Sometimes you might need to adjust many objects at once, so being able to select them and run a script on them at the same time is a real time saver.

The first type of selection in MAXScript is the use of the character *$*. If you have one object selected and need to relate to it in MAXScript, just use $. It's also an easy way to assign an object to a variable because you can say `b = $` and assign the currently selected object to a variable very easily. $ also returns the current selection if more than one object is selected. But there's not much you can do if you have more than one object selected because you cannot access each separated object, only the collection as a whole. That's why you need to use *selection*.

To manage selections with more than one object, it's better to use the *selection* global variable. *Selection* is an array that contains all objects that are selected. Its use is the same if one object is selected or if multiple objects are selected. But what's an array? An *array* is a variable type that has the peculiarity of having multiple elements. You can check how many elements it has by using the *count* property, for instance, `selection.count` will return the number of selected objects.

Now, to access each element, you must use a different syntax: *array[i]*, where *i* is the number of the element and is an integer greater than zero and less than or equal to the number of elements returned by the *count* property. For instance, to access the fifth object selected, you'd use `selection[5]`.

Let's play a bit with selections. Open the file `corridor.max` from your CD-ROM and select all five boxes in the scene.

Now, let's apply a Taper modifier to one of them, like this:

```
addmodifier selection[3] (taper())
selection[3].taper.amount = -0.2
```

Next, let's apply a Skew modifier to another one as follows:

```
addmodifier selection[4] (skew amount:5 direction:90 axis:3)
```

In this example, besides adding the modifier, you are assigning the modifier and defining its properties in a single line. This is valid elsewhere in MAXScript, even to create objects.

Notice that when you specified the modifier's properties, you did not use the `()` *(parentheses) elsewhere. This is valid elsewhere in MAXScript. When you created a box in the Game Box script, you used* `box()` *because you were not specifying any property. If you wanted to specify the position, you would use* `box pos:pt`*, not using the* `()` *anywhere.*

Another way to access an object in MAXScript, other than selections or variables, is through its name. This is done by using the *$* character before the name. In the `corridor.max` scene, `$Box01` would refer to the first box to the right, as seen from the camera.

Referring to objects by their name isn't a good practice. MAXScript does not understand capital letters. Also, MAX allows you to have two objects with the same name. So if you have one object named Box, another named box, and a third one cloned with the same name, using `$Box` *will pick one of them, but you wouldn't know which one.*

Loop Functions

MAXScript also provides commands that allow us to step through all of the selected elements or through all the elements of an array, thereby automating a series of tasks. These expressions allow us to manage selections of objects, materials, and modifiers, and to search for the data that we want and to adjust it.

This can be done using the For expression. Its syntax is *for...in...to...do.* For instance, if you want to count from 1 to 10, you would use the following syntax:

```
for i in 1 to 10 do
```

This will repeat the block of commands 10 times. Notice that we used `for i in 1 to 10`, where *i* is one variable that will be assigned to the number of the step that the For expression is executing. This syntax allows us to use the i value as the index of the array, since it'll change incrementally.

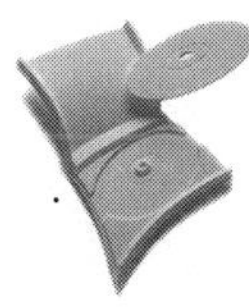

Let's use an example to better understand how it works. Open the file `area_light.max` on the CD-ROM. It contains an array of 20 lights to imitate an area light. Render it to see the result.

It's over illuminated, so we'll need to adjust the multipliers. The problem is that each of these lights might not have the same color value, so they are not instanced, which means that you have to adjust them manually, one by one. This is where the script will save you time.

Select all the lights and type the following command in the Listener:

```
for i in 1 to selection.count do (selection[i].multiplier = 0.05)
```

This command will step through all the selected objects (`i in 1 to selection.count`) and will change each multiplier to 0.05. Render the file again and adjust the multipliers until you get a good result.

Another way of adjusting the multipliers is to using following code:

```
for i in selection do (i.multiplier = 0.05)
```

This code will step through each element assigning it to the i variable. This syntax requires that `selection` be an array. (`selection` will always be an array, but if you use other variables, these need to be arrays also.)

Animating with MAXScript

You can use MAXScript to help you animate objects. MAXScript can manipulate the objects for you, and if you have the Animate button on, it also creates an animation.

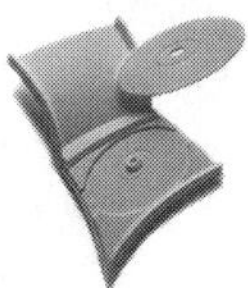

Let's open the file `Eyes.max` from the book's CD-ROM and create a script that will animate the eyes and allow them to move around.

The Slider User Interface

A *slider* is different from the spinner because it allows a bit more flexibility visually, when we do not need precision. A slider is perfect for managing the eyes because it relates exactly to a vertical and horizontal movement, instead of needing to translate this movement into numbers (see Figure 1.12). A slider has the same parameters as a spinner, with an additional parameter that specifies its orientation.

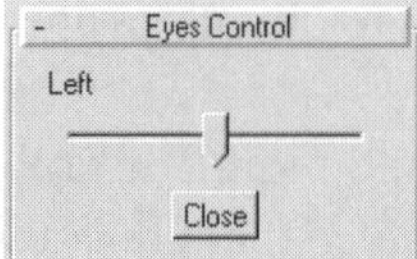

Figure 1.12 *The Eye Control script's slider*

Open the script file `utility_eyes01.ms` and evaluate and play with it. Notice that the slider code is very similar to the spinner code. Also, notice how rotation was implemented on the object.

You are going to edit this script a bit and change some of the parameters. Edit the *slider* line and add the following code at the end of it:

```
orient:#vertical offset:[-30,0]
```

The *orient* property will make it vertical. The syntax of the property requires that you use the variables *#vertical* or *#horizontal*. The *offset* property moves it 30 pixels to the left from the default position. (A positive number would move it to the right.) This value is usually empirical, guessed by trying different values until you get the desired effect.

Now, duplicate the slider by renaming *l_eye_v* to *r_eye_v* and renaming *"Left"* to *"Right"*. Duplicate the event also by renaming the object to $eye01. Edit the *offset* of *r_eye_v* to [30,–100]. See the result in Figure 1.13.

We're referring to the objects by name in this script. Therefore, the script will only work in this file, or if the objects always have the same name. An option is to use a pickbutton and have the user select the objects in the script.

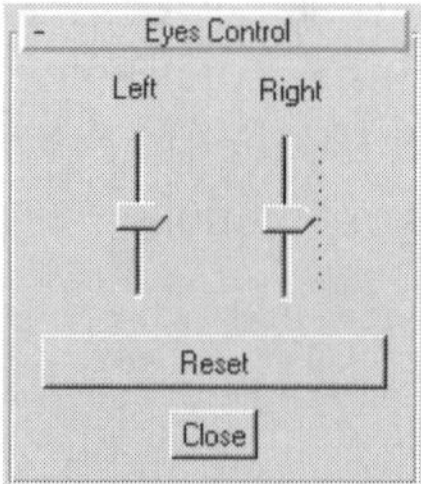

Figure 1.13 *The Eyes Control script with two sliders*

As you can see, there's no way to reset the eyes back to the original position because the slider has no precision. The file `utility_eyes02.ms` on the CD-ROM has an example of a button to reset the rotation, as well as all the other changes that we just made.

The Checkbox User Interface

A *checkbox* is a simple on or off control. You can use it in the script to define which action to take based on whether it's on or off.

Let's add a checkbox to the previous script that locks both sliders or unlocks them (see Figure 1.14). To do so, add a new line before the button and enter the following:

```
checkbox lockv "Lock"
```

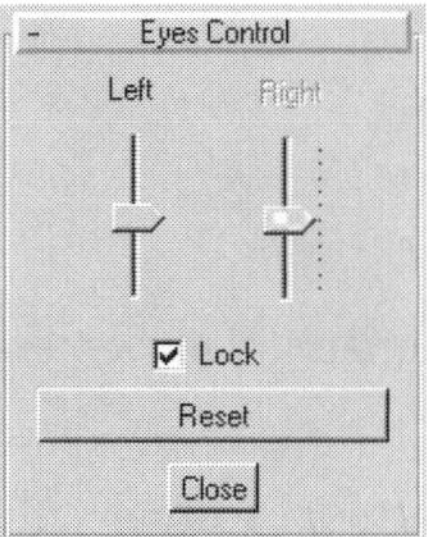

Figure 1.14 *The Eyes Control script with a checkbox*

Now, edit the *l_eye_v changed* event to make both sliders move together if the checkbox is locked. To do so, add the following code:

```
if lockv.checked do
(
   r_eye_v.value = val
   $eye01.rotation.x_rotation = -val + 90
)
```

Now, add another event for the checkbox among any of the existing events. If the checkbox is on, the right slider will be disabled:

```
on lockv changed state do
(
   if state then r_eye_v.enabled = false
      else r_eye_v.enabled = true
)
```

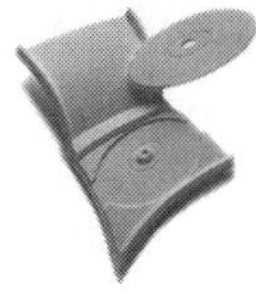

The final version of this script can be found in file `utility_eyes03.ms` on the CD-ROM. An additional file, `utility_eyes04.ms` has been supplied with both vertical and horizontal movements, as in Figure 1.15.

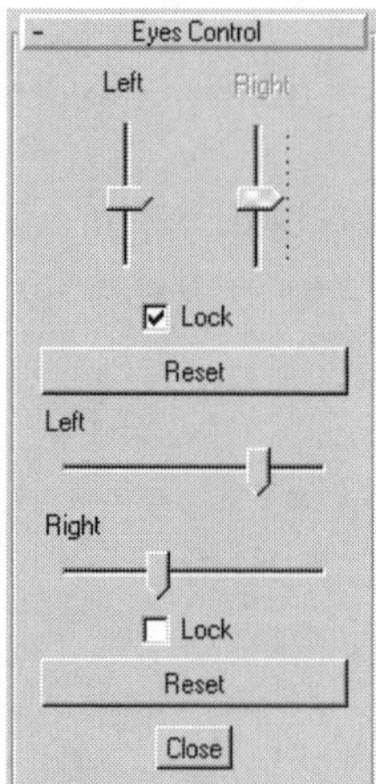

Figure 1.15 *The Eyes Control script with vertical and horizontal movements*

To create an animation of the eyes moving, just turn on Animate, move the slider to the desired frame, and adjust the eyes', positions by using the sliders.

Summary

In this chapter, you took your first steps in MAXScript by working through a series of exercises and examples. These were simple, but you can already begin to see what can be done with MAXScript.

In the next chapter, you will learn how to work with the Macro Recorder to create scripts. You will also learn functions and structures, as well as materials, maps, and material libraries.

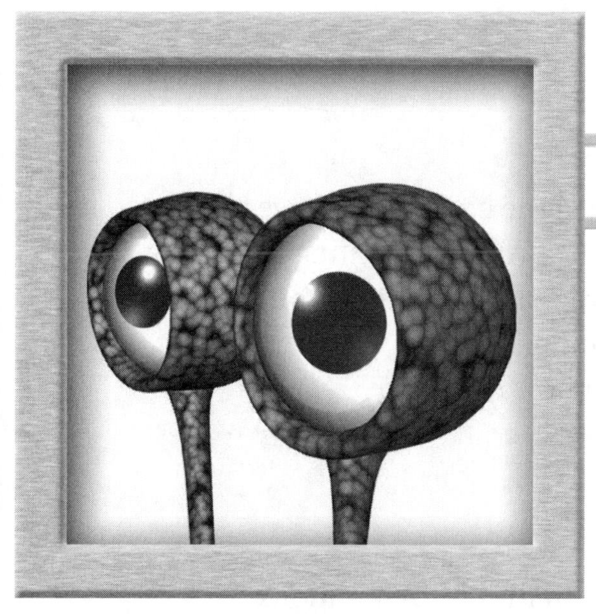

The Macro Recorder and Materials

MAXSCRIPT

Chapter 2

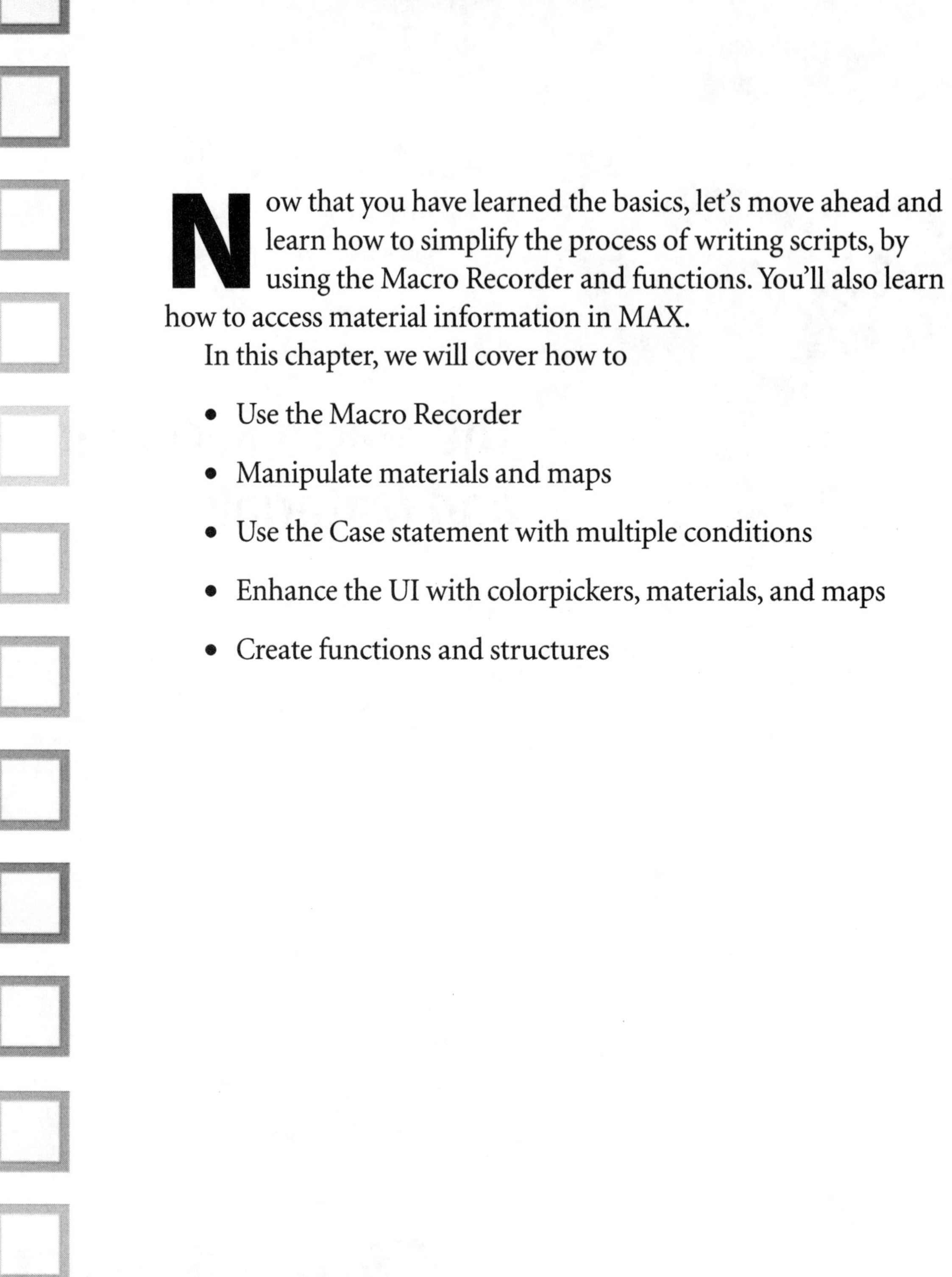

Now that you have learned the basics, let's move ahead and learn how to simplify the process of writing scripts, by using the Macro Recorder and functions. You'll also learn how to access material information in MAX.

In this chapter, we will cover how to

- Use the Macro Recorder
- Manipulate materials and maps
- Use the Case statement with multiple conditions
- Enhance the UI with colorpickers, materials, and maps
- Create functions and structures

The Macro Recorder

The Macro Recorder's main function is to record each step that you're doing in MAX. You will expand this idea by using the recorded steps to create your own scripts without having to memorize lots of code.

Exercise 2.1 illustrates how the Macro Recorder works. You will rewrite the first utility you created in Chapter 1, the file `utility_box09.ms`, but this time, you'll do it using the Macro Recorder.

EXERCISE 2.1: USING THE MACRO RECORDER

1. Turn on the Macro Recorder by going to the main menu and selecting MAXScript ➔ Macro Recorder.
2. Open the MAXScript Listener.
3. Create a box of any size and position.
4. In the Modify Panel, adjust the following properties:
   - Height = 30
   - Width = 40
   - Length = 40
   - Mapping Coords. = On
   - Height segs = 5
5. Add the *Taper* modifier and change its amount to –0.2.
6. Select all the recorded lines in the pink area of the Listener.
7. Drag and drop the selection into the Objects toolbar (see Figure 2.1).
8. Turn off the Macro Recorder and click the button that you just created.

You created the same script that you did in the first chapter, but this time, in a much easier way. This script still has the same problem that the first one had: It will always be created in the same position.

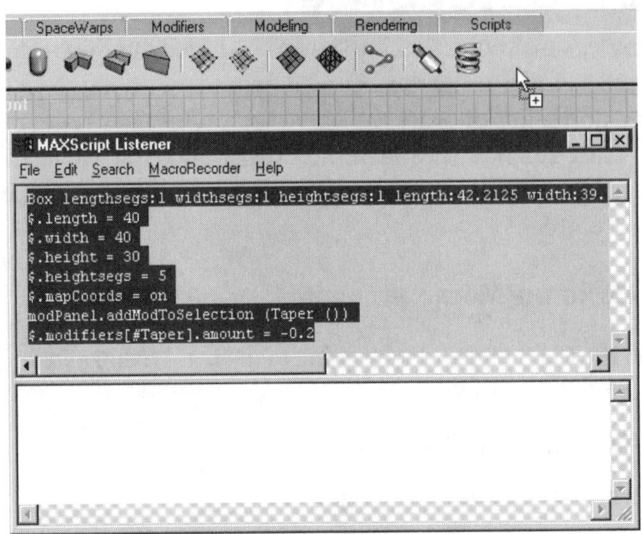

Figure 2.1 *Drag and drop the recorded actions to create scripts.*

Now, you will edit the script and add the *pickpoint* function, just as you did in Chapter 1. To do so, follow these steps:

1. Right-click the button that you just created and select Edit Macro Script, as shown in Figure 2.2.

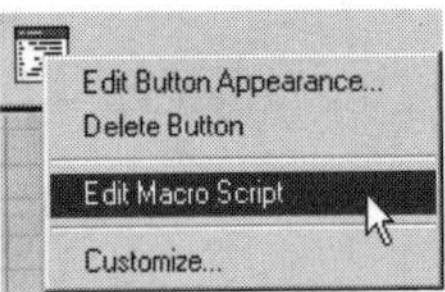

Figure 2.2 *Right-click the Button menu.*

2. Before *Box*, add the following code:

```
pt = pickpoint prompt:"Select Position"
```

3. Locate *pos:[...]* and change it to `pos:pt`.
4. Save and evaluate your script.

Now, press the button again and notice that you can specify the object's position on-screen.

Configuring the Macro Recorder

Using the Macro Recorder is very simple, as you can see from the previous exercise. You will now learn how to configure the Macro Recorder.

Begin by opening the MAXScript Listener and looking at the Macro Recorder pull-down menu (see Figure 2.3). This menu is where you configure the Macro Recorder. Basically, it configures if the Macro Recorder works in absolute or relative mode.

Exercise 2.2 shows how the Macro Recorder works in each mode using a simple exercise.

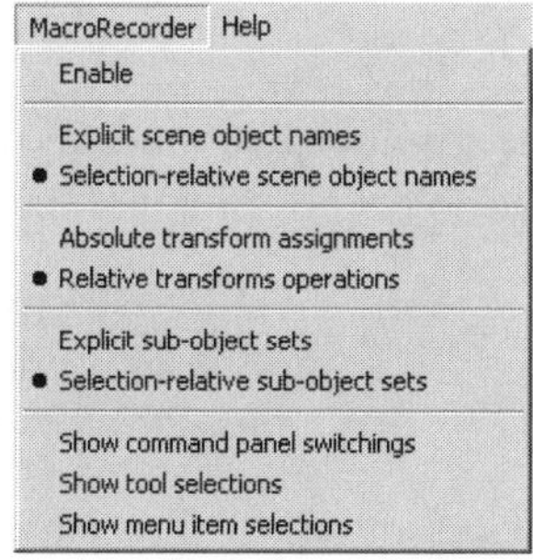

Figure 2.3 *The Macro Recorder pull-down menu*

Exercise 2.2: Using Different Macro Recorder Configurations

1. Create a sphere and collapse it to an editable mesh.
2. Turn on the Macro Recorder.
3. Make sure it is configured as in Figure 2.3. The following options should be selected:
   - Selection-relative scene object names
   - Relative transforms operations
   - Selection-relative sub-object sets

4. Move the sphere in the scene. You should have something like this recorded:

```
move $ [40.7545,-27.9609,0]
```

5. Change the Macro Recorder configuration to *Explicit scene object names* and repeat step 4. You should have something like this recorded:

```
move $Sphere01 [24.2707,19.4362,0]
```

   Notice that now you have the object name recorded, instead of having the selection recorded ($). It's not good to have the object name recorded because you cannot reuse the code unless you edit the object name for each case that you need. Using $ makes the code repeatable.

6. Return to *Selection-Relative scene object names* and change the other option to *Absolute transform assignments*. Repeat the object movement, and you should see something like this recorded:

```
$.pos = [-8.17357,-42.9315,0]
```

   Now, instead of recording the move, the absolute position is recorded. This is also not useful because it sets the precise object position, not the movement relative to the previous position.

7. Return the options to the default ones. Now change the last option to *Explicit sub-object sets*.

8. In the Modify Panel, select a couple of faces and move them around. You should see something like this as your last recorded line:

```
move $.faces[#{259..260}] [4.45065,-7.11286,0]
```

   In this line of code, you can see the list of faces that are moving. If you select *Selection-relative sub-object sets*, you would see the following recorded:

```
move $.selectedFaces [1.49587,-11.5157,0]
```

Again, this allows you to use a previous selection or to specify precisely which faces are being moved. If you know the exact topology of your object in a script, this might be handy, but if not, you'd probably end up using the *Selection-relative sub-objects sets* method.

The other three options will allow you to record or not record certain actions.

The *Show command panel switchings* option will record Command Panel changes. For instance, when you move from one panel to another, this action will be recorded, allowing the user to see the steps that you used to build the script.

The *Show tool selections* option will record when you have selected any of these tools: Selection, Move, Rotate, Non-uniform Scale, Uniform Scale, or Squash.

The *Show menu items selections* option will record some menu commands, like Mirror, Select All, or Select Invert.

Now that you know how to use the Macro Recorder, you will use it many times in the future to help you write your scripts, especially when accessing a new feature or a property so that you do not need to memorize it.

Material and Map Manipulation

Much like any feature in MAX, MAXScript can also access materials and maps. This is important because besides working on an object or a modifier, you can also assign materials and maps or prepare them to be assigned to a scene. MAXScript also works with *material libraries,* which allow you to manage the materials into assets, making your life a lot easier.

This ability comes in handy if you are developing a game and you have a lot of material presets. Instead of each animator choosing the presets from the Materials Editor, they can select them from an organized list in the Utilities Panel.

You can assign a material to any object or shape. This is done using the *.material* property in this object. As an example, the command, `obj.material = standardmaterial()` assigns a new default Standard material to `obj`.

Next, you will now learn how to work with the materials and their properties.

The Standard Material

The *Standard material* is the default basic material in MAX, and the most often used. Of course, MAXScript accesses any information in this material.

You can refer to a material in three ways.

- You can assign a material to a variable and access the variable.
- You can assign a material to an object and access the object's material.
- You can access any active material in the Materials Editor.

The easiest way is the first: Assign the material to a variable, accessing the variable. To assign a Standard material to a variable, you can use one of the following examples:

```
glass_mat = standardmaterial()
```

or

```
glass_mat = standard()
```

Both ways will assign the material to the object.

You can now use `showproperties glass_mat` to list the properties of this material. If you want to see the list, you may access it from the CD-ROM in the file `material_properties.txt`. As you can see in the text file, there are many properties in a material. In addition, these properties might vary depending on the shader of that material.

We will cover the main properties in this chapter, and you can access the rest of them using the Macro Recorder, which saves you from memorizing them.

The Color Property

You can access the material's color using the following properties:

- *.diffusecolor*, *.diffuse_color*, or *.diffuse*
- *.ambientcolor*, *.ambient_color*, or *.ambient*
- *.specularcolor*, *.specular_color*, or *.specular*
- *.filter_color* or *.filter*

You can supply the color using one of the following formats:

- `glass_mat.diffusecolor = [255,0,0]`, specifying the colors as a point3 variable where the values are r,g,b
- `glass_mat.diffusecolor = color 255 0 0 255`, where you're asking MAXScript to create a color mixing r, g, b, a values (Alpha is ignored for material colors but might be useful elsewhere.)
- `glass_mat.diffusecolor.r = 255`, specifying each color channel separately

Other Properties of the Standard Material Type

You can also access several other properties of the Standard material.

The *.shadertype* and *.shaderbyname* properties allow you to select an active shader. *Shadertype* is zero based. The first option in the drop-down list sets shadertype equal to zero (see Figure 2.4). *Shaderbyname* allows you to specify the shader name. For instance,

```
glass_mat.shadertype = 2
```

sets the shader to *Metal*, and

```
glass_mat.shaderbyname = "blinn"
```

sets the shader to *Blinn*.

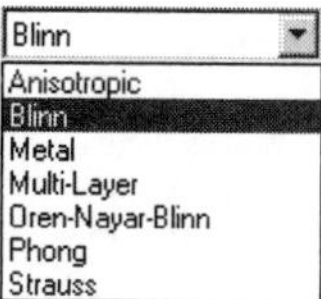

Figure 2.4 *Shader options*

To set the other options, just turn on the Macro Recorder and play with them. Write down the property name and use it in your script.

Exercise 2.3 is an example of the *opacity* property.

EXERCISE 2.3: ASSIGNING A *OPACITY* PROPERTY TO A SCRIPT

Let's create a simple utility that assigns a new material and allows you to set the object color and its transparency.

1. Open the script file named `material_utility01.ms` on the CD-ROM. Notice how the script works: It uses a pickbutton to select an object and assigns a Standard material to it. It also has a spinner but lacks an event to link it to the material's *opacity* property. Let's create the *spinner* event.
2. Run the script and select an object with the pickbutton.
3. Open the Materials Editor and copy the material from the object using the *Pick Material from Object* tool.
4. Turn on the Macro Recorder.
5. Change the object's opacity to 50%. You should have the following line recorded:

   ```
   meditMaterials[1].opacity = 50
   ```

   As you can see, the Macro Recorder records the materials based on the Materials Editor. But, you need it to be based on your own material in the script, so edit this line to reflect these changes:

   ```
   mat.opacity = val
   ```

6. Now, edit your script and add the line in step 5 as the *spinner* event.

Now you have the script assigning a material to an object and editing its transparency. The final script is named `material_utility02.ms` on the CD-ROM.

Let's move ahead and edit the material's color.

The Colorpicker

You can use a colorpicker on the UI to allow the user to select the material's color, as shown in Figure 2.5. Exercise 2.4 shows you how.

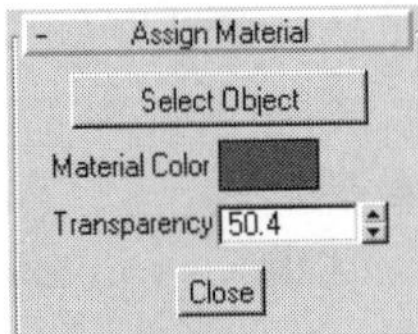

***Figure 2.5** A colorpicker*

Exercise 2.4: Using a Colorpicker to Assign the Color

Let's assign a color using the colorpicker.

1. Open the script file named `material_utility02.ms` on the CD-ROM.

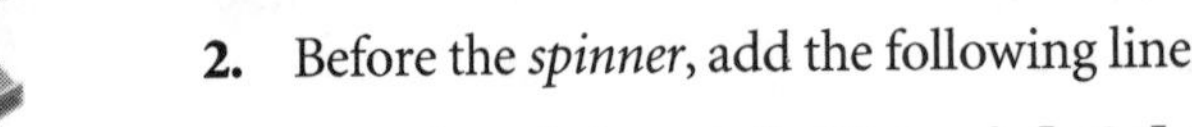

2. Before the *spinner*, add the following line:

```
colorpicker col "Material Color" default:[180,180,180]
```

3. Add a new event for the colorpicker:

```
on col changed val do
   (
   mat.diffusecolor = val
   mat.ambientcolor = val/2
   )
```

This event sets the diffuse color to the same color selected in the colorpicker and sets the ambient color to half the value, making the ambient color darker.

The final script is named `material_utility03.ms` on the CD-ROM.

The Bitmap Map

As the Standard material is the most popular material, the *bitmap* is the most often used map type.

In Exercise 2.5, you'll now create a script that allows the user to select a bitmap and assign it to the Diffuse map.

Remember that the object needs to have UVW Mapping coordinates to render correctly.

Exercise 2.5: Assigning a Bitmap to a Material

Let's create a script that assigns a bitmap to the Diffuse map.

1. Open the script file named `material_utility04.ms` on the CD-ROM.
2. Run the script and select any object in your scene using the pickbutton.
3. Using the "Pick Material from Scene" button, copy the object's material into the Materials Editor.
4. Turn on the Macro Recorder.
5. Assign any bitmap to the Diffuse map. You should have something like this recorded:

```
meditMaterials[1].diffuseMap = Bitmaptexture
   fileName:"D:\DUSKCLD1.JPG"
```

6. Now, you need to edit this to fit your script:

```
mat.diffuseMap = Bitmaptexture fileName:"D:\DUSKCLD1.JPG"
```

7. Edit your script and add the edited line as the *select bitmap* event.

The *Selectbitmap* Function

To allow the user to select the bitmap that will be assigned to the object, just use the *Selectbitmap()* function. It will display a dialog requesting the user to select a bitmap, as shown in Figure 2.6.

The dialog created by the *Selectbitmap()* function selects a bitmap and returns a bitmap variable. Instead of assigning the bitmap texture using its *filename* property, you will use the *bitmap* property.

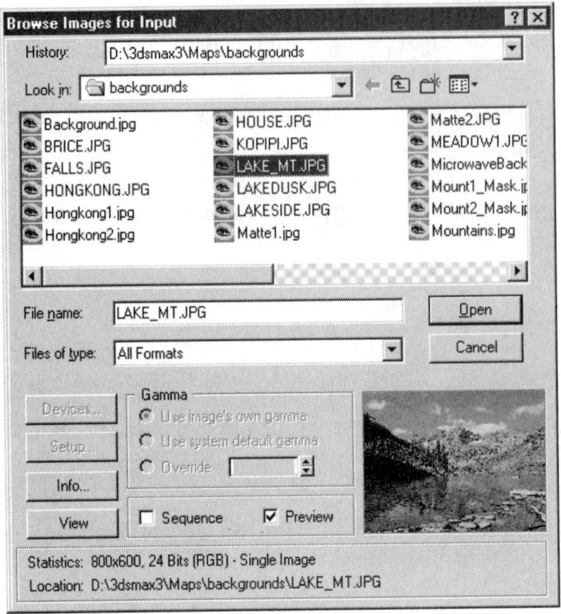

Figure 2.6 *Selecting a bitmap*

Exercise 2.5a: Assigning a Bitmap to a Material (continued)

1. Before the *mat.diffusemap* line, add the following line of code:

```
bmp = selectbitmap()
```

2. Edit the *mat.diffusemap* line as follows:

```
mat.diffuseMap = Bitmaptexture bitmap:bmp
```

The final script is named `material_utility05.ms` on the CD-ROM.

Showing a Map in a Viewport

It would be nice if the bitmap had an option to show the map in the viewport, but it works differently because one material can't have more than one map displayed in the viewport. Enabling one map automatically disables the other.

To enable a map in viewport, you should use the *showtexturemap* function, which will require you to specify the material and the map that will be shown. For example,

```
showtexturemap mat mat.diffusemap on
```

turns on the *Show Map* option in the *diffusemap* map in Exercise 2.5a.

Working with the Materials Editor

As you can see in both the exercises we did with materials, all the content recorded is recorded based on the Materials Editor. This is one of the ways that we can work with materials.

To access any of the materials in the Materials Editor, you can use `meditmaterials [index]`, where index is an integer from 1 to 24 (the maximum number of slots you can have in the Materials Editor). You can read a material parameter using *meditmaterials*, as well as create new materials using it. Also, if you use the "Get Material from Scene" button, it records this action, allowing you to use all the recorded data inside your script.

In Exercise 2.6, let's redo Exercise 2.3 using the Materials Editor and the Macro Recorder.

EXERCISE 2.6: ASSIGNING AN *OPACITY* PROPERTY TO A SCRIPT USING THE MATERIALS EDITOR

1. Open the script file named `material_utility05.ms` on the CD-ROM.
2. Run the script and select an object with the pickbutton.
3. Turn on the Macro Recorder.
4. Open the Materials Editor and copy the material from the object using the *Pick Material from Object* tool. You should have something like this recorded:

   ```
   meditMaterials[1] = $Sphere01.material
   ```

5. As you will notice, the Macro Recorder recorded the material copy from the object to the Materials Editor. In your script, this line should be

   ```
   meditMaterials[1] = obj.material
   ```

   Enter the edited line below `obj.material = mat`.

6. Change the object's opacity to 50%. You should have the following line recorded:

```
meditMaterials[1].opacity = 50
```

7. Change 50 to val, reflecting the spinner value, and copy this line to the *spinner* event.

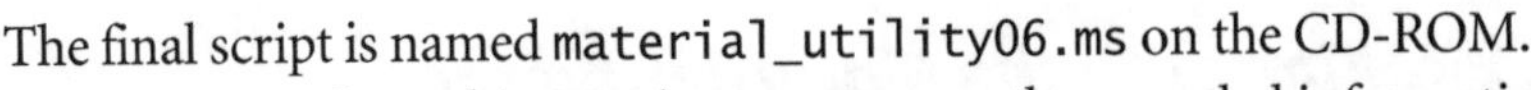

The final script is named `material_utility06.ms` on the CD-ROM.

As you can see from this exercise, you can use the recorded information from the Materials Editor directly in your script, as long as you place a copy of the material in the Materials Editor. From then on, MAXScript behaves just like MAX: Any changes made to the material in the Materials Editor reflect immediately in the object.

You can read or write materials to the Materials Editor using two other functions: *getmeditmaterial* and *setmeditmaterial*. Both require a material index from 1 to 24, and work like the example here:

```
mat01 = getmeditmaterial 1
setmeditmaterial 2 mat01
```

This will read the material in the first slot and copy it to the second slot.

Other Maps

MAX has many other maps besides Bitmap, and these maps can be assigned elsewhere than in the Diffuse map. The best thing to do is to play with these maps using the Macro Recorder, adapting the recorded data to fit your script. Table 2.1 provides a list of the existing maps that are supported through MAXScript.

Table 2.1 Maps and Their MAXScript Functions

MAP	MAXSCRIPT FUNCTION
Adobe Photoshop Plug-in Filter	*adobe_Photoshop_Plug_In_Filter()*
Adobe Premiere Plug-in Filter	*adobe_Premiere_Video_Filter()*
Bitmap	*bitmaptexture()*
Bricks	*bricks()*
Cellular	*cellular()*
Checker	*checker()*
Composite	*compositetexturemap()*

Table 2.1 Maps and Their MAXScript Functions (continued)

Map	MAXScript Function
Dent	*dent()*
Falloff	*falloff()*
Flat Mirror	*flatmirror()*
Gradient	*gradient()*
Gradient Ramp	*gradient_ramp()*
Marble	*marble()*
Mask	*mask()*
Mix	*mix()*
Noise	*noise()*
Output	*output()*
Paint	*paint()*
Particle Age	*particle_age()*
Particle Mblur	*particle_mblur()*
Perlin Marble	*perlin_marble()*
Planet	*planet()*
Raytrace	*raytrace()*
Reflect/Refract	*reflect_refract()*
RGB Multiply	*rgb_multiply()*
RGB Tint	*rgb_tint()*
Smoke	*smoke()*
Speckle	*speckle()*
Splat	*splat()*
Stucco	*stucco()*
Swirl	*swirl()*
Thin Wall Refraction	*thin_wall_refraction()*
Vertex Color	*vertex_color()*
Water	*water()*
Wood	*wood()*

Multi-Sub Material

The *Multi-Sub material* is probably the second most used material in MAX. It's where you define different materials for different parts of a single object. In MAXScript, the Multi-Sub material is an array of materials, where you can place any material you want in any of the elements.

In Exercise 2.7, we'll play a bit with Multi-Sub materials.

Exercise 2.7: Creating Multi-Sub Materials

1. Open the file `multi_sub01.max` on your CD-ROM. This file contains two objects created in MAX. These objects were converted to editable meshes, so they work even if you do not have the Door and Window plug-ins installed. These objects are interesting because they already have Material IDs specified for their different parts, which makes it easier for us to manage them using Multi-Sub objects.
2. In the Listener, type the following code:

   ```
   doormat = multimaterial()
   ```

   This will assign a Multi-Sub material to a variable.
3. Set the number of materials to 4:

   ```
   doormat.count = 4
   ```

4. Now create each of the four materials using the following code:

   ```
   doormat[1] = standardmaterial name:"Front"
   \diffusecolor:[183,156,132]
   doormat[2] = standardmaterial name:"Back"
   \diffusecolor:[231,221,206]
   doormat[3] = standardmaterial name:"Glass"
   \diffusecolor:[110,201,207]
   doormat[4] = standardmaterial name:"Frame"
   \diffusecolor:[120,98,74]
   ```

The MAXScript Listener and the MAXScript Editor are not limited in width, therefore, you can enter as many characters as you wish in one line. If you want to break a line and continue it below, just add a \ character (backslash) at the end, and MAXScript will understand that the line continues. We'll use this notation in the book because we have limited space for the code, but, if you prefer, you can ignore the \ character and the line break and place all the text in a single line.

5. Now assign this material to the PivotDoor01 object:

```
$pivotdoor01.material = doormat
```

6. Change the Glass transparency by adjusting its opacity:

```
doormat[3].opacity = 30
```

7. Repeat the steps 2–6 above, creating a material (*windowmat*) for the window with the following properties:

ID	Name	Color	Opacity
1	Front	183,156,132	100
2	Back	231,221,206	100
3	Glass	110,201,207	30
4	Frame1	120,98,74	100
5	Frame1	120,98,74	100

Since ID 4 and 5 are the same material, you can copy one to the other.

Take a look at the file `window_mat.ms` on the CD-ROM. It contains all the code you need to create and assign the materials to the window.

Raytrace Material and Map

Raytrace material and map work the same way as other materials and maps, but some of their parameters are not recordable. To access these parameters, you will need to use *showproperties* to list them and access them manually.

On the CD-ROM you will find two files, `raytracemap_properties.txt` and `raytracematerial_properties.txt`, which list the properties of both the Raytrace material and map. Notice that the Raytrace map itself has only one property: *.parameters*. Inside the *.parameters* property, you will find all properties of the map.

Global Raytrace Tracks

Through the Raytrace material and map, you can access the local options but not the global options. The global options are accessible only through the Track View.

For instance, to turn Raytrace on or off , you should use the following line of code:

```
trackviewnodes.raytrace_engine_globals.options.raytracer_enable.value
```

Specifying a value of 1.0 turns Raytrace on, and a value of 0.0 turns it off.

The rule of thumb is to use the syntax *trackviewnodes.level1.level2.level3.value* to access these properties. Level 1, 2, 3, and so on are nested levels that you see in the Track View. If the level has spaces, hyphens, slashes (/), or other special characters, simply substitute them with an underscore character (_). For instance, *Reflect/Refract Material ID's* would be

```
reflect_refract_material_id_s
```

You will learn more about how to access Track View nodes and controllers in Chapter 7.

You can use the Raytracer Setup Macro Script sample that comes with MAX to control global Raytrace properties.

Other Materials

The remaining MAX materials are also accessible through the Macro Recorder, and they have very few options. More often than not, you will work with their submaterials, which will probably be the Standard material or the Raytrace material. As always, the best method is to use the Macro Recorder to adapt the results.

Table 2.2 shows a list of the remaining materials and how you can create them in MAXScript.

Table 2.2 More MAX Materials and Their MAXScript Functions

MATERIAL	MAXSCRIPT FUNCTION
Blend	*blend()*
Composite	*compositematerial()*
Double Sided	*doublesided()*
Matte/Shadow	*matteshadow()*
Morpher	*morphermaterial()*
Shellac	*shellac()*
Top/Bottom	*topbottom()*

Material Libraries

MAXScript can access the current material library or any other material library as an array of materials. The *currentmateriallibrary* variable returns all materials in the current library indexed as an array.

Since it is an array, you can use the function *append* to add materials to the library. Since *currentmateriallibrary* is an array, you can also use *.count* (which lists the number of elements in the array):

```
currentmateriallibrary.count
```

to know how many materials are in the library, and

```
currentmateriallibrary[i]
```

to read any material from the library by substituting *i* with an integer number.

You can use the *loadmateriallibrary* and *savemateriallibrary* functions to load and save the current material library. These two functions will require you to specify a filename string to load or save the file.

If the Material/Map Browser is opened, the material library is not updated automatically. You must either close and re-open it, or choose another filter and reselect the material library.

If you do not know the name and path of the material library, you can use the *fileopenmatlib*, *filesavematlib*, and *filesaveasmatlib* methods to display a dialog box where you can choose the material library file that you want to open or save, as shown in Figure 2.7.

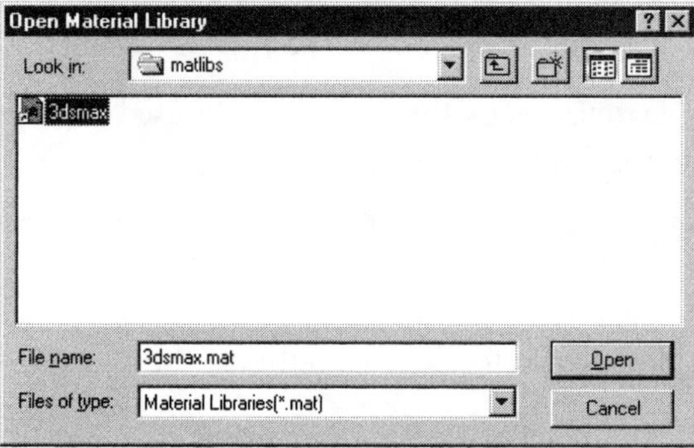

Figure 2.7 *The Open Material Library dialog box*

New User Interface Items

Let's take a look at some helpful UI items and functions for working with materials and other scripts.

Radio Buttons

Radio buttons allow us to choose one option among several. Examples of radio buttons include the choice between Chop and Squash in the Sphere's rollout, or the choice of Particle Type in any of the Particle Systems.

You can use radio buttons to choose which Bump map should be applied to an object, as in Figure 2.8.

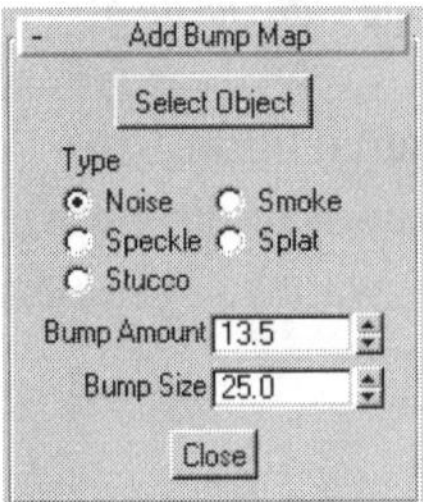

Figure 2.8 *An example of radio buttons*

Look at file `utility_bump01.ms` on the CD-ROM. We used radio buttons in it. The radio buttons line has the following syntax:

```
radiobuttons type "Type" labels:#("Noise","Smoke") columns:2
```

where

- `type` is the variable assigned to the radio buttons.
- `"Type"` is the caption text displayed in the UI.
- `labels:#("Noise","Smoke")` are the options displayed, which need to be an array with strings as elements.
- `columns` defines the number of columns, where the default is a single stacked column.

Notice also that the script reads the radio buttons using the *.state* property. Each element in the *labels'* arrays will return its index value and will allow you to design a specific action, depending on which one was selected.

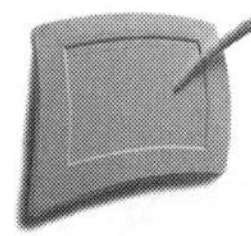

We also used max mtledit *in the script. This command opens the Materials Editor dialog, which makes it easier for the user to visualize the material changes.*

In Exercise 2.8, we will add the missing parts to this script.

Exercise 2.8: Using Radio Buttons to Select One Option among Many

1. Open the script file `utility_bump01.ms` on the CD-ROM.

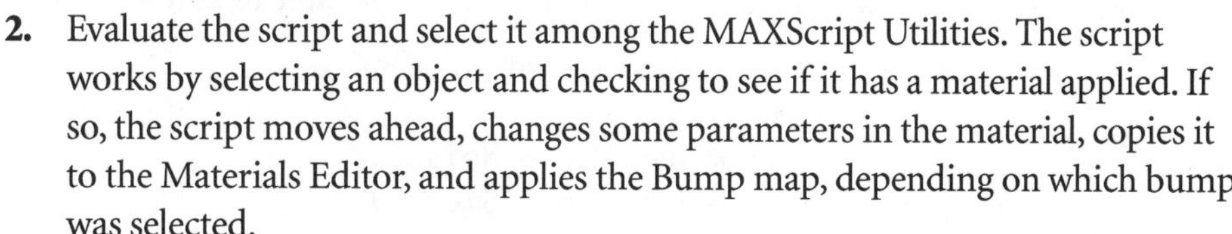

2. Evaluate the script and select it among the MAXScript Utilities. The script works by selecting an object and checking to see if it has a material applied. If so, the script moves ahead, changes some parameters in the material, copies it to the Materials Editor, and applies the Bump map, depending on which bump was selected.
3. You will now define the events that will happen when the user selects a different radio button or changes the bump amount or the size. First, you will write the *radiobutton* event. It's very similar to a *checkbox* event:

```
on type changed state do
  (
  if type.state == 1 then m.bumpMap = Noise()
  if type.state == 2 then m.bumpMap = Smoke()
  m.bumpMapAmount = amount.value
  m.bumpMap.size = size.value
  )
```

   You still need to specify the amount and the size because the Bump map created is a new one and has default values.

4. Create the events for the spinners.

The final script is named `utility_bump02.ms` on the CD-ROM.

Multiple Conditions

What would happen if we had a very large number of radio buttons? Basically, we could copy and paste a series of lines of `if type.state == n` and edit the rest. But

MAXScript offers us a better solution: the Case statement. The *Case statement* tests a variable for various values, and when it reaches the desired value, it executes the variable's related event.

Exercise 2.9 is a practical example of using the Case statement. In this exercise, we will continue using the script from Exercise 2.8.

Exercise 2.9: Using the Case Statement to Test for Multiple Conditions

1. Open the script file `utility_bump03.ms` on the CD-ROM. Currently, we have five items in the radio button and five If statements in the code. Let's edit these If statements and change them to Case statements.

2. Change the content in the five *if type.state* lines to the following:

```
case type.state of
   (
   1: m.bumpMap = Noise()
   2: m.bumpMap = Smoke()
   3: m.bumpMap = Speckle()
   4: m.bumpMap = Splat()
   5: m.bumpMap = Stucco()
   )
```

   This will have the same result as the If Then sequence, but it's easier to manage and has much clearer code.

3. Repeat the change in step 2 in the *radiobutton* event.

The final script is named `utility_bump04.ms` on the CD-ROM.

Creating Functions

If you take a look at the code in Exercise 2.8 and 2.9, you will see that a block of commands is repeated twice. *Functions* can help us avoid this repetition, making the script faster and easier to manipulate.

You can create several types of functions: functions that need arguments, functions that output values, functions that just perform a series of commands, and so on. In Exercise 2.10, you will create a function that simply reads the values from the UI and performs the necessary actions.

EXERCISE 2.10: USING FUNCTIONS TO REMOVE REPEATED CODE

1. Open the script file `utility_bump04.ms` on the CD-ROM.
2. Before the code *on pick_obj*, enter the following lines:

```
fn update_material =
(
```

3. Cut and paste all content from the *on type changed state* event.
4. Close the parenthesis.
5. In the *on type changed state* event, add the following code:

```
update_material()
```

6. Substitute the repeated content in the *pick_obj* event with the same line.

You should have the same content as file `utility_bump05.ms` on the CD-ROM.

The `fn update_material` code creates a function named *update_material*. This function will execute the code that is inside its block of code (whatever is inside the parenthesis). To call this function, simply use its name followed by a *()* (parentheses) because this function does not require any argument.

As you can see in Exercise 2.10, we substituted two repeated pieces of code with one function and two function calls. Functions are often used in this way to automate tasks and to simplify code.

Filtering User Interface Items

One use for a function is to filter objects to be selected. How does this work? Basically, you define a function that returns true if the object meets your requirements and then you link the function to a pickbutton.

In Exercise 2.11, we will do this using the script from Exercise 2.10.

EXERCISE 2.11: USING A FUNCTION FILTER TO SELECT THE CORRECT OBJECTS

1. Open the script file `utility_bump06.ms` from the CD-ROM. Notice that the code that checks to see if the selected object has a Standard material applied has been removed. This is simply because you are going to create a function that does this.

2. Before the *pickbutton*, write the following function:

```
fn object_has_material obj =
   (
   return_value = false
   if classof obj.material == StandardMaterial then
   return_value = true
   return_value
   )
```

This function has two features: It requires an argument (obj), and it returns a value. This function will return true if obj has a valid material and will return false in any other situation.

3. Edit the pickbutton line as follows:

```
pickbutton pick_obj "Select Object"
filter:object_has_material
```

Now, you linked the function to the pickbutton. Try it using two objects: one that has a Standard material and another without a material. Notice that the cursor doesn't even allow you to select the object without a material.

The final script is named utility_bump07.ms on the CD-ROM.

Using *Materialbutton* and *Mapbutton*

In the script you used in the previous examples, you allowed the user to choose a Bump map from five predefined ones. You could also allow the user to select among all the maps available in MAX using *mapbutton* (see Figure 2.9).

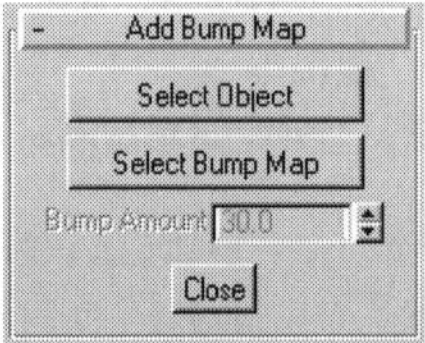

Figure 2.9 *An example of* mapbutton

When you need to select a material in a script, you can do the same using *materialbutton*. Both *materialbutton* and *mapbutton* work in the same way.

In Exercise 2.12, we'll edit the script you created in Exercise 2.11 and use *mapbutton* to allow the user to select a map for the bump.

Exercise 2.12: Using *Mapbutton* to Select the Bump Map

1. Open the script file `utility_bump08.ms` from the CD-ROM. Notice that this file has no radio buttons and no code that assigns a map to the material.
2. Add the following line after the pickbutton:

    ```
    mapbutton map "Select Bump Map" width:120
    ```

3. Add the following event code in the script:

    ```
    on map picked bumpmap do
       (
       m.bumpmap = bumpmap
       m.bumpMapAmount = amount.value
       map.text = classof bumpmap as string
       )
    ```

4. Evaluate and test the code.

The use of *mapbutton* makes the script much simpler and more flexible. Now, the user simply selects any map, and it will be placed as the Bump map. Notice that the size was removed because not every map has a *Size* option.

The final script is named `utility_bump09.ms` on the CD-ROM.

Structures

To organize complex data in MAXScript, you can use *structures*. Structures are useful to help you understand variables and their properties. A structure is a compound variable where you can define properties. To define a structure, simply type **`struct`** ***`variable-name`*** **(*`property1name`*, *`property2name`*, ...)**.

For instance, you can create a structure to manage a project. This structure will have three properties: the name of the person who is working, the starting time, and the ending time. The following code defines a structure type and then creates one variable using that type:

```
struct project (name, start, end)
oct2599 = project (name:"John", start:11.5, end:14.25)
```

To access this data later, all you would need to do is type **`variable.value`**. For instance, `oct2599.name` will return "John". The same applies to all other properties.

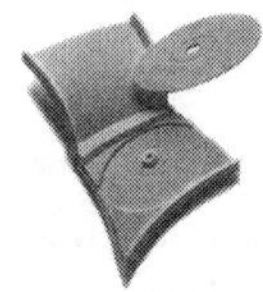

You can find a sample script called `Time_functions.ms` on the CD-ROM that will convert the local time to a structure variable that stores the date and the number of seconds. We will use this script later in other chapters.

The script will check to see whether the time configuration in your system is A.M./P.M. or 24-hour, but it will not accept dates in *dd/mm/yyyy* format. It works by cropping the *localtime* global variable, outputting the date and time as integer values. Then the script converts the hour, minute, and second values to seconds only. Manipulating only the seconds and converting the output result to hours, minutes, and seconds later saves script code and processing time.

All the result values are placed in a structure variable, which separates the data to be reused easily later.

To execute this script, simply assign a new variable to the function *right_now*. This will assign the current time to this variable. This script is useful for calculating how long a certain function takes to process. For instance, `start = right_now()` will return "#clock(day:27, month:2, year:98, sec:23119)". You can later assign a new variable and compare it with this one, calculating the time lapse.

Summary

In this chapter, you learned the concepts that will allow you to work with materials and maps in MAXScript. You also learned how to use the Macro Recorder.

In the next chapter, you will learn how to work with Editable Mesh and Editable Spline objects, hierarchies, and compound objects. You will also learn how to create simple animations using MAXScript.

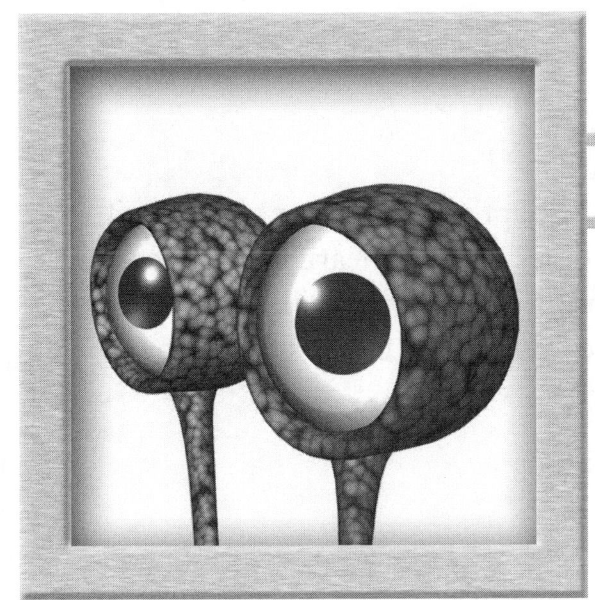

Transforms, Modifiers, and Sub-Objects

MAXSCRIPT

Chapter 3

Let's move ahead into MAXScript and learn how to work with transformations and modifiers. You will learn how to work with sub-objects and gizmos, how to work with editable meshes and editable splines, and even how to create splines from scratch. This chapter will cover:

- Working with transformations
- Managing hierarchies
- Using the coordinate system context
- Working with modifiers and sub-objects
- Manipulating editable meshes
- Manipulating editable splines

Working with Transforms

Everyone confuses transforms and modifiers. *Modifiers* change the topology of the object, while *transforms* only position and orient the object in space. Even seasoned MAX users often confuse transforms and modifiers, and it's easy to understand why. Both items make changes to objects, but the differences are important for you to remember. Modifiers change the topology of the object, while transforms only position and orient the object in space.

For example, a Bend modifier in a cylinder changes its topology, bending it to the right, while a Rotate transform rotates the cylinder in the World Coordinate System.

It's very important for you to learn how to transform an object using MAXScript. It is also important to learn how to manipulate hierarchies and to understand where the transformation takes place.

Let's start by learning how to position and orient an object in 3D space.

Adjusting Position, Rotation, and Scale

It's very important for you to know where the object is in space and which transformation has been applied to it. You might access a Box object in MAXScript and read its height, but this information will not be useful if you don't read which Z scale was applied to it.

All transformations ultimately depend on which controller has been assigned to an object. Usually, you access position, rotation, and scale simply by adding *.position*, *.rotation*, and *.scale* properties to an object.

Position and Scale

Position is the easiest to work with. Simply adding *.pos* or *.position*, as we did in Chapter 1, will usually access the object's position. Position's value is a point3 variable, where you can access independently *.x*, *.y*, and *.z*.

Position values can also be specified when the object is created (as in `b = box pos:[10,20,10]`), just like any other object option.

Some objects may not allow you to access position data using *.pos* because they have a special controller. For example, because bone objects have an IK controller, using *.pos* will return a value of invalid or undefined. Only bones with End Effectors or without the IK controller will allow *.pos*. To know their position in space, you can use the *.transform.translation* property, which will read the current position (or translation) of the object in 3D space. This command works for all objects in MAX, no matter which controller has been applied.

Scale works exactly the same way as position. In some cases, if the *.scale* property fails, you can use the *.transform.scale* property.

Rotation

Rotation might be a little bit difficult to understand. This is because MAX uses TCB rotation by default. TCB rotation uses a quaternium algebra (or quats) to calculate the rotation. TCB rotations are smooth for animation, but it's a little hard to manipulate TCB values in MAXScript because the quaternium doesn't directly show us the rotation of the object. For more information on quats and TCB rotation, refer to the MAXScript Online Help.

We'll make rotation simple and use a different rotation method, called eulerangles. *Eulerangles* are X/Y/Z rotation vectors that work the same way as position and scale. In order to access the rotation without using quats, you need to access each axis independently, using the property *object.rotation.axis_rotation*, substituting *x*, *y*, or *z* for *axis*. Eulerangles can be used regardless of the controller assigned to the rotation track.

For instance, to access a box's Z rotation for an object named b, you can use the `b.rotation.z_rotation` command.

Managing Hierarchies

You can create and manage hierarchies in MAXScript. It's the same as using the Link and Unlink tools, but you can also list and check the object relations in MAXScript.

You can link objects the same way you do manually in the viewports, selecting the children and linking them to a parent. It's done using the *.parent* property, which is valid for all objects.

For example, let's create two objects and link them:

```
b = box pos:[100,0,0]
c = cylinder pos:[50,0,0]
c.parent = b
```

In this example, `b` is the parent, and `c` is the child. You can check it using the Select By Name dialog with the *Display Subtree* checkbox selected, as in Figure 3.1

Figure 3.1 *The Select By Name dialog box*

Of course, you could use any means you wish to specify the objects: `$name`, `selection[index]`, etc.

You can use *.children* property to see which objects are linked to one object, and you can also append child objects. For example, let's create a sphere and link it to the box, continuing the previous example:

```
s = sphere()
append b.children s
```

To simply list the child objects, use the `b.children` command. If you want to know how many child objects you have, use the `b.children.count` command. Since the index of children is an array, you can also use the `b.children[`*index*`]` syntax to access each child object.

Using the Coordinate System Context

The transforms that we saw are based in the World Coordinate System. But, if you need to know an object's position based on another object, or based on a grid, how would you do it? This can be done using the *coordinate system context.*

To use the *coordinate system context*, just enter the following:

```
in coordsys <coord_base> <transform>
```

As an example, let's play with a simple file:

1. Open the file `dummy_hand.max` on your CD-ROM. In this file, you have a Hand object and a series of fingers named A–E, with each finger containing two or three divisions, as seen in Figure 3.2.

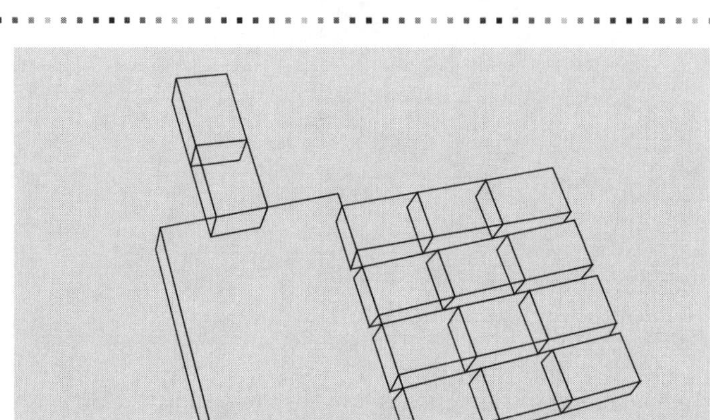

Figure 3.2 *The dummy Hand object*

2. Open the MAXScript Listener.
3. Select *HandA_01* and type the following:

   ```
   $.rotation.z_rotation += 45
   ```

4. Observe the results and then undo the results.
5. Now, type the following:

   ```
   in coordsys local $.rotation.z_rotation = 45
   ```

   Now you have a nice result. The first rotation did not work well because the objects are not aligned to the XYZ world.

6. Repeat step 5. Notice how the rotation is adding 45 degrees to the last state. That's what the `coordsys local` context does: The current state is considered to be [0,0,0], and any transformation to the object is based on its current state.
7. Undo all rotations until the object returns to its initial state.
8. Now, select *HandB_01* and type the following:

```
in coordsys parent $.rotation.x_rotation = -30
```

Now you have the finger correctly rotated. And, most importantly, the finger is rotating based on a *coordsys* that will not be altered, as `coordsys local` was.

Take a look at the `hand_controller.ms` script in the CD-ROM to see how the coordinate system context is used.

Besides using `local` and `parent coordsys`, you can also use `world`, `grid`, and `node`, where `node` is any object in the scene.

Duplicating Objects

MAX allows objects to be duplicated using three procedures: copy, instance, and reference. MAXScript also allows this sort of duplication. However, it's easier to copy and instance parameters, materials, modifiers, maps, objects, and even controllers through MAXScript than it is through the UI.

Using the *copy* function, you can create copies of anything. For example, you created a box using `b = box()`. Now, you can create a copy using `c = copy b`. The same happens for materials, maps, and controllers. This copy is not instanced; it's just a clone object with the same parameters. The copy does not retain any relation to the original.

You can also use *copy* to copy any variable or parameter. When the parameter has nested elements, like an array, the base array is copied, but the elements are instanced. This also happens with a material that has maps: The maps remain instanced. To copy a variable or parameter, you need to implement a loop that will copy the nested elements one by one. For instance, using the `m.diffusemap = copy m.diffusemap` command will create a copy without references, acting just like the *Make Unique* button.

You can create an instance of any object, using the *instance* function. If you want to create an instance of materials, maps, controllers, and modifiers, simply assign them again to the instanced value without using `copy`. For instance, the command `m.diffusemap = n.diffusemap` will create an instance of the *diffusemap* in *n*. If you need to create an instance with objects in the scene, you will need to use the *instance* function. For example, `c = instance b` duplicates `b`, creating an instance.

If you want a reference of any object, just use the *reference* function. References only work for objects in the scene.

Working with Modifiers and Sub-Objects

Sub-objects are a constant in MAX. Almost everything you do in MAX will require you to adjust something at a sub-object level. Modifiers, editable meshes, and editable splines require us to manipulate and adjust sub-object information. Some of these features even have several new options that are dependant on the sub-object level.

You'll now see how MAXScript can access this information and help you create scripts that can do things you couldn't do before. Let's start working with modifiers.

Working with Modifiers

Modifiers are part of our daily life in MAX. You played with modifiers in Chapter 1, but now you will get a better idea of how to work with them. You saw how to add modifiers using the *addmodifier* function. You also learned how to query the modifier for its properties, using the *showproperties* function.

Now you will learn how to work with modifiers, how to change their properties and how to access their sub-objects levels.

Adding Modifiers

As you saw in Chapter 1, you can add modifiers to an object using the *addmodifier* function. But this function will not work all the time, especially if you have an object that cannot have that modifier applied. Let's see how this happens:

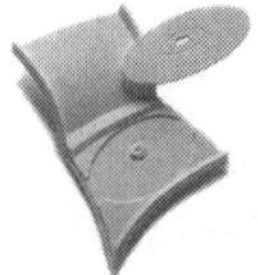

1. Open the `modifier_sample.max` file on your CD-ROM. This file looks like Figure 3.3.
2. Select the *Text01* object.
3. In the Listener, type the following:

```
addmodifier $ (extrude())
```

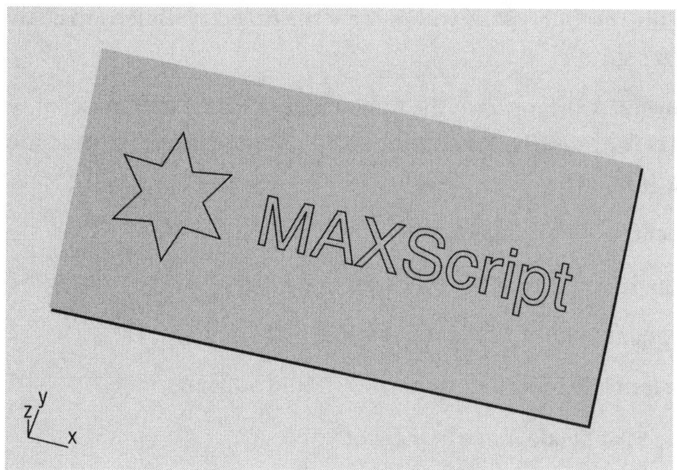

Figure 3.3 *The modifier_sample MAX file*

4. Select *Box01* and repeat step 3. You will receive the following error message:

```
-- Runtime error: Modifier is not appropriate: Extrude:Extrude
```

   That happens because the Box object is not a 2D element, thus, it cannot have an *Extrude* modifier applied. This kind of error would stop a script from executing, leaving you with a problem: How can you know which modifiers can be applied to an object? That's simple, use the *validmodifier* function.

5. In the Listener, type the following:

```
validmodifier $ (Extrude())
```

MAXScript will return false, which means that this object cannot have an Extrude modifier applied.

Validmodifier can also be used in selections, and if a single object in the selection doesn't fit the modifier rules, the entire selection will return false.

Editing Modifiers

You already learned how to access a modifier property. But so far, you have not yet learned the subtleties of how accessing a modifier property works.

You can access a modifier using *obj.modifier*, where *obj* is the object and *modifier* is the name of the modifier. So, if you rename the object, you need to change the way you access it. That's simple:

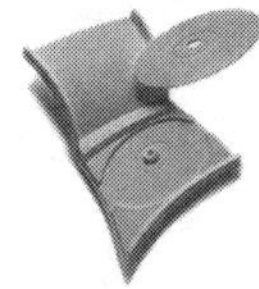

1. Continue working with the same file from the last exercise, or open the file `modifier_sample.max` on the CD-ROM and add a Extrude modifier to the *Text01* object.
2. Select the *Text01* object.
3. In the Listener, type the following:

   ```
   showproperties $.extrude
   ```

   The Extrude modifier properties should appear.
4. Type **`$.extrude.name = "Z vector"`**.
5. Repeat step 3. MAXScript will return the following message:

   ```
   -- Unknown property: "Extrude" in $Editable_Mesh:Text01
   ```

This happens because you have renamed the modifier. Now, you need to access it using one of the methods shown in Table 3.1:

Table 3.1 Accessing a Modifier Sample

METHOD TO ACCESS MODIFIERS	SAMPLE
By name (directly)	`$.z_vector` or `$.'Z vector'`
By index	`$.modifiers[1]` or `$[4][1]`
By name (using modifiers)	`$.modifiers["Z vector"]` or `$.modifiers[#z_vector]`

Every time you have a name with a space or a special character, you can access it in MAXScript by substituting it with an underscore (_) character or by encapsulating the string inside single quote characters ('). In the previous example, "Z vector" is accessed as `z_vector` *or* `'z vector'`.

To remove a modifier, you can simply use the *deletemodifier* function.

To remove the modifier in the previous example, just use the `deletemodifier $ $.z_vector` command.

Listing Properties

Besides using the *showproperties* function, you can list the properties of anything using the *getpropnames* function. This function is more useful for modifiers because it allows you to know not only what the properties are but also to access them.

Let's see an example of how *getpropnames* works:

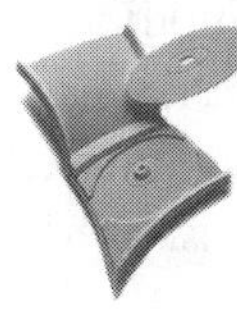

1. Continue working with the same file from the last exercise, or open the file `modifier_sample.max` on the CD-ROM.
2. Select Box01.
3. Add a Taper modifier using the following code:

```
addmodifier $ (taper amount:-2 curve:2 primaryaxis:0 effectaxis:1)
```

4. Copy a list of the properties to a variable using the following command:

```
prop = getpropnames $.taper
```

This will generate an array containing all the properties of that modifier. We can read and set these properties using the *getproperty* and *setproperty* methods. The `getproperty $.taper #curve` command will read the value of the curve property in that modifier. To set the amount value, you would use the command `setproperty $.taper "amount" -2`.

A good example of the usage of *getpropnames*, *getproperty*, and *setproperty* is the Copy Property script (`tools-copy_prop.mcr`), included as a sample on the CD-ROM.

Global Modifier Properties

Besides the *.name* property, a modifier has a couple more properties. These properties define if the modifier is enabled or disabled both in the viewport and at rendering time.

Using the *.enabled* property allows you to turn a modifier on or off, both in viewport and in rendering.

Using the *.enabledinviews* property turns off a modifier in the viewport only, leaving it on at the render time.

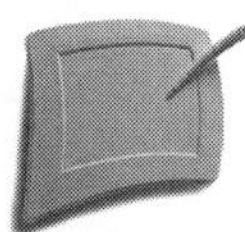

Turning off some modifiers in the viewport, such as Meshsmooth and Optimize, will speed your screen redraw, making it faster to manipulate your models.

Manipulating Sub-Objects in Modifiers

Many of the modifiers have sub-objects. Usually they're a gizmo that defines the area to be affected by the modifier.

The sub-object appears as one of the properties of the object, when called through the *showproperties* or *getpropnames* functions.

One of the modifiers that has a gizmo is the Slice modifier. Let's use this modifier to recreate a real-life scenario and show how MAXScript can help automate tasks.

In the following exercise, we have a Mesh object with a bitmap texture on it. This object, due to its irregular shape, has problems loading into lightscape or into discreet's frost*. The best scenario is to break it into smaller objects, making the irregular areas smaller.

How can you do this? Simple: Just add a Slice modifier to divide it in two, and then divide these parts in two again. Where does MAXScript fit in? By automating this task with a script. With a script, you can repeat this action in many objects if you need to.

Exercise 3.1: Using the Slice Modifier to Split Meshes

1. Open the file `slice_object.max` on your CD-ROM. It should look like Figure 3.4.
2. Open the script file `slice_object01.ms`. Observe the script and notice that it already contains the UI, and it also applies the Slice modifiers. You need to add a series of commands that will rotate the gizmos in the Slice modifier, called slice_plane.

Figure 3.4 *The slice_object MAX file*

3. After *obj4 = copy obj*, add the following code:

```
obj.modifiers[1].slice_plane.rotation.x_rotation = 90
obj.modifiers[2].slice_plane.rotation.y_rotation = 90
```

4. Repeat the same for the other three objects, rotating the planes according to Table 3.2.

Table 3.2 Slice Plane Rotation

OBJECT	AXIS	ANGLE
obj2	x	–90
	y	90
obj3	x	90
	y	–90
obj4	x	–90
	y	–90

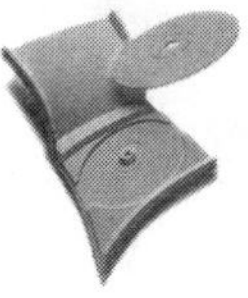

Your script file should look like `slice_object02.ms`, which is on the CD-ROM.

After learning how to manipulate bitmaps in Chapter 5, and after learning how to work with texture vertices later in this chapter, you will be able to finish this script, splitting the bitmap into four smaller bitmaps and applying each of them to the respective slice that you created.

Working with Editable Meshes

An important use of MAXScript is to access and manipulate editable meshes. You can access vertex and face information, allowing you to change almost any parameter on the sub-object level. You can even create objects from scratch using these commands.

MAXScript also provides access to the editable mesh UI commands. These commands will not be executed, but instead will keep waiting for the user's input in the viewport. Using a MAXScript extension, you can also execute these commands directly from MAXScript (see Chapter 11).

Converting Objects to Editable Meshes

The first way we can create Editable Mesh objects is by converting objects to editable mesh or by collapsing the modifier stack. This can be done using either of the commands *collapsestack* or *converttomesh*.

The *collapsestack* command will work the same way as the *Collapse All* button in Edit Stack, as in Figure 3.5.

Here's an example of how it can be done:

```
obj1 = sphere pos:[-30,0,0]
obj2 = box pos:[25,0,0]
addmodifier obj2 (taper())
collapsestack obj1
collapsestack obj2
```

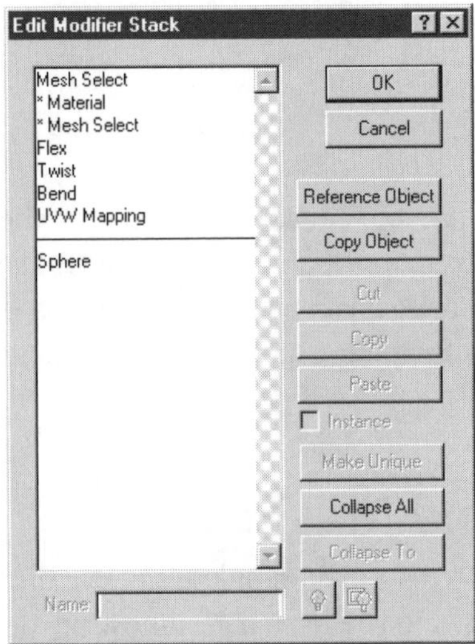

Figure 3.5 *The Edit Modifier Stack dialog box*

In order to convert your object to editable mesh using the *collapsestack* command, it needs to have a modifier on top of it, or else it will be converted to its base object. In the previous code, notice that the sphere remains a Sphere object because it has no modifiers on top.

To remove this limitation, you can use the *converttomesh* function, which will convert the object to an Editable Mesh object, regardless of the modifiers it has. To make sure that this conversion is possible, you can use the *canconvertto* function to see if it can be converted to mesh.

Continuing the previous example, entering `canconvertto obj1 mesh` will return true, telling you that the sphere can be converted to a mesh. Using `converttomesh obj1` will convert the sphere to an Editable Mesh object.

The editable mesh conversion considers every modifier, except space warps. To have the space warp effect considered, you need to use the *snapshot* function, which will make a copy of the object in its current state as an editable mesh.

Another way to have an object converted to editable mesh is by attaching it to an Editable Mesh object. This can be done using the *attach* function. In the previous example, using `attach obj1 obj2` will attach obj2 to obj1, leaving you with a single Editable Mesh object.

Accessing Vertex Information

Another benefit of knowing how to access editable mesh information is that you also can obtain and modify vertex information.

MAXScript accesses all information available for vertices, as seen in in Table 3.3.

Table 3.3 Vertex Manipulation Methods

INFORMATION	READ	SET
Number of vertices	*getnumverts*	*setnumverts*
Vertex position	*getvert*	*setvert*
Vertex normal	*getnormal*	*setnormal*
Vertex selection	*getvertselection*	*setvertselection*
Average selection center	*averageselvertcenter*	
Average selection normal	*averageselvertnormal*	

All this information can be read or set, meaning that you can modify an Editable Mesh object. You can also modify vertex selections in Edit Mesh and Mesh Select modifiers.

Let's play with vertices.

1. Reset your MAX scene and create the following object:

   ```
   b = box pos:[20,20,0] width:30 height:30 length:30
   ```

2. Convert it to editable mesh using the `converttomesh b` command.
3. Read the number of vertices using `getnumverts b`. It should return 8.
4. Read the position of vertex #1 using the command `getvert b 1`. It should return [5,5,0].
5. Now, move vertex #1 to [0,0,0] using the command `setvert b 1 [0,0,0]`.
6. Nothing happens because all mesh operations need to be updated using the `update b` command.
7. Go to the Modify panel and select three vertices in the base and two in the top of the box. Turn off Sub-Object mode.
8. In the Listener, query which vertices are selected using the `getvertselection b` command. It should return something like this:

   ```
   #{1..3, 5,7}
   ```

   This is called *Bitarray*. It defines a series of elements that define the selection. These elements can be defined as an interval or as single elements. Here, *1..3* defines an interval, and *5* and *7* are isolated elements. In total, elements 1, 2, 3, 5, and 7 are selected.

9. Let's specify that vertices 1–4 and 7 are selected using the command `setvertselection b #{1..4,7}`.
10. Go to the Modify panel and enter Sub-Object mode to see which vertices are selected.
11. To know what the average center of the vertex selection is, use the `getselvertcenter b` command. It should return [–4,2,6].

The value returned is in object space. To know this point in world space, simply multiply it by `b.transform`.

Accessing Color Per Vertex

Besides vertex position, normal, and selection, you can also access Color Per Vertex (CPV). This is used together with the Assign Color Per Vertex utility in MAX, or even using the Vertex Paint or other modifiers.

Through MAXScript, you can read and set the vertex color, using the methods shown in Table 3.4.

Table 3.4 Color Per Vertex Manipulation Methods

INFORMATION	READ	SET
Number of CPV vertices	*getnumcpvverts*	*setnumcpvverts*
Vertex color	*getvertcolor*	*setvertcolor*

Let's see how it works.

1. Open the file `cpv_sample.max` on your CD-ROM. It looks like Figure 3.6.
2. Select the cylinder.
3. Using the Listener, list the number of CPV vertices using the command `getnumcpvverts $`. It should return 648.

Figure 3.6 *The CPV_sample MAX file*

4. Read the vertex colors or the first vertex using the command `getcpvccolor $ 1`. It should return `(color 0 0 0)`.
5. Repeat step 4 for vertices 100, 200, 300, 400, 500, and 600.
6. Change the vertex color of vertex #648 using the command `setvertcolor $ 648 (color 255 255 255)`.
7. For you to see the changes on-screen, use the command `update $`.

Notice the white triangle on top of the cylinder.

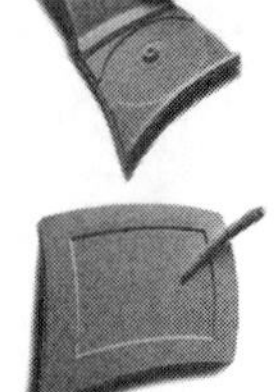

The `cpv_adjust.ms` file found in the CD-ROM is an example of script that adjusts CPV information.

The `cpv_sample.max` file you used has a large number of vertices with Color Per Vertex. Using the sample script to adjust this information might take a long time, depending on your system speed.

Accessing Face Information

By connecting three vertices, you can create a face. A *face* has more information than a vertex. Besides its location and its normal, a face also has a smoothing group and a material ID. Also, a face can be extruded, collapsed and deleted. And, you can do all of this through MAXScript. Table 3.5 shows you the methods associated with faces.

Table 3.5 Face Manipulation Methods

INFORMATION	READ	SET
Number of faces	*getnumfaces*	*setnumfaces*
Face vertices	*getface*	*setface*
Face normal	*getfacenormal*	*setfacenormal*
Material ID	*getfacematid*	*setfacematid*
Smoothing group	*getfacesmoothgroup*	*setfacesmoothgroup*
Face selection	*getfaceselection*	*setfaceselection*
Delete face		*deleteface*
Collapse face		*collapseface*
Extrude face		*extrudeface*

All these properties work exactly like the ones for vertices.

For instance, you can write a script that will extrude each pair of faces of an object. Let's see how it is done:

1. Draw a sphere in MAX using the command `sph = sphere radius:30 segments:15`.
2. Convert it to editable mesh using the command `converttomesh sph`.
3. Define the variable that will contain the number of faces using the command `numfaces = getnumfaces sph/2`.
4. You need a *For* expression to create a loop stepping through the faces. You will also define the *Extrude* method, so create both in a single line, as follows:

   ```
   for i in 1 to numfaces do (extrudeface sph #{i*2..(i*2)+1} 4 50)
   ```

5. Now, update the object using the `update sph` command.

Do not forget to update the mesh when manipulating vertices and faces.

6. Now you can set the colors of these faces using Material IDs, as follows:

   ```
   for i in 1 to (getnumfaces sph) do setfacematid sph i 1
   for i in 1 to (numfaces*2) do setfacematid sph i 2
   ```

7. Repeat step 5 to update it.

You just set all faces to Material ID 1 and then extrude all the faces. Then you set Material ID 2 to all the faces that were extruded, creating a nice multi-colored object, as seen in Figure 3.7. If you want to see it in the viewport, create a Multi-Sub material with two different colors.

Other Properties in Editable Mesh Objects

You can also access edge visibility and texture vertex (UVW Map) information. In addition, many of the methods we saw here are also defined as properties of an editable mesh. Table 3.6 shows these properties.

Table 3.6 Editable Mesh Object Properties

Property	Description
.numverts	Number of vertices
.numfaces	Number of faces

Table 3.6 Editable Mesh Object Properties (continued)

PROPERTY	DESCRIPTION
.numcpvverts	Number of CPV vertices
.selectedverts	Selected vertices
.verts	A selection with all vertices
.selectedfaces	Selected faces
.faces	A selection with all faces
.selectededges	Selected edges
.edges	A selection with all edges

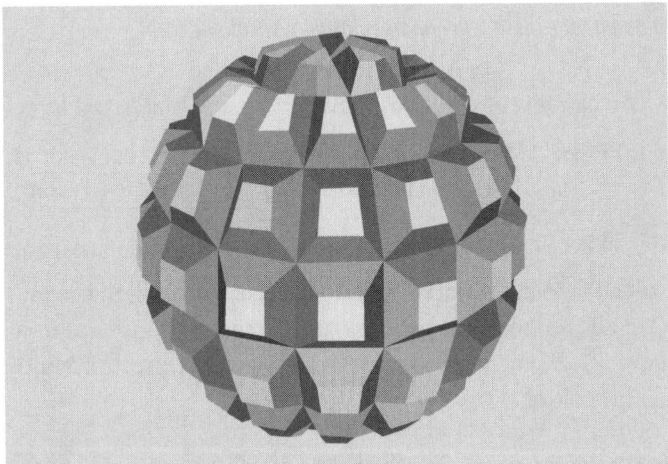

Figure 3.7 *A sphere with extruded faces*

The properties that list the number of vertices, faces, and edges can substitute the *getvertnumber* method and the others. The selection properties are used for transformation only. For instance, the `move sph.selectedfaces [10,10,10]` command moves all selected faces in the *sph* object the specified distance.

Texture vertex (TV) works similarly to CPVs, but instead of color, the texture coordinate will be adjusted. A texture vertex of 0 defines the bottom left of the map, and a texture vertex index of 1 defines the top-right point of the map. The methods that adjust texture vertex can be seen in Table 3.7.

Table 3.7 Texture Vertex Manipulation Methods

INFORMATION	READ	SET
Number of TV vertices	*getnumtverts*	*setnumtverts*
Texture Vertex	*gettvert*	*settvert*

Manipulating these properties might be very complicated, mathematically speaking. Make sure you know what you're doing, and make backup copies of your models before working with the texture vertices.

Hands-On MAXScript: Designing a Scatter Utility

Using all the knowledge you have to work with Editable Mesh objects, you can design your own Scatter utility. It might not be as complex as the Scatter compound object in MAX, but at least it allows you to scatter any type of object, not only geometry.

You will create a simple Scatter utility that has the following features. It selects a 3D object that will be the base object. Then it selects the object that will be scattered. It offers you two scatter methods: *vertex* and *face center*. By clicking a button, the scatter is created using the chosen method.

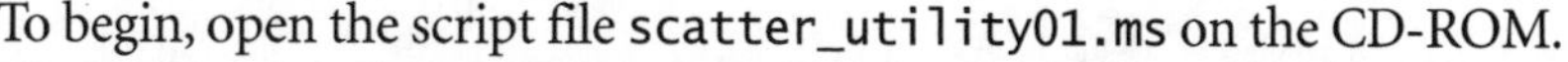

To begin, open the script file `scatter_utility01.ms` on the CD-ROM.

This file has the UI ready and a few of the commands, as in Figure 3.8. When the user clicks the *base_obj pickbutton*, a *snapshot* of the object is created, so it will be converted to editable mesh automatically, and all the space warps and modifiers will be collapsed.

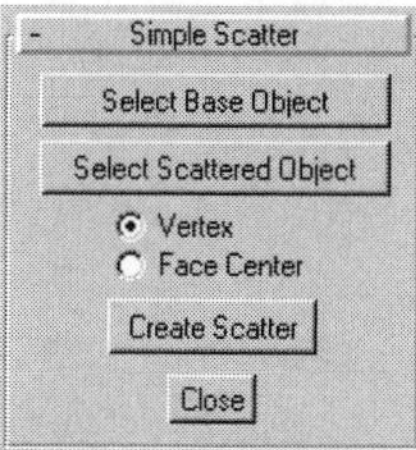

Figure 3.8 *The Scatter utility script*

The script already defines the two objects that you will work with: *base* and *sc*. The code is also ready and just needs the *scatter* function to be created. You will create the code for the first scatter type: *vertex*. The idea is to create an instance of the *sc* object at each vertex position. To do so, after `1: (`, enter the following:

```
numsc = base.numverts
for i in 1 to numsc do
      (
      pos = getvert base i
      temp = instance sc
      temp.pos = pos
      )
delete base
```

`Numsc` reads the number of vertices. Then, for each vertex, read its position using `getvert` and assign this position to an instance of the original object.

Your script should look like file `scatter_utility02.ms` on the CD.

Think a little bit and play with the file to create the *face center* part of the script. The idea is to read each face, identify the vertices positions, and position the instanced object in the average position. Figure 3.9 shows the different results you should get using the *face center* or *vertex* methods in the scatter.

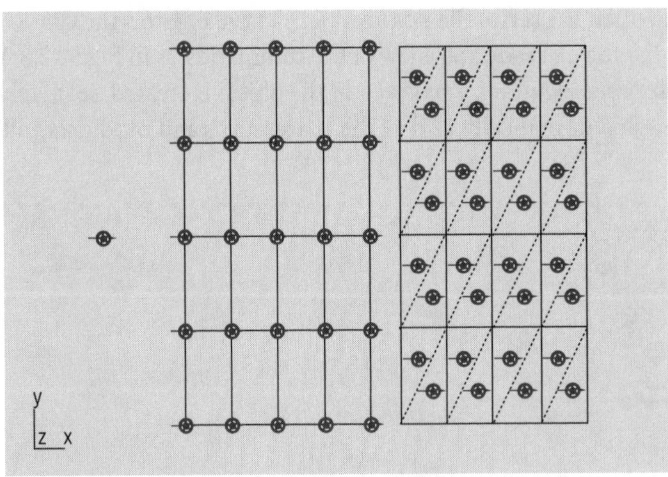

Figure 3.9 *Scatter using* vertex *and* face center *methods*

The *face center* part is ready in the file `scatter_utility03.ms` on the CD-ROM.

Working with Editable Splines

Editable Spline objects are very similar to editable meshes. The main difference comes from the topology of the objects and their properties. You can work with splines, segments, and vertices, manipulating all of their properties.

As with editable meshes, you can convert shapes to editable splines using the *converttospline* function. To test if an object can be converted to an editable spline, use the command `canconvertto obj splineshape`.

Manipulating Shapes

Shape is the entire Spline object. A shape has various splines, which are made of vertices and segments. When manipulating shapes, it's very important to identify which spline, segment, and vertex you want to access.

MAXScript provides lots of methods and properties for shapes so that you can access all of their information. Table 3.8 shows the *shape* methods.

Table 3.8 Shape Methods

METHOD	DESCRIPTION
resetshape	Removes all splines from the shape.
setfirstspline	Defines which is the first spline in the shape.
materialID	Reads the material ID of the segment.
hideselectedsplines	Hides the selected splines.
hideselectedsegments	Hides the selected segments.
hideselectedverts	Hides the selected vertices.
updateshape	Same as update for editable meshes.
curvelength	Returns the length of a spline.
pathinterp	Returns a XYZ point in the spline that is segment based.
lengthinterp	Returns a XYZ point in the spline that is overall-length based.

Curvelength, *pathinterp*, and *lengthinterp* are probably the most important methods. They allow us to query the spline for its length, which might be useful for many tasks.

Pathinterp and *lengthinterp* are functions that calculate a point in the spline, interpolating the position using two different methods. *Pathinterp* interpolates segments, which means that if a spline has five segments, segment #1 will be 0–20% of the spline, segment #2 will be 20–40%, and so on. This can lead to strange results if the segments are not normalized (if they have different lengths).

Lengthinterp interpolates the point based in the overall spline length. This is similar to the effect of the *Constant Velocity* option in the Path Controller, which will evenly space the animation along the overall spline length.

Let's move on to the other elements of an editable spline. At the end, you will create an exercise gathering all the information.

Manipulating Vertices

Vertices are called *knots* in MAXScript. This is to differentiate them from Editable Mesh vertices.

MAXScript allows you to create knots and adjust their position, type, and tangent vector (when possible). You can also work with selections, the same way as editable meshes. Table 3.9 shows the methods used to work with knots.

Table 3.9 Knot Methods

INFORMATION	READ	SET
Knot position	*getknotpoint*	*setknotpoint*
Knot in tangent	*getinvec*	*setinvec*
Knot out tangent	*getoutvec*	*setoutvec*
Knot type	*getknottype*	*setknottype*
Knot selection	*getknotselection*	*setknotselection*
Add knot		*addknot*
Delete knot		*deleteknot*

As an example, let's modify a Circle shape adjusting its information.

1. Create a circle using the command `c = circle radius:30`.
2. Convert the circle to an editable spline using the command `convertto-splineshape c`.

3. Query which knot type is knot #2 using `getknottype c 1 2`, where *1* is the number of the spline, and *2* is the number of the knot. It should return "`#bezier`".

4. Change the knot type to corner using the command `setknottype c 1 2 #corner`.

5. Update the changes on-screen using the command `updateshape c`. You should see the shape shown in Figure 3.10.

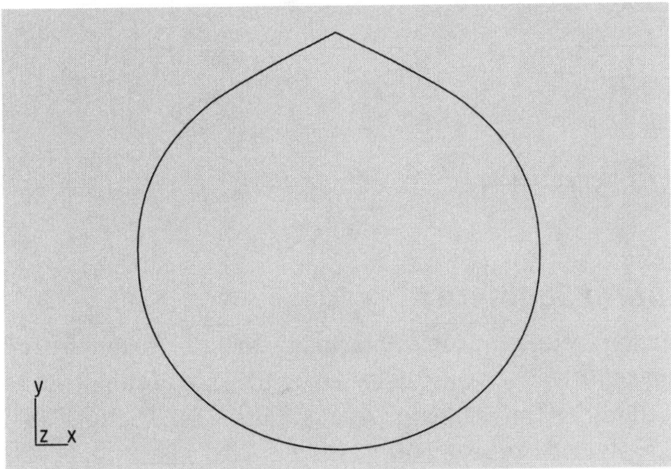

Figure 3.10 *Circle with top vertex changed to corner*

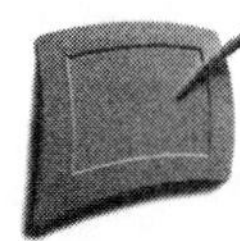

Similar to an editable mesh, you need to use the `updateshape` method to see the changes to an editable spline.

6. Now, move this knot up using the command `setknotpoint c 1 2 (getknotpoint c 1 2 + [0,30,0])`.

7. Repeat the `updateshape c` command to update your viewport.

You should have a droplet-shape object, as in Figure 3.11

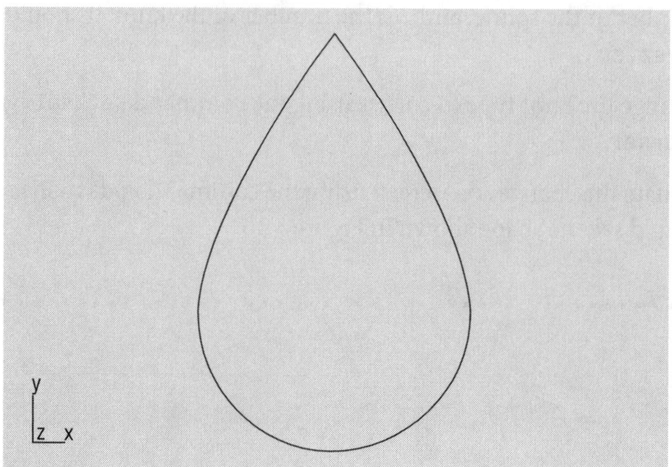

Figure 3.11 *A Droplet shape*

Manipulating Segments

MAXScript manipulates segments very similarly to how it manipulates knots. You cannot set a segment position because it's based on the knot position, but you can set its type and selection. You can also refine segments using MAXScript. Table 3.10 shows a list of available methods for segments.

Table 3.10 Segment Methods

INFORMATION	READ	SET
Segment type	*getsegmenttype*	*setsegmenttype*
Knot selection	*getsegmentselection*	*setsegmentselection*
Refine segment		*refinesegment*

Let's refine the droplet, creating two more vertices in the pointed portion of the shape:

1. Continue using the example we started in the "Manipulating Vertices" section.
2. Refine the right segment using the command `refinesegment c 1 1 0.5`. The *refinesegment* method needs the spline number (1), the segment number (1), and the percentage where it will break the segment, which can vary from 0 to 1.0.
3. Update the droplet on-screen using the command `updateshape c`.
4. To view the segments, go to the Display Panel and turn on the *Vertex Ticks* option in the Display Properties rollout. Now you see little marks where the vertices are located.
5. Refine the left segment using the command `refinesegment c 1 3 0.5`. Notice that it's not segment #2, but instead #3 because the first refine created an extra segment that needs to be considered.
6. Repeat step 5.

Now you should have the same Droplet shape, but with with extra vertices, as in Figure 3.12.

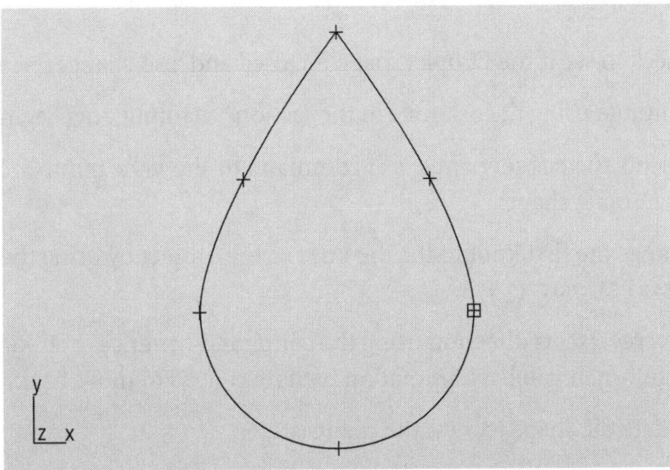

Figure 3.12 *The Droplet shape with two more vertices*

Manipulating Splines

A *spline* is a group of segments. MAXScript allows you to create and delete splines, to query the number of segments and vertices, to close or open them, and also to manipulate their selection. The methods available for splines are explained in Table 3.11.

Table 3.11 Spline Methods

INFORMATION	READ	SET
Spline selection	*getsplineselection*	*setsplineselection*
Add spline		*addspline*
Delete spline		*deletespline*
Number of segments	*numsegments*	
Number of knots	*numknots*	
Is spline closed	*isclose*	
Close spline		*close*
Open spline		*open*
Reverse its direction		*reverse*
Set first knot		*setfirstknot*

Let's check to see if the Droplet shape is closed and also change its first vertex.

1. Continue using the example in the section "Manipulating Segments."
2. Execute the `numsegments c 1` command to show the number of segments in the Droplet shape.
3. Change the first knot to the top knot of the droplet by using the command `setfirstknot c 1 3`.
4. Now reverse its direction using the command `reverse c 1`. Reverse is very useful when you have animation paths and need to move backward.
5. Update the shape to view the changes.

Creating Splines from Scratch

You can create splines manually in MAXScript, specifying each vertex and spline position. It's not simple, but sometimes it's the only way that it can be done.

You can create splines by creating and connecting vertices (using *addknot*) and also by creating splines in the same shape (using *addnewspline*). This way, you can create splines and vertices, which will be connected sequentially.

Let's create a rectangle as an example. To do so, enter the following code in the Listener:

```
ss = splineshape()
addnewspline ss
addknot ss 1 #corner #curve [0,0,0]
addknot ss 1 #corner #curve [10,0,0]
addknot ss 1 #corner #curve [10,10,0]
addknot ss 1 #corner #curve [0,10,0]
close ss 1
updateshape ss
```

The first command, `ss = splineshape()`, creates an Editable Spline object with no vertex or spline. Then, you manually create the spline and the vertices, which are automatically connected in sequence.

The Edit Spline Command

MAXScript allows you to access a series of commands in Edit Spline. Most of these commands will start one action and wait for the user input. Some of them, like *weld*, will perform the action on the selected elements.

The Edit Spline commands are all present in the shortcut menu shown in Figure 3.13. In MAXScript, all of these commands start with *splineops*. For instance, you can delete the selected vertices, segments, or splines simply by selecting the sub-object level and using the command `splineops.delete`.

Hands-On MAXScript: The Measure Spline Utility

The Normalize Spline modifier works by dividing the spline in segments of the same length. Sometimes a user might need to divide the spline in segments of equal size, regardless of its length. We will now design such a utility.

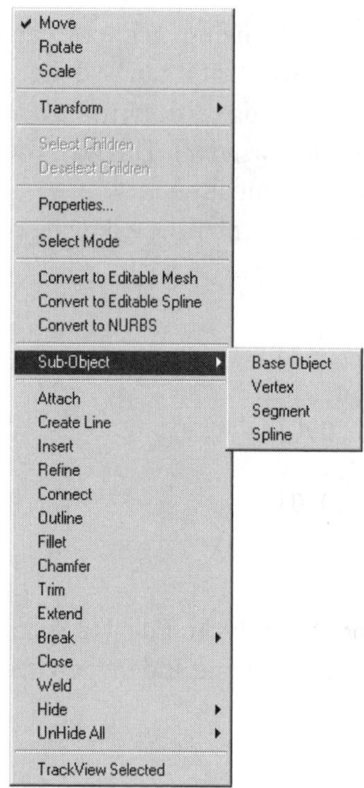

Figure 3.13 *The Splines shortcut menu*

The main idea is to use the *lengthinterp* method to read points on the curve at the needed positions and then a new spline will be created using these points.

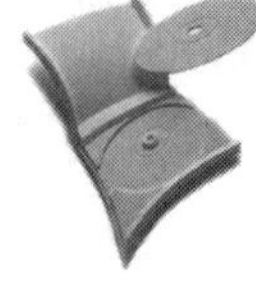

1. Open file `utility_divide01.ms` on the CD-ROM. This file has the skeleton of the UI coded (see Figure 3.14) and only needs the "engine" to work.

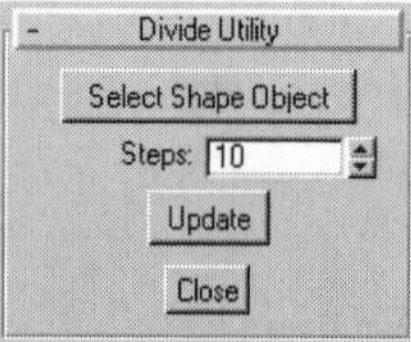

Figure 3.14 *The Divide utility script*

2. After *upd.enabled* = *true*, enter the following:

```
rate = 1.0/steps.value
new = splineshape()
addnewspline new
pt = lengthinterp shp 1 0
addknot new 1 #smooth #curve pt
for j in 1 to steps.value do
     (
     pt = lengthinterp shp 1 (rate*j)
     addknot new 1 #smooth #curve pt
     )
   updateshape new
```

In this code, `rate` defines the percentage of the curve that will be used in the calculation in *lengthinterp*. If the number of segments is 10, `rate` will be 0.1, which is the step to be used. The formula is *step#*rate*, which will range from 0 to 1.0.

A new spline is created using *splineshape*. Then, the first vertex is calculated and created. From then on, each new vertex is calculated for each defined step, using *lenghinterp*.

This script calculates only the first spline of the shape. It also does not close the spline if the original one was also closed.

Use the tools you learned to finish this script, adding the needed code to the Update button. Remember, you need to reset the new shape before adding new vertices. File `utility_divide03.ms` in the CD-ROM has this code ready.

Take a look at the script file `utility_divide_final.ms` on the CD-ROM, which calculates all splines and checks to ensure that they're closed correctly.

Working with Edit Mesh, Edit Patch, and Edit Spline

It's possible to work with Edit Mesh, Edit Patch, and Edit Spline in MAXScript. These commands are the same ones that are displayed for you when you right-click an object.

Working with Edit Mesh and Edit Patch is the same as working with Edit Spline. Edit Mesh commands will start with *meshops,* and Edit Patch commands will start with *patchops.*

Most of these commands will only start actions, but some of them will work automatically. All these commands require a previous sub-object selection. For instance, if you want to delete the selected faces of an object, you can use the command `meshops.delete object`. In this case, the script will display a dialog box to confirm whether it should delete the isolated vertices.

These commands require MAX to be in the Modify Panel with one of the sub-objects selected. To change to the Modify Panel, type **`max modify mode`**. To select the sub-object that you want, use the command *subobjectlevel*.

In an editable spline, sub-object levels are

Sub-Object Level	Level
1	Vertex
2	Segment
3	Spline

In an editable mesh, sub-object levels are

Sub-Object Level	Level
1	Vertex
2	Edge
3	Face
4	Polygon
5	Element

In an editable patch, sub-object levels are

Sub-Object Level	Level
1	Vertex
2	Edge
3	Patch

In Chapter 11, you will see how we can work with these commands using a MAXScript extension so that you can actually enter values and execute the functions without needing to wait for user interaction.

Summary

You learned how to access the object's properties and its sub-objects levels in this chapter. This allows you to create scripts that manipulate geometry at a deeper level, or even create geometry, as you did with shapes.

In the next chapter, you will see how to script the Render Effects and the Environment features, and you will learn how to create animation using scripts. You will also learn how to create compound and custom objects through MAXScript.

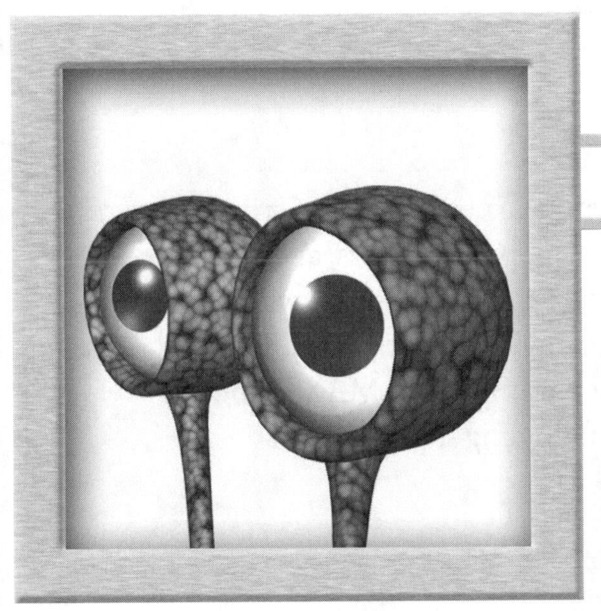

Objects and the Render and Environment Effects

MAXSCRIPT

Chapter 4

In the past three chapters, you learned the MAXScript basics: how to work with materials, maps, modifiers, and sub-objects levels. In this chapter, you will learn how to work with the remaining objects and with render and environment effects. This will finish our coverage of all the creation parameters in MAXScript.

This chapter will cover the following topics:

- Lights
- Cameras
- Helpers
- Compound objects
- NURBS and patches
- Custom object creation
- VIZ objects
- Object parameters
- Render effects
- Environment effects

Objects

In the first chapter, you learned how to create a box object using the *box()* constructor. Later, you learned to query an object's property using the *showproperties* and *getpropnames* functions. In Chapter 2, you learned how to use the Macro Recorder to record the steps in creating an object so that you do not have to memorize the object's MAXScript name or any specific property.

In this section, you will see all the remaining objects that have some particular features and properties. You will also see how you can create compound and custom objects, allowing you to create your own objects in a scene.

For those of you who also work with 3D Studio VIZ, we will also see how you can script VIZ objects.

Creating Lights

MAXScript allows you to create five out of the six light types in MAX. Only the Sunlight system is not creatable through MAXScript, but you can access all the parameters of a created Sunlight. Lights can be created using the constructors shown in Table 4.1.

Table 4.1 Light Constructors

LIGHT TYPE	CONSTRUCTOR
Omni	*omnilight()*
Target Spot	*targetspot()*
Free Spot	*freespot()*
Target Direct	*targetdirectionallight()*
Free Direct	*directionallight()*

When creating Target lights (Target Spot and Target Direct), you will also need to create the target object (using *targetobject*) and associate it to the light using the *.target* property. For instance, you would write the following code:

```
light01 = targetspot pos:[50,50,50]
target01 = targetobject pos:[0,0,0]
light01.target = target01
```

Light Properties

MAXScript gives you access to all properties in a light. You can even change a light, as you would do in the UI, but keep in mind that changing the light type will give you different options. For instance, an Omni Light does not have a Falloff or a Hotspot option, as seen in Figure 4.1.

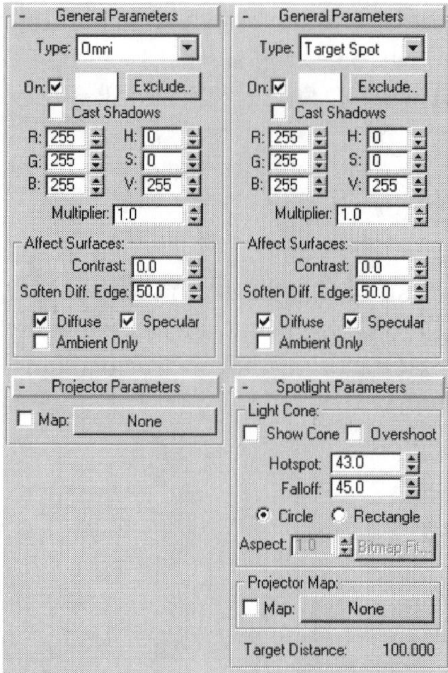

Figure 4.1 *Omni and Target Spot properties*

Be careful when changing light types after setting additional properties. The parameters that are not shared between light types will be lost or changed.

Continuing to use the last example, `light01.type = #omni` changes the light from Target Spot to Omni. Changing it back to Target Spot recreates the target object, so you do not need to worry about it. The different light types are simply the light name without the space.

Assigning Include and Exclude Objects

MAXScript allows you to easily assign Include and Exclude objects. Just collect the objects in an array and assign them to either *.includelist* or *.excludelist* properties. For instance, using `$light02.includelist = selection as array` will include the current selected objects in the $light02 include list.

Assigning the *includelist* automatically clears the *excludelist*, and the opposite is also true. Figure 4.2 shows the Exclude/Include dialog.

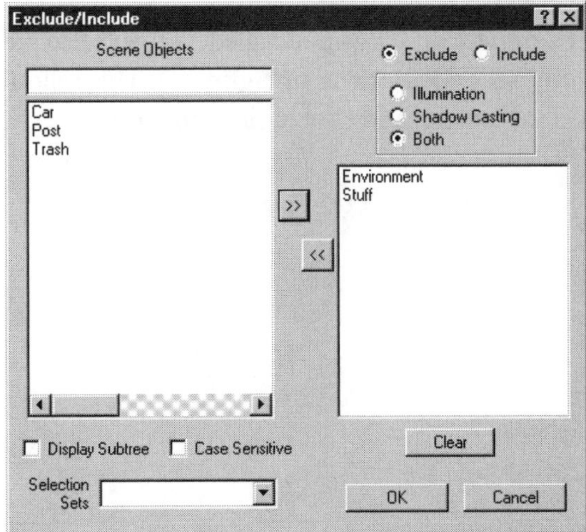

Figure 4.2 *The Exclude/Include dialog*

Always remember that the Exclude/Include lists are based on the object's name. If the object is renamed, you need to update the Exclude/Include list.

Shadow Parameters

Shadow parameters might be a tricky part in MAXScript. MAXScript only allows you to turn on or off the Raytraced Shadows light, so if you have a Shadow plug-in installed, it cannot be set through MAXScript, only through the UI.

To define if a light will use raytraced shadows, you will use the *.raytracedshadows* property. Setting the property to true uses raytraced shadows, and setting it to false uses Shadow Maps.

If you are using a Shadow plug-in, it will probably return true to the *.raytracedshadows* property, but you will not be able to assure if it has been defined unless you check for any specific property that plug-in might have.

Having defined which Shadow plug-in to use, each of them will define a new set of properties. Use *showproperties*, and these properties will appear at the end of the list.

mental ray Properties

If you have the mental ray Connection Plug-in installed, you will also see a new rollout in your lights: Indirect Illumination Params, as in Figure 4.3. This rollout will setup the light parameters to be used in Caustics and Global Illumination.

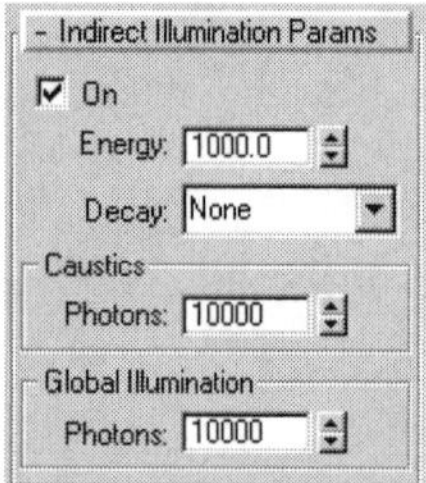

Figure 4.3 *The Indirect Illumination rollout*

To access these properties, just use the properties found in Table 4.2.

Table 4.2 Indirect Illumination Parameters

PARAMETER	PROPERTY
On/Off	*.indirect_illumination_params.emitter_enable*
Energy	*.indirect_illumination_params.emitter_energy*
Caustic Photons	*.indirect_illumination_params.caustic_photons*
Global Illumination Photons	*.indirect_illumination_params.global_illumination_photons*

Creating Cameras

Cameras work exactly the same way as lights. There are two types of cameras available in MAX. Table 4.3 shows how they are created in MAXScript:

Table 4.3 Camera Constructors

CAMERA TYPE	CONSTRUCTOR
Free camera	*freecamera()*
Target camera	*targetcamera()*

Just like lights, when creating a target camera, you need to create and assign a target object. This example illustrates creating a target camera:

```
cam01 = targetcamera pos:[-50,-20,30]
target01 = targetobject pos:[0,0,10]
cam01.target = target01
```

Unlike a light, no property is lost if you change a camera type, except if you have any animation assigned to the target object.

Cameras also have specific mental ray properties, as seen in Figure 4.4. These properties are related to the Depth Of Field setting and are listed in Table 4.4.

Table 4.4 Depth of Field Parameters for mental ray

PARAMETER	PROPERTY
On/Off	*.depth_of_field.enable*
fStop	*.depth_of_field.fstop*

Working with Helpers

Among the helpers, the most used are the dummy and the atmospheric gizmos. Usually, the grid also deserves attention, but with the new AutoGrid feature, it's not used much anymore.

Helpers have properties as any other objects, with the exception of the dummy, which has a hidden property that does not show in the UI. This property is *.boxsize* and defines the size of the Dummy object on-screen.

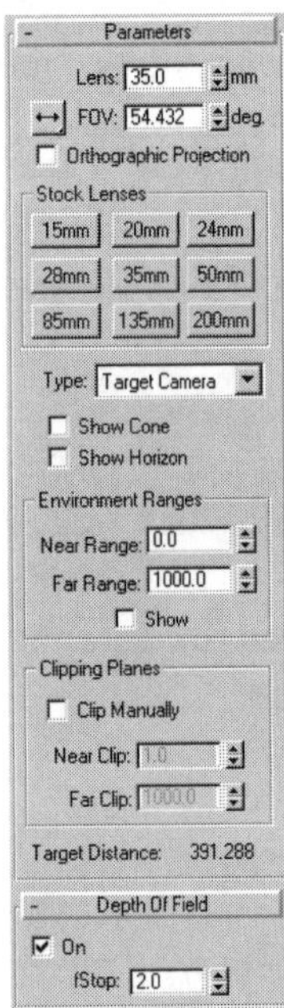

Figure 4.4 *Camera properties*

The use of a Scale transform in a dummy might affect the hierarchy underneath the dummy, so it's better to use the boxsize *property to adjust its format.*

For instance, `d = dummy boxsize:[5,10,20]` will create a dummy that does not have a cuboid format and does not have any scale applied to it; it only has a modified size. This is the same concept used to create the `dummy_hand.max` file you used in Chapter 2, where the dummies aren't cubes and have the format of fingers to create the hand.

To know how to use the remaining helpers, use the Macro Recorder and the *showproperties* function.

Creating Atmospheric Gizmos

Atmospheric gizmos are necessary to work with Atmospheric Environments, such as Volume Fog and Combustion. There are three atmospheric gizmos: Box, Sphere, and Cylinder.

All three have properties to define their sizes, as well as a property called *seed*. The *seed* property randomizes the format of the atmospheric gizmo. Clicking the New Seed button in the UI generates a random integer number that will define the seed, as in Figure 4.5. You can do this in MAXScript using the *random* function.

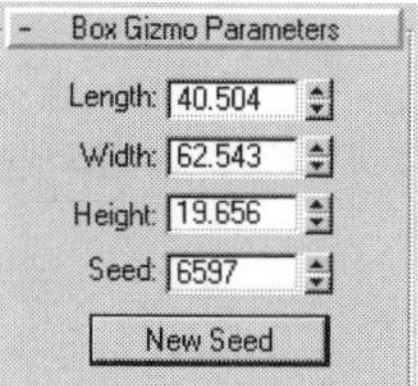

Figure 4.5 *Box Gizmo properties*

The *random* function generates a random value in a given interval, with the same type as the given interval. For instance, `random 0 10` will generate an integer value between 0 and 10. If you need a random color, you can use `random [0,0,0] [255,255,255]`, and a new color value will be created.

In the following example, let's create a Box gizmo and assign a random seed value to it:

```
gizmo1 = boxgizmo pos:[10,19,0] width:10 height:10 length:10
gizmo1.seed = random 0 32768
```

If you reassign the seed value repeating the last line, you'll notice that different values are generated.

Particle Systems

Besides the object parameters you can access, MAXScript accesses other information that might help you create scripts.

The *particlecount* method will read the number of particles in a particle system. The *particlepos* method will read the position of a specific particle, and the *particleage* method will read the particle age in frames.

With these three values, you can create a script that positions objects and makes them follow the particles, and that can even change their color based on the particle's age.

For instance, create a *superspray* and select it. Move ahead to frame 20 and type the following:

```
particlecount $
particlepos $ 1
partileage $ 1
```

Move ahead to frame 25 and repeat all three. The number of particles should not have changed, but the position and age should change.

If the particle does not exist at the specified time, particleage *or* particlepos *will return undefined.*

Working with Space Warps

Space warps are different objects. They're gizmo objects that affect other objects. You need to bind a space warp to an object for space warp to be affected. The same happens in MAXScript.

Space Warp objects are created the same way any other object is created. You can use the Macro Recorder and *showproperties* to know how to work with any of them. The tricky part in MAXScript is how to bind a space warp to an object. This is done using *bindspacewarp*. Let's see an example of how it works:

```
p = plane width:200 length:200 lengthsegs:40 widthsegs:40
r = spaceripple()
bindspacewarp p r
```

Now, you should see the Space Warp effect in the plane, as in Figure 4.6.

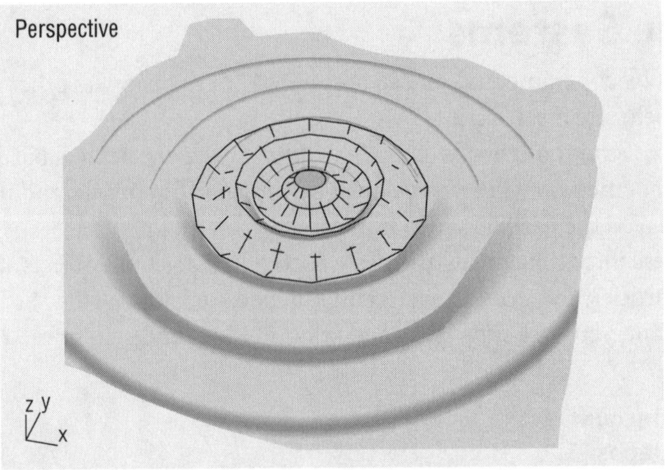

Figure 4.6 *A Plane object affected by a Ripple space warp*

There are a couple of tricks you need to learn when working with space warps. First of all, the space warp is a regular object, so if you want to modify its effect, all you need to do is come back to it and adjust its properties. That's simple to do. You can also animate space warps in MAX. In the example we just built, you can change the *wave length* property of the ripple using `r.wavelength = 40`.

Second, the space warp appears on top of the modifier stack of the objects it was associated to. Many space warps have options through the modifier stack, as shown in Figure 4.7. These properties can be accessed through MAXScript, too; then, the space warp reacts as a regular modifier.

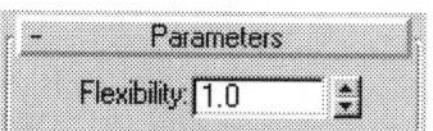

***Figure 4.7** Ripple space warp options in the modifier stack*

Looking on the modifier stack of the *Plane01* object you created in the last example, you will see the Space Warp effect, and it's called *Ripple Binding*. So, to access it in MAXScript, you would use

```
p.ripple_binding
```

or

```
p.modifiers[#ripple_binding].
```

In this case, the only property you have is *.flexibility*. But in many space warps, many properties would appear here.

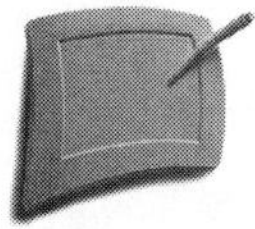

World Space modifiers are also space warps, but they do not need any gizmo or object to be created. They are simply applied as normal modifiers. You can add them to the objects using addmodifier *and can manipulate them normally as you would any modifier.*

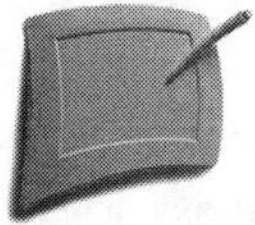

A good trick is to rename the Space Warp modifier because if you bind many space warps to the same object, their names will always be the same in the modifier stack regardless of the name of the space warp.

System Objects

System objects are not creatable through MAXScript. There are two types of System objects: the ones that simply create a series of regular objects, as Ring Array; and the ones that create objects with particular animation controllers, like the Sunlight or Bones objects.

Even though MAXScript cannot create a System object, you can access its properties and modify them in MAXScript. For example, you can access the Sunlight properties just as if you were accessing them through the Motion Panel, as in Figure 4.8. Since the Sunlight properties are motion properties, they are tied to a special controller, so you can access them using *.controller*.

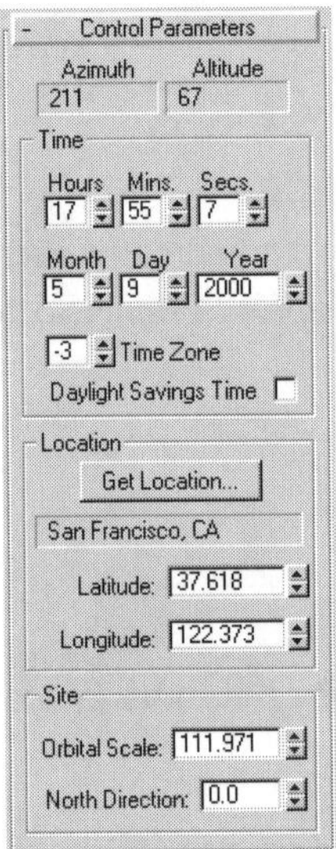

Figure 4.8 *The Sunlight control parameters in the Motion Panel*

As an example, create a Sunlight object in MAX and select its light. Now, in MAXScript, list its properties using `showproperties $.controller`. Now, change the local time to noon using the command `$.controller.solar_time = 12`.

Notice that you can change the latitude, longitude, and the orbital scale, but you cannot change the north direction. This should be done by rotating the Compass object.

The .solar_date *property is based on the current date, so it returns a value of 0 for today, –1 for yesterday, 1 for tomorrow, and so on.*

Accessing Bones and IK Controllers

You can create Bones objects in MAXScript using *bone()*, but these bones will have a regular PRS controller, not an IK controller. You can only create bones with an IK controller using the UI.

MAXScript does not access the IK controller information, but it allows you to position the End Effector using *.controller.end_effector_position*.

Since an IK Bone does not have a PRS controller, you cannot use .position *to read its position. Instead, use* .transform.translation *to do so.*

Compound Objects

Among the compound objects, Boolean and Morph are the only ones created by MAXScript. Terrain is also creatable, but in VIZ R3 only. All other compound objects have some properties that are accessible, but only after they have been created, and even then, only for a few of their properties.

Use *showproperties* to see which properties are available.

Many of the compound objects allow you to access the sub-object levels and modify them. Each compound object will do this in a different way, so refer to the Online Help to see how it's done.

Booleans

You can create Booleans in two ways: using a compound object or using editable meshes.

Using editable meshes is the simplest way. Just assign an operand to two 3D objects, and MAXScript will perform a Boolean operation with an editable mesh as a result. Here is an example of how it works:

```
b = box()
s = sphere pos:[15,0,0]
b - s
delete s
```

This will subtract the sphere from the box, leaving an Editable Mesh object as the result. Notice that the last object was not modified, so you had to delete it manually. Using + performs a union, and * creates an intersection.

This Boolean is simple, but it does not give you the flexibility of the compound object, where you can come back and edit the end result at any time. MAXScript also allows you to create the Boolean compound object, although it's a little more difficult to do. You can use *boolobj.createbooleanobject* to create it.

Let's repeat the previous example using compound Booleans:

```
b = box()
s = sphere pos:[15,0,0]
boolobj.createbooleanobject b s 4 3
```

Now, if you select the result object and check the Modify Panel, you will see that it's a Boolean object, as in Figure 4.9.

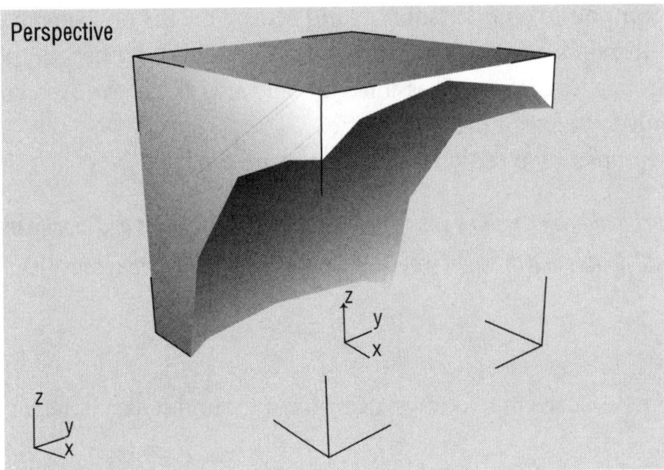

Figure 4.9 *Boolean results*

So far, this is easy to understand. But what does the `4 3` in the last line of code mean? `Boolobj.createbooleanobject` needs four parameters:

- Object A
- Object B
- A method to use Object B, which can be one of the following:
  1 *Instance*
  2 *Reference*

3 *Copy*

4 *Move*

- A material-handling procedure, which can be one of the following:

1 Combine materials without changing IDs

2 Match IDs to materials, combining materials

3 Match materials to IDs, combining IDs

4 Use only original material from Object A

After a Boolean is created, you can access both original objects as if they were properties of the original Boolean object. Using the previous example, you could access the original Box using `b.box01` (if box was named Box01).

Boolobj is a structure that contains several functions and methods that manipulate Boolean objects. These methods are described in Table 4.5.

Table 4.5 Boolobj Methods

DESCRIPTION	READ	SET
Operand B		*setoperandb*
Selected operand	*getoperandsel*	*setoperandsel*
Operation type	*getboolop*	*setboolop*
Cut type	*getboolcuttype*	*setboolcuttype*
Display results	*getdisplayresult*	*setdisplayresult*
Results + Hidden operands	*getshowhiddenops*	*setshowhiddenops*
Update mode	*getupdatemode*	*setupdatemode*
Optimize	*getoptimize*	*setoptimize*

In Table 4.5, Operation type can be any of the following options:

1 Union

2 Intersection

3 Subtraction (A–B)

4 Subtraction (B–A)

5 Cut

Cut type can be any of the following options:

1 Refine

2 Split

3 Remove Inside

4 Remove Outside

Update Mode can be one of the following options:

1 Always

2 When Rendering

3 Manually

Let's create an example of a Boolean object, using the methods we just learned:

```
c = cylinder radius:20 height:80 name:"C01"
s = sphere radius:30 pos:[0,0,40] name:"S01"
boolobj.createbooleanobject c s 4 1
boolobj.setboolop c 2
redrawviews()
c.s01.segments = 64
c.c01.sides = 32
```

After changing any Boolean object, you need to use redrawviews() *to redraw the screen and see the changes.*

This illustrates how to create and modify a Boolean object and how to set parameters in its sub-object operands.

Terrain

Terrain objects cannot be created in MAX R3, but some of their properties can be accessed. In VIZ R3, you can create and manipulate terrains just like a Boolean object, using *terrainops*.

Terrainops is a structure that contains all functions and methods needed to create and manipulate terrains. Table 4.6 lists them.

Table 4.6 Terrainops Methods

Description	Method
Add operand	*addoperand*
Delete operand	*depeteoperand*
Read one operand	*getoperand*
Update viewport	*update*

If you have VIZ R3, load the file `terrain.max` on the CD-ROM and execute this sequence of commands:

```
t = terrain()
terrainops.addoperand t $100
```

Repeat these lines for all the other curves (105,110,115,120,125) and see the results. Notice that the terrain is shaped as you add new curves, as in Figure 4.10.

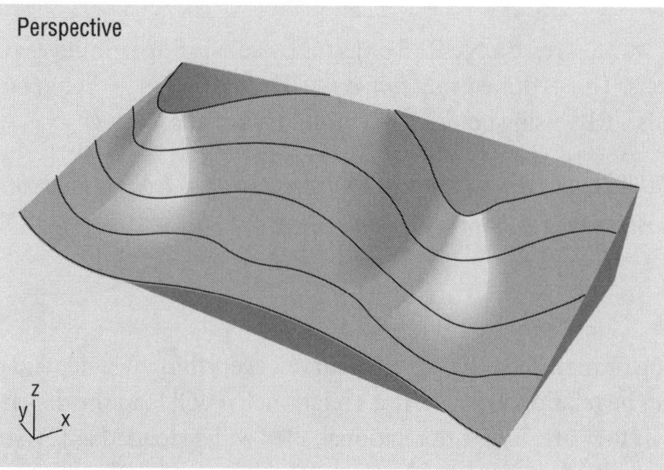

Figure 4.10 *The Terrain object*

Patches

MAXScript only allows you to create patches using the Tripatch or Quadpatch commands in the Create Panel using the Surface modifier, or by converting any object to an editable patch. The Tripatch and Quadpatch objects and the Surface modifier behave just like any other scriptable objects in MAX.

You can convert any object to editable patch using *convertto*. For instance, if you create a sphere using `s = sphere()`, you can convert it to an Editable Patch object using `convertto s patch`.

You can read and set the number of steps on an Editable Patch object using *getpatchsteps* and *setpatchsteps*. For instance, if you want to set the example sphere with 10 steps, you would use `setpatchsteps s 10`.

No other property or information can be accessed in MAXScript. The best way to have access to a Patch object in MAXScript is to design it using the Surface modifier. This way, you can manipulate the splines underneath the modifier.

NURBS

NURBS objects are fully creatable and accessible through MAXScript. However, it's not an easy task.

The first way to create a NURBS object is by converting primitives or patches to NURBS objects. This is done using *convertto*. For instance, `s = sphere()` would be converted to NURBS using `convertto s nurbssurface`.

Working with NURBS can be very complicated. We'll cover just a few topics in this book. You can find complimentary information in the MAXScript Online Help.

Nurbsset

When creating or manipulating NURBS curves, everything will depend on a *nurbsset*. A *nurbsset* can be relational or not. If it's relational, it will load the dependent curves and surfaces as they are. If it's not relational, they will be loaded as CV surfaces and CV curves. If you make changes to *nurbssets* and they are not relational, they might not be updated on-screen.

To understand how it works, let's use an exercise. In Exercise 4.1, we will adjust a NURBS curve and turn on its *trim* property. You will also see the differences in loading a relational or non-relational *nurbsset*.

Exercise 4.1: Working with NURBS

1. Open the file `nurbs.max` on your CD-ROM.
2. Select the NURBS object. It's made of two planes, one Blend surface, and a CVCurveOnSurface.
3. In the Listener, define the `nurbsset using n = getnurbsset $`. This loads the *nurbsset* without loading the dependant Blend curve.
4. Check to see how many sub-objects exist using `n.count`. It should return 4.
5. Let's see which sub-objects they are. Enter **`n[1]`**. It should return "<NURBSCVSurface:0x0000ac78>".
6. Repeat the same with the **`n[2]`**, **`n[3]`**, and **`n[4]`**.

Every time you load a nurbsset*, the order of the objects may change. In our example, we will consider the BlendSurface as* `n[3]` *and CVCurveOnSurface as* `n[4]`*. It might be different on your system, so this step is very important.*

7. Now, turn on the trim in the curve using `n[4].trim = true`. Nothing happens because you are working on a non-relational *nurbsset.*
8. Load a new *nurbsset* using `n = getnurbsset $ #relational`.
9. Repeat step 7 and see the *nurbsset* updating on-screen.
10. Flip the trim using `n[4].fliptrim = true`.
11. Adjust the tension of the Blend Surface using `n[3].tension1 = 0` and `n[3].tension2 = 0`.

You should now have the same results as in Figure 4.11.

The properties seen in this exercise will execute the same actions as if you were adjusting them in the UI.

Take a look at the NURBS 2 Spline script that comes with MAX. It's similar to the `utility_divide.ms` you developed in Chapter 3, but it works with NURBS curves.

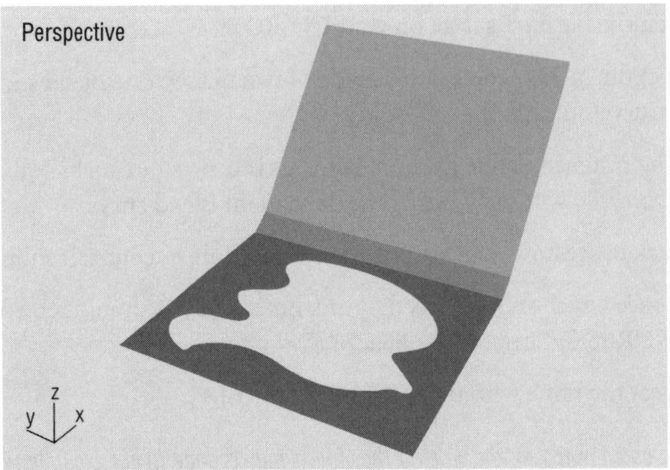

Figure 4.11 *A NURBS surface trimmed through MAXScript*

VIZ Objects

MAXScript in VIZ works exactly the same as in MAX, with minor differences. The Macro Recorder does not record some modifier parameters, and some properties are not available in VIZ, such as Sub-Object Animation.

VIZ also does not have space warps and particles, but has other objects that MAX does not have. These objects are Railing, Foliage, Wall, and Stairs. Doors and Windows are also present in MAX if you do a custom install and select the bonus plug-ins. You also have the RPC bonus plug-in in VIZ R3. Figure 4.12 shows some VIZ objects.

With the exception of Stairs, all other VIZ objects cannot be created through MAXScript, but can have their parameters modified. For instance, the Railing object can have any of its parameters modified, except the Pick Path option, which would allow you to create a Railing object.

A Wall object can only be modified through MAXScript if you did not modify any property in its sub-objects.

Figure 4.12 *VIZ objects*

MAXScript is a good tool to help you randomize RPC and Foliage objects. For instance, this code will randomize all foliage objects in your scene:

```
for i in objects do
   if classof i == foliage do i.seed = random 1 5000000
```

You can take a look at the `rpc_randomizer.ms` sample script on the CD-ROM. It randomizes RPC objects, changing their height and rotation.

Global Object Properties

Besides the properties each object has, all objects share some properties, like *name*, *screen color*, and so on. Most of these properties are found in the Object Properties dialog box, seen in Figure 4.13. You can access and change all these properties in MAXScript. Table 4.7 shows the global object properties.

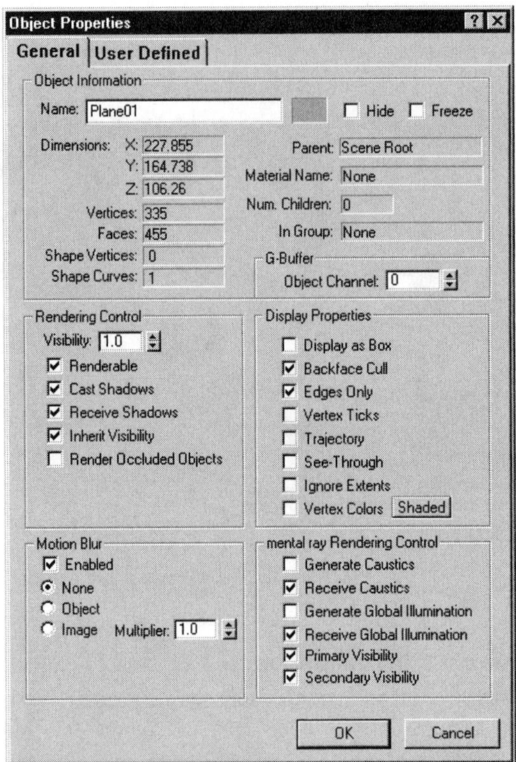

Figure 4.13 *The Object Properties dialog box*

Table 4.7 Global Object Properties

Property	**Description**
name	Object name.
baseobject	Returns the base node without the modifiers on top.
isselected	Defines if the object is selected.
xray	Turns the *xray* property on or off.
ignoreextents	Turns the *ignore extents* property on or off.
boxmode	Displays the object in Box mode.

Table 4.7 Global Object Properties (*continued*)

Property	Description
alledges	Displays all object edges, regardless of the visibility.
backfacecull	Displays the object as two-sided.
wirecolor	Defines the color in wirefame viewports.
showlinks	Shows the object links.
showtrajectory	Shows the animation trajectory on-screen.
showvertexcolors	Shows the vertex colors on-screen.
vertexcolorsshaded	Displays the vertex colors that are shaded on-screen. If set to false, the vertex colors will be shown flat.
castshadows	Defines if the object will cast shadows.
receiveshadows	Defines if the object will receive shadows.
gbufferchannel	Defines the object ID number.
renderable	Defines if the object is renderable.
renderoccluded	Defines if the objects behind this one should be rendered.
motionbluron	Defines if *Motion Blur* is on or off.
motionblur	Defines the type of motion blur (#none, #object, or #image).
imagemotionblurmultiplier	Defines the value of the *Image Motion Blur* multiplier.

For instance, you can create a script to quickly randomize object IDs in the scene using the following code:

```
for i in geometry do i.gbufferchannel = random 1 255.
```

When assigning a new name to an object, use uniquename <string>. *This will automatically create a new unique name by appending 01, 02, or the next available number.*

Pivot Point

Besides all object properties, you can also find the object size, centroid, and pivot point. Table 4.8 shows these properties.

Table 4.8 Object Size Properties

PROPERTY	DESCRIPTION
min	Minimum coordinates of the object's bounding box
max	Maximum coordinates of the object's bounding box
center	Center coordinates of the object's bounding box
pivot	Coordinates of the pivot point of the object

You can center the pivot point of the object making it equal to the object's center. For instance, `b.pivot = b.center` will do so in object b.

Visibility

The visibility properties are very important in MAX because they allow you to remove an object from the scene during a specific time. Visibility is now an integer value and is no longer an on or off property. Now you can animate these properties and create object fades.

MAXScript accesses the *visibility* property using *visibility*. A value of 0 will turn visibility off, while a value of 1 will turn it on. Animating it will create the Fade effect.

You can also define if a parent's visibility will affect the children by using the *.inheritvisibility* option. If it's on, the current object's visibility will be controlled by its parents.

Hiding, Unhiding, and Freezing Objects

You can hide, unhide, freeze, and unfreeze objects using MAXScript. This is done using two properties: *.ishidden* and *.isfrozen.*

When using objects, geometry, or other built-in arrays, MAXScript will access all objects regardless if they're hidden or frozen. This allows you to manipulate even objects that are not seen on-screen.

Another way you do it is to use the *hide*, *unhide*, *freeze*, and *unfreeze* commands.

A nice example is the Layer Manager script, by David Humpherys, included as a sample script on the CD-ROM. Among its other features, it orders objects by layers and hides and unhides them.

Appdata

Appdata is a way to store and retrieve custom information for objects in MAX. This information will be saved with that object and usually is accessed through plug-ins. You can also set and read appdata information, but MAXScript will only allow you to work with string data, not with binary data as the SDK does.

You can set appdata information using *setappdata*. In an example `s = sphere()` object, you can set appdata information using `setappdata s 1 "Appdata Sample"`. To retrieve this data, use `getappdata s 1`. The appdata index can be any integer number.

Deleteappdata allows you to reset any appdata index, while *clearallappdata* resets all appdata indexes.

Hands-On MAXScript: Creating a Custom Object

One of the uses of MAXScript is to create custom objects. These objects help you automate tasks, either by using template objects or by adding pre-defined options for the user.

Creating a custom object script is very simple. In Exercise 4.2, you will create a custom object script using the Macro Recorder.

Exercise 4.2: Creating a Fountain Object

Using the Macro Recorder, you will create a Fountain object preset. It will include all of the parameters needed: the object, the space warp assignment, and the material.

1. Open the MAXScript Listener and turn on the Macro Recorder.
2. In the Top viewport, create a *Superspray* object and adjust its properties as follows:
   - Off Axis Spread = 30
   - Off Plane Spread = 180
   - Viewport Display = Mesh
   - Use Rate = 30
   - Emit Start = -100
   - Emit Stop = 500
   - Display Until = 500
   - Life = 100
   - Size = 10
   - Variation = 50
   - Particle type = Tetra

3. Right-click the particle and select *Properties*. Turn on *Image Motion Blur* and set its value to 5.
4. Now create a Gravity space warp and set its strength to 0.12
5. Bind the Gravity space warp to the particle.
6. Open the Materials Editor.
7. Using *Get Material*, select a new Standard material.
8. Specify Diffuse Color = R:0, G:105, B:128; and Opacity = 50. Turn on two-sided.
9. Click the *Assign Material to Selection* button.
10. Select all lines in the Macro Recorder. Drag and drop them to any toolbar.
11. Right-Click the icon you just created and select the Edit Macro Script button. You will now assign the Superspray object to a variable and define its position using *pickpoint*.
12. Before *superspray*, add a new line:

    ```
    pt = pickpoint prompt:"Select Fountain Location"
    ```

13. Add `ss =` just before *superspray* in the same line, and add `select ss` in the line that follows.
14. Add `ss.pos = pt` in the next line. You will now assign Gravity to a variable and adjust the lines that follow.
15. Add `g =` just before *gravity* in the same line.
16. Edit *$.strength = 0.12* and substitute *$* with `g`.
17. Edit *bindtospacewarp* as follows:

    ```
    bindtospacewarp ss g
    ```

18. Add `select ss` to the line after *bindtospacewarp*.
19. Save and evaluate your script.

It should look similar to the file `macro_fountain.mcr` on the CD-ROM. Your rendered results should be the same as Figure 4.14.

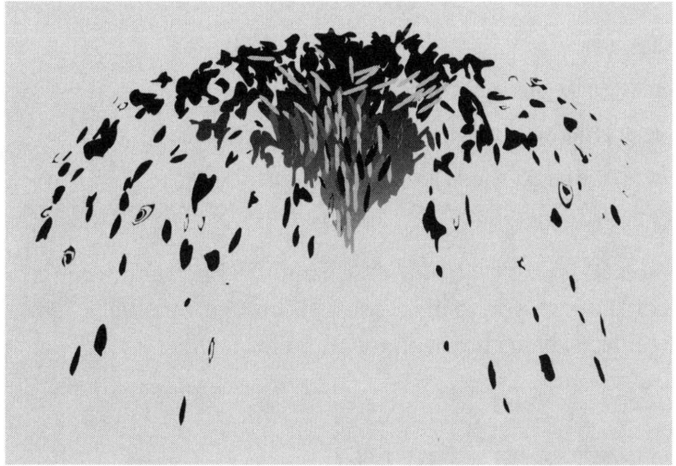

Figure 4.14 The rendered fountain

You can see how simple it is to create a custom template object by recording a series of steps, even when the steps involves materials, space warps, and object properties. You can also create other objects using Booleans, the surface modifier, or any other process you learned so far.

Render and Environment Effects

Render and environment effects add realism to your renders by creating nice effects. MAXScript accesses all information in both of them.

Unfortunately, MAXScript cannot access any information in the Video Post dialog window.

Let's see how you can work with render and environment effects. To illustrate, we will create a script that automates an object explosion.

Render Effects

Render effects are post-processing effects that are added after the image has been rendered. MAX has several built-in render effects. Table 4.9 lists the methods associated with render effects.

Table 4.9 Methods for Render Effects

METHOD	DESCRIPTION
addeffect	Adds render effects, similarly to *addmodifier*.
Numeffects	Returns the number of render effects present in the scene.
Geteffect	Reads the render effects present in the scene.

For instance, `addeffect (blur())` will add the Blur render effect to the scene. `b = geteffect 1` allows you to manipulate it through variable *b*. Figure 4.15 shows the Rendering Effects dialog box with the Blur effect added.

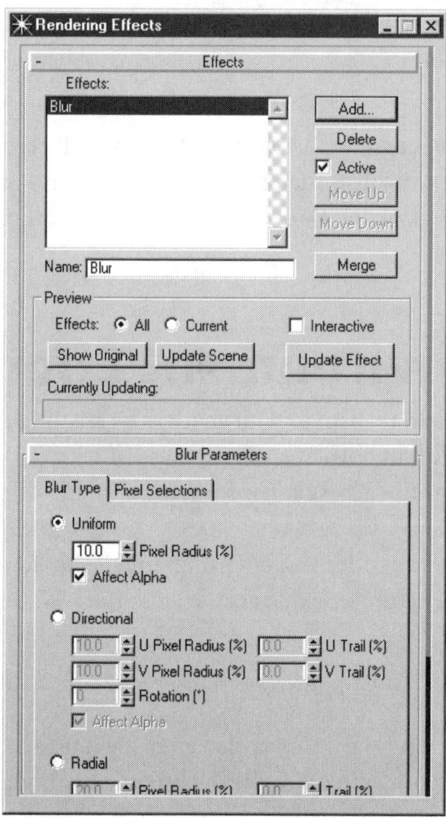

Figure 4.15 *The Blur render effect*

The only render effect that behaves differently is Lens Effects. Once you add a Lens Effects render effect using `lens = lens_effects()` and `addeffect lens`, you adjust each individual parameter of the Lens Effects using the *le* structure, as in Table 4.10.

Table 4.10 Lens Effects Parameters

PARAMETER	METHOD
Add Glow	*le.addglow*
Add Auto Secondary	*le.addasec*
Add Manual Secondary	*le.addmsec*
Add Ring	*le.addring*
Add Star	*le.addstar*
Add Ray	*le.addray*
Add Streak	*le.addstreak*
Add Light	*le.addlightnode or le.addlight*
Delete Light	*le.deletelight or le.deletelightbyname*
Delete Element	*le.deleteelement or le.deleteelementbyname*

Using the previous Lens Effects example, you could add a Glow element using `le.addglow lens`. Then, you would access its properties using `lens.glow`. To remove the glow, use `le.deleteelement lens 0` or `le.deleteelementbyname lens "Glow"`.

le.deleteelement *is zero based, which means that the first element is 0, not 1.*

Environment Effects

Environment effects are controlled by the Environment dialog box. The Environment dialog box is divided in two rollouts. The first rollout defines common scene parameters, which include background image, ambient light, and so on. The second rollout defines atmospheric effects, such as fog and combustion, as in Figure 4.16.

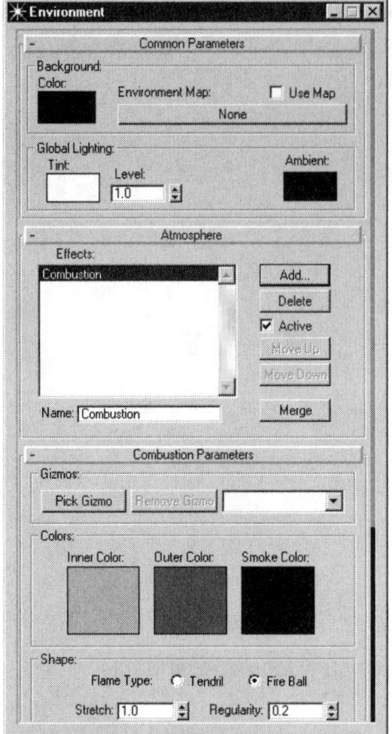

Figure 4.16 *The Environment dialog box*

Table 4.11 shows the common parameters that are accessible through MAXScript.

Table 4.11 Common Parameters for Environment Effects

PARAMETER	METHOD
Background color	*backgroundcolor*
Environment map on or off	*useenvironmentmap*
Environment map	*environmentmap*
Ambient color	*ambientcolor*
Global lighting tint color	*Lighttintcolor*
Global lighting level	*lightlevel*

These properties will adjust the parameters as if you were adjusting them in the dialog box. Use them cautiously because they can easily mess up your scene.

Atmospheric Effects

Atmospheric effects work exactly the same as render effects, with a single difference: some effects require a gizmo association. Table 4.12 lists the methods for atmospheric effects.

Table 4.12 Methods for Atmospheric Effects

METHOD	DESCRIPTION
addatmospheric	Adds the atmospheric effect to the scene.
getatmospheric	Reads an atmospheric effect present in the scene.
deleteatmospheric	Removes an atmospheric effect present in the scene.
numatmospherics	Returns how many atmospheric effects are present in the scene.
appendgizmo	Associates a gizmo to an atmospheric effect.
deletegizmo	Deletes the gizmo from the atmospheric effect.

As an example, let's create an Omni light and add a Volume Light effect to it:

```
l = omnilight nearattenend:20 farattenstart:20 farattenend:40
v = volume_light()
appendgizmo v l
addatmospheric v
```

Now, render the scene and see the Volume Light effect.

Pay attention to the gizmo type. Volume Light gizmos are Light *objects. Volume Fog and Combustion require* atmospheric gizmos *to work.*

Animation Context

When you use a Combustion atmosphere effect, there's an option that automatically creates an explosion. It asks you for a start frame and an end frame. If you pay attention, all it's doing is animating the *phase* property from 0 to 300 in the requested interval. You can do this in MAXScript using the animation context.

The animation context works similar to the coordinate system context, but instead, defines an animation.

For example, if you create `s = sphere`, you can animate its properties using `animate on (at time 100 s.radius = 50)`. This will turn on, animate, and set the *radius* property at frame 100.

Using the animation context, you can manually set an explosion using any start and end frames simply by animating the *phase* property.

Hands-On MAXScript: Setting Up an Explosion

In Exercise 4.3, you will adjust a script that automates the explosion process. It allows you to select an object and define start and end frames. The script will then perform the following operations:

- Create a Particle Array object with the picked object as emitter.
- Setup the particle array to appear only at the start frame, and explode the object into pieces.
- Hide the original object using its Visibility track.
- Create an atmospheric gizmo at the object's start position.
- Setup a combustion as the Explosion effect.

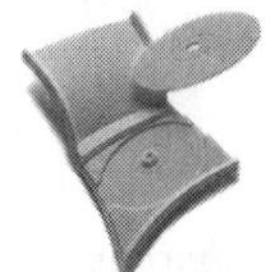

Exercise 4.3: Adjusting an Explosion Script

1. Load the file `street.max` on your CD-ROM. It contains an animation of a car moving and throwing an object into the trash, as in Figure 4.17.
2. Load the file `utility_explosion01.ms` from your CD-ROM and evaluate it. This file contains the script UI and the Particle Array object. All you will need to do is add the combustion code and the Sphere gizmo.
3. Before *animate on*, enter:

```
size = (distance explode.max explode.min)/2
at time start.value gizmo = spheregizmo radius:size pos:explode.pos
 c = combustion explosion:1
```

The *size* variable reads the size of the object, based on its bounding box, so this size can be used as the gizmo's radius. Also, you're using `at time start.value` here to position the gizmo in the same position as the object will be in when the explosion starts.

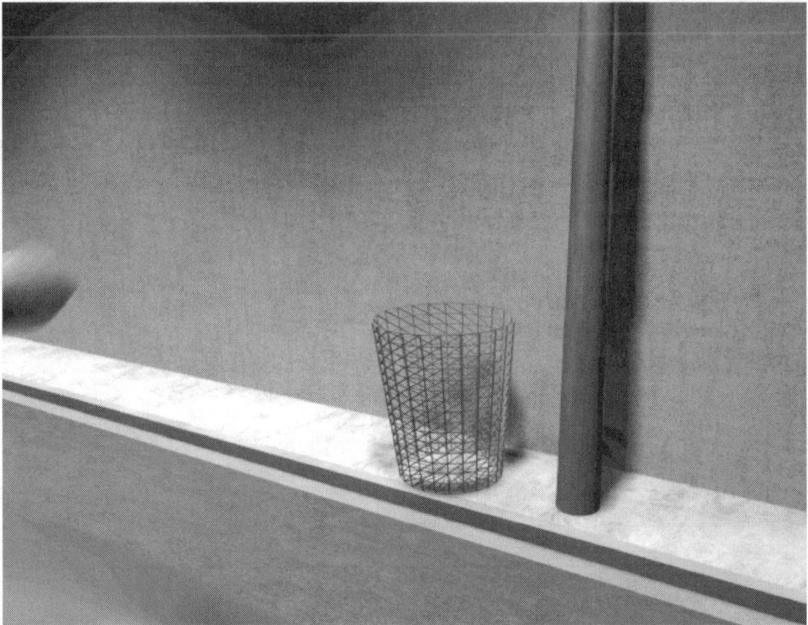

Figure 4.17 *The* Street.max *file*

4. In the *animate on* block, enter:

```
at time start.value c.phase = 0
at time end.value c.phase = 300
```

   These two properties will animate the combustion to create the explosion.

5. After the *animate on* block, enter:

```
appendgizmo c gizmo
addatmospheric c
```

6. Save and evaluate your script.

7. Try your script on the file, selecting *Stuff* as the object to be exploded, start frame 40, and end frame 100.

8. Reload the MAX file later and try other time ranges.

The script file should look like `utility_explode02.ms` on the CD-ROM.

Summary

This chapter taught you how to create and access properties in all object types in MAX and VIZ. You also learned how to use environment, atmospheric, and render effects to enhance your scene.

In the next chapter, you will learn how to use different user interfaces in MAXScript, creating floaters and rollouts, and using other UI items. You will also learn how to render a scene and manipulate bitmaps.

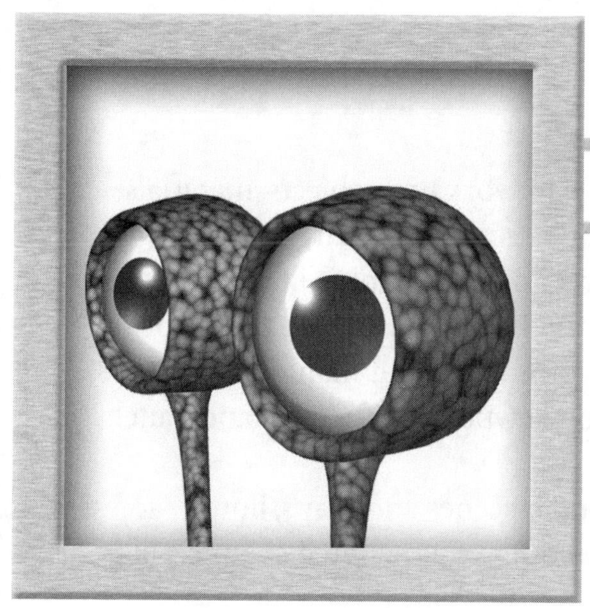

User Interface and Bitmap Manipulation

MAXSCRIPT

Chapter 5

Now that you learned how to work with objects, materials, and effects, you will move ahead and learn how to create a better user interface for your scripts. You will learn how to work with rollouts and floaters and how to customize the Right-Click menu. You will also learn commands that manipulate MAX's interface, allowing you to control viewports, the Command Panel, and the menus.

You will also learn how to render scenes and maps, how to access bitmap color information, and about extra rendered channels like Z-Buffer and Object ID.

This chapter covers the following topics:

- Enhancing the IU with rollouts and floaters
- Interface driven events
- Alert messages
- The Right-Click menu
- Manipulating viewports
- Rendering images
- Extra channel access
- Bitmap variables
- Rendering maps

Enhancing the User Interface

In Chapter 1, you learned how to create a utility script. You also learned how to work with the Macro Recorder to create a Macro Script. You will now learn how to work with rollouts and floaters to enhance your script. At the end of this section, you will learn how to customize the Right-Click menu and how to control the viewport's appearance.

Using Rollouts

Let's refresh the first lesson in Chapter 1. In Chapter 1, you created a simple utility:

```
utility simple_utility "Example"
(
)
```

If you evaluate and execute this script, all you see added to the Utilities Panel is a new rollout with a Close button, as in Figure 5.1. All utility scripts have a single rollout and a Close button. But you can add new rollouts if you wish. This is done in two steps: First, you create the rollout, and then you add it to the utility or to a floater, as you'll see later in this section.

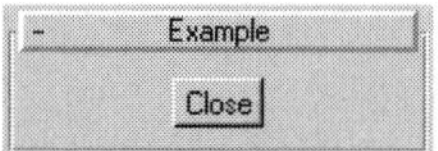

Figure 5.1 *The default utility script UI*

A rollout is created exactly the same way as a utility is, but it's not executed until you add it somewhere. Exercise 5.1 contains an example of how you can work with rollouts.

Exercise 5.1: Working with Rollouts

1. Open `rollout01.ms` on the CD-ROM. This script contains two declared rollouts and one utility script. You will now create the events that will add the rollouts to the utility.
2. Add the following event to the utility:

   ```
   on open_1 pressed do addrollout one rollout_test
   ```

   The *addrollout* method will add the rollout to the specified utility.

The rollout needs to be declared before the utility so that it exists when the event calls it.

3. Add the following code, which creates the event to remove the added rollout that is assigned to the Close button:

```
on close_1 pressed do removerollout one rollout_test
```

4. Now, add the events to add and remove rollout *two*, which is already declared in the script. They will have the same code that you used to add and remove rollout *one*.
5. Add the last event. Close both rollouts.

Removerollout *works even if the rollout is not open and does not return any error message. Using* addrollout *to add a rollout that already exists will also do nothing.*

Your script should look like `rollout02.ms` on the CD-ROM, and the UI should look like Figure 5.2.

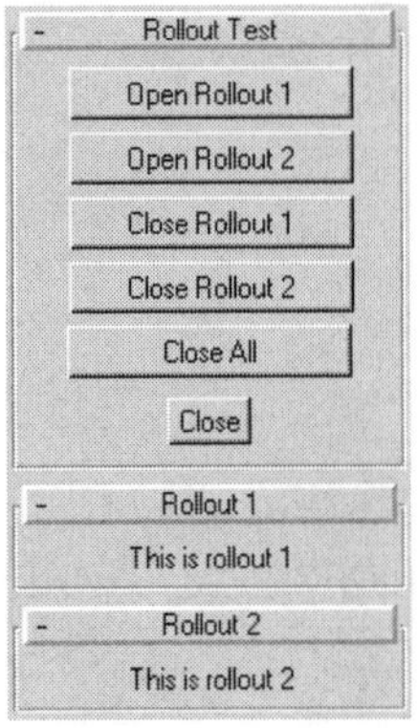

Figure 5.2 *The utility script with multiple rollouts*

Organizing the UI

Organizing the UI is the tricky part. As you can see in Figure 5.2, the script you created in Exercise 5.1 does not have an attractive UI. We can create one using a few tricks.

All UI items can be aligned in the UI to the left, center, or right, using *align:#left* and the respective other *align* functions. Some items have default alignment. For instance, the buttons default to center alignment, and spinners default to right alignment.

Besides the alignment, you can reposition each UI item specifying an absolute position or an offset from the default alignment. This is done using *pos:[x,y]* or *offset:[x,y]*. The position is based on the top-left corner of the rollout, which is [0,0].

Using offset *makes it easier to position your UI items because you specify the position based on the default location, instead of needing to specify each item's position.*

The *label* UI item is also useful to help us add text to the UI, either as captions or as return messages.

Look at `rollout03.ms` on the CD-ROM and notice how it looks better organized now, as in Figure 5.3.

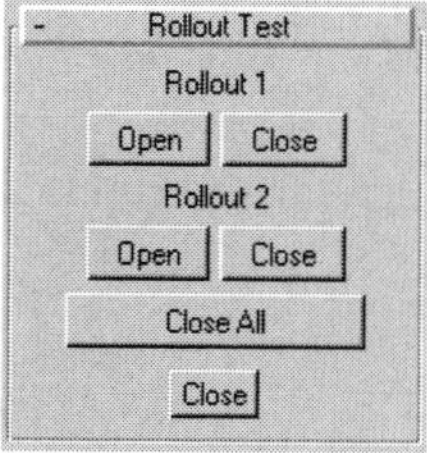

Figure 5.3 *Button re-organization*

Another way to organize the UI is using *groups*. UI groups will draw an outline around a group of options and write a caption, like most common scripts.

File `rollout04.ms` contains an example of groups, instead of using label captions. It looks like Figure 5.4.

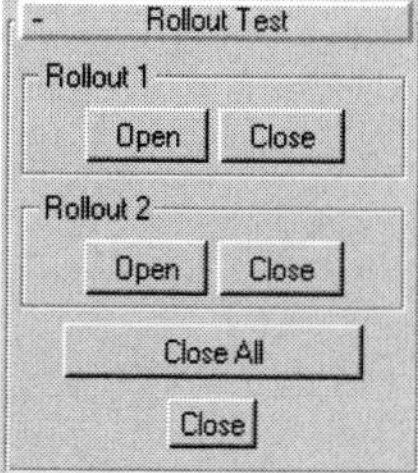

Figure 5.4 *Using groups to organize the UI*

The last alignment option is *across*. It's used to easily align UI items in columns. For instance, previously, we manually aligned the file, using offset. This is an example of using across to align two buttons side by side:

```
button open_1 "Open" width:60 across:2
button close_1 "Close" width:60
```

File rollout05.ms on the CD-ROM has an example of across, which saves us a lot of tweaking.

Using Floaters

Another important way to write a script UI is using floaters. Utility scripts are a bit limited in the UI. They are always the same width so they can be difficult to manage when you need a lot of information. In addition, you need to be in the Utilities Panel to open a utility script. Floaters can be opened from utility scripts, from Macro Scripts, or even from the Right-Click menu.

Floaters can be placed wherever you wish on the screen and can be any size. Figure 5.5 shows a floater example.

***Figure 5.5** A floater example*

A floater needs a rollout to work because a floater itself cannot have any UI item. You also need to be careful not to open the same floater many times, which can mess up the interface and can also cause some strange behaviors in the scripts because MAXScript will not know which of the floaters to handle when many are open.

Exercise 5.2 shows you how to convert a utility to a floater.

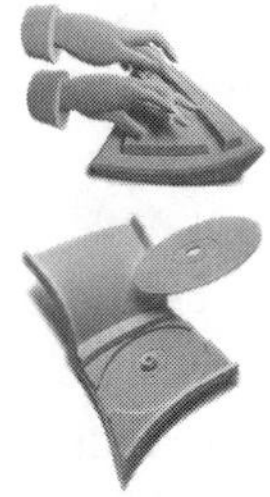

EXERCISE 5.2: CONVERTING A UTILITY TO A FLOATER

Let's make our script from Exercise 5.1 a floater. It's not difficult.

1. Open file `floater01.ms` on the CD-ROM.
2. In the script code, substitute *utility* with `rollout.`
3. At the end of the script, write the following code:

```
floater_test = newrolloutfloater "Floater Test" 200 250
addrollout rollout_test floater_test
```

4. Evaluate the script and see the rollout in the floater.
5. Edit the rollout events, changing *addrollout one rollout_test* to `addrollout one floater_test.`
6. Repeat the same edit for the remaining events.

Your script should look like `floater02.ms` on the CD-ROM. Figure 5.6 shows the floater with the rollouts open.

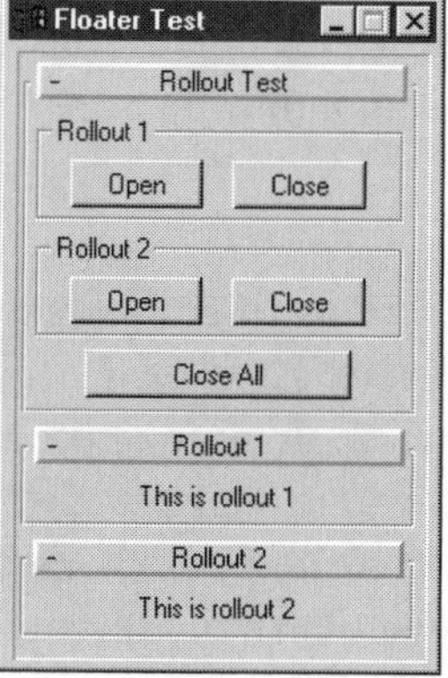

Figure 5.6 *The floater with multiple rollouts*

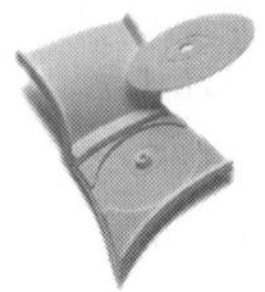

This script has two problems. If you evaluate it, it will load multiple floaters, one on top of the other. Also, there's no UI that calls the script; it only opens when evaluated. To create a Macro Script out of it, just select the entire script and drag it to a toolbar, or enter the Macro Script code yourself, as in file `floater03.ms` on the CD-ROM.

The Try *and* Catch *Functions*

MAXScript has a function that tries to execute a command and does not stop the script even in case of an error. This function is *try*. *Try* requires you to use another function called *catch*. The *catch* function is called if the command you tried fails.

We can use both the *try* and *catch* functions in situations where we do not know what to expect or if we do not know if a specific property is available or not. For example if you are adjusting shadow properties in a light, since the light only returns two states for the Shadow plug-in even if you have more than two states, it would be nice to adjust shadow properties using *try* and *catch* so that, in case of an error, MAXScript will not stop your script.

You will use *try* and *catch* to check if a floater is open, and you will have the script close this floater if it is open in Exercise 5.3.

For instance, *try(closerolloutfloater floater_test)* will try to close the floater you designed in Exercise 5.2. Two options are possible here:

- The rollout may be open.
- The rollout may be closed.

If the rollout is open, *try* will close it. If it's closed, nothing will happen, and you can open a new copy of it.

Open file `floater04.ms` on the CD-ROM and evaluate it. Now, configure a button in the toolbar and click it to start the script. Notice that you only have one Floater window, and it blinks when closing one and opening the other. If you remove the *try catch* line, you will have many windows opening one on top of the other.

Using Rollout Events

You can associate events to rollouts and utilities. There are three events that can be associated: *on rollout open*, *on rollout close,* and *on rollout oktoclose*. The *oktoclose* event allows you to block a user from closing a floater, forcing an input or other action.

These events are very useful because they allow you to load a predefined set of variables when a rollout is open. For instance, you could create a rollout and load all lights in a variable to be manipulated later. The same happens on a *close* event, where you can dump all information from the script.

An example of using rollout events is to turn on or off UI items that are dependent one on the other. In Exercise 5.3, we'll work on the `floater04.ms` script and add a couple of rollout events.

Exercise 5.3: Using Rollout Events

1. Open the file `floater05.ms` on your CD-ROM.
2. Evaluate the script and customize a toolbar, creating an icon to load the script.
3. In rollout one, add the following event:

```
on one open do
   (
   rollout_test.open_1.enabled = false
   rollout_test.close_1.enabled = true
   rollout_test.close_all.enabled = true
   )
```

This event will toggle the buttons in the main rollout so that when this rollout is open, the Open button is disabled, and the Close buttons are enabled.

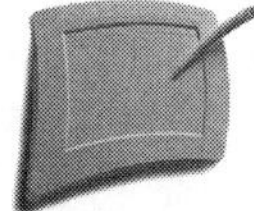

UI Items only exist inside the rollout they belong to. To access a UI item from outside its rollout, simply use rollout.item.

4. Add an *on one close* event and invert the button states without disabling the *close_all* button.
5. Add the same events to rollout two.

Your script should look like the one in file `floater06.ms` and should produce the same results seen in Figure 5.7.

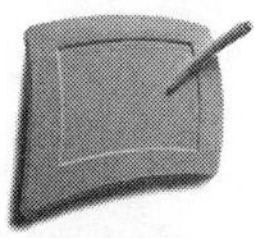

Notice that you did not need to add any code in the Close All *button, because all the action is triggered by the rollout's state.*

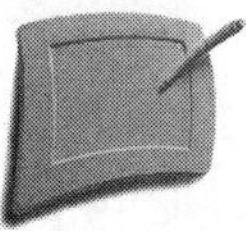

It's easier to add rollout-driven events than events driven by buttons. Sometimes, more than one button triggers the event, in which case you would have to add the custom code for each button.

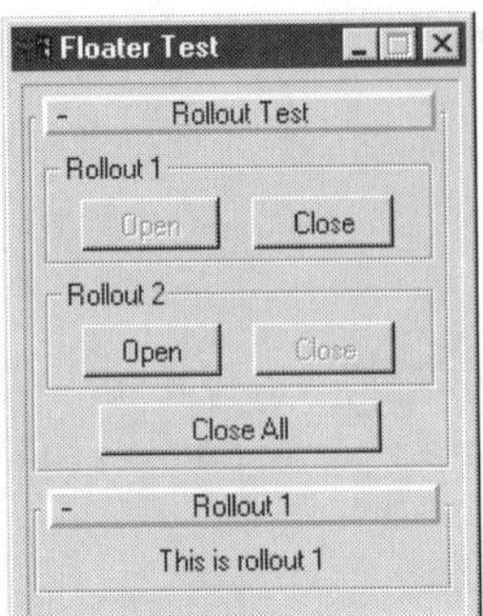

***Figure 5.7** Buttons toggled by a rollout event*

The Drop-Down List and Listbox

The drop-down list (*dropdownlist* in MAXScript)and listbox UI items work similarly. Their difference is their appearance in the UI. Both are used to allow the user to select an item in a list, which will trigger a specific action, such as which Anti-alias filter to use or which object property to select. Figure 5.8 shows an example of both UI items.

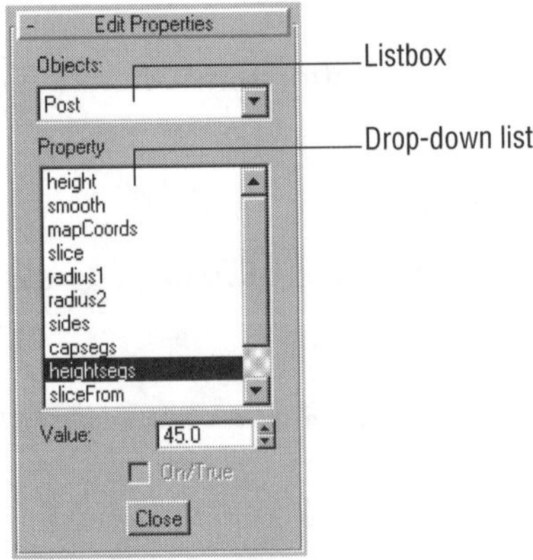

***Figure 5.8** Examples of a listbox and a drop-down list*

The key to using the drop-down list and the listbox is the *items* property. This is an array of strings, which will be listed. The trick is to store a copy of this array, as well as an array of the related objects, nodes, etc. This way you know which object has been selected.

Another useful property is *selection*. It lists which item is selected so you can use it as an index to the array.

Take a look at the `edit_properties.ms` script on the CD-ROM. It shows you how to use a *on open* event and how to collect two arrays, one with objects and another with their names, so they can be displayed in the drop-down list. You can then use *getpropnames*, *getproperty*, and *setproperty* to read and set any object property.

Using Macro Scripts

Macro Scripts are scripts created either by using the Macro Recorder or by typing them manually. There are several properties we can add to a Macro Script: the `category` where the Macro Script will be added, the `text` that will appear when using a text button, the `tool tip` of the button, and the bitmap `icon`. When you drag and drop, MAX automatically fills these properties for you, auto-numbering the Macro Script and defining it inside the drag-and-drop category.

This is an example of a Macro Script:

```
macroscript example
   category:"Mastering 3D Studio MAX"
   buttontext:"Example"
   tooltip:"Macro Script Example"
   icon:#("example",1)
(

script code...

)
```

Using Icons

You can use a bitmap icon to define your Macro Script button. It can be automatically defined using the *icon* property. To create these icons, use any painting program or use the Custom Icon Maker script supplied with MAX as a bonus script.

This bitmap is nothing more than a BMP file with two different resolutions (for large and small icons) and a mask file. You can use more than one icon in the same BMP file, simply placing them side by side (see Figure 5.9).

Figure 5.9 *Sample bitmap icons*

When specifying the *icon* property, you need two parameters: the *filename* (without path or extension) and the *icon number*. Icons are numbered left to right, starting at 1. For instance, in the previous Macro Script, we used `icon:#("example",1)`, where `example` is the BMP file with the icon, and we want to use the first icon in this file.

Loading Macro Scripts

There's no need to load a Macro Script file. Just place it in the `UI\Macroscripts` folder or evaluate it (MAX automatically copies it to that folder), and it will be loaded automatically when MAX starts.

If you remove any MCR file, MAX will not load its button in the UI since it will not find the related script. The opposite does not happen, which means, if you remove a button from the UI, the script file will not be removed.

After you add a new Macro Script, you will need to customize a toolbar and add a new button for it so that it can be executed.

Using Alert Messages

We often need to advise the user that something went wrong, or we may need to advise the user of a path to follow. This can be done using alert messages.

MAXScript offers three alert messages: *messagebox*, *querybox*, and *yesnocancelbox*. You already saw messagebox in chapter 1, so let's see how the other two work.

Querybox stops the script and waits for the user to press yes or no, as in Figure 5.10. You can then route the script to take the necessary action.

***Figure 5.10** An example of a querybox alert message*

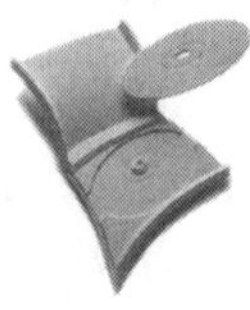

For instance, in the script `floater06.ms` on the CD-ROM, you can create an *oktoclose* event and ask the user if he really wants to close the script. File `floater07.ms` has this event added. Take a look and see how it works.

Querybox returns true or false, depending on the user response, so you can easily query the user. The *yesnocancel* box returns *#yes*, *#no*, or *#cancel*.

Using the Right-Click Menu

One of the nice features in MAX R3 is the context-sensitive Right-Click menu. Part of this menu is entirely made in MAXScript and is 100% customizable.

There are two ways that you can create a Right-Click menu (RCMenu): by editing the original RCMenu files in MAX or by adding new menu options using other script files.

The RCMenus have three UI items: *menuitem*, *submenu*, and *separator*. Menuitem defines a new item in the menu. If it's followed by submenus, the menuitem will open a new menu to the side, just like Figure 5.11. The *separator* is the horizontal line that divides the menu.

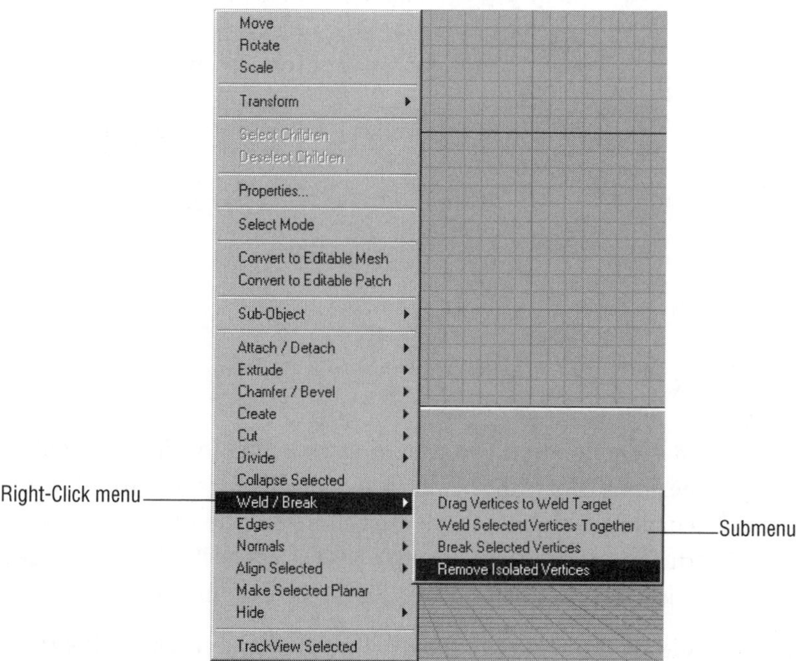

Figure 5.11 *A Right-Click menu with a submenu*

What makes the RCMenus context sensitive is the ability to filter each UI item. This way, you can specify when you want the UI item to appear. For instance, you can create an RCMenu to manipulate groups, so that it will only appear if the selected object is a group or part of a group. Let's do this in Exercise 5.4.

Exercise 5.4: Creating an RCMenu

In this exercise, you will create and register an RCMenu, appending it to the end of the original RCMenu in MAX.

1. Open the file `rcmenu_group01.ms` on the CD-ROM. This file has the RCMenu ready, with all menuitems and all events associated. But, it's missing the filters that allow you to load it only when a group is selected.
2. To add these filters, enter the following before *submenu*:

```
fn is_group =
   (
   if selection.count > 0 do
      (
      head = isgrouphead selection[1]
      members = true
      for i in 2 to selection.count do
         (
         if selection[i].parent != selection[1] then
            (
            members = false
            exit
            )
         )
      members and head
      )
   )
```

   This function tests two conditions: whether the first object of the selection is the group *Head* (the helper object that defines the group), and whether all the remaining selected objects are children of this object. If both conditions return true, you have a single group object selected. If no object is selected, or if the object is not a single group, this function returns false.

3. Add this function as a filter to the submenu, adding `filter:is_group after submenu "Group"`. You need to specify a filter to show as open or closed, depending on the group state. Since the Open or Close options are under the submenu, and the submenu is already filtered, the object is certainly a group. Now, all you need to do is test to see if the selected group is closed or open and add the correct filters.

4. Before *submenu*, add the following function:

```
fn is_open = isopengrouphead selection[1]
fn is_closed = not isopengrouphead selection[1]
```

5. Now, add `filter:is_closed` to the *open_group* menu item and add `filter:is_open` to the *close_group* menu item. Your script should look like file `rcmenu_group02.ms` on the CD-ROM.

6. To add this RCMenu to MAX's RCMenu, evaluate the script and then register it using `registerrightclickmenu group_mgr`. When loaded, it should look like Figure 5.12.

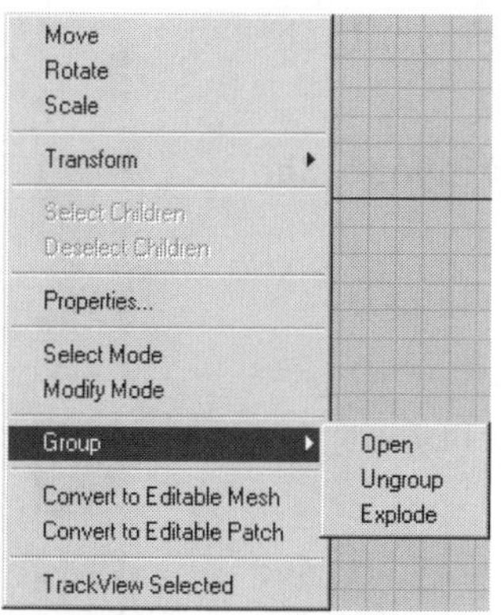

Figure 5.12 *Group Manager RCMenu*

Now, test it by selecting any object or group on-screen. You will notice that there are times when the group menu should appear, and it doesn't. This is because we forgot to add to the correct filters, such as the filters that select an object that is part of the group when it's open. File `rcmenu_group03.ms` has all the correct filters set. Notice that it also has *registerrightclickmenu*, which will automatically load the script in the RCMenu.

Place your RCMenus in the `scripts/startup` folder in your 3D Studio MAX path, and MAX will load them automatically when starting.

MAX has an extra RCMenu that is executed when pressing the CTRL key and right-clicking. This RCMenu has an option that opens it for customization. All default RCMenu files are located in the `stdplugs/stdscripts` folder in MAX.

Customizing Viewports

You can control the viewport layout and the viewport type using MAXScript. It is also possible to adjust several parameters in each viewport.

Viewport Layout

You can set 14 different viewport layouts using MAXScript. This is done using the *viewport.setlayout layout* method. Layouts are named as shown in Table 5.1.

Table 5.1 Viewport Layout Names

NAME	LAYOUT	NAME	LAYOUT
#layout_1		#layout_3ht	
#layout_2v		#layout_3hb	
#layout_2h		#layout_4	
#layout_2ht		#layout_4vl	
#layout_2hb		#layout_4vr	
#layout_3vl		#layout_4ht	
#layout_3vr		#layout_4hb	

Viewport Type

MAXScript allows us to control the 3D viewports. You are able to set any type of viewport, but if this viewport is a 2D viewport (Track View, Schematic View, Asset Manager, and MAXScript Listener), you will not be able to change it.

To get and set viewport types, you can use *viewport.gettype* and *viewport.settype* respectively. The supported viewport types are shown in Table 5.2.

Table 5.2 Viewport Names

NAME	VIEWPORT
`#view_top`	Top view
`#view_bottom`	Bottom view
`#view_right`	Right view
`#view_left`	Left view
`#view_bront`	Front view
`#view_back`	Back view
`#view_persp_user`	Perspective view
`#view_iso_user`	User view
`#view_camera`	Camera view
`#view_spot`	Spot view
`#view_shape`	Shape view
`#view_grid`	Grid view
`#view_track`	Track view

If there is no camera or spot selected when setting the Camera or Spot views, the Select Camera or Spot dialog window will be shown.

You can set the active viewport using *viewport.activeviewport*. It will require an index number that will identify the viewport. You can use *viewport.numviews* to inquire how many viewports you have.

Track View, Schematic View, Asset Manager, and MAXScript Listener will not be considered in any of these commands. Once you change a viewport to any of them, you cannot change it back using MAXScript.

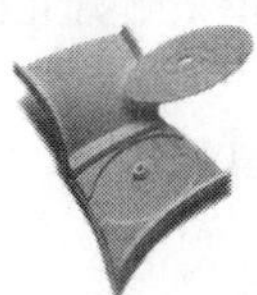

Check the ViewportsLayout Macro Script by Borislav Petrov on the CD-ROM, which provide viewport management (`vpLayout02.zip` on the CD-ROM).

Camera Views

You can manipulate Camera views to define which camera will be used and also to find out which camera is being used in a viewport. *Getactivecamera* or *viewport.getcamera()* will list the camera that is used by the current Camera view.

Viewport.setcamera will allow us to set a camera in the current Camera view. For instance, `viewport.setcamera $Camera02` will set the current Camera view as Camera02. If the current view is not a camera, it will return undefined.

Redrawing

Some actions require us to force a redraw on-screen. There are three ways to do this: *redrawviews()*, *completeredraw()*, and *max views redraw*.

Redrawviews() will redraw only what has changed on-screen, providing a fast but not so accurate redraw. *Completeredraw()* and *max views redraw* will redraw the entire screen, regardless of what was or was not changed, which is slower but more accurate.

Safe Frames

You can turn the safe frames on or off . To do so, you can use two commands: *displaysafeframes* or *max safeframe toggle*. The latter will toggle the status of the safe frames (if they were off, they will be turned on, and vice versa). The viewports with safe frames are automatically redrawn.

To use *displaysafeframes*, you need to say whether it is true or false. For instance, `displaysafeframes = true` will turn *displaysafeframes* on for the active viewport. The viewport is not redrawn automatically, so you will need to use *completeredraw()* or *max views redraw* to refresh the viewport and display the safe frame.

Accessing the MAX UI

Besides creating your own interface and manipulating viewports, you can also work with MAX's interface, controlling the Command Panel, the prompt line, and transform tools, and even changing the cursor arrow. You'll see some of these features in this section.

Cursors

Sometimes you may want to let the user know that MAX didn't freeze while the script is still processing. A way to do this is to change the cursor to the system wait cursor (usually an hourglass) until the process is over, and then switch the cursor back to normal. To do this, you can use *setwaitcursor()* and *setarrowcursor()*. They will set the cursor to the wait cursor and back to the normal arrow, respectively.

Controlling the Command Panel

You can use *setcommandpaneltaskmode* to control which of the tabs is open in the Command Panel. Similarly, you can use *getcommandpaneltaskmode* to know which panel is activated. This is useful because some options—sub-object level, for instance—will not run if a specified Command Panel tab isn't activated.

To set any panel as active, simply specify `setcommandpaneltaskmode #panel`, where `panel` is one of the six Command Panel tabs: *create, modify, hierarchy, motion, display,* or *utility*. Instead of using *setcommandpaneltaskmode*, you can use *max mode panel*, substituting `panel` with the panel name, just like in the previous example.

Using Transform Tools

You can activate all transform tools using scripts. See Table 5.3 for a list of the commands you can use to activate each transform tool.

Table 5.3 Transform Tool Commands

COMMAND	TRANSFORM TOOL
max move	Move tool
max rotate	Rotate tool
toolmode.nonuniformscale()	Non-Uniform Scale tool
toolmode.uniformscale()	Uniform Scale tool
toolmode.squashscale()	Squash tool
max select	Select tool

Toolmode commands also allow us to set the active coordinate system and which pivot point will be used. *Toolmode.coordsys* will set the active coordinate system, which you need to choose from among `#view`, `#screen`, `#world`, `#parent`, `#local`, or `#grid`.

To set the coordinate system center, you can use the properties of *toolmode*: `.pivotcenter()`, `.selectioncenter()`, or `.transformcenter()`. These will set the coordinate system center to each object's pivot, to the center of the selection, or to the origin of the coordinate system, respectively.

The Prompt Line

MAX commands use the prompt line to ask the user to perform certain actions, and also display the status of the last command issued, such as the rendering time taken by the last *render* command. You can also use the prompt line in MAXScript.

You can use *pushprompt* to add a string to the prompt line. The previous string will be stored in a temporary buffer. To restore the previous string, you can use *popprompt()*. For instance, type:

```
pushprompt "Select Shapes to be trimmed:"
```

The text string will be displayed in the prompt. If you enter `popprompt()`, the previous prompt will be restored.

You can use *pushprompt* as many times as needed, and the previous prompts will be stored in memory. *Popprompt()* can restore each prompt backward, one at a time, until the first prompt is reached.

The *replaceprompt* command will substitute the actual prompt with a specified string, regardless of the use of *pushprompt* and *popprompt*. The only drawback is that the old prompt cannot be restored; essentially, the *popprompt* buffer is cleared.

Displaying Calculation Progress

Some plug-ins show a progress bar in the status bar, as in Figure 5.13, to show the user that some processing is taking place. You can do this with scripts also.

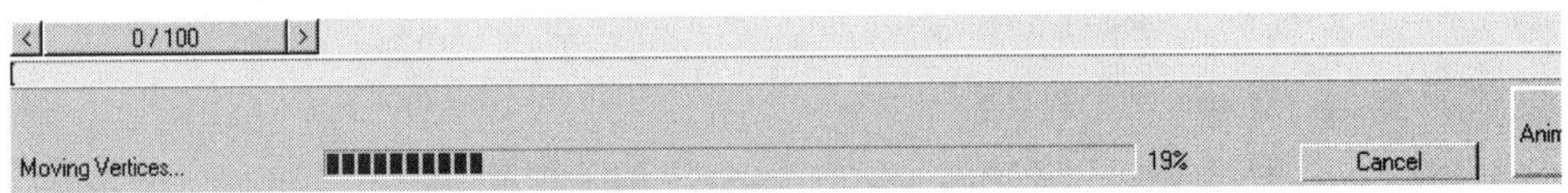

***Figure 5.13** A sample progress bar*

The *progressstart* command creates a progress bar and sets it to 0%. Its only argument is the title of the progress bar. You need *progressupdate* to update the progress bar, specifying the actual percentage as an integer number. At the end of the process, you need *progressend()* to remove the progress bar.

Do not enter `progressstart` *in the Listener because it may lock MAX, and you will not be allowed to cancel the command.*

MAX Commands

MAXScript allows us to access almost all commands found in the toolbars and menus. These commands usually only invoke the action and require user input.

For instance, *max file open* will do the same as picking File → Open from the menu.

Several MAX commands are also executable within MAXScript, like *max views redraw*, which is the same as *redrawviews()*.

To see a list of all MAX commands, just enter **`MAX ?`** in the Listener, or enter **`max views ?`** for a list of MAX view commands.

The Online Help has a list of all these commands.

Bitmap Manipulation

One of the important steps in MAXScript is bitmap manipulation. You can render images or maps and manipulate them through MAXScript, or even load and save any supported MAX format.

What's even more interesting in MAXScript is that you can access all the extended information in the rendered image, such as Z-Buffer, G-Buffer, Node ID, and so on.

Rendering Images

You can invoke the renderer within MAXScript to render your current scene. MAXScript supports all rendering features, except Network Rendering and which Plug-in Render is active.

You can set some parameters in the Render Scene dialog (see Figure 5.14) using the methods shown in Table 5.4.

Table 5.4 Render Scene Dialog Methods

METHOD	DESCRIPTION
renderwidth	Defines the render width in pixels.
renderheight	Defines the render height in pixels.
renderpixelaspect	Defines the pixel aspect.
renderoutputfilename	Defines the output filename.
renderdisplacements	Turns on or off the rendering of Displacement maps.
rendereffects	Turns on or off the rendering of render effects.
skiprenderedframes	Turns on or off Skip Existing Images.
renderer	Defines if the current renderer is #draft or #production.

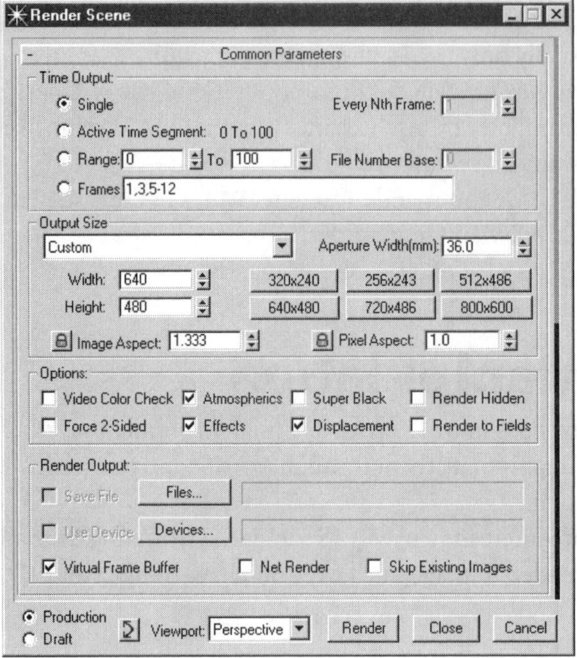

Figure 5.14 *The Render Scene dialog*

Besides these properties, MAXScript also accesses the Anti-aliasing filter in the Scanline renderer. If the Scanline renderer is not the active renderer, these properties return undefined. They're listed in Table 5.5.

Table 5.5 Anti-Aliasing Properties

PROPERTY	DESCRIPTION
scanlinerender.antialiasfilter	Defines which is the active anti-aliasing filter.
scanlinerender.antialiasfiltersize	Defines the size of the current filter.
scanlinerender.enablepixelsampler	Turns on or off the Global SuperSampling.

To render a scene, you simply need to use the *render()* function. It will render the current viewport with the current values set, or you can specify the parameters you wish. Take a look at the Online Help for a list of all these parameters.

For example, `render camera:$camera01 framerange:#(0,100) nthframe:2` renders the specified camera with the given settings.

A good example of the *render()* function is in the Batch Renderer sample script from Ravi Karra that comes with MAX.

Extended Channel Access

MAX renders various channels besides the colors you see on the screen. It renders the Object IDs, Material IDs, UVW map, Normals, Z Depth, and more. This information is useful for post-processing in MAX or in any other external program. These channels are enabled when you render RLA or RPF files.

MAXScript has full access to these channels, allowing us to directly read their information or to read them as grayscale images. Then, you can output these images and use them as masks inside or outside MAX. You can access these channels by rendering an image and asking the renderer to calculate these channels, or by loading an RLA or RPF file.

To render the channels, you need to add `channels:#(channel array)`, where `channel array` is an array of the channels you want to render. The channels you can list in this array are *#zdepth, #matid, #objectid, #uvcoords, #normal, #unclamped, #coverage, #node, #shadercolor, #shadertransparency, #velocity,* and *#weight*.

To read channel information, use *getchannel*, which returns the channel parameters for the specified pixel. This information is extremely technical and differs for each channel. If the bitmap does not have that channel, it will return undefined.

To read the channel information as a grayscale bitmap, you can use *getchannelasmask*. The grayscale is similar to the images you see in the VFB when you select these channels. This bitmap can be saved and used anywhere in MAX or in external post-processing software. Figure 5.15 shows an example of a grayscale mask.

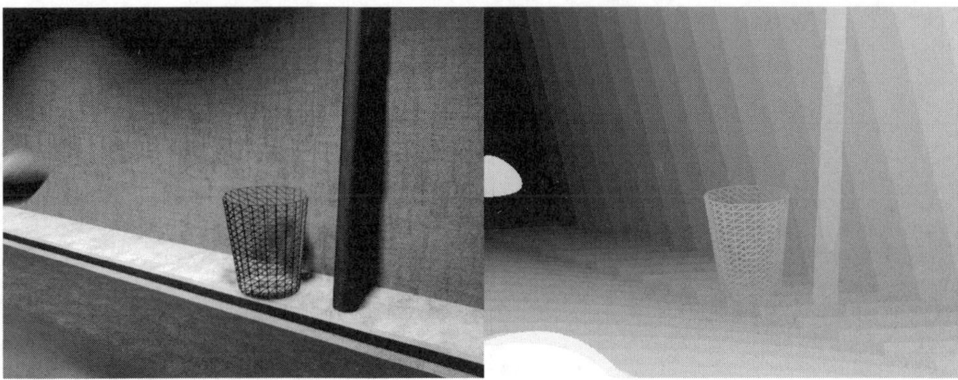

Figure 5.15 *A Z-Buffer grayscale channel*

Bitmap Variables

`Bitmap` is also a variable type. It can hold a bitmap that was loaded from a file, rendered in MAX, or even created through a script.

A bitmap can be created simply by specifying its size. For instance, `b = bitmap 640 480` creates an empty bitmap with the specified size.

Create bitmaps carefully. The sample bitmap created here occupies more than 1Mb of RAM.

You can also load an existing bitmap from disk. This is done using *openbitmap* or *selectbitmap*. *Openbitmap* requires you to specify the whole path, while *selectbitmap* displays a dialog box, which is user friendly.

Another way to create a bitmap is by rendering an image. This can be done in two ways:

```
b = bitmap 640 480
render to:b
```

or

```
b = render()
```

Both ways will assign the rendering result to *b*.

Bitmap Properties and Methods

The `bitmap` variable has several properties to help you work with them. Table 5.6 lists the `bitmap` properties.

Table 5.6 *Bitmap* Properties

Property	Description
filename	Defines the filename associated with it.
width	Returns the width of the bitmap.
height	Returns the height of the bitmap.
numframes	Defines the number of frames on an animated bitmap (IFL, AVI, or other sequence).
frame	Defines the current frame (0-based).

These methods allow you to read and set important information to a bitmap. For instance, it's important to set the *filename*, so that you can later save this bitmap to a file. Also, *numframes* and *frame* are important properties when working with animated bitmaps, like AVI, File Sequence, or others.

Besides these properties, MAXScript also has some methods that will help you manipulate bitmaps. They're listed in Table 5.7.

Table 5.7 Bitmap Methods

METHOD	DESCRIPTION
display	Displays the bitmap on the Virtual Frame Buffer (VFB).
undisplay	Closes the VFB with the bitmap.
save	Saves the bitmap to the specified filename.
close	Closes the bitmap file.
copy	Copies the bitmap to another one.
gotoframe	Positions the bitmap in the specified frame.

There are other methods that will manipulate pixel information, which you will see later. These methods allow you to save, display, and close a bitmap.

The following example shows the entire process, from creating a bitmap to rendering, saving, and closing it.

```
b = bitmap 640 480
render to:b
b.filename = "c:\\temp\\test.tga"
save b
close b
```

Always use two \ (backslash) characters to specify a file path. The \ (backslash) character is a special character for string variables.

Cleaning Memory

You can easily lose track of your memory if you do not take the necessary precautions. The first of them, as mentioned before, is to close the bitmap files when you are finished using them.

But, in case you don't, MAXScript has two functions that can help you. The first is *gc()*, which stands for garbage collector. This function frees memory by closing unused files and other free references that might have been left open. As a rule of thumb, always use *gc()* after working with bitmaps, especially in For and While loops.

The second function that helps free memory is *freescenebitmaps()*. When you render a scene in MAX, the renderer loads all bitmaps in memory and keeps them. Calling *freescenebitmaps()* releases this memory, but the next render will take longer because MAX will need to reload all the bitmaps.

Manipulating Pixel Information

MAXScript offers access to pixel information, such as color or channel information, if available. You can read or set color information to any pixel in an image.

The methods available to manipulate pixel information are listed in Table 5.8.

Table 5.8 Methods to Manipulate Pixel Data

METHOD	DESCRIPTION
getpixels	Reads the color of a specified pixel or array.
setpixels	Sets the color of a specified pixel or array.
getchannel	Reads the channel information for the given pixel.
getchannelasmask	Reads the channel information as a grayscale image.

Using *getpixels* and *setpixels* can be very slow when adjusting lots of information in bitmaps.

In Exercise 5.5, you will work on a script that renders an image and allows you to select whether you want to save it or any of its channels as a grayscale image.

EXERCISE 5.5: CREATING THE RENDER CHANNELS SCRIPT

1. Open `render_channels01.ms` on your CD-ROM. This script is partially ready. It works by selecting an existing bitmap or by rendering the current scene. Then, it shows which channels are available and allows you to select a bitmap to save the selected channel. After evaluated, it looks like Figure 5.16.

2. Enter the following code in the *on channel selected i* event:

```
bmp_channel = channel.selected
save_it.enabled = true
```

These actions specify which channel is selected and enable the Save button.

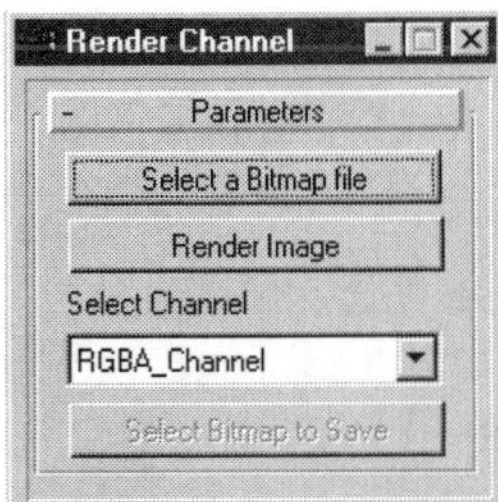

Figure 5.16 *The Render Channels script*

3. Add the following code in the on *save_it pressed* event:

```
if img2 != undefined then (close img2)
if bmp_channel == "RGBA_Channel" then img2 = copy img
else img2 = getchannelasmask img bmp_channel
img2.filename = selectsavebitmap()
save img2
display img2
gc()
```

This event creates a copy of the image named *img2*. If the channel is *RGBA*, this means it's the original object color, so all you need to do is copy it. If the channel is something else, you need to use *getchannelasmask* to retrieve it. At the end, the script just saves the file and wisely invokes the *gc()* to clean unused memory.

Your script should look similar to `render_channels02.ms` on the CD-ROM.

Bitmaps in the UI

It is possible to see bitmaps in the user interface. Just use the *bitmap* UI item to do so.

The bitmap interface item only needs its size, and the bitmap that will be loaded in it. Let's continue Exercise 5.5 and add a bitmap preview to it.

EXERCISE 5.5A: ADDING A BITMAP TO THE RENDER CHANNELS SCRIPT

1. Open file `render_channels02.ms` if you're not working with it.
2. Below button *save_it*, add a new interface item:

```
bitmap uibmp width:150 height:120
```

3. Evaluate the script and notice that the floater needs to be taller. Edit the *channel_floater* line and change *195* to *321*.
4. You need to have the bitmap displayed when the channel is selected, so move these lines from *on save_it* to *on channel*:

```
if img2 != undefined then (close img2)
if bmp_channel == "RGBA_Channel" then img2 = copy img
else img2 = getchannelasmask img bmp_channel
```

5. Now, adjust the image size to be displayed. MAXScript can do it for you using the *copy bitmap* method. Add the following lines after the code you entered in step 4:

```
tmpbmp = bitmap 150 120
copy img2 tmpbmp
```

6. Now that you have the bitmap, display it in the UI and continue to add the following code:

```
uibmp.bitmap = tmpbmp
```

7. Make sure you add `gc()` at the end to clear unused memory.

Your script file should look like file `render_channels03.ms` on the CD-ROM. The UI should look like Figure 5.17.

***Figure 5.17** The bitmap UI item*

Rendering Maps

A nice feature in MAX is the ability to render maps. You can create a complex map hierarchy and have it rendered to a bitmap file, saving you render time; or you can create nice effects to be used later. This can be done using *rendermap*.

Using *rendermap* is a lot faster than accessing pixel information directly. Of course, some operations cannot be done with render maps, but if you can find a way using this feature, it will save you a lot of time.

In Exercise 5.6, we will illustrate the two processes, one using direct pixel manipulation and the other using *rendermap*.

EXERCISE 5.6: CREATING A CROSS FADE TRANSITION

1. Open `cross_fade01.ms` on your CD-ROM and evaluate it. You should see the rollout in Figure 5.18.

   This script has the UI ready, along with the events for loading both bitmaps. Notice that when *bmp2* is loaded, it is copied to *tmpbmp2*. This is done to rescale *bmp2* to match the same size of *bmp1*.

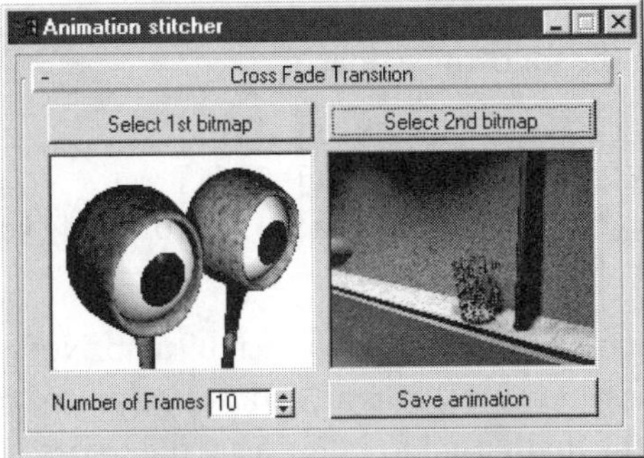

Figure 5.18 *The Cross Fade Transition script*

2. You will now start adding the event to create the transition. Enter the following in *on go pressed:*

```
bmpout = bitmap  bmp1.width bmp1.height
bmpout.filename = selectsavebitmap()
```

This creates the output bitmap and asks the user to select the output filename.

3. Continue adding the following code after the lines in step 2:

```
if bmpout.filename != undefined do
(
total = nof.value
progressstart "Calculating..."
for i in 1 to total do
(
```

This code checks to see if the bitmap filename is set. If so, a variable is created to hold the total number of frames in the transition. It also starts a progress bar to display the calculation progress. You have just defined the loop that will run for each frame in the transition.

4. Continue adding the following code:

```
for y in 1 to bmp1.height do
for x in 1 to bmp1.width do
(
```

These two *fors* will step through each pixel. The first *for* steps through each line, and the second *for* steps through each pixel of that line.

5. Continue again, adding the following code:

```
col01 = (getpixels bmp1 [x-1,y-1] 1)[1]
col02 = (getpixels bmp2 [x-1,y-1] 1)[1]
col03 = col01 * (total - i)/total + col02 * i/total
setpixels bmpout [x,y] #(col03)
```

Col01 and *col02* are the color of each pixel in each bitmap. Notice that you used *[1]*. This is because *getpixels* returns an array of colors, so you only need a pixel out of it. *Col03* is the math used to interpolate the colors, and *setpixels* writes it to the new bitmap.

6. Now, finish by adding the following code:

```
)
save bmpout frame:i
progressupdate (100*i/total)
)
```

```
progressend()
)
gc()
```

Save saves each frame of the animation. *Progressupdate* updates the progress bar, and *progressend* removes it after the calculation is done. As always, you'll finish with a *gc()*.

Your script should look like `cross_fade02.ms` on the CD-ROM.

This script can take a long time to process images. It took five minutes to create a 10-frame transition between two 640 × 480 images in a Dual 500.

To continue Exercise 5.6a, you will rewrite the main engine using *rendermap* to calculate the transition. To use *rendermap*, you need to use a map. In this case, the best one is surely Mix.

Exercise 5.6a: Rewriting the Cross Fade Transition Script

1. Open the file `cross_fade02.ms` if you're not working with it.
2. Remove the nested *for y* and *for x* and all of its content.
3. After *progressstart*, add the following code:

   ```
   bmpmap = mix()
   bmpmap.map1 = bitmaptexture bitmap:bmp1
   bmpmap.map2 = bitmaptexture bitmap:bmp2
   ```

   This creates the Mix map and loads each bitmap in one submap.
4. Before *save bmpout*, add the following:

   ```
   bmpmap.mixamount = 100.0*i/total
   rendermap bmpmap into:bmpout
   ```

   This will set the Mix amount and render the map, placing the result in the `bmpout` variable.
5. In *on load2 pressed*, remove the following lines:

   ```
   tmpbmp2 = bitmap bmp1.width bmp1.height
   copy bmp2 tmpbmp2
   bmp2 = tmpbmp2
   ```

These lines need to be removed so that the bitmap loaded in Mix reflects the one in the hard drive. We do not need to loose time rescaling it through MAXScript. Mix does it for you.

Your script is now ready and should look like `cross_fade03.ms` on the CD-ROM.

This script now takes less than 20 seconds to execute the same sequence.

Summary

In this chapter, you learned how to work with the MAXScript interface and with the MAX interface. You also learned how to work with bitmaps and rendered images.

In the next chapter, you will work with everything related to file I/O. You will learn how to work with MAX files, how to import other files, and how to use external data to drive objects in MAX. You will even work with Xref files and binary file I/O.

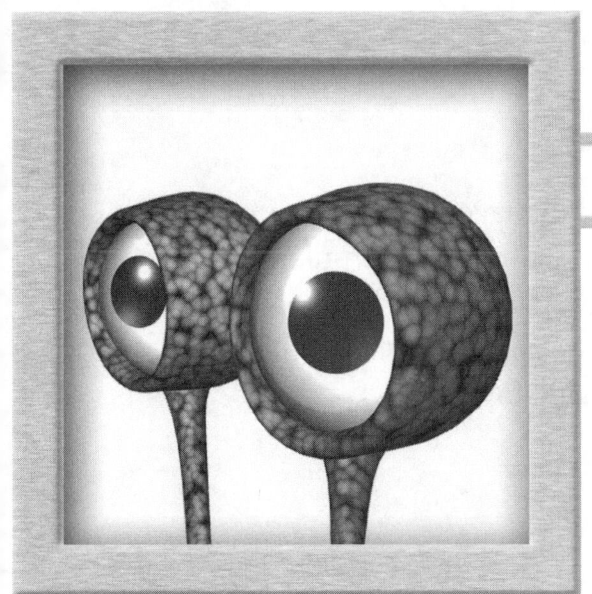

File I/O

MAXSCRIPT

Chapter 6

File input/output (I/O) and management is very important and useful. MAXScript allows you to manipulate its file formats and to read and write ASCII files. Using a MAXScript Extension plug-in, you will even be able to work with binary files.

This chapter covers the following topics:

- Text file I/O
- INI file I/O
- Managing files
- Binary file I/O
- Working with MAX files
- Importing and exporting files
- Using Xref
- MAX file properties

MAXScript File I/O

MAXScript allows you to access text files (ASCII) and to read and write information to them. You can also load and execute script files, access and modify file properties (such as read-only and archive), and you can read or write binary files using a MAXScript Extension plug-in.

You will start by learning how MAXScript handles strings, and then you will learn how to input and output strings from MAX.

Strings

Variables that contain text are called *strings*. Strings are needed in various places in MAX. When you create a button, you have a string that is the button's label. When you create an alert message, you need a string that will be the alert, and so on.

All strings have a *.count* property, which lists the number of characters in it (spaces are also included). Strings also work as an array of characters, so using `[i]` retrieves the character present in "i".

For example, in `s = "MAXScript"`, `s.count` returns 9, and `s[3]` returns "X".

Manipulating Strings

MAXScript gives you a lot of flexibility when working with strings. You can convert any variable to a string variable, allowing you to output numerical values or other variables easily. This is done using *as string*.

For instance, if you have `a = [10,2,-35]`, you can convert it to a string using `b = a as string`, and *b* would then be "[10,2,–35]".

The opposite is also valid: You can also convert any string to other variable types, if that's possible. For instance, in `a = "2.5"`, `b = 2.5 as float` *would convert it to a float variable. In* `c = "a2.5"`, `d = c as float` *would return undefined because this conversion would not be possible.*

You can also join two or more scripts using +. For instance, if you had `a = 150` and you wanted to create a nice output message, you could use `message = "The final result is " + a as string`. The message variable would return "The final result is 150". This operation is called concatenation.

MAXScript offers other methods to manipulate scripts, as listed in Table 6.1.

Table 6.1 String Methods

Method	Description
findstring	Finds an expression in a string.
substring	Returns a specified part of a script.
filterstring	Breaks the string into an array of strings based on a given separator.
replace	Replaces part of a string with another string.
matchpattern	Checks to see if a string matches a wildcard pattern.
execute	Executes the string as if it were a MAXScript command.

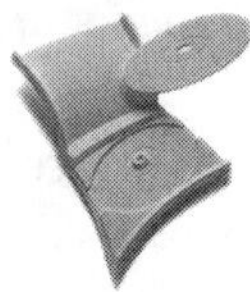

A good example of the use of *findstring* and *substring* is the `Time_functions.ms` script on the CD-ROM. It's a script that reads the local time using the *localtime* function. *Localtime* returns the current time as a string variable, so the script will use *findstring* and *substring* to break it into day, month, year, time, minutes, and seconds.

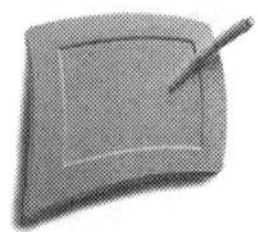

You can use execute *to access an object by knowing its name. For instance,* `b = "Sphere01"` *is the name of the object.* `C = execute ("$" + b)` *will execute "$sphere01", which will then return the object in the scene. If you did not use this method, you would need to loop through all objects and search for their names, or use a MAXScript Extension plug-in, which is discussed in Chapter 11.*

Outputting Strings

There are a couple ways you can output a string. You already learned how to use alert messages and how to use the status bar. You can also output strings to the Listener or even to a New Script window.

This is done using *format* or *print*. *Print* will display the variable in the Listener or in the output file or stream, without formatting or changing it. Using *print*, you can print a variable directly without converting it to a string.

On the other hand, *format* requires a string to be printed but allows you to create a template that will be filled with variables.

As an example, suppose you have the following variables:

```
name = "John"
age = 25
```

You can output the name and age using *format*, as shown here:

```
format "Name:% Age:%" name age
```

Format will replace each percent sign (%) with the respective variable value listed later. The result would be `"Name:John Age:25"`.

Working with Special Characters

If you use *format* all the time, MAXScript will write everything in a single line. You surely do not want it displayed like that. There are also other characters that might not work, so MAXScript has special characters and extended hexadecimal characters. They're listed in Table 6.2.

Table 6.2 Special Characters

CHARACTER	DESCRIPTION
\n	Jumps to the next line.
\t	A tab character.
\"	A double quote character.
\%	A percent character.
*	An asterisk character.
\?	A question mark character.
\\	A single \ character.
\x*n*	A hexadecimal character, where *n* is the hex number.

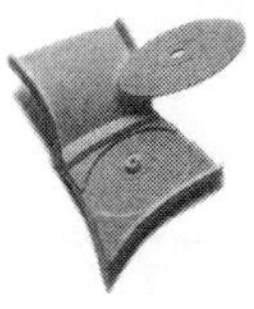

Execute the script `print_chars.ms` on the CD-ROM to see a list of all of the hexadecimal characters. Notice how the script uses *execute* to create the command that will form the hexadecimal string. Also, notice how you can use a function call inside *format* by using the percent character (%) substitution. Also, notice that *try* and *catch* were used because some ASCII characters invoke commands when executed and cannot be printed.

Text File I/O

Now that you know how to use strings, let's create and output strings to text files.

You can create a text file using *createfile*. To do so, you need to specify the filename and path. This will create a *filestream*.

For instance, `f = createfile "c:\\output.txt"` will create this file and prepare it to be written.

You can then format or print anything to this file. For instance, `format "This is the first line" to:f` will write the string "This is the first line" to the specified file.

After a file is written, you can use *close* to close the file and stop the output. For instance, `close f` will write everything that is in the memory buffers to the file and will then close it.

When a file is opened by MAXScript, Windows locks access to this file. The only way to open this file is either by closing it through MAXScript or by closing MAX.

Always close a file when you're finished using it to clean memory and to free the file. Closing a file performs automatic garbage collection.

Besides creating a file, you can also open an existing file using *openfile*. *Openfile* requires an extra parameter that specifies if the file is open for reading only or for appending. For instance, `f2 = openfile "c:\\output.txt" mode:"a"` will open the specified file for appending.

Open files also need to be closed.

Always remember to use \\ when specifying file paths.

Table 6.3 shows all the remaining methods associated to text file I/O.

Table 6.3 Text File I/O Methods

METHOD	DESCRIPTION
readline	Reads the next line.
readchar	Reads the next character.
readchars	Reads the specified number of characters.
readdelimitedstring	Reads the next block of strings in delimited files (CSV, SDF, etc).
readvalue	Reads the next value.
readexpr	Reads the next expression and evaluates it.

Table 6.3 Text File I/O Methods (*continued*)

execute	Reads and evaluates all the expressions in the file.
eof	Tells you whether there is more data available to read in the file.
seek	Positions the file so that the next read takes place from that point on.
filepos	Returns the current file position.
skiptostring	Positions the file at the place where a specified string is found.
skiptonextline	Positions the file in the beginning of the next line.

These methods allow you to read all kinds of data in a text file. You can select the way you will read the data, with or without evaluating the expressions in it. You can also position the file at any given point and continue working from there.

When appending or writing to a file, be careful using seek *or other positioning methods. They will overwrite whatever was previously in the file.*

Using Dialogs to Select Files

As you saw before, MAXScript requires you to type in the entire filename and path to open or create a file. You can use dialogs to make opening or creating a file more user-friendly.

Getopenfilename and *getsavefilename* display a dialog asking you to select a filename to open or save, respectively. This dialog is shown in Figure 6.1. You can specify three parameters: caption, default filename, and supported file types.

For instance, `fname = getopenfilename caption:"Select File" types:"CSV Files (*.csv) |*.csv|All Files (*.*)|*.*|"` will show a dialog box and allow you to select CSV files, and also all files, as a standard File Open dialog box. Notice how *types* works: You list the description, then the pipeline character (|), and then the file mask. You can repeat it as many times as you wish. It always ends with a pipeline character (|).

The MAXScript Listener and the MAXScript Editor are not limited in width, so you can enter as many characters as you wish in one line. If you want to break a line and continue below, just add a backslash character (\) at the end, and MAXScript will understand that it continues in the next line. You cannot break a line in the middle of a word; you have to break lines in spaces only. Also, you cannot break a line in the middle of a string, the "...." block must remain on a single line.

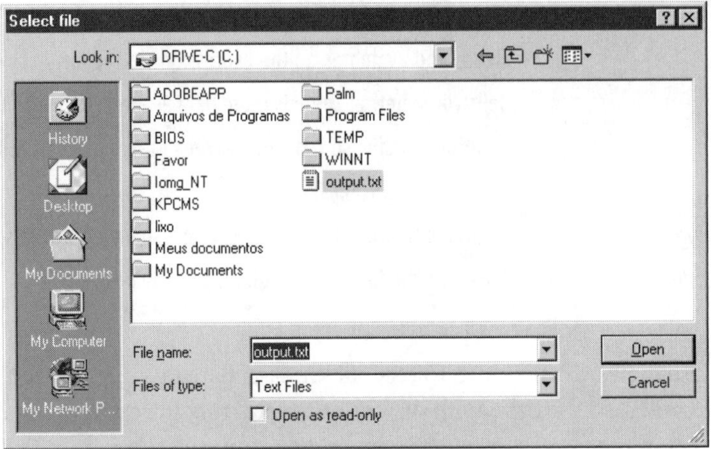

Figure 6.1 *The standard Select File dialog*

Sometimes, all you need to know is a file path. You can get this information using *getsavepath*. The only property you can set is the *caption*. For instance, `fpath = getsavepath caption:"Select path"` will ask you for a file path and will display a dialog as in Figure 6.2.

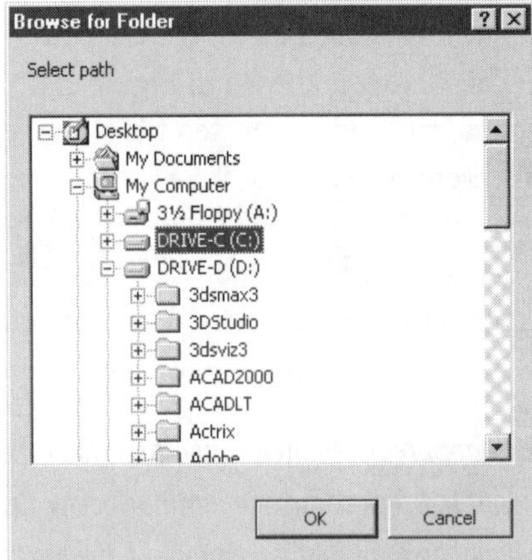

Figure 6.2 *The standard Select Path dialog box*

Working with Filenames and Paths

Sometimes you need to create more files out of a filename, or you need to know which path a file will be located in. Or, you may need to create files at known paths, such as in the MAX root path. MAXScript has functions that will help you do this. Table 6.4 lists filename and path methods.

Table 6.4 Filename and Path Methods

Method	**Description**
getfilenamepath	Retrieves the file path.
getfilenamefile	Retrieves the filename.
getfilenametype	Retrieves the file extension.
filenamefrompath	Retrieves the filename and extension.
getdir	Returns MAX-related paths.
scriptspath	Returns the Scripts folder in MAX.

These methods are very handy if you need to place several files in a specific folder, or if you need to create another file in the same folder. Also, you might want to create a `.cfg` file in the *plugcfg* folder, so all you need to do is use `getdir #plugcfg` to know the path.

It's a good habit to place configuration files for your scripts in known MAX folders. This way, when the user reloads the script, you can read the configuration file and load the values in your script.

When using scriptspath, *MAXScript already adds the backslash character (\) at the end of the path. This does not happen when using* getdir *or* getfilenamepath, *so you will need to do it manually.*

Besides these paths, you can also read and set map paths and Xref paths. This is done using two structs, *mappaths* and *xrefpaths*, which have the same methods listed in Table 6.5.

Table 6.5 *Mappaths* and *Xrefpaths* Methods

METHOD	DESCRIPTION
add	Adds a new path.
count()	Lists the number of paths.
get	Retrieves a path.
delete	Removes a path.

For example, `mappaths.count` will return the number of map paths that are set. `Mappaths.get 1` will return the first map path. *Xrefpaths* works exactly the same way.

Do not set more than 50 map paths. MAX R3.x and VIZ R3 are limited to 50 map paths in the INI file. If you need files outside of the map paths, simply use the UNC path format (`\\computer\shared_folder\folder\file`).

Working with Script Files

Besides outputting to a file or to the Listener, you can also open a New Script window and output data to it.

Instead of creating a new file or opening another, just use *newscript()* to open a New Script window, and then format all needed data to it.

You can also load and execute a script file, allowing you to break larger scripts into smaller ones. This is done by using *filein,* which loads and compiles the script, acting just like MAXScript ➜ Run Script...

Hands-On MAXScript: Creating a Script to Animate Objects through External Data

You will now create a script that reads and writes animation data to a file. Basically, the script will manage position and rotation, but the process is the same for any other property you wish to add later.

After working on Chapter 7, you will be able to add more features to this script, like a keyframe reducer or the ability to write only the keyframes.

You will start working on a file that already has the UI and part of the script done. It already has the export part ready, and you will complete it by writing the import code. This script is made to manage a CSV (Comma Separated Value) file with seven values per line: frame number; x,y,z position; and x,y,z rotation.

1. Open file `animation_io01.ms` on the CD-ROM and evaluate it. It should look like Figure 6.3.

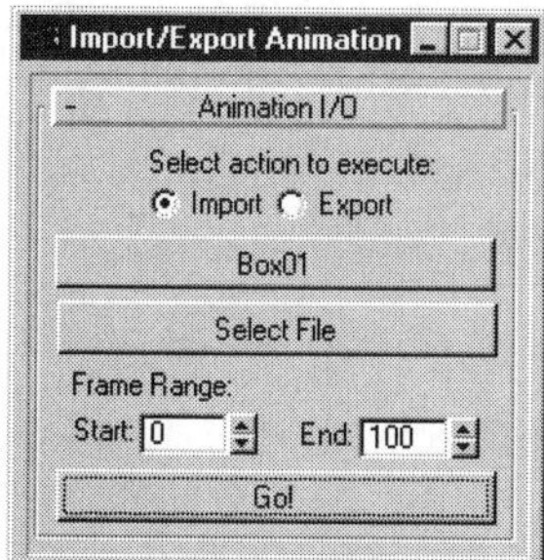

Figure 6.3 *The Import Export Animation script*

2. In *go pressed, if action.state == 1,* enter the following:

```
f = openfile fname
while not eof f do
(
```

   These actions will define the starting conditions for the script. You are opening the file and creating a loop that will read all data until you reach the end of the file.

3. Continue writing the following code:

```
animate on
(
tempvar = filterstring (readline f) ","
```

   This code will turn the animation on and will read a new line in the file. *Filterstring* will separate all the data in an array, making it easier for you to manipulate it later.

4. Continue writing the following code:

```
at time (tempvar[1] as integer)
(
obj.pos.x = tempvar[2] as float
```

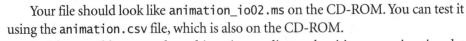

This will position the animation at the specified frame and will position the object in X.

5. Repeat the last line for the remaining position and rotation values.
6. Close all needed brackets and add *close f* after the *While* loop to close the file.

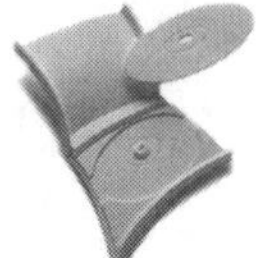

Your file should look like `animation_io02.ms` on the CD-ROM. You can test it using the `animation.csv` file, which is also on the CD-ROM.

Feel free to add more code to this script, reading and writing any animation data you wish. You can even allow the user to select which values are related to the CSV columns.

INI File I/O

INI files are easier to manage through MAXScript because you will not need to worry about opening and closing files. All you will need to do is ask MAXScript to read or write the information you need, and it will be written using the INI format.

The two commands used to manipulate INI files are *getinisetting* and *setinisetting*. They need the filename, the section, and the key. This is how an INI file looks:

```
[Section01]
key01 = value01
key02 = value02
...
```

For example, `getinisetting (getdir #maxroot + "\\3dsmax.ini") "RenderDialogPosition" "Dimension"` returns the position and dimension of the Render dialog box, which is saved to the INI file.

You can create INI files to store your script's data. For example, `setinisetting (getdir #plugcfg + "\\sample.cfg") "Settings" "Reload" "true"` creates the file and writes the specified data to it.

DOS Management

You may need to manage files and folders within MAXScript. This is possible using the methods listed in Table 6.6.

Table 6.6 File and Folder Methods

METHOD	DESCRIPTION
getfiles	Lists all files that match the wildcard.
getdirectories	Lists all directories that match the wildcard.
copyfile	Copies the specified file.
renamefile	Renames the specified file.
deletefile	Deletes the specified file.
makedir	Creates the specified directory.
getfileattribute	Reads the file attribute.
setfileattribute	Sets the file attribute.
getfilecreatedate	Reads the file creation date.
getfilemoddate	Reads the date that the file was last modified.
getfileversion	Reads the `.exe` or `.dll` file version.

These methods are important because they allow you to search for files and modify them. You can search for all MAX files in a folder and render a preview of each of them. Using these methods, you can also create a function to test if a specific file exists or not.

Working with Encrypted Files

MAXScript allows you to encrypt your script files and also to encrypt any other ASCII file. Encrypting your scripts is a good way to protect your code, allowing you to sell it and even attach it to MAX's hardware lock, similar to the way plug-ins work.

Using the *encryptscript* method creates a copy of the specified script, using an MSE extension, and encodes it as a binary file. This file can be read in any 3D Studio MAX but cannot be accessed or edited.

MAXScript does not support the encryption of Macro Script files (`.MCR`). If you want to encrypt these files, place your code in an `.MSE` file and use filein *to load it into the Macro Script.*

Besides encrypting MAXScript files, you can encrypt any other ASCII file using the *encryptfile* method. You need to specify the input and output files, as well as an encryption key, which can be any integer number.

You can read this file in MAXScript using the *openencryptedfile* method, which will be used instead of *openfile*, producing the exact same results. *Openencryptedfile* requires the correct key so that it can open the encrypted file.

An interesting trick is to encrypt files using the Hardware Lock ID, which will prevent the user from opening the file in another MAX system.

You can query the Hardware Lock ID using the `hardwarelockid` *variable.*

Binary File I/O (MAXScript Extension)

MAXScript does not provide built in binary file I/O, but this can be done using a MAXScript Extension plug-in developed by Simon Feltman, who just happens to be the author of Chapters 12–18 of this book.

Chapter 11 explains all about MAXScript extensions. Just unzip `binstream.zip` from your CD-ROM and place `binstream.dlx` in the Plug-ins folder. Then, restart MAX so that the plug-in is loaded.

After that, the methods listed in Table 6.7 will be exposed.

Table 6.7 Binary File Methods

Method	Description
fopen	Opens the file for reading or writing.
fclose	Closes the file.
writebyte	Writes an integer as one byte.
readbyte	Reads a one-byte integer.
writeshort	Writes an integer as two bytes.
readshort	Reads a two-byte integer.
writelong	Writes an integer as four bytes.
readlong	Reads a four-byte integer.
writestring	Writes a string to the file.
readstring	Reads a string.
fseek	Positions the file.
ftell	Returns the file position.

These methods allow you to access any info you might need in the binary file. In order to work with these parameters, all you will need to know is the binary file structure.

MAX File I/O

You can manipulate MAX files through MAXScript. You can load, save, merge, save selected, import, and export files through MAXScript.

Combining these features with the ones you learned before, you can create powerful scripts that will automate tedious tasks, such as batch converting and batch rendering files.

Loading and Saving MAX Files

You can load max files through MAXScript using *loadmaxfile*. All it needs is a valid MAX file and path. You can use *getopenfilename* to select the file.

If a MAX file is open, MAXScript will not prompt to save it; all changes will be discarded. To avoid losing data, you can use *checkforsave()*, which will check to see if the file has been saved or not. If the user presses the *Yes* button, the file will be saved.

If you want to save a MAX file and specify the filename and path, you can use *savemaxfile*. If you do not specify a file path, MAXScript will save the file in the default scene path.

To retrieve the current MAX filename and path, you can use two global variables: `maxfilename` and `maxfilepath`.

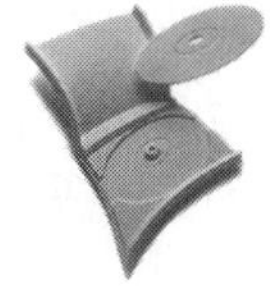

The `render_folder.ms` script on the CD-ROM asks the user to select a folder. Then, all MAX files in that folder are rendered at 320 × 240, and the result is saved to a JPEG file with the same name as the MAX file.

Merging Files

Merging files with MAXScript is a two-step process. First, you need to know the object names, and then you tell MAXScript which of them you want to merge.

You can get a list of the objects in a MAX file using *getmaxfileobjectnames*. The result will be an array with the names of the objects.

You can the use *mergemaxfile* to merge the objects from that file. *Mergemaxfile* has a lot of options that you can specify. These options are listed in Table 6.8.

Table 6.8 *Mergemaxfile* Options

Option	Description
#prompt	Shows the dialog to select the objects.
#select	Selects the merged objects.
#noredraw	Does not redraw the screen after the merge.
#deleteolddups	Deletes duplicated objects. If not used, the dialog will appear.
#mergedups	Merges the objects even if they have duplicate names.
#promptdups	Requests an action in case of duplicated objects.

If you still have duplicated materials, or Raytrace Tracks, the dialog will appear anyway, and there's no way to skip it.

Besides these parameters, *mergemaxfile* needs you to specify a filename and a list of object names. If you do not specify the object names, all objects will be merged.

The reverse operation (Save Selected) is done in MAXScript using *savenodes*. *Savenodes* requires an array of nodes and a filename.

Hold, Fetch, and Undo

When you do any operation using MAXScript, MAX stores this operation in the Undo buffer, usually naming it MAXScript. Some operations do not allow Undo in MAX, then the Undo buffer is cleared, and you will not be able to come back to the original scenario.

The trick is to use Hold and Fetch. In MAXScript, these functions are *holdmaxfile()* and *fetchmaxfile()*, which perform the exact same action as the menu options. You can also use *max hold* or *max fetch*, which will work exactly the same.

MAXScript also offers some control over the Undo. You can turn Undo off, or you can even clear the Undo buffer.

The Undo context allows you to turn on or off the Undo option for a set of actions. If you turn Undo on, this will force the Undo to record an action and place it in the Undo list. This is useful if you want to allow the user to undo the various steps in your script.

For instance, if you execute these commands (`b = sphere();b.material = standard diffusecolor:red`), MAXScript will only show a single MAXScript entry in the Undo list. If you do not want these operations to be undoable, just use *undo off* before them. If you want to define an Undo for a set of actions, just use *undo on.*

You can join several commands in a single line, separating them with a semi-colon (;).

Some operations might use a lot of memory to save the Undo buffer. You can free this memory using *clearundobuffer().*

If needed, you can invoke the Undo and Redo commands in MAXScript using *max undo* and *max redo.*

Sometimes it's nice to remind the user to do a hold by adding a button with this option. Also, at the end of an operation, you can add an Undo option for the user.

Other File Commands

You can reset or exit MAX through MAXScript. Both operations need to be performed with caution because you can loose your scene contents. And of course, shutting down MAX will stop any script execution.

To reset MAX, you use *resetmaxfile()* or *max reset file.* Both functions will have the same effect as using File ➜ Reset. If you use *resetmaxfile #noprompt*, MAX will not display any dialog and will reset automatically.

To exit MAX, use *quitmax().* Similarly to *resetmaxfile*, you can also use *#noprompt* and skip the confirmation dialog.

Make sure you use checkforsave() *before using either of these commands to allow the user to save the current scene.*

File Properties

MAXScript also can access file properties. You can assign the properties through scripts and you can create useful utilities.

To access these properties, use the *fileproperties* structure, which has a series of methods to manage file properties, as listed in Table 6.9.

Table 6.9 File Property Methods

Property	**Description**
getnumproperties	Lists the number of properties.
addproperty	Adds a new property and sets its value.
findproperty	Searches for a property index.
getpropertyname	Returns the name of a specified property based on its index.
getpropertyvalue	Returns the value of a property.
getitems	Returns the values of a given item.
deleteproperty	Removes a property and clears its value.

The File Properties dialog box (see Figure 6.4) is divided into three tabs: Summary, Contents, and Custom. You access these through `#summary`, `#contents`, and `#custom`, respectively.

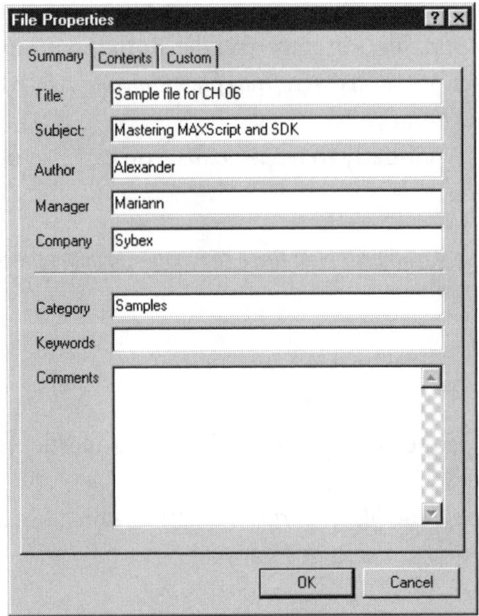

Figure 6.4 *The File Properties dialog box*

You can use *fileproperties.addproperty* to add properties to each of the sections. For example, `fileproperties.addproperty #summary "Title" "Animation Project"` adds this text to the Title field in the Summary section. The Summary section has the following fields: Title, Subject, Author, Keywords, and Comments. The Contents section has Manager and Company, despite the fact that they are also located in the Summary page in the dialog.

Use `max hold` *after changing any property in the Contents section because they are only updated when saved.*

To retrieve a property's value, you can use *fileproperties.getpropertyvalue*, but to do so, you need to know the index of the property. This is done using *fileproperties.findproperty*. If a property does not exist, it returns 0; if the property does exist, it returns the index of that property.

You can add some properties and retrieve their values later, such as in the following examples:

```
fileproperties.addproperty #summary "Title" "Animation Project"
fileproperties.addproperty #summary "Subject" "First Shot"
fileproperties.addproperty #summary "Author" "Alexander"
t = fileproperties.findproperty #summary "Title"
v_value = fileproperties.getpropertyvalue #summary t
```

As you can see, the correct property value was retrieved and stored in `v_value`.

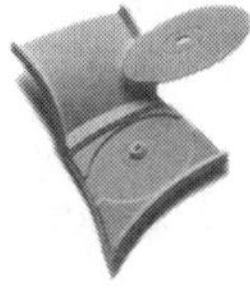

Take a look at the `Manage_properties.ms` example script on the CD-ROM. It's a rollout (see Figure 6.5) that requires the user to fill in the data. If the data is not filled in, the *on oktoclose* event does not allow you to dismiss the dialog. Any data you enter is automatically saved because each *edittext* event writes the property directly. The Edit Values button is available on subsequent uses of this script to edit the values that have already been entered.

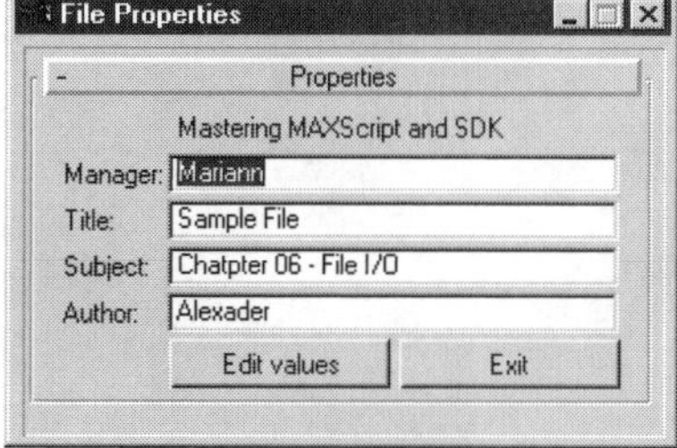

Figure 6.5 *The Manage Properties script*

Importing and Exporting Files

You can import and export files from MAX using *importfile* and *exportfile*. Both options define the file type based on the file extension that you supply.

Both *importfile* or *exportfile* have a *#noprompt* option, which suppresses all configuration dialogs and works with the default values.

There's no way to change any Import or Export options through MAXScript. Some plug-ins remember the last settings used, and some use their default values.

Some Import and Export plug-ins have limitations, such as the 3DS Importer and Exporter, which can only handle a maximum of 64K faces or vertices. If your mesh does not fit this condition, you will need to break the mesh into smaller objects. You can use *numverts* or *numfaces* to check the number of faces and vertices in the objects to see if they will fit the criteria.

Hands-On MAXScript: Creating a 3DS Animation Exporter

You will now create a script that exports each frame of an object animation as a single 3DS file. This is needed for some game engines that use 3DS files to create their animation.

The script will create a snapshot of the object at every frame. This snapshot is saved by using *savenodes* and creating a series of `.MAX` files. These MAX files will then be opened, one by one, and they will be exported to 3DS. At the end, the series of MAX files will be deleted.

We will base the script UI on the Animation I/O script that you developed earlier in this chapter.

1. Open file `3ds_io01.ms` and evaluate it. The interface should look like Figure 6.6.

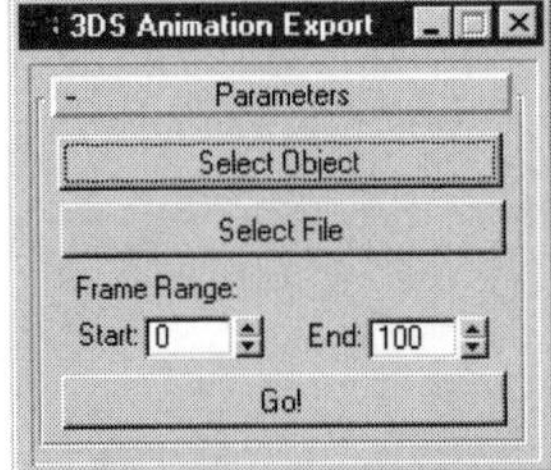

Figure 6.6 *A 3DS Animation Export script*

2. In the *on go pressed* event, add `checkforsave()` so that the user can save the current file.
3. Continue adding the following code after `checkforsave()`:

```
for i in start.value to end.value do
(
at time i m = snapshot obj
savenodes m (getfilenamepath fname + "\\temp3dsexport" + i \
   as string)
delete m
)
```

This is the first part of the script. A *snapshot* is created at each frame and is saved to a MAX file.

4. Now add the 3DS exporting code:

```
for i in start.value to end.value do
(
loadmaxfile (getfilenamepath fname + "\\temp3dsexport" + \
   i as string + ".max")
exportfile (getfilenamepath fname + "\\" + getfilenamefile \
   fname + i as string + ".3ds") #noprompt
deletefile (getfilenamepath fname + "\\temp3dsexport" + i \
   as string + ".max")
)
```

This is the last part of the script. It will load each saved MAX file and export it to 3DS, deleting the original one.

The code in step 4 does not fit in a single line of the book, so we added a backslash character (\) at the end of the line. MAXScript works the same way: If you want to break a line, just use a backslash character (\) at the end, and MAXScript will understand that the line is a continuation of the previous line. Or if you prefer, you can write everything on a single line.

Your script should look like `3ds_io02.ms` on the CD-ROM. The script can take a long time to process your animation, so it might be nice to add a progress bar to the script, such as in file `3ds_io03.ms` on the CD-ROM.

Xref Management

MAXScript allows you to load, unload, merge, and discard Xref scenes and objects. You can also access all properties in the Xref, such as *Bind* and *Proxy*.

MAXScript goes one step beyond the MAX UI and gives you access to any scene property in the Xref, such as *materials*, *scene nodes*, *animation*, and *controllers*.

Xref Scenes

You can add an Xref scene to the scene by using *xrefs.addnewxreffile()*. For example, `xrefs.addnewxreffile "vase.max"` adds *vase.max* as an Xref scene in the current scene.

Xref scene properties are listed in Table 6.10. They relate to the properties of the Xref Scenes dialog box, shown in Figure 6.7.

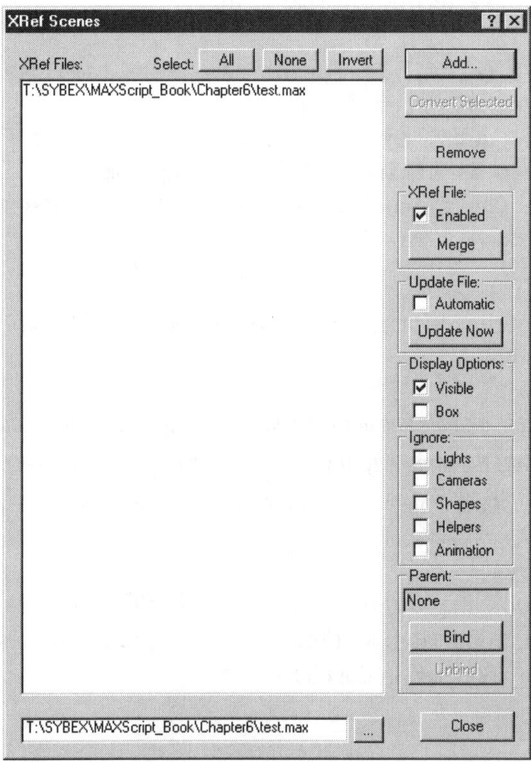

***Figure 6.7** The Xref Scenes dialog box*

Table 6.10 Xref Scene Properties

Property	**Description**
filename	Returns the Xref filename.
autoupdate	Turns on or off the *autoupdate*.
boxdisp	Turns on or off display in Box mode.
hidden	Defines whether the Xref scene is hidden.
disabled	Defines whether the Xref scene is disabled.
ignorelights	Turns on or off the Ignore Lights checkbox.
ignorecameras	Turns on or off the Ignore Cameras checkbox.
ignoreshapes	Turns on or off the Ignore Shapes checkbox.
ignorehelpers	Turns on or off the Ignore Helpers checkbox.
ignoreanimation	Turns on or off the Ignore Animation checkbox.
tree	Returns the Xref root object in case of nested Xref scenes.
parent	Displays the Xref parent if the Xref scene is bound to any scene object.

You cannot select or manipulate an Xref scene in MAX. Because they do not appear as objects, you have to use *xrefs.getxreffile* to access any Xref present in the current scene. For example, `xrefs.getxreffile 1` will retrieve the first Xref in this scene. You can then use the methods listed in Table 6.11 to manipulate the Xref.

Table 6.11 Xref Scene Methods

Method	**Description**
delete	Removes the Xref.
merge	Merges the Xref.
updatexref	Reloads the Xref from the file.
xrefs.getxreffilecount	Lists the number of Xrefs in the scene.
xrefs.deleteallxrefs	Removes all Xrefs from the scene.
xrefs.updatechangedsrefs	Updates all Xrefs that were changed.
xrefs.findunresolvedxrefs	Lists all Xrefs that were not found.
xrefs.attemptunresolvedxrefs	Tries to update the Xrefs that were not found.

When an Xref is not found, you can specify a series of paths where MAX can search for them. You can add more paths in MAXScript using xrefpaths.add()*, which is explained earlier in this chapter.*

Xref Scene Data

MAXScript allows you to access any information in the objects inside of an Xref scene. This is done as if the objects were part of a hierarchy.

Using the *tree* property, you can access the objects inside the Xref scene. For example, `scene01 = xrefs.addnewxreffile "vase.max"` loads the `vase.max` file as an Xref scene. Then, `scene01.tree.children` lists all the objects that are part of this scene.

You can read any property, but you cannot change them. To do so, you would need to open the original file and then reload the Xref.

Xref Objects

You can add an Xref object to the scene using *xrefs.addnewxrefobject()*. This will add a new object to the scene, which different from the Xref scene.

The Xref object can be manipulated as a regular MAX object and has some other properties, which are listed in Table 6.12. These properties appear in the Modify Panel, as in Figure 6.8.

Figure 6.8 *An Xref object in the modifier stack*

Table 6.12 Xref Object Properties

PROPERTY	DESCRIPTION
filename	Returns the Xref filename.
proxyfilename	Returns the proxy filename.
currentfilename	Returns the filename that is active on-screen.
objectname	Returns the name of the object in the original file.
proxyobjectname	Returns the name of the proxy object in the original file.
currentobjectname	Returns the original name of the active object on-screen.
useproxy	Defines whether the proxy object will be displayed.
renderproxy	Defines whether the proxy object will be rendered.
updatematerial	Turns on or off the Update Material checkbox.
ignoreanimation	Turns on or off the Ignore Animation checkbox.

The only method associated with Xref objects is *updatexref*, which will reload the Xref object and its proxy.

For example, `obj = xrefs.addnewxrefobject "vase.max" "vase01"` adds *vase.max* as an Xref object. You can access its position, rotation, scale, and all object properties (*renderable*, *cast shadows*, *material*, and so on) as a regular MAX object. Then, you can add a proxy object using `obj.proxyfilename = "vasebox.max"`, and `obj.proxyobjectname = "box01"` will load the proxy object, and `obj.useproxy = true` will display the proxy on-screen.

Summary

In this chapter, you learned how to work with files, read and write data, work with filenames and paths, and work with supported MAX files. These skills give you a lot of flexibility and allow you to automate tedious tasks, such as batch importing and rendering.

In the next chapter, you will learn how MAXScript works with animation, how to add and manipulate controllers and keyframes, and also how to work with the Track View and its options.

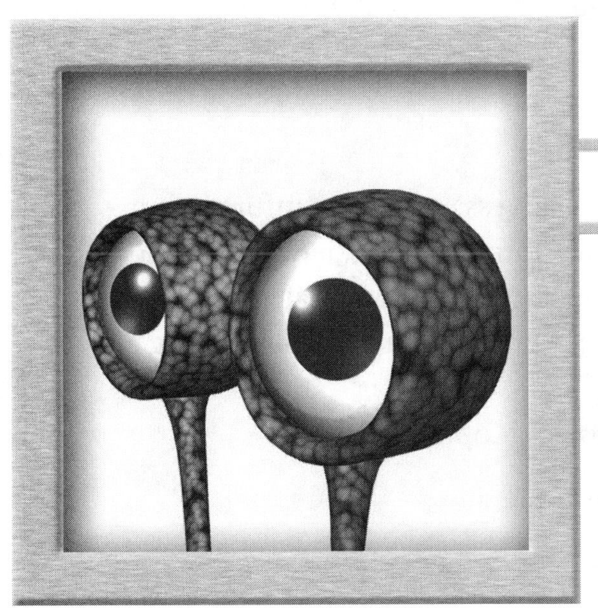

Creating and Manipulating Animation Parameters

MAXSCRIPT

Chapter 7

You can use MAXScript to access animation information, including controllers, keyframes, Track View nodes, and even Track View time operations such as scale and reverse time. You can also create a script that acts as a controller, using Script controllers.

This chapter covers the following topics:

- Working with animation controllers
- Manipulating keyframes
- Accessing time functions
- Animating with Script controllers
- Animating FFD and vertices
- Creating Track View nodes

Working with Animation Controllers

Every animated parameter in MAX requires an *animation controller* to define how the animation will happen. MAX has many different animation controllers for different parameters and with different purposes.

Through MAXScript, you can assign any controller and change its parameters, adding or modifying the animation of any property.

Adding and Accessing Controllers

You can access any parameter's controller by adding *.controller* after the parameter's name. For instance, to access the position controller of an object named *Sphere01*, you could use `$Sphere01.position.controller`.

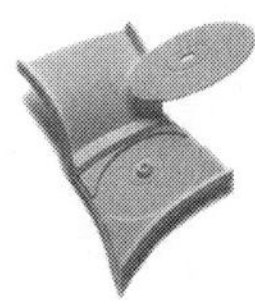

You can find a list of all controllers available in MAX in the file `animation_controller.txt` on the CD-ROM. Notice that the controllers are divided into types. This is because you need to know the correct controller for each parameter. For example, you need to assign a *Point3controller* to a color parameter, a *Floatcontroller* to the *Y* property of a *Position_XYZ* controller, and so on.

The following sequence creates an object and sets its position controllers:

```
s = sphere()
s.pos.controller = position_xyz()
s.pos.z_position.controller = noise_float()
```

Controller Properties

Some other controllers, such as Noise, Reactor, Look At, Link Control, Path, and Surface, have several properties that depend on a dialog or on the Motion Panel. All of these properties are accessible through MAXScript.

To list a controller's properties, you can use *showproperties*. Continuing the previous example, `showproperties s.pos.z_position.controller` will list the properties of the *noise_float* controller.

Track View Properties

You can access the object properties as they appear in the Track View. To do so, you need to add *`[index]`* after the object name. `Obj[3]` is the transform track and ***`obj[4]`*** is the node track (the object track as listed in the Track View). These properties are called *subanims*. Table 7.1 lists the subanims that an object can have.

Table 7.1 Subanims

SUBANIM	NAME
1	Visibility
2	Space warps
3	Transform
4	Node (Modified Object)
5	Material
6	Image Motion Blur multiplier
7	Object Motion Blur on_off

Notice that some objects will not have all subanims, since the property in that subanim cannot be assigned to that object. For instance, lights will not have materials assigned.

To know how many subanims a node or parameter has, you can use the *numsubs* property.

The methods associated with subanims are listed in Table 7.2.

Table 7.2 Subanim Methods

METHOD	DESCRIPTION
getsubanim	Retrieves the indexed subanim.
getsubanimname	Retrieves the name of the subanim.
getsubanimnames	Retrieves an array with all subanim names.

You can change the controller of any subanim and any of its properties. You can also know if the subanim is or is not animated by using the `.isanimated` property.

The `.value` property will list the value of a subanim. If an object is animated, the `.value` property will show the subanim value at the current frame.

For example, to create a sphere and access its subanims, type the following:

```
obj = sphere()
obj.numsubs
getsubanimname obj 3
obj[3].numsubs
getsubanimname obj[3] 1
obj[3][1].value
```

Notice that `obj.numsubs` returns 7, which is the number of subanims that an object has. `Getsubanimname obj 3` lists the name of the third subanim, which returns `#transform`.

Next, we checked to see how many subanims transform by using `obj 3.numsubs`. As we know, it should return 3 because the sphere has a PRS transform controller.

Finally, we asked for the name of the first subanim in transform, and we asked for its value. Notice that we used `[3][1]`, which means that we're accessing the first subanim of the third subanim. If the position controller was an XYZ position, we still would have three subanims in it, which means that the Y axis would be `obj[3][1][2]`.

The subanim structure can be seen in Figure 7.1, which shows an example of all properties and subanims of an object and how they appear in the Track View.

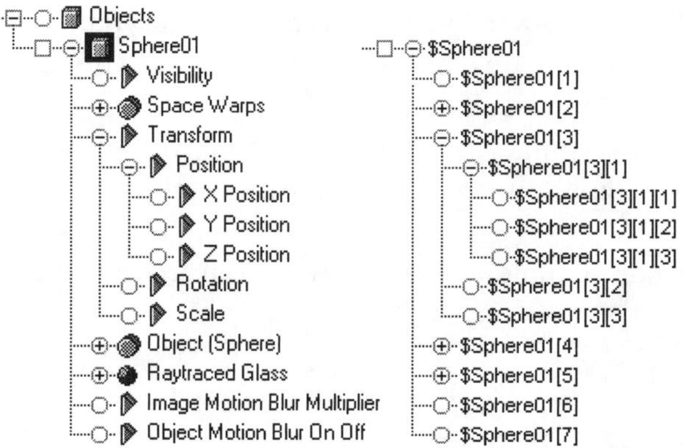

Figure 7.1 *Subanim structure*

The script in Listing 7.1 searches for all materials in the scene, as well as all of their subanims, and then collects all files associated with them. With this information, you can substitute maps, check for missing files, and so on.

LISTING 7.1: A FILENAME COLLECTOR SCRIPT

```
mat_array = #()
for i in scenematerials do append mat_array i
counter = 0
while counter < mat_array.count do
(
counter += 1
num_subs = mat_array[counter].numsubs
for i = 1 to num_subs do append mat_array mat_array[counter][i]
)
fname = #()
for i in mat_array do
(
try (append fname i.filename)catch()
)
```

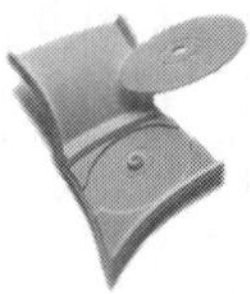

The `vizable_maker15.ms` sample script on the CD-ROM is an example of a script that uses subanims to collect the maps, just like Listing 7.1.

Manipulating Keyframe Information

The main reason for using MAXScript to control animation is its ability to control keyframe information. In MAXScript, you can change any keyframe information, such as time and tangents, and you can even adjust keyframes using the *Edit Time* functions in the Track View, such as *Scale* and *Reverse*.

You can access the keyframes in any controller using the *keys* property. It will return an array of keys, and you can manipulate each of them using their respective index.

The following code example illustrates how you can access keyframes:

```
s = sphere()
animate on
(
at time 30 move s [20,0,10]
at time 60 move s [0,20,-10]
at time 90 move s [-20,-20,0]
)
s.pos.keys
s.pos.keys[1]
```

`S.pos.keys` returns the array of keys. `S.pos.keys[1]` accesses the first keyframe. You can use the keyframe properties to modify the animation. These properties depend directly on the type of controller assigned. The keyframe properties are listed in Table 7.3.

Table 7.3 Keys Properties

PROPERTY	DESCRIPTION
All Controllers	
time	Accesses the time of the keyframe.
value	Accesses the value of the keyframe.
selected	Specifies if the keyframe is selected.
Bezier Controller	
intangent	Specifies the value of the In tangent.
outtangent	Specifies the value of the Out tangent.
intangenttype	Specifies the type of the In tangent.
outtangenttype	Specifies the type of the Out tangent.
x_locked	Defines if the x_lock is on.
y_locked	Defines if the y_lock is on.
z_locked	Defines if the z_lock is on.
constantvelocity	Specifies if constant velocity is on or off.
TCB Controller	
tension	Specifies the Tension value.
continuity	Specifies the Continuity value.
bias	Specifies the Bias value.
easefrom	Specifies the Ease From value.
easeto	Specifies the Ease To value.

Every controller has specific properties. The Bezier controller and the TCB controller are used most often in MAX. The properties listed in Table 7.3 are the properties shown in the Bezier Controller dialog box (see Figure 7.2) and in the TCB Controller dialog box (See Figure 7.3).

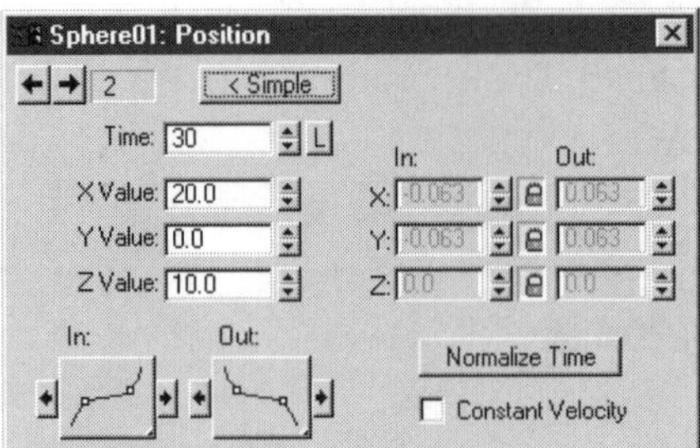

Figure 7.2 *The Bezier controller keyframe property dialog box*

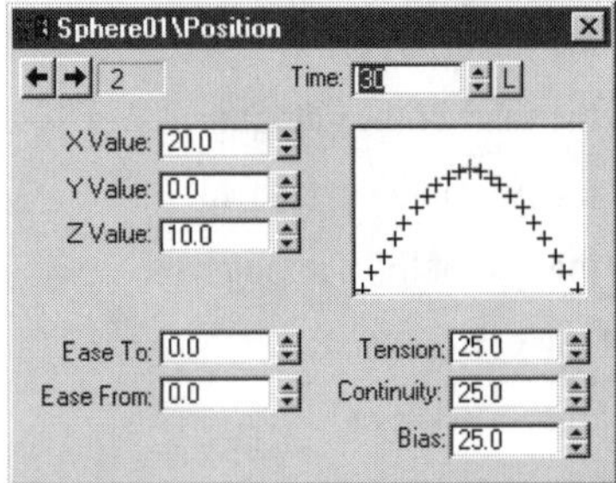

Figure 7.3 *The TCB controller keyframe property dialog box*

Using the previous example, you can change the keyframe time using `s.pos.keys[1].time = 10`. If you want to change the tangent type on Bezier controllers, you can specify one of the following tangents: *#smooth*, *#linear*, *#step*, *#fast*, *#slow*, or *#custom.*

Using our previous example, you can set the last keyframe In tangent to decelerated movement by using `s.pos.keys[4].intangenttype = #slow.`

Select the sphere before entering these commands in the Listener, and you will see the changes reflected in the Track Bar.

Working with Keyframes

MAXScript has a series of functions that allow you to add, delete, move, and select keys. These functions are listed in Table 7.4.

Table 7.4 Keys Functions

FUNCTION	DESCRIPTION
addnewkey	Adds a new keyframe at the specified time.
deletekey	Deletes the specified keyframe.
deletekeys	Deletes the keyframes specified (*#allkeys* or *#selection*).
selectkey	Selects the specified keyframe.
selectkeys	Selects the keyframes in the given interval.
deselectkey	Removes the specified keyframe from the selection.
iskeyselected	Indicates if the keyframe is selected or not.
movekey	Moves the specified keyframe.
movekeys	Moves the keyframes in the given interval.
numkeys	Returns the number of keyframes in a controller (the same as *controller.keys.count*).
numselkeys	Returns the number of selected keyframes.
getkey	Returns the specified keyframe (same as *controller.keys[index]*).
getkeytime	Returns the time of the specified keyframe.
getkeyindex	Returns the index of the keyframe at a given time.
createlockkey	Copies the previous keyframe value and holds it.

You can use these functions to manually create an animation or to modify it, by moving, removing, or adding new keyframes. These functions reflect the Edit Time section of the Track View, as in Figure 7.4, with the exception of Scale Keys, which does not exist in MAXScript.

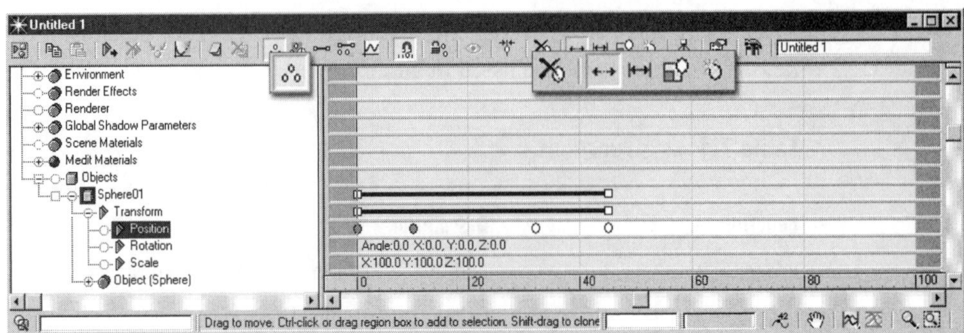

Figure 7.4 *The Edit Keys toolbar in Track View*

The following example illustrates the use of the functions in Table 7.4:

```
s = sphere()
addnewkey s.pos.controller 10
addnewkey s.pos.controller 30
k2 = getkey s.pos.controller 2
k2.value = [20,30,-10]
movekey s.pos.controller 2 20
addnewkey s.pos.controller 30
n = getkeyindex s.pos.controller 30
s.pos.controller.keys[n].value = [-20,10,0]
createlockkey s.pos.controller 40 0
```

Notice that *addnewkey* adds a new keyframe with the position of the object at the specified frame, which is the same as using the Track View, or right-clicking the Time Slider. *Movekey* also uses the same format and does the same as `k2.time += 20`. *Getkeyindex* returns the index of the keyframe at the given time so you can modify the keyframe on the other commands that will require the index. We also used *createlockkey*, which simply copies the previous keyframe and sets the tangents so that it holds the object in place.

When adding or moving keyframes, the keyframes index may change. Make sure you adjust your script to check for the index before manipulating other keyframes.

The following functions can be applied to multiple objects or nested controllers and will affect all of them: addnewkey, deletekeys, selectkeys, deselectkeys, *and* movekeys.

Assigning Out-of-Range Curves

One of the advantages of CG animation is the ability to design a piece of a cyclic animation and repeat it over and over. MAX does this through the Parameter Curve Out-of-Range and offers six different curves, as seen in Figure 7.5.

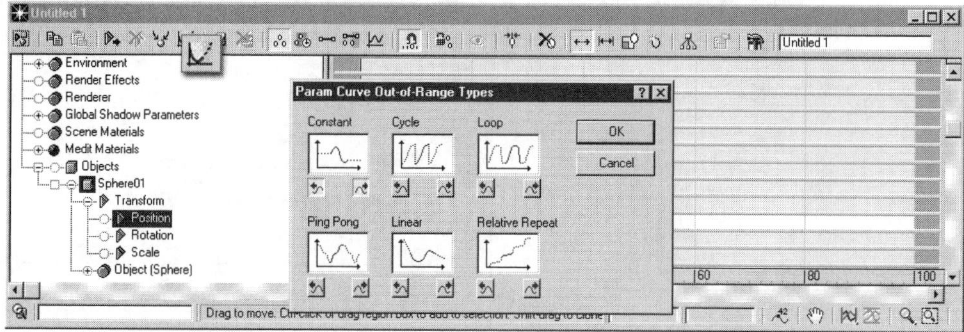

Figure 7.5 *Parameter Out-of-Range curves*

You can access the Out-of-Range curves in MAXScript, using the functions described in Table 7.5.

Table 7.5 Parameter Out-of-Range Functions

FUNCTION	DESCRIPTION
getbeforeort	Returns the Out-of-Range type to the left (before).
getafterort	Returns the Out-of-Range type to the right (after).
setbeforeort	Sets the Out-of-Range type to the left.
setafterort	Sets the Out-of-Range type to the right.
enableorts	Enables or disables Out-of-Range for the controller.

There are six different Out-of-Range types: `#constant`, `#cycle`, `#loop`, `#pingpong`, `#linear`, and `#relativerepeat`.

For instance, `setbeforeort $box* #cycle` sets the Out-of-Range curve to loop in all the controllers of the objects whose names start with *box*. Setting *enableorts* to false produces the same result as setting the Out-of-Range types to *#constant*.

The setbeforeort, setafterort, *and* enableorts *functions work with multiple objects and nested controllers.*

Time Functions

MAXScript accesses all commands in the Edit Time mode of the Track View, as shown in Figure 7.6.

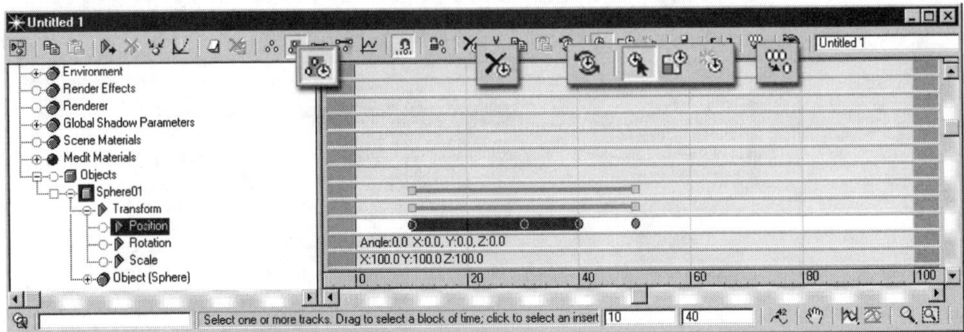

***Figure 7.6** The Edit Time toolbar in Track View*

These commands and their respective MAXScript functions are listed in Table 7.6.

Table 7.6 Edit Time Functions

FUNCTION	DESCRIPTION
supportstimeoperations	Indicates if the controller supports these functions.
deletetime	Deletes the keyframes in the specified interval.
settimerange	Sets the time range for any specified interval.
gettimerange	Returns the time range for three cases: *#allkeys*, *#selonly*, and *#children*.
scaletime	Scales the time in the given interval.
inserttime	Slides the keyframes adding a blank area.
reversetime	Reverses the time in the given interval.

It's important to test the controllers to see if they support the time functions by using *supportstimeoperations*. For instance, the PRS controller does not support time operations, but the controllers beneath it do support them.

When using *deletetime* and *reversetime*, two parameters can be specified, indicating if the keyframe present on the start or end of the interval will be affected. These parameters are *#incleft* and *#incright*, respectively. *Deletetime* also has another parameter, which will instruct MAX to remove the keyframes and will not move the remaining others to fill the empty space. This parameter is *#noslide*.

The following script exemplifies the use of the functions in Table 7.6:

```
s = sphere()
animate on
(
at time 30 move s [40,30,20]
at time 80 move s [-60,10,-30]
)
addnewkey s.pos.controller 15
addnewkey s.pos.controller 50
addnewkey s.pos.controller 65
supportstimeoperations s.pos.controller
t = gettimerange s.pos.controller #allkeys
reversetime s.pos.controller t #incleft incright
scaletime s.pos.controller t (100.0/80)
```

Notice that *reversetime* included the keyframes in frames 0 and 80 because you used *#incleft* and *#incright*.

Only gettimerange *and* supportstimeoperations *cannot be used in multiple objects and controllers.*

Reducing Keys

Sometimes a plug-in or a script may create many keyframes for a controller. You can reduce them using the function *reducekeys*. It has the same effect as the Reduce Keys button in the the Track View, as shown in Figure 7.6.

All you need to specify is the *threshold* and the *step*. If the values of two keyframes inside a given range (the step) are closer than the threshold, the reducer will delete the extra keyframe.

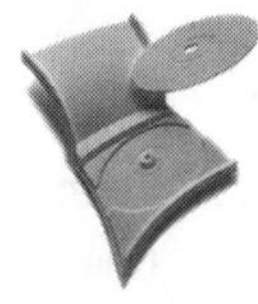

Take a look at the `Collapse_prs.ms` script on the CD-ROM, which converts any animation controller to a Bezier controller and places a keyframe at each given interval. It also features a Keyframe Reducer, which removes unnecessary keyframes.

Using Ease Curves

Ease curves are a nice way to control the overall animation speed. MAXScript allows you to add ease curves and multiplier curves to any controller using *addeasecurve* and *addmultipliercurve*, respectively.

To add an ease curve, you need to specify a float controller, and you also need to add the keyframes to it because they are not automatically created.

The following example adds an ease curve to the position track of a sphere:

```
s = sphere()
animate on
(
at time 30 move s [40,30,20]
at time 80 move s [-60,10,-30]
)
fc = bezier_float()
end = animationrange.end
animate on at time end fc.value = end as integer
addeasecurve s.pos.controller fc
```

In this code, we created a controller and animated it. Then we added it as an ease curve to the position controller. And you already know how to manipulate its keyframes to get any desired effect.

The methods listed in Table 7.7 are also associated with ease curves.

Table 7.7 Ease Curve and Multiplier Curve Methods

METHOD	DESCRIPTION
numeasecurves	Lists the number of ease curves of a controller.
nummultipliercurves	Lists the number of multiplier curves of a controller.
deleteeasecurve	Removes the ease curve from a controller.
deletemultipliercurve	Removes the multiplier curve from a controller.
applyeasecurve	Returns the controller value with the Ease Curve effect applied.
getmuultipliercurve	Returns the controller value with the Multiplier Curve effect applied.

Script Controllers

Besides working with scripts, MAXScript offers you the ability to use a script as a controller. This means you can use a math formula that uses values from a scene to animate a property in MAX.

Besides the math part, a Script controller is a regular script, which means that you can add conditions to it, making it even more interesting.

Let's compare the same animation using an Expression controller and a Script controller so that you can see each one's strengths and weaknesess.

Hands-On MAX: The Expression Controller

Expressions aren't scripts, but they are very useful and sometimes easier to use than scripts. *Expression controllers* allow the user to assign math formulas to any parameter. These math formulas can depend on any other object's parameters; for example, you can change an object's color depending on another object's position.

You can assign an Expression controller to any parameter in MAX. To do so, select the parameter in the Motion tab or in the Track View and assign a float, position, scale, or point3 expression to it.

Right-click the Track View and select Properties, as in Figure 7.7. This opens the Expression Controller dialog box (see Figure 7.8). This is a *modeless dialog*, which means that you can manipulate objects and properties in the scene while still accessing this dialog. You cannot close the Track View.

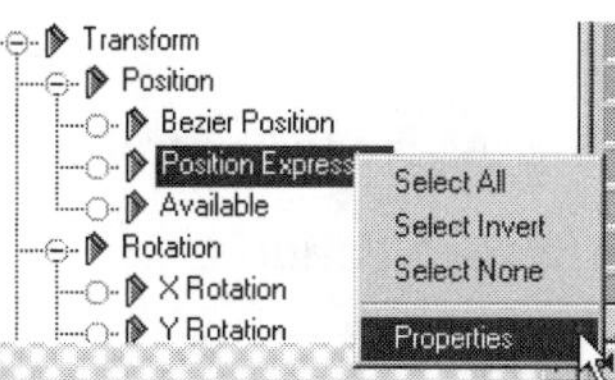

Figure 7.7 *Defining the position expression*

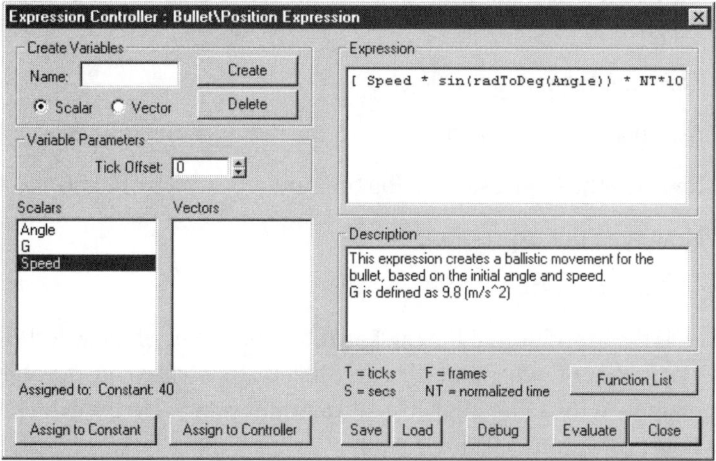

Figure 7.8 *The Expression Controller dialog box*

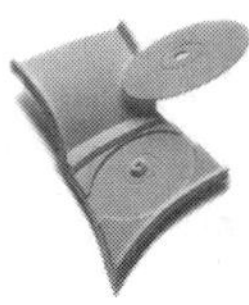

To define an expression, you need to know how you want the object to behave. Let's create an expression using a previously modeled example. Open the file `Wheel_expression.max` on the CD-ROM. It contains a box and a cylinder, which is attached to the box. You want the wheel to rotate according to the box movement. Let's create an expression for this:

1. Open the Track View and locate the wheel's rotation track.
2. Change the Rotation controller to Euler XYZ.
3. Expand the rotation and select Y Rotation.
4. Assign a Float expression to the rotation.
5. Right-click the Track View and select Properties.
6. Type **Car** in the Name field, select Vector, and click Create. This creates a variable that is defined by the car's position. The wheel rotation will be based on this variable.
7. Select Car from the Vectors list and click "Assign to Controller".
8. In the Track View, select Car ➜ Transform ➜ Position.
9. Create a new scalar variable named `Radius`.
10. Select it and click "Assign to Controller".
11. Try to select Wheel ➜ ModifiedObject ➜ Object ➜ Radius. You will not be allowed to select this property because it needs to have a Bezier Float controller assigned to it.
12. Close the Expression dialog box.
13. Assign a Bezier Float controller to the radius of the cylinder.
14. Re-open the Expression dialog box and repeat steps 10 and 11.
15. Now, type this expression:

```
Car.x/Radius
```

`Car.x` is the X position of the car. `Radius` is the radius of the wheel. This expression returns the number of radians, or the curve length, that will rotate the object accordingly. If it rotates in the wrong direction, just add a minus sign (–) to the expression. You can see the whole expression in Figure 7.9.

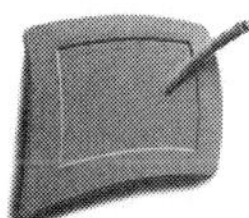

In an Expression controller, rotations are always calculated in radians.

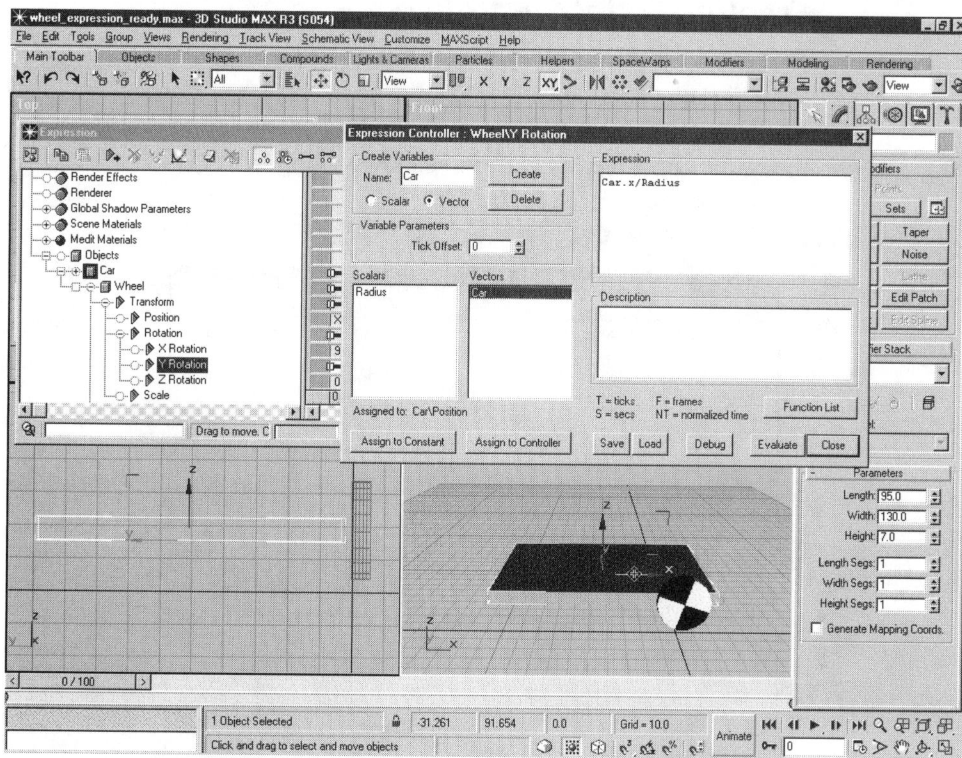

Figure 7.9 *The Car Wheel expression*

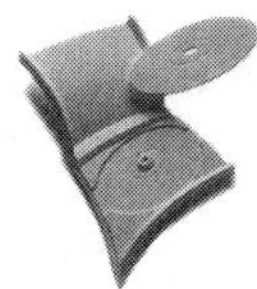

The file `Wheel_expression_ready.max` on the CD-ROM contains the finished expression and a small animation example. There's another example on the CD-ROM, `Bullet_expression.max`, which shows an example of ballistics movement applied as an expression.

Using Script Controllers

A *Script controller* works the same way as an Expression controller, with a small difference: It's a script. There's no need to learn new techniques or formulas—just write it as a regular script. Script controllers are very useful because you can access and modify any property in any object, not only in the local object. You can even call functions and read and write files from Script controllers.

Creating Script Controllers

To create a Script controller, use the same process as used to create an Expression controller. Simply select any Object track and assign a position, rotation, scale, float, or point3 Script controller. Right-click the Track View and select Properties; it will display the Script Controller dialog box, as shown in Figure 7.10.

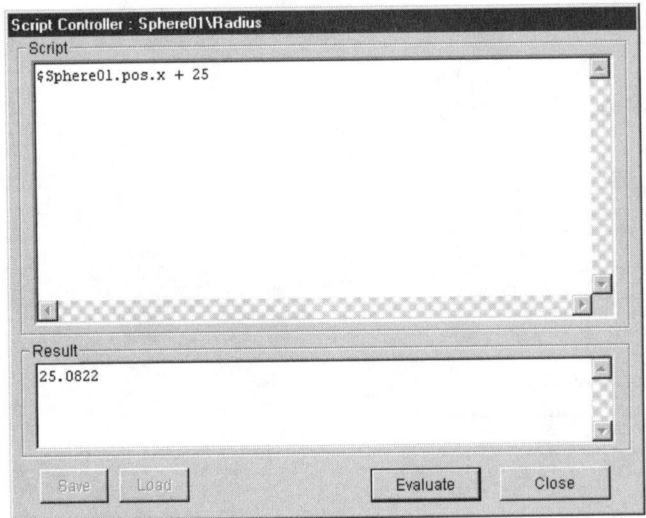

Figure 7.10 *The Script Controller dialog box*

The Script controller must return a result to the script, which is different from the scripts you've written so far, where you always used variables to store values.

Let's repeat the Expression controller example, this time using a Script controller. Open the file `Wheel_script.max` on your CD-ROM and follow these steps:

1. Locate the rotation track of the wheel and assign an Euler XYZ controller to it.
2. Locate the Y rotation track and assign a float Script controller to it.

3. From the Track View shortcut menu, select Properties. In the script area, type **`$Car.pos.x/$Wheel.radius`**.
4. Animate the car, moving it from left to right, and notice the wheel animation.

A Script controller does not update on-screen automatically when you change a parameter. Objects update when you move the Time Slider or when you change the current frame.

The file `Wheel_script_ready.max` on the CD-ROM contains the finished expression and a small animation example.

To easily update the objects from a Script controller, move to the next frame and then move back to the current frame.

Using Conditions

The great advantage of Script controllers is that you can actually write any script in them, using conditions and making decisions about what actions to take.

Take a look at the `auto_optimizer.ms` script on your CD-ROM. This script automatically increases the optimize strength according to the distance of the object; if the object is farther than a certain distance, it'll retain its value.

The following script creates a Script controller and writes the following script (if the camera is named $Camera01 and the object is a sphere named Sphere01):

```
d = distance $Camera01 $Sphere01
if d > min and d < max then
f = threshold*pi*2*((distance $Camera01 $Sphere01)- min)/
(max-min)/360
else if d < min then f=0 else f = threshold*pi/180
f
```

First, it checks the distance between objects. If it's between *min* and *max*, it calculates the face angle threshold. This value is interpolated from 0 to Threshold, and it's calculated in radians. (This explains `*2*pi/360`.)

If the distance isn't between those two values, the script checks if it's above or below them and will set the correct values.

To animate an object, move outward from the camera. Then, using this script, specify the optimize value and the distances. Play the animation and notice how it gradually reduces the number of faces.

Limitations of Script Controllers

The biggest limitation of a Script controller is that it's not interactive, which means that you'll have to move one frame back and forth to see it working. You can make a small script for it, with only two lines: `max time forward` and `max time back`.

Another script problem is that it relates to objects by their names ($camera01, for instance), so the script will fail if an object is renamed or deleted.

You can turn off the Script controllers through the MAXScript option in the Preference Settings dialog box, as shown in Figure 7.11. This might be helpful when you have too many controllers, or when you have controllers crashing and many error messages popping up. Just disable Load Controller Scripts, and they will not be executed.

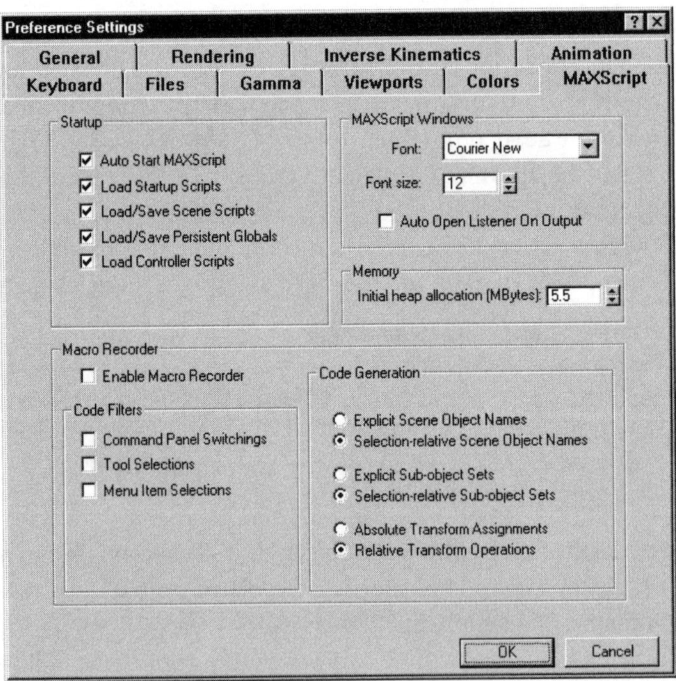

Figure 7.11 *The MAXScript tab in the Preference Settings dialog box*

Animating Vertices and FFDs

You can animate vertices in editable meshes, editable splines, and FFDs. To do so, you need to tell MAX that you want to animate a specific vertex by using *animatevertex*.

If you animate a single vertex in an editable mesh, you will see that it shows in the Track View, as in Figure 7.12. This is because, to save memory and resources, MAX only creates the animation tracks for the vertices once they're animated. This is what *animatevertex* does: It creates the animation track so that you can animate the vertex.

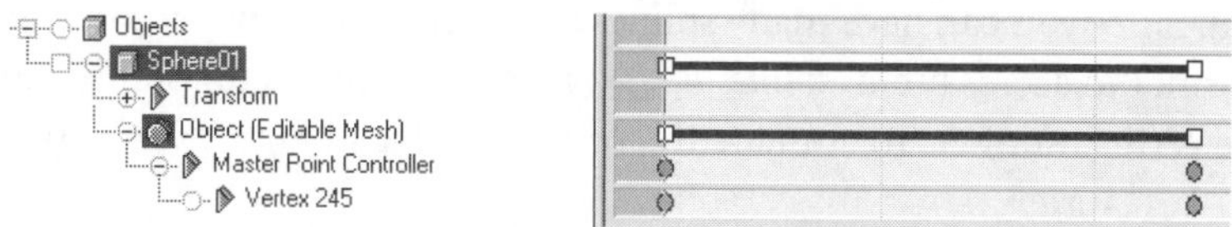

Figure 7.12 *The vertex animation track*

The following example will create a vertex animation:

```
b = box()
converttomesh b
animatevertex b 2
animate on at time 30 b.vertex_2 = [20,-20,0]
```

Notice how you accessed the vertex position and name through MAXScript. Another way to access the vertex is *b[4][1][n].value*, where *n* is the vertex number.

Remember that when using vertex animation, MAXScript uses the object space coordinate system. If you wish to use world space coordinates, you need to multiply the object space coordinates by inverse obj.transform, *where* obj *is the object you're manipulating.*

Editable Splines

Editable splines are animated in the same way that editable meshes are. There are some peculiarities, which we will see.

When animating editable splines, MAX displays three tracks per vertex, as seen in Figure 7.13:

- In vector
- Vertex position
- Out vector

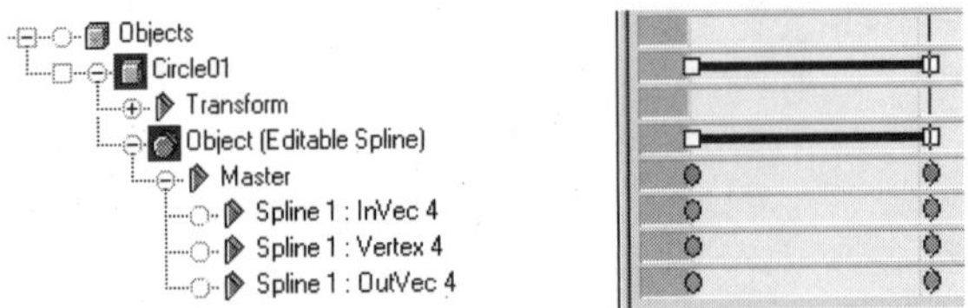

***Figure 7.13** Editable spline vertex tracks*

The difference in the editable spline is the way you will access the vertex to animate it. Since you can have many splines and vertices per shape, you will need to use this format to access them: *spline_n___vertex_i*, where *n* is the spline number and *i* is the vertex number. To animate the vertex you see in Figure 7.13, you would need *spline_1___vertex_4*.

This is a simple example of editable spline vertex animation:

```
c = circle()
convertto c splineshape
animatevertex c #all
animate on at time 30 c.spline_1___vertex_1 = [0,0,0]
animate on at time 30 c.spline_1___vertex_3 = [0,0,0]
animate on at time 60 c.spline_1___vertex_1 = [25,0,0]
animate on at time 60 c.spline_1___vertex_3 = [-25,0,0]
animate on at time 60 c.spline_1___vertex_2 = [0,0,0]
animate on at time 60 c.spline_1___vertex_4 = [0,0,0]
c.spline_1___vertex_2.keys[1].time = 30
c.spline_1___vertex_4.keys[1].time = 30
```

Again, all the coordinates are local when using editable spline vertex animation.

FFD Animation

There is one thing you need to remember when animating FFD vertices: FFD is a modifier, so all the position data it returns will be object-based and not world-based.

You can access the vertices of the FFD using *control_point_n*, where *n* is the vertex number.

The following example illustrates the animation of a FFD control point:

```
c = cylinder height:100 heightsegs:20
ffd = ffd_4x4x4()
```

```
addmodifier c ffd
animatevertex ffd #all
animate on for i in 1 to 16 do
(
execute ("at time 30 ffd.control_point_" + i as string + \
" += [0,0,0.5]")
)
```

Since all coordinates are in modifier space, [1,1,1] is equal to the object's dimensions, so using 0.5 means that we moved the FFD points half the height of the object.

To move a FFD vertex in the world coordinate system, you need to use a small trick. First, you need to convert the FFD coordinates to object space, and then you convert them to world space. This is done in two steps because you can have the modifier applied only to a selection and not to the whole object.

To convert the coordinates from FFD space to object space, you will use two functions: *getmodcontextbboxmin* and *getmodcontextbboxmax*. They will return the boundaries of the FFD in object space. Using the previous example, you would use the following code:

```
min = getmodcontextbboxmin c ffd
max = getmodcontextbboxmax c ffd
obj_space = (ffd.control_point_27*(max-min))+min
```

Now that you have the control point in object space, all you need to do is multiply by *obj.transform* to convert it to world space. In our example, it would be `world_space = obj_space * c.transform`.

Creating and Accessing Track View Nodes

MAXScript allows you to access any track in the Track View so that you can manipulate its information. You can also create your own tracks and even attach controllers to them so that you can animate custom parameters.

You can access the tracks in the Track View using the following syntax:

```
trackviewnodes.track.subtrack1.subtrack2
```

Tracks are unlimited, which means that you can have as many nested tracks as are available. You simply substitute *track* and *subtrack* for the track name that appears in the

Track View. If it has spaces or special characters, just substitute them with a backslash character (\). For instance, *Reflect/Refract Material ID's* would be *reflect_refract_material_id_s*, as seen in Figure 7.14.

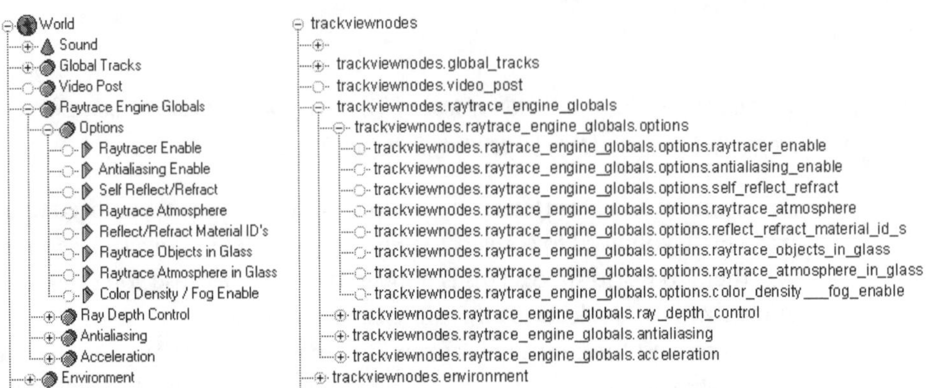

Figure 7.14 *Track View nodes in MAXScript*

Some properties and plug-ins are configured by the Track View, such as the Raytrace global parameters. There's no way to access these properties except by using *trackviewnodes*.

Creating Track View Nodes

You can create your own tracks using *newtrackviewnode*. This function adds a new track to the root tracks or under an existing track.

For instance, `newtrackviewnode "My Track"` creates a new root track, while `newtrackviewnode trackviewnodes.my_track "Subtrack1"` creates a new track under the first one you created.

The track is useless if it does not have a controller. You can add one using *addtrackviewcontroller*. For instance, you can create a Bezier controller and add it to "My Track" in the Track View using:

```
c = bezier_position()
addtrackviewcontroller trackviewnodes.my_track c \
"My Controller"
```

This shows as a regular position controller, as in Figure 7.15, and you can change it to any other position controller. You can then add keyframes and assign the controller to any object using *trackviewnodes.my_track.my_controller.*

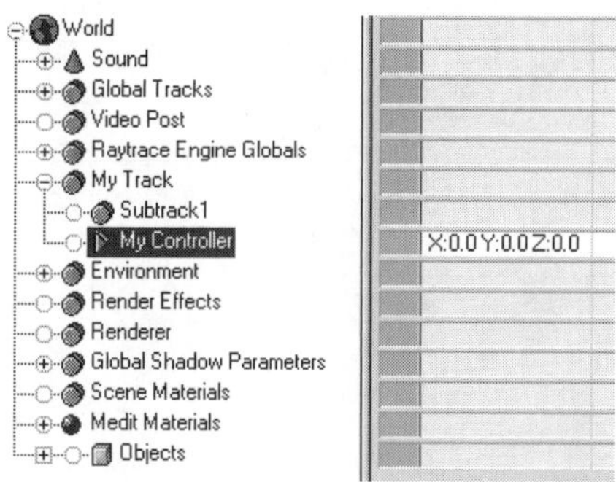

Figure 7.15 *New tracks created with MAXScript*

You can remove the tracks and the controllers using *deletetrackviewnode* and *deletetrackviewcontroller*, respectively.

The Material Animator sample script on the CD-ROM is a good example of the use of Track View nodes. It adds Materials to the Track View in VIZ and adds a series of tracks that allow the user to create material animation, which cannot be done by default in VIZ. It also uses callbacks, which you will learn about in Chapter 8.

Summary

This chapter led you through animation in MAXScript, teaching you how to work with controllers, keyframes, time functions, Script controllers, and Track View nodes. With these tools, you can create and manipulate any kind of animation information.

In the next chapter, you will learn how to work with callbacks and persistent variables, which allow you to create functions that are triggered by specific scene conditions and also to create variables that can be saved with the MAX file.

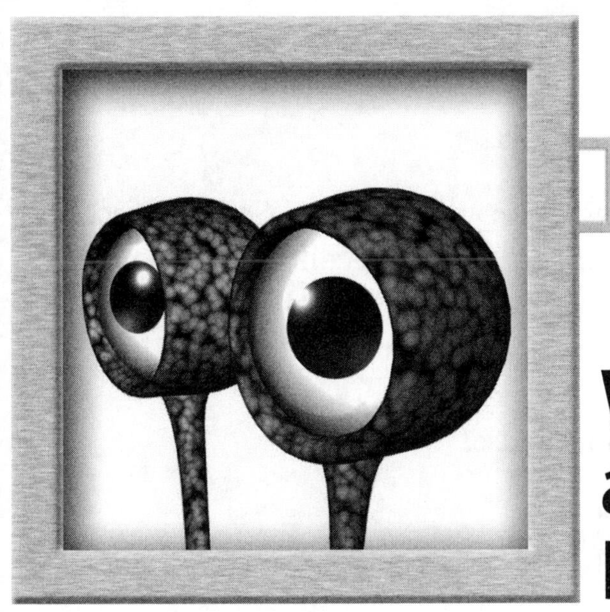

Variables, Callbacks, and Additional MAX Features

MAXSCRIPT

Chapter 8

By now, you've seen almost everything in MAXScript: object manipulation, user interface, animation control, and file I/O. Now you will learn some advanced topics: variable scope, callbacks, and a couple of extra functions that might help you in MAXScript.

In this chapter, you'll see how to use:

- Global and local variables
- Persistent variables
- The Time Change callback
- The Change Handler callback
- The General callback
- Auto-run scripts
- MAXScript features to control timing

Variables

You have worked with variables since Chapter 1, but we haven't discussed them in depth. In this section, we'll do just that, so you can avoid problems and even learn how to save variables in the MAX scene.

Global and Local Variables

When writing a script, we often create simple variable names, since they're easier to type and remember; but this might be a problem in MAXScript, especially if you have two variables with the same name in different scripts.

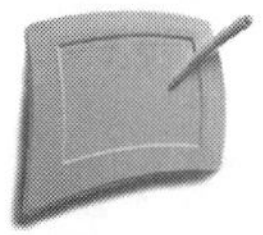

Avoid using simple names for variables. Instead of using `s = sphere()`, *use* `rcm_sphere = sphere()`. *Using different naming conventions will make it harder to have the same variable name in another script.*

Another problem you can face in scripts is that the variables are left in memory after you close the script. That might be OK for some variables but might also cause problems for other variables. This is why you should use *global* and *local* variables.

A *local variable* exists only in the block that it was declared in. Once that block ends, the variable will return undefined and will be cleared. This is very useful for temporary variables but might cause you a problem if you need that variable outside of that block.

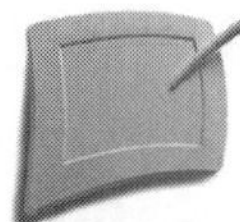

A block *is the code defined inside a pair of parentheses, such as "(...)".*

Declare all local variables in the head of a utility or a rollout, and you will not need to declare them or free the memory associated with them later in the script.

Sometimes you may need global variables. *Global variables* are valid until you shut down MAX and allow you to exchange data between scripts, scenes, or even to reclaim data later.

To avoid conflicts between scripts, make sure you create a unique name for a global variable.

An example of a global variable is a floater. When you declare a floater, make sure you declare its variable as global, so you can use the *try* and *catch* functions later to close any open instance of this rollout, no mater where it was opened. Why should you worry about it? Here's a simple example. If you open a floater from inside a utility and the floater variable is declared as local, it only exists while the utility is open. If you close the utility and reopen it, using *try* and *catch* will not close the older floater because it does not exist anymore. If you declare the floater variable as global, it will work all the time.

Take a look at files `local_floater.ms` and `global_floater.ms` on the CD-ROM. The difference between them is just the variable scope, and you will notice that the floater does not close in the first file, but it closes in the second.

When declaring a variable as local or global, you can also declare its value. For example, `global sphere_radius = 20` declares this variable and also sets its value.

The most common process, though, is to declare a series of variables and then set their values as needed within the script. For example,

```
local sphere_radius, cube_size, tmp_var
```

will define these three local variables, and later in the script, you can use them as you wish without worrying about whether they have been declared.

It's very common for the first lines of a rollout to list all local and global variables.

Persistent Variables

Persistent variables are variables that will be saved with the MAX file. It is interesting to use these variables to save information that can be reused by the script later.

Besides any variable type, persistent variables can also save node information, which means objects, modifiers, materials, and so on. But there's a limitation: Persistent variables can save node information only if this node exists in the scene. For instance, `persistent global sphere_radius = 20` will create this variable and save it. Do a test, saving this file and reopening it. The variable will be there with the value saved.

On the other hand, executing this script will show you that nodes that do not exist in the file cannot be saved:

```
persistent global sphere_global = sphere()
persistent global cube_global = box()
delete cube_global
```

Now, save the MAX file and reopen it. Notice that `cube_global` is now undefined.

The methods listed in Table 8.1 allow you to manipulate persistent variables.

Table 8.1 Persistent Global Variables Methods

Method	**Description**
persistents.show()	Lists all persistent variables.
persistents.remove	Removes the specified variable.
persistents.removeall()	Removes all persistent variables.

When removing a persistent variable, it will become a global variable and will be erased only when you close MAX, or when a new variable is defined with the same name.

For instance, `persistents.remove #cube_global` will remove the variable called `cube_global`.

Using Callbacks

Callbacks are used to activate functions depending on certain scene conditions or events. MAX has four types of callbacks:

Time Change callbacks Executed when the current frame changes by moving the time slider

Redraw Views callbacks Executed when a scene redraw happens

Change Handler callbacks Executed when an object's property changes

General callbacks Executed when a scene property changes, such as the render being executed, a new scene being loaded, and so on

Next, we'll examine these callbacks in detail.

Using Time Change and Redraw Views Callbacks

In Chapter 1, you learned how to animate objects using MAXScript. We used the Eye Control example script, which works fine for what we needed. But this script fails in one task: If you move back the time slider, the sliders in the script are not updated with the object's animation. This means that you can create the animation, but it will be hard to edit it.

That's where the Time Change callbacks fit in: They can call a function that will be executed when the time slider moves. Then you can have this function update the UI based on the object's state. Let's do this in Exercise 8.1.

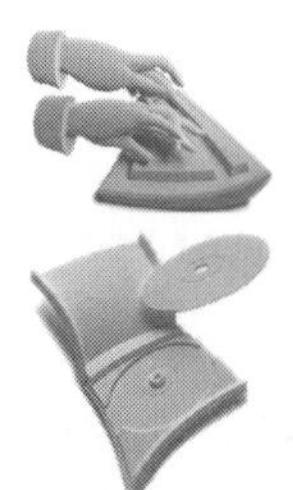

Exercise 8.1: Adding Callbacks to the Eye Control Script

1. Open the file Eyes.max on your CD-ROM. It should look like Figure 8.1.
2. Open and execute the utility_eyes01.ms script on your CD-ROM.
3. "Scrub" the time slider back and forth and notice that the script is not updated with the eyes' movement.
4. You will now create a function that updates the sliders according to the eyes' movement. Enter this function in the script before *Vertical Movement*:

```
fn update_eye_slider =
(
   eyes.l_eye_v.value = 90- $eye.rotation.x_rotation
   eyes.r_eye_v.value = 90- $eye01.rotation.x_rotation
   eyes.l_eye_h.value = $eye.rotation.z_rotation
   eyes.r_eye_h.value = $eye01.rotation.z_rotation
)
```

Figure 8.1 *The* Eyes.max *file*

Always access user interface elements using rollout.element *because the callback is executed outside the rollout scope. Also, If you need to use variables in the callback function, these need to be global variables.*

5. Now, you need to create the callback when the script is open and remove it when it's closed. You will also need to update the UI when the script opens. Edit the script and add the following code after the line *button reseth*:

```
on eyes open do
(
   registertimecallback update_eye_slider
   update_eye_slider()
)
on eyes close do unregistertimecallback update_eye_slider
```

Registertimecallback will create the callback, calling the function every time the slider changes the current time. *Unregistertimecallback* removes the callback, avoiding future crashes and cleaning memory and resources.

If the function returns an error message, the callback will be disabled.

6. Evaluate and reload the script. Drag the time slider and notice that it is updating the interface according to the animation.

The final script can be found on the CD-ROM in the file `utility_eyes02.ms`.

The Redraw Views Callback

The *Redraw Views callback* works exactly the same way as the Time Change callback, and, of course, it is executed when the screen is redrawn.

The method used to register this callback is *registerredrawviewscallback,* and the method used to remove the callback is *unregisterredrawviewscallback.*

Change Handlers

Change handlers are different from the Time Change and Redraw Views callbacks. *Change handlers* will be called when an object's property has been changed.

There are two types of change handlers. The first type notifies you when an object is deleted. For example, if you have an object named sphere01 in your scene, this change handler will notify you if this object is deleted:

```
deletealert = when $sphere01 deleted do
messagebox "Sphere01 was deleted"
```

The second type of change handler notifies you if a property is modified. These properties are listed in Table 8.2.

Table 8.2 Properties That Will Notify the Change Handler

PROPERTY	NOTIFIES WHEN
topology	The object topology has changed (face count, object type, and so on).
geometry	The object geometry has changed (such as vertex position).
transform	The object has been moved, rotated, or scaled.
select	The object has been selected or deselected.
parameters	Any property of the object has changed.
subanimstructure	There's any change in subanims.
controller	A new controller is assigned.
children	The object hierarchy has changed.

You can create a change handler that will prevent an object from being selected, using the handlers in Table 8.2. For example,

```
unselectsph = when select $sphere01 changes do
$sphere01.isselected = false
```

prevents you from selecting *sphere01*.

The following script creates a new Track View node and creates a track for the selected object. The callback renames this track if the object gets renamed:

```
my_nodes = #()
my_track = newtrackviewnode "My Objects"
my_nodes[1] = newtrackviewnode my_track $.name
namechange = when name $ changes do my_nodes[1].name = $.name
```

Be careful when playing with these callbacks. You can easily lock MAX by using recursive callbacks, so save often.

To remove a callback, use *deletechangehandler*. For example, to remove a callback named *namechange*, use `deletechangehandler namechange`. If you need to remove all change handlers, use *deleteallchangehandlers*.

When creating a change handler, you can specify an ID *property. This property allows you to identify and group the handlers, making it easier to remove them using* deleteallchangehandlers.

General Callbacks

General callbacks are called when a *scene* event happens in MAX. This *scene* event can be a File Open, a File Save, a Reset, and so on.

These callbacks can also be grouped into IDs, making them easier to manage. They can also be *persistent*, which means they will be saved with the MAX file.

Table 8.3 lists all the *General callback* events, and Table 8.4 lists the methods to create, list, and remove General callbacks.

Table 8.3 *General Callback* Events

EVENT	WHEN IT'S CALLED
#filepreopen	Before a file is opened
#filepostopen	After a file is opened
#filepresave	Before a file is saved
#filepostsave	After a file is saved
#filepremerge	Before a file is merged
#filepostmerge	After a file is merged
#systemprereset	Before MAX is reset
#systempostreset	After MAX is reset
#preimport	Before a file is imported
#postimport	After a file is imported
#importfailed	When import fails
#preexport	Before a file is exported
#postexport	After a file is exported
#exportfailed	When export fails
#prerender	Before the render starts
#postrender	After the render ends
#prerenderframe	Before each frame is rendered

Table 8.3 *General Callback* Events (*continued*)

EVENT	WHEN IT'S CALLED
#postrenderframe	After each frame is rendered
#noderenamed	When a scene node is renamed
#selectionsetchanged	When the selection has changed
#bitmapchanged	After a bitmap is reloaded
#viewportchange	After the user changes the viewport layout
#timeunitschange	After the user changes the time format
#unitschange	After the user changes the system units
#spacemodechange	After the user changes the current coordinate system
#modpanelselchanged	After the Modify Panel refreshes with a new selection

Table 8.4 General Callback Methods

METHOD	DESCRIPTION
callbacks.addscript	Registers a new callback script.
callbacks.removescripts	Removes a callback script.
callbacks.show()	Lists all callback scripts.
callbacks.broadcastcallback	Executes the specified script, simulating the *callback* event.

Next, we will illustrate the use of General callbacks. Exercise 8.2 creates a floater that contains some useful object properties, one that will refresh automatically as soon as you change the current selection.

EXERCISE 8.2: UPDATING THE SELECTION IN A FLOATER

1. Create a couple of objects in MAX, or open a scene with some objects. Select a few of them.

2. Open the file `object_properties01.ms` on the CD-ROM and evaluate it. You will see a floater like in Figure 8.2.

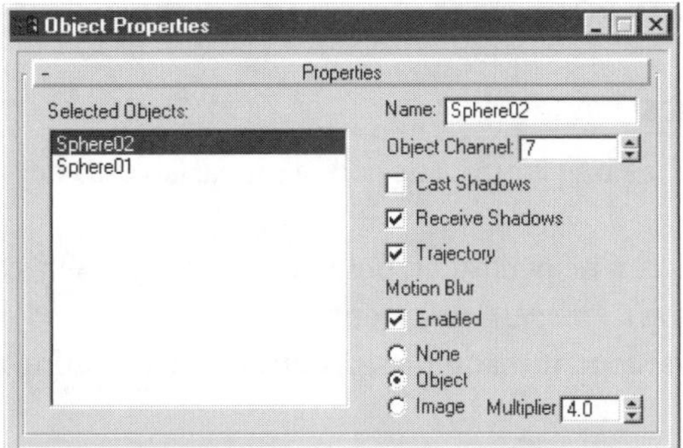

Figure 8.2 *Object Properties Script floater*

The script loads the selection and places it in the listbox. Every time an object is selected, the right part of the floater is updated to reflect the current properties, and you can change them as you wish.

3. Now, you will create a callback to update the floater when the selection changes. In the *on object_properties open* event, add a new statement, as follows:

```
callbacks.addscript #selectionsetchanged \
"collect_selection()" id:#updUI
```

   This code creates a callback that is called when the selection changes. The *collect_selection* function is declared outside of the rollout, and it updates the properties according to the selection set.

4. You need to remove the callback when the rollout is closed. To do so, add the following event to the script:

```
on object_properties close do callbacks.removescripts \
id:#updUI
```

   This event removes the callback when the rollout is closed.

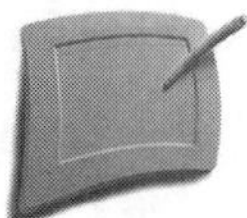

Use IDs to identify your callbacks and to remove them easily.

The final script with all these changes can be found in the file `object_properties02.ms` on the CD-ROM.

Persistent Callbacks

Persistent callbacks follow the same concept as persistent variables: They are saved with the MAX file.

Only General callbacks can be persistent, but you can make a General callback initiate any other callback using a *#filepostopen* event.

To make a callback persistent, just add *persistent:true* when creating a new callback. For example,

```
callbacks.addscript #prerender "checkForSave()" persistent:true
```

creates a persistent callback that always requests the user to save the file before rendering.

Do not use IDs in persistent callbacks because the callback will not be saved. This is a bug in Max 3.x.

The `working_time.ms` script on the CD-ROM is another example of a callback script using IDs instead of persistent callbacks.

Additional MAX Features

You have seen just about everything in MAXScript so far, with the exception of plug-in scripts, tools, and MAXScript extensions, which we will cover in the next three chapters.

In this section, we will explore some MAXScript concepts and functions that allow us to control timing, set the animation timing scheme, and configure MAX, including features like preferences and snap mode.

Auto-Run Scripts

MAXScript allows you to create scripts that load automatically when MAX starts. When MAX is launched, MAXScript executes the `startup.ms` script file, searching for it in the following folders:

- `Scripts` folder
- `Scripts/Startup` folder
- `3DS MAX` main folder

If MAXScript finds a `startup.ms` file, it will stop searching for another one.

After this, MAXScript loads any script file that is placed in the `Scripts/Startup` and `Plugins` folders.

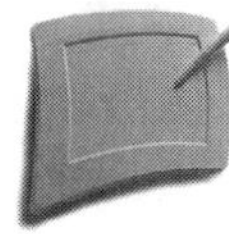

If you want to load a file that is not in any of these folders, you can create a startup script file and use filein *to load your files.*

If you do not want MAXScript to automatically load startup scripts, you can disable the option in the Preferences dialog, shown in Figure 8.3. (It's the second item in the Startup area.)

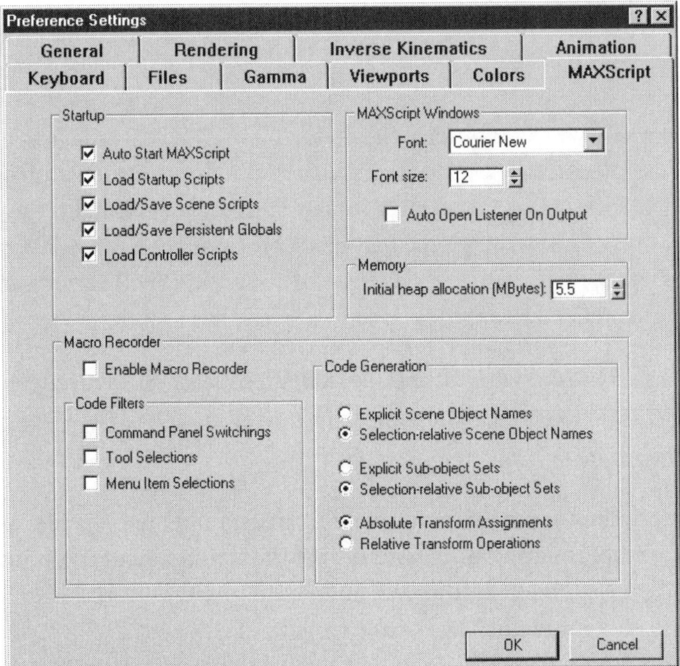

Figure 8.3 *MAXScript preferences*

You can also disable scene scripts (persistent callbacks) and persistent globals in the MAXScript Preferences dialog.

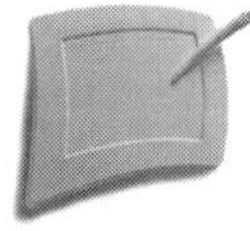

If you're using VIZ R3, the Preferences dialog can be found in the main menu, under Tools → Options.

Controlling Timing

MAXScript allows you to control the animation timing and also gives you some functions to access the real-time clock of the machine.

The *sleep* function allows you to stop script execution for a specified amount of time. This may be useful if you're using an external application and you need to wait for it to process. Using `sleep 5` will pause the script for 5 seconds, after which the script will continue ahead.

You can use the ESC key to cancel sleep.

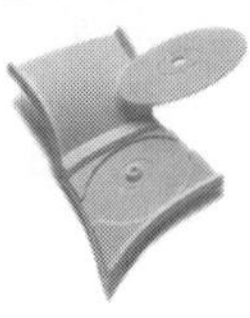

In the `working_time.ms` script file on the CD-ROM, you can find a couple of functions that calculate the elapsed time. These functions make use of a global MAX variable called `localtime`. `Localtime` returns a string that contains the current time, according to the Windows Regional Settings. For instance, entering `localtime` would return "31/7/2000 11:40:24 AM" right now. Of course, this will vary depending on your configuration and the current time.

The major drawback to using `localtime` *is that different computers can have different regional settings configured; one may use* mm/dd/yy, *while another may use* dd/mm/yyyy. *Also, time can be* AM/PM *or* 24hrs, *so use this variable with caution.*

To count time, you can use *timestamp()*. Timestamp() returns the number of milliseconds since 0:00. You can call *timestamp()* at the start and end of a function, and then calculate the elapsed time, but this will not work if the time goes past midnight. Of course, if you pass midnight, the elapsed time will be negative; so just add 86,400,000 (the number of milliseconds in a day), and you will have the correct elapsed time.

Adjusting the Time Configuration in MAX

You can access and adjust all the information found in the Time Configuration dialog box (see Figure 8.4). You can also access internal MAXScript variables that will tell you the current frame and even play or stop the animation.

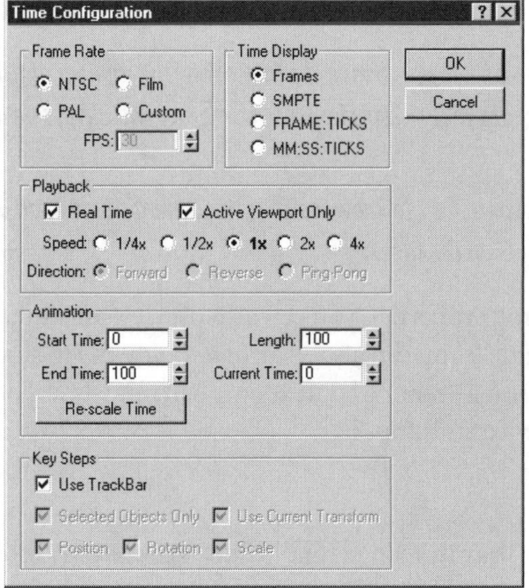

Figure 8.4 *The Time Configuration dialog box*

The methods that will adjust the parameters in the Time Configuration dialog box are listed in Table 8.5.

Table 8.5 Time Configuration Methods

METHOD	DESCRIPTION
animationrange	Defines the current animation range.
framerate	Defines the number of frames per second.
ticksperframe	Changes the number of ticks per frame.
currenttime	Returns the current frame.
slidertime	Defines the current frame.
playactiveonly, or timeconfiguration.playactiveonly	Turns on or off Active Viewport Only.
realtimeplayback, or timeconfiguration.realtimeplayback	Turns on or off Real Time.
timeconfiguration.playbackspeed	Defines the playback speed.

You can use *animationrange* to define the active time segment in MAX. For example, `animationrange.start = 10f` sets frame 10 as the beginning of the segment.

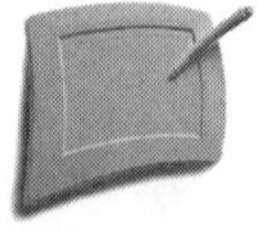

MAX always has 4,800 ticks per second. If you change the frame rate, the number of ticks per frame will be adjusted automatically. This means that ticksperframe × framerate *will always be 4,800.*

You can use currenttime *in Script controllers to know which is the current frame in an animation. It's useful when the animation depends on the time.*

Besides adjusting the time properties, you can also preview an animation on-screen by using *playanimation()*. You can also use *stopanimation()* to stop it, but *stopanimation()* needs to be on a separate context or it will not work. The following script plays the animation once and stops it:

```
fn stop_it =
(
if slidertime == animationrange.end then stopanimation()
)
registertimecallback stop_it
playanimation()
unregistertimecallback stop_it
```

You can drag and drop it to a toolbar and create a button to see it. Modifying this example, you can even create a Play 1 Second option, or others.

Dialog Options and Configurations

You can also access and define other dialog options through MAXScript. You can open and close dialogs and set a couple of options in some of them.

You can open and close the Track View and the Schematic View. Both dialogs have the same methods, which are listed in Table 8.6.

Table 8.6 Track View and Schematic View Methods

METHOD	DESCRIPTION
Track View	
trackview.open	Opens the dialog and names it.
trackview.close	Closes the specified dialog.

Table 8.6 Track View and Schematic View Methods (*continued*)

Method	Description
Track View	
trackview.setfilter	Defines the filter for the specified dialog.
trackview.clearfilter	Removes the filter for the specified dialog.
trackview.zoomselected	Zooms to the selected object in Track View.
trackview.numtrackviews()	Returns the number of Track Views defined.
trackview.gettrackviewname	Returns the name of the specified Track View.
Schematic View	
schematicview.open	Opens the dialog and names it.
schematicview.close	Closes the specified dialog.
schematicview.zoomselected	Zooms to the selected objects in Schematic View.
schematicview.numschematicviews()	Returns the number of Schematic Views defined.
schematicview.getschematicviewname	Returns the name of the specified Schematic View.

For example, the following script opens the Track View and displays and zooms only the selected objects:

```
trackview.open "My Track view"
trackview.setfilter "My Track View" #selectedobjects
trackview.zoomselected "My Track View"
```

Accessing the Preferences Dialog Box

You can access some properties in the Preferences dialog box. Although there are few scriptable options among the number of settings in the dialog, they may be useful to you.

Table 8.7 lists the methods that allow you to access these properties.

There is no MAXScript access for the remaining properties in the Preferences dialog box.

When accessing UI colors, look at the Online Help for a list of the UI color items.

Table 8.7 Preferences Dialog Methods

METHOD	DESCRIPTION
General	
preferences.constantreferencesystem	Turns on or off the Constant Reference coordinate system.
preferences.flyofftime	Defines the flyout time.
preferences.spinnerwrap	Turns Wrap Cursor Near Spinner on or off.
Viewport	
preferences.usevertexdots	Turns on or off Use Show Vertices as Dots.
preferences.uselargevertexdots	Specifies the size of the vertices dots.
preferences.usetransformgizmos	Turns the Transform gizmo on or off.
Rendering	
preferences.maximumgbufferlayers	Defines the maximum number of G-Buffer layers.
Keyboard Shortcuts	
shortcuts.getallshortcuts()	Lists all keyboard shortcuts.
shortcuts.getcount()	Returns the number of keyboard shortcuts.
shortcuts.getshortcut	Returns the indexed keyboard shortcut.
shortcuts.getcommandname	Returns the command name of the indexed keyboard shortcut.
shortcuts.runshortcut	Executes the specified keyboard shortcut.
shortcuts.runcommand	Executes the specified command.
Colors	
getuicolor	Returns the current UI color for the specified item.
setuicolor	Sets the UI color for the specified item.
getdefaultuicolor	Returns the default UI color for the specified item.

Using the RAM Player

You can open the RAM Player (see Figure 8.5) and place the clips in A or B buffer using MAXScript. To do so, just use *ramplayer clipA clipB*, where *clipA* and *clipB* are the files to be loaded. For example, `ramplayer "myavi.avi" ""` loads `myavi.avi` in the A buffer and will not load anything in the B buffer.

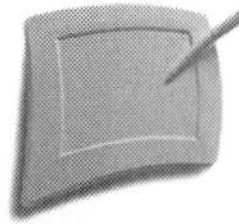

You need to specify an empty string in clipB *if you do not want to load any footage in it. If you do not specify anything, the function will fail because it requires two arguments.*

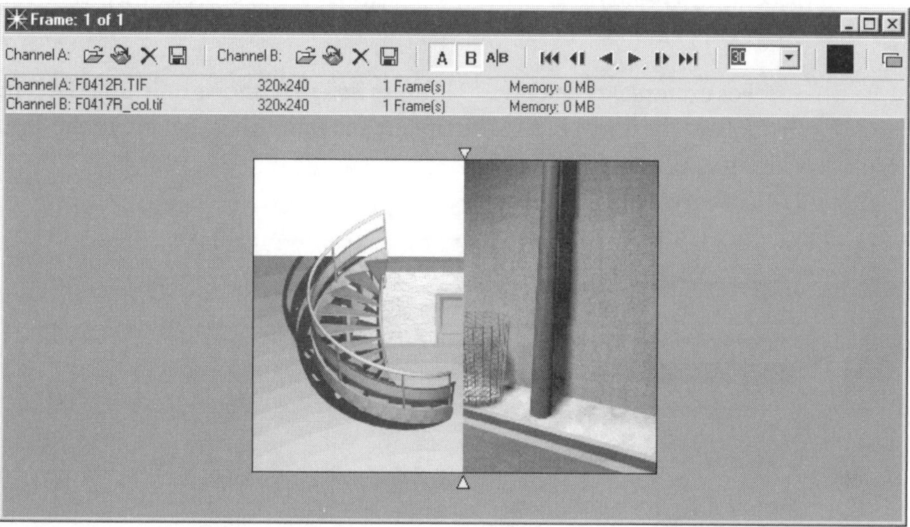

Figure 8.5 *The RAM Player*

Controlling the Track Bar and the Animate Button

An interesting feature in MAXScript is the ability to turn off the Animate button to prevent the user from animating properties. This is done using *animbuttonenabled*. For example, `animbuttonenabled = false` disables the Animate button.

You can control the Animate Button state using *animbuttonstate*. This sets the Animate button the way you direct, regardless of whether the button is enabled or not. For example, `animbuttonstate = on` turns the Animate button on.

MAXScript also allows you to control the Track Bar. The methods associated with the Track Bar are listed in Table 8.8.

Table 8.8 Track Bar Methods

METHOD	DESCRIPTION
trackbar.visible	Turns on or off the Track Bar in the interface.
trackbar.filter	Defines the Track Bar filters.
trackbar.getpreviouskeytime()	Returns the time of the previous keyframe.
trackbar.getpreviouskey()	Returns the time of the next keyframe.

For example, `trackbar.filter = #object` shows only object keyframes in the Track Bar. The filters in MAXScript are the same ones that are in the Track Bar Right-Click menu, as in Figure 8.6.

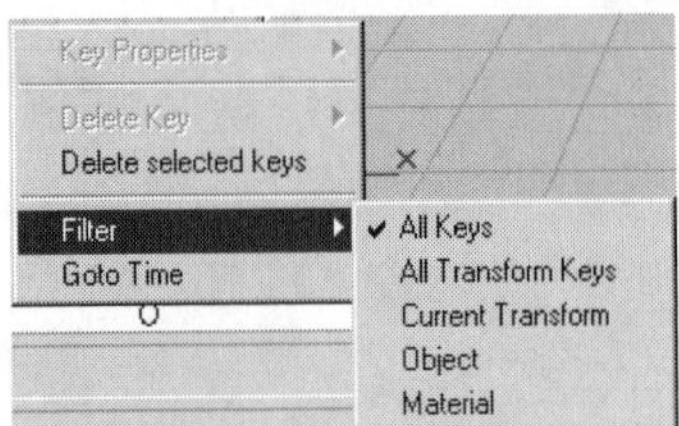

***Figure 8.6** Track Bar filters*

Other Dialog Boxes

You can call some known MAX dialogs to help you write your scripts. These include the Exclude/Include dialog box, the Material/Map Browser, the Object Color dialog box, and the Configure Bitmap Paths dialog box.

To call the Exclude/Include dialog box, use *exclusionlistdlg()*. A dialog like Figure 8.7 is displayed, and an array of the node names is returned. No other option set on this dialog will be returned.

To call the Material/Map Browser, use *materialbrowsedlg*. You can use *#mats* to list only materials, *#maps* to list only maps, and *#incnone* to include the None material and map. For example, `mymap = materialbrowsedlg #maps #incnone` displays the dialog in Figure 8.8 and returns the selected map to the variable `mymap`.

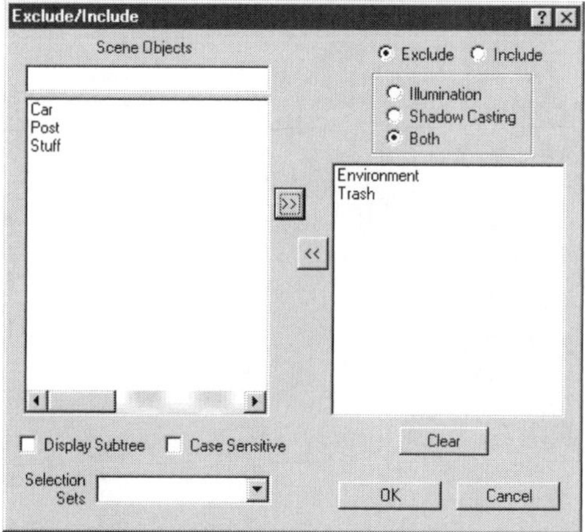

Figure 8.7 *The Exclude/Include dialog box*

Figure 8.8 *The Material/Map Browser dialog box*

To select a color, use *nodecolorpicker()*. It displays the dialog box in Figure 8.9 and returns the selected color value.

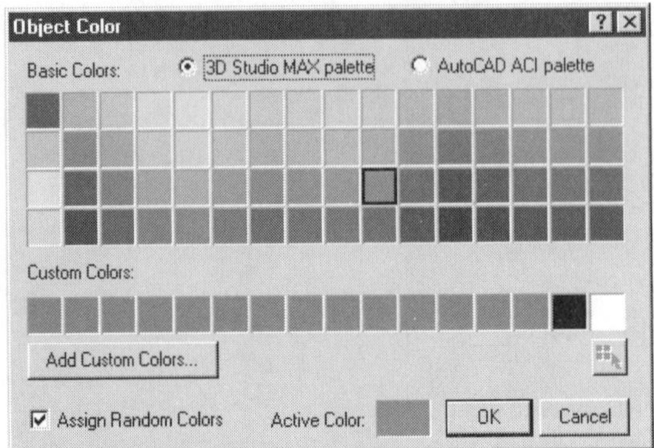

Figure 8.9 *The Object Color dialog box*

If you want the user to specify a map path, you can call the Configure Bitmap Paths dialog box (see Figure 8.10) using *configurebitmappaths()*. It's useful in combination with *enumeratefiles*, which lists the bitmaps associated with the nodes or scene or lists the missing files.

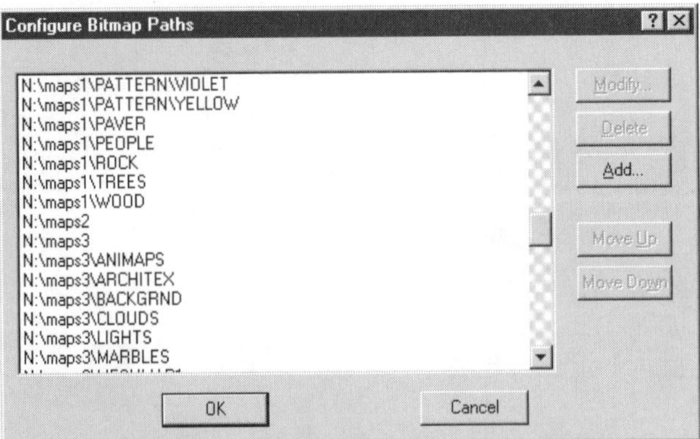

Figure 8.10 *The Configure Bitmap Paths dialog box*

The following script calls the Configure Bitmap Paths dialog box in case a missing bitmap is found, and retests for missing maps after the user has added the missing bitmap paths:

```
function get_names name a = append a name
miss_files = #()
enumeratefiles get_names miss_files #missing
if miss_files.count > 0 do configurebitmappaths()
miss_files = #()
enumerateFiles get_names miss_files #missing
if miss_files.count > 0 do (messagebox "Missing Map files";exit)
```

More Functions

Similar to *gc()*, which reclaims unused memory in MAXScript, you can use *freescenebitmaps()* to reclaim the memory used by the bitmaps after a scene has been rendered or after a bitmap has been loaded in the Materials Editor. It's a very useful function because MAX always maintains the bitmaps in memory after rendering them, which can use a lot of RAM depending on the scene. Do a test with this function: render a scene and open the Task Manager. Then, call `freescenebitmaps()` in the Listener and notice the amount of RAM that is freed.

Another interesting function is *swap*, which swaps the content of two variables or nodes.

If you want to load plug-ins that were not loaded when MAX started, you can use *loaddllsfromdir*. It's not documented correctly in the Online Help, and you need to specify the *folder* and *plug-in wildcard* so that the function loads all the plug-ins that match that wildcard. For example,

```
loaddllsfromdir "d:\\3dsmax3\\plugins\\digimation\\" "*.dlt"
```

loads all *dlt* plug-ins found in that folder.

If you need to check whether MAX is running in network rendering mode, use *isnetserver()*. This function is useful when you have auto-run scripts that need to run (or not run) when MAX is in this mode. A nice example of *isnetserver()* is the Region Net Render sample script on the CD-ROM (`Tools-Render_Calculator.mcr`).

Summary

In this chapter, you have seen how to work with variables, callbacks, and plenty of other very useful functions. This information might seem extremely detailed, but will prove to be very handy on a daily basis.

Next, we will introduce you to plug-in scripts, giving you the power to create your own plug-ins by customizing the existing ones in MAX.

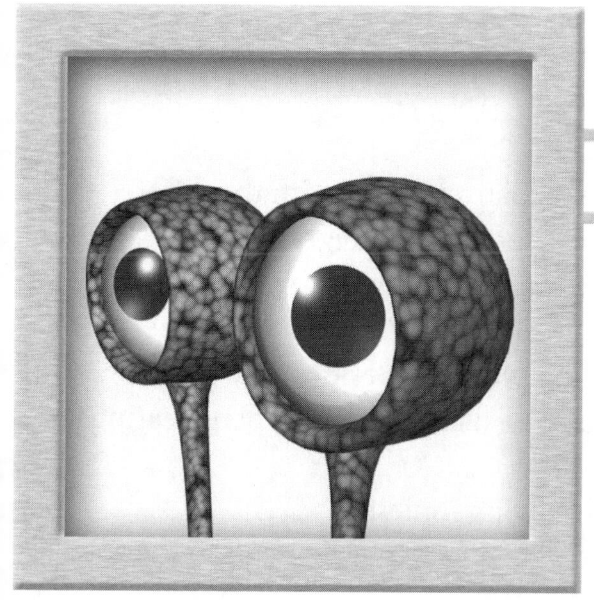

Plug-In Scripts

MAXSCRIPT

Chapter 9

P*lug-in scripts* are just like regular plug-ins, with the difference that they're scripts. As such, they integrate seamlessly in the UI and behave like C++ plug-ins.

There are several types of plug-ins. In this chapter, you'll see system-like plug-ins and extending plug-ins. Besides plug-ins, you'll also learn how to use tools, which are essential when creating plug-ins.

This chapter will cover the following topics:

- Creating tools
- Creating extending plug-ins
- Creating system-like plug-ins

Creating Tools

Tools are scripts that use mouse clicks. They're used when you need to click and drag, similar to the way you create an object in the viewport.

Tools are essential for plug-in scripts because they define how the objects are created in the viewport, but they can also be useful for other tasks.

A tool can be created using the *tool* construct. You will need to use the *starttool* method to execute the tool you created. MAXScript also allows you to abort a tool execution using the *stoptool* method.

When you create a tool, you're expecting it to drive your script through the mouse clicks and drags. Besides mouse clicks and drags, there are a series of events that a tool can call. These events are listed in Table 9.1.

Table 9.1 Tool Events

EVENT	DESCRIPTION
on start do	Called when the tool starts
on end do	Called when the tool ends
on mousepoint do	Called for each mouse click
on mousemove do	Called for each mouse drag or move
on mouseabort do	Called when the user right-clicks or presses the ESC key
on freemove do	Called prior to the first click

These events can return a series of values, which you can use in your script. These values are listed in Table 9.2.

Table 9.2 Values Returned When a Tool Is Executed

VALUE	DESCRIPTION
viewpoint	The current mouse position in screen coordinates
worldpoint	The current mouse position in world coordinates
gridpoint	The current mouse position in the active grid coordinates
worldangle	The angle between the current and the previous position in world coordinates

Table 9.2 Values Returned When a Tool Is Executed (*continued*)

VALUE	DESCRIPTION
gridangle	The angle between the current and the previous position in the active grid coordinates
worlddist	The distance between the current and the previous position in world coordinates
griddist	The distance between the current and the previous position in the active grid coordinates
shiftkey	If the Shift key is pressed
ctrlkey	If the Control key is pressed
altkey	If the Alt key is pressed
lbutton	If the left mouse button is pressed
mbutton	If the middle mouse button is pressed
rbutton	If the right mouse button is pressed

The following example creates and executes a tool that creates a sphere:

```
tool sph
(
local s
on mousepoint clickno do
   (
   if clickno == 1 do in coordsys grid s = sphere pos:pt radius:0
   if clickno == 2 do #stop
)
on mousemove clickno do
   (
   if clickno == 2 do
      (
      if shiftkey then
         (
         in coordsys grid s.pos = gridpoint - griddist/2
         s.radius = length [griddist.x,griddist.y]/2
         )
         else s.radius = length [griddist.x,griddist.y]
      )
   )
on mouseabort clickno do
   if clickno > 1 then delete s
)
starttool sph
```

The *mousepoint* event defines the mouse clicks or releases. The *mousemove* event defines the mouse drag, where the first drag is considered when the button is pressed, and the other ones are considered with the mouse up. Also, the *mousemove* events are counted for the event to come, not for the past event. For instance, in the previous example, the *mousemove* event calls the second click, which still hasn't happened.

In this example, you can also notice that if *shiftkey* returns true, the sphere is created by specifying its diameter and not its radius. You can use different keys to create different effects, such as to create a hemisphere, to increase or decrease the number of segments, and so on.

At the end of the code, *mouseabort* deletes the object if the creation is aborted.

Tools can be used as Macro Scripts or can be called from any other script.

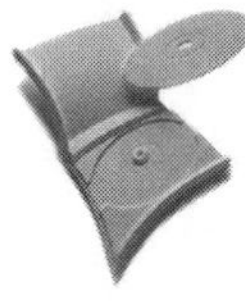

You can find another tool example in the file `tool_nurbsbox.ms` on the CD-ROM. It's a tool that automatically creates a Box object and converts it to NURBS.

Creating Extending Plug-Ins

The general syntax to create a scripted plug-in is

plug-in <superclass> <variable> [options]

where *superclass* defines the plug-in class, *variable* is the plug-in's variable name, and *options* can be any of the options listed in Table 9.3.

Table 9.3 Plug-In Script Options

OPTION	DESCRIPTION
name	Defines the plug-in name string that will appear in the Command Panel.
category	Defines the category the plug-in will show in the Command Panel.
classid	Defines the plug-in Class ID and needs to be unique for each plug-in.
extends	Defines which class the plug-in extends.
replaceui	Defines whether the script will replace the UI of the base class.
version	Defines the plug-in version.
invisible	Defines whether the plug-in appears in the UI.
silenterrors	Turns off any error message that might be caused by the script.

There are a couple of required options, like *classid* and *name*. All remaining properties will depend on the plug-in you're creating.

The first type of plug-in script you will learn is an *extending plug-in*. This plug-in will extend an existing plug-in class, adding or modifying its features.

Using extending plug-ins, you can add your own properties to an existing plug-in, customizing it to fit your needs.

Creating Geometry Plug-Ins

You will start by working with plug-ins that extend objects, like the Standard and Extended objects.

Let's begin with a series of exercises so you can learn how plug-in scripts work. In Exercise 9.1, we'll begin by creating a plug-in script that creates a Cube object.

EXERCISE 9.1: CREATING A CUBE PLUG-IN SCRIPT

1. Start a new script and enter the following code:

```
plugin geometry cube
name:"Cube"
category:"Mastering MAXScript & SDK"
classID:#(0x36b2b16a, 0x60b9a8bb)
extends:Box
```

In this code, you defined a new Geometry plug-in called *Cube*. Next, you specified the name and category of the plug-in, which will define where it appears in the Create tab. The plug-in script also requires a *Class ID*. The Class ID is a hexadecimal number that allows MAX to identify which plug-in is being used. This value is given using the *genclassid()* function, which generates a new Class ID for you to use in your scripts.

The Class ID must be unique to each plug-in or plug-in script.

The last option is *extends*, which defines the object that is being extended. In your example, you're extending the Box object, so you used `extends:Box`.

2. Now, you will continue writing the script by defining the tool. The plug-in script automatically executes the tool named *create*. Continue typing the following code:

```
tool create
(
   on mousePoint clickNo do
   (
```

```
            if clickNo == 1 do nodeTM.translation = gridPoint
            if clickNo == 2 do #stop
        )
        on MouseMove clickNo do
        (
            if clickNo == 2 do
            (
                delegate.width = length gridDist
                delegate.height = delegate.length = delegate.width
            )
        )
    )
)
```

This tool needs the following mouse movements: the first click, mouse drag, and release. The first click defines the object's position. In plug-in scripts, this is done using `nodeTM.translation`. `NodeTM` stores the plug-in object's transformation matrix (TM) without requiring the use of *gridpoint* or *worldpoint*. You will not need to use `in coordsys grid` either.

The drag movement defines the size of the cube. It is done using `delegate.parameter`. When you need to define any parameter of the object that's being extended, use *delegate*. In our example, the width, height, and length are all equal and are defined by the distance between the first click and the mouse drag position. The distance is specified using *griddist*. Here we used *length*, which will tell us the resultant of the *griddist* vector.

When the mouse is released (`clickNo = = 2`), the plug-in stops. Note that the Box rollout appears on the screen, and if you select Modify, it will continue appearing there. If you open the Track View and expand the Object track, you will see that the box is now a subanim of the cube. This is how extending plug-ins work.

Once you add a plug-in script to a scene, it will behave just like a regular plug-in, which means that you will need to have the plug-in loaded to open the scene again. Placing the `.ms` *file in any plug-in folder will load it as a regular plug-in.*

The final script looks like Figure 9.1 and can be found in the `plugin_cube01.ms` file on the CD-ROM.

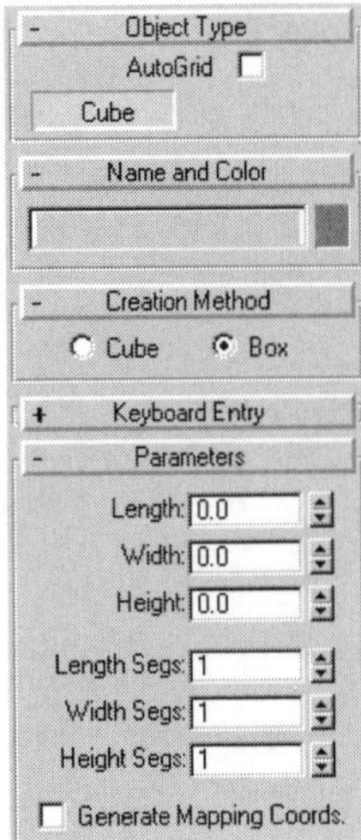

Figure 9.1 *The Cube plug-in script*

You can still add more options and flexibility to this plug-in. A plug-in script also can have a rollout, which will define the properties that you want to give to the object. For example, it would be nice to have a Size option in our cube.

To add a rollout to a plug-in script, simply add it before the tool. If the plug-in script extends another plug-in, you need to specify whether this rollout will or will not replace the object's user interface (UI).

In Exercise 9.2, we will add a rollout to the script you created in Exercise 9.1, which will allow the user to specify the size of the cube.

Exercise 9.2: Adding Rollouts to a Plug-In Script

1. Edit the script you created in Exercise 9.1, adding `replaceUI:true` to the plug-in statement as follows:

```
plugin geometry cube
name:"Cube"
category:"Mastering MAXScript & SDK"
classID:#(0x36b2b16a, 0x60b9a8bb)
extends:Box
replaceUI:true
```

2. Then, add the Rollout clause before the tool:

```
rollout params "Parameters"
(
spinner size "Size: " range:[0,10000,0]
on size changed val do
   delegate.width = delegate.height = delegate.length = val
on params open do size.value = delegate.width
)
```

3. You will also need to modify the MouseMove action so that it updates the spinner value when dragging the mouse:

```
if clickNo == 2 do
(
val = length griddist
delegate.width = delegate.height = delegate.length = val
params.size.value = val
)
```

4. Now, the script is ready. Evaluate and play with it.

Notice that now your object has a new rollout, as in Figure 9.2. When creating a new object, this rollout sometimes appears below the object's rollouts, or sometimes it appears alone. In the Modify tab, only this rollout appears, unless you specify `replaceUI:false`, in which case, all rollouts will appear.

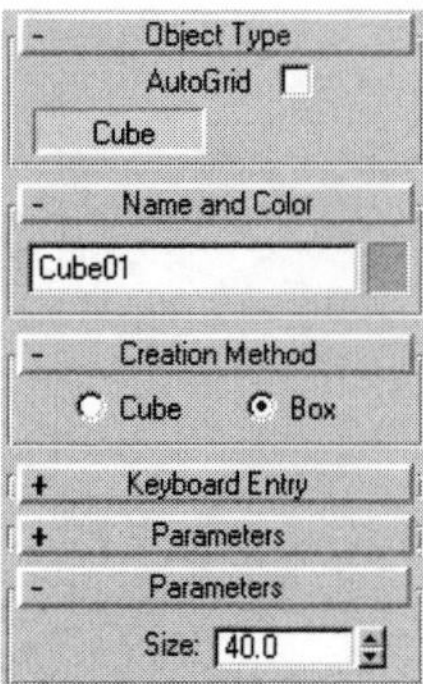

***Figure 9.2** The Cube rollout*

This script can be found in the `plugin_cube02.ms` file on the CD-ROM.

Using Parameter Blocks

If you check the Track View, even though this object now has an interface, it still does not have any parameters. This is because you need to create a *parameter block*.

Parameter blocks are special parameters that are saved with the object and allow direct animation of their values. Using parameter blocks creates tracks in Track View for each property you want to access, making animation easier to edit and visualize. Parameter blocks are essential for creation plug-ins, since creation plug-ins do not extend any plug-in that already has parameters. A parameter block can be linked to a rollout, which will automatically link the variables with the UI items. This makes it easier for you to write the script because you will not need to write any event handler code for the UI item.

The parameter can have a series of properties, but the most important is the type. This defines which kind of variable the parameter is—integer, float, color, point3, Boolean, and so on. Table 9.4 lists the parameter block types. In Exercise 9.3, you will use *worldunits*, which will allow the user to specify this value using any configured unit in the system. This makes the script usable for different measuring systems.

Table 9.4 Parameter Block Types

UI Item	Parameter Type
spinner or slider	`#float`
	`#integer`
	`#time`
	`#angle`
	`#percent`
	`#colorchannel`
	`#worldunits`
radio button	`#integer`
	`#radiobtnindex`
checkbox or checkbutton	`#integer`
	`#boolean`
colorpicker	`#color`
pickbutton	`#node`
map button	`#texturemap`
material button	`#material`

You can also specify whether or not the parameter is animatable. If it's not animatable, it will not be displayed in the Track View, but its value will be stored and retrieved when you open the scene again or re-select the object.

All parameters in a parameter block can be accessed using MAXScript, and they are accessed just like any object property by using the *object.property* syntax. In Exercise 9.3, we will add a parameter block to the plug-in we created in Exercise 9.2.

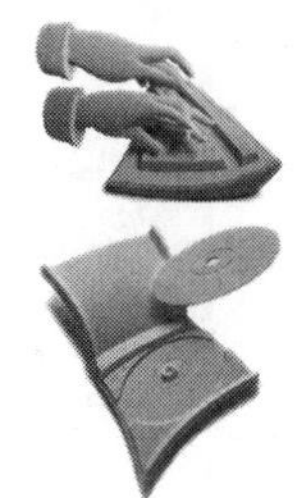

Exercise 9.3: Adding Parameters Blocks

1. Continue working on the file from Exercise 9.2 or open the file `plugin_cube02.ms` on the CD-ROM.

2. Add a parameter block to your cube plug-in by adding the following lines before the Rollout clause:

```
parameters pblock rollout:params
(
cube_size animatable:true type:#worldunits ui:size
on cube_size set val do
   delegate.width = delegate.height = delegate.length = val
)
```

   The parameter block is linked to the *params* rollout, since you used *rollout:params*. The variable `cube_size` will be linked to the size spinner in this rollout because you used *ui:size*.

3. Now that you defined the parameter block, you can adjust the rest of the script so that it uses the parameter block. Replace the code in the rollout with the following:

```
rollout params "Parameters"
(
spinner size "Size: " range:[0,10000,0]
)
```

4. Now, edit the *MouseMove* event:

```
on MouseMove clickNo do
(
if clickNo == 2 do
   cube_size = length gridDist
)
```

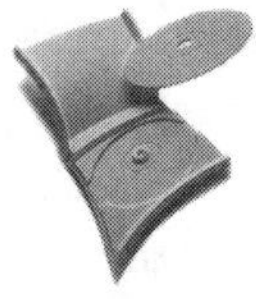

Evaluate the script and play with it. Notice that the *Size* parameter also appears in the Track View, as in Figure 9.3. This script can be found on the CD-ROM in the file `plugin_cube03.ms`.

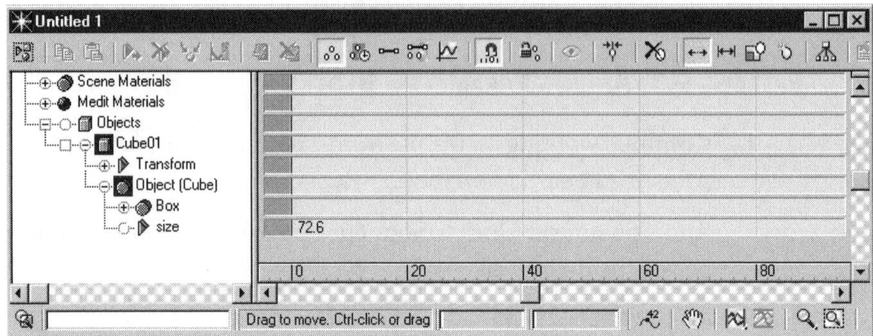

Figure 9.3 *Cube properties in Track View*

You can now animate the script like any regular object. You can save this plug-in in the Plugins folder.

Always place your plug-in script files in any plug-in folder. MAX searches for plug-in scripts in the same path it searches for regular plug-ins.

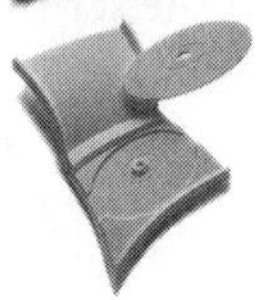

On the CD-ROM, you can find another Geometry plug-in example in the file `plugin_hemisphere.ms`. This plug-in automatically creates a Hemisphere object. It also features a new event: *on create*. This event is called when the object is created, and you usually use it to preset the delegate object.

Creating Shape Plug-Ins

Extending Shape plug-ins is very similar to extending Geometry plug-ins. The same syntax is used; the only difference is the object that's being manipulated.

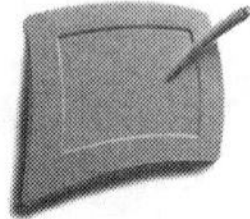

You cannot extend the Line, Point Curve, and CV Curve shapes. Only the parametric ones can be extended.

The file `plugin_circle2.ms` creates a plug-in script that extends the NGon shape in order to create circles with a variable number of vertices. The Circle2 plug-in script has two parameters: *Radius* and *Segments*. When loaded, this plug-in shows in the Command Panel, as in Figure 9.4.

Figure 9.4 *The Multi Circle plug-in script*

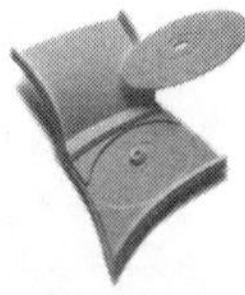

The file `plugin_newstar.ms` on the CD-ROM is another example of a Shape plug-in.

Helpers and lights can be extended in the same way as geometry and shapes can. Check the `plugin_dummy2.ms` *file on the CD-ROM for an example of a Helper plug-in.*

Creating Modifier Plug-Ins

Modifier plug-ins are similar to the plug-ins that you have already learned about, but they do not require a tool because modifiers cannot be drawn in the viewport.

Any modifier can be extended as long as it supports MAXScript.

The script in Listing 9.1 extends the Optimize script, creating four presets: None, Low, Medium, and High.

LISTING 9.1: THE OPTIMIZE2 PLUG-IN SCRIPT (*PLUGIN_OPTIMIZE2.MS*)

```
plugin modifier optimize2
name:"Optimize2"
extends:optimize
replaceui:true
classID:#(0x52ef94f8, 0xadb373cb)
(
parameters pblock rollout:params
   (
   power type:#integer default:1 ui:str
   on power set val do
      (
      case val of
         (
         1:   delegate.facethreshold1 = 0
         2:   delegate.facethreshold1 = 2.5
         3:   delegate.facethreshold1 = 5
         4:   delegate.facethreshold1 = 10
         )
      )
   )

rollout params "Parameters"
   (
   group "Optimize"
      (
      radiobuttons str "Strength:" \
         labels:#("None","Low","Medium","High")
      )
   )
)
```

Once this plug-in is evaluated, the new modifier will appear in the Modifiers list, as in Figure 9.5

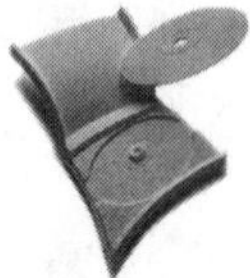

Another Modifier plug-in example is the `plugin_normalize2.ms` file on the CD-ROM. This plug-in extends the Normalize Spline plug-in and allows it to accept values smaller than 1.0, which is not acceptable in the current version.

You can also create your own modifiers using MAXScript. We'll see how this is done in Chapter 10.

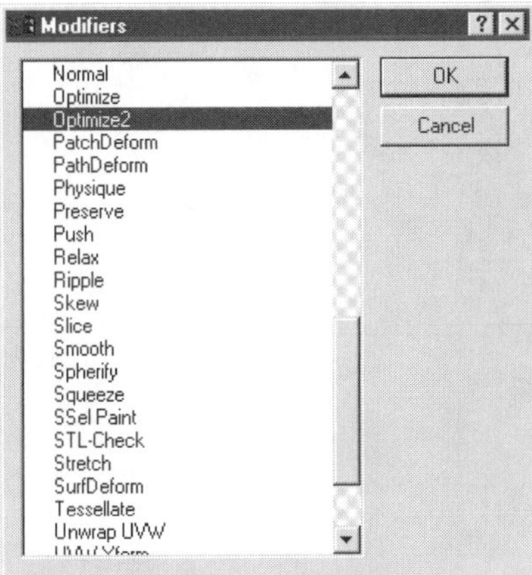

Figure 9.5 *The Modifiers list*

Creating Material and Texture Map Plug-Ins

The Material and Texture Map plug-ins work just like the Modifier plug-in. They extend an existing material or texture map, allowing you to predefine and automate a series of values.

Their biggest advantage is the ability to use material buttons and map buttons to allow the user to select a material or map to be used in the plug-in.

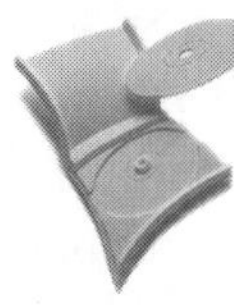

The `plugin_rayglass.ms` script found on the CD-ROM is a good example of a Material plug-in. It has three properties: *Color*, *Transparency*, and *Index of Refraction*. These three properties will be used on an extended Standard material, which has the Raytrace map applied to the Reflect and Refract maps.

Besides these properties, this plug-in features some options to control the Raytrace global parameters, accessing them through *trackviewnodes*, as you saw in Chapter 7. This plug-in's interface is shown in Figure 9.6.

An example of a Texture Map plug-in is the `plugin_gamemap.ms` file on the CD-ROM. It allows you to pick a folder and displays all the available JPEG, TGA, and GIF files in a drop-down list. Once you select the desired file name, it will be assigned as the bitmap texture. Notice that most of the work here is done to display and update the user interface, and not much is done in the plug-in code itself.

You can customize this script to fit your needs, adding more file extensions and defining a fixed file path so that, for example, all game artists will be using the same textures.

Figure 9.6 *The Raytraced Glass Material plug-in*

Creating Render Effect and Atmosphere Plug-Ins

Render Effect plug-ins can be created in two different ways: by extending an existing plug-in or by creating a whole new effect. We'll see how you can extend a plug-in script in this chapter, and you will see how you can create your own render effect in Chapter 10.

Extending Render Effect and Atmosphere plug-ins works the same way as the materials, texture maps, and modifiers did, with no difference at all.

The file `plugin_blur2.ms` on the CD-ROM shows an example of an extended render effect. This plug-in extends the Blur render effect, limiting it to Radial Blur, based on a center object. The parameter block shows a *Node* parameter, which will store the selected object.

Once the plug-in is loaded and added to the Render Effects dialog, it looks like Figure 9.7.

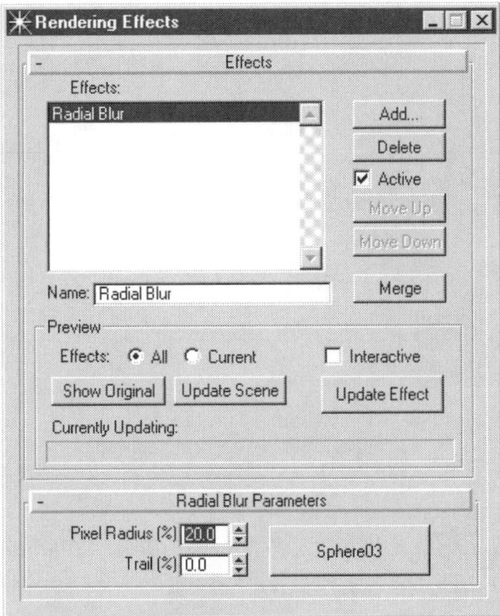

Figure 9.7 *The Radial Blur Render Effect plug-in*

Creating System-Like Plug-Ins

You will now learn how to create a system-like plug-in script. This plug-in script creates geometry, but once it's created, you cannot adjust its parameters anymore.

System-like plug-ins are basically an interface for tools. You can use system-like plug-ins to create several objects and manipulate them the way you need to. When you leave the Create Panel, each object will behave like a regular object, without having any connection to the group.

The `plugin_hand.ms` file on the CD-ROM shows you an example of a system-like plug-in script. It creates a dummy Hand object, the same one you used in Chapter 3. It doesn't even have an interface; it just has the tool that creates the object. Once it's created, it will look like Figure 9.8.

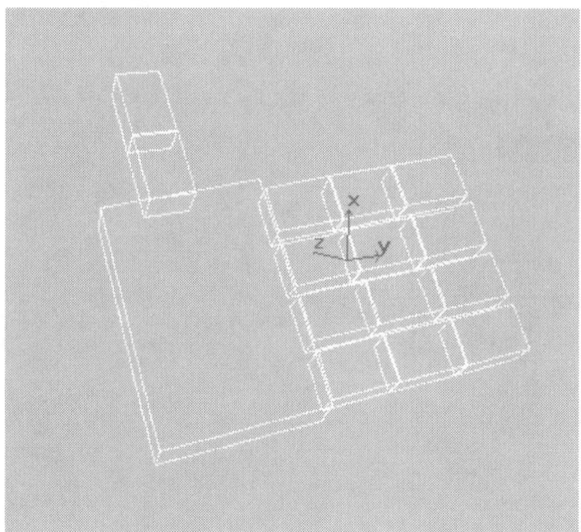

Figure 9.8 *The dummy Hand*

System-like plug-ins do not have a Class ID. These plug-ins do not save any information in the MAX scene and do not need to be present for the scene to be loaded.

Summary

You learned how to create tools and plug-in scripts. Extending plug-ins help you customize MAX, while system-like plug-ins allow you to create custom objects.

In the next chapter, you will build on your knowledge of plug-in scripts and learn how to create new modifiers and render effects. You will also learn how to create objects and how to assign mapping coordinates and smoothing groups to them.

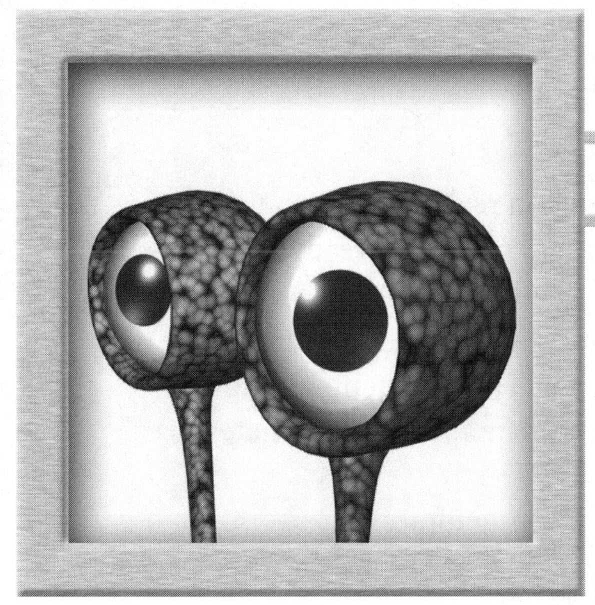

Creating Plug-In Scripts from Scratch

MAXSCRIPT

Chapter 10

Now you will start working on real plug-ins; you are not going to extend or use anything that is ready, but you will create your own plug-in code. This is done with three plug-ins: Render Effects, Modifiers, and Geometry. Besides learning how to create Geometry plug-ins, you will also learn how to add smoothing, material IDs, and texture mapping coordinates to the objects that you create.

This chapter will cover the following topics:

- Creating Render Effect plug-ins
- Creating Modifier plug-ins
- Creating Geometry plug-ins
- Adding mapping coordinates to Geometry plug-ins
- Working with materials and other information

Creating Render Effect Plug-Ins

You can create Render Effect plug-ins that manipulate the rendered image, changing the pixel colors according to the parameters that you specify.

Besides manipulating the pixel colors, MAXScript also has access to all extended channels, which allows you to create pixel masks that are dependent on the object ID or any other parameter.

When creating a render effect, you need to use the *on apply bmp* event. This event allows you to access the rendered image using the `bmp` variable. Exercise 10.1 will help us see how this works.

Exercise 10.1: The Colorize Effect Script

This script will allow the user to select a color that will be added to the rendered image.

1. Open file `plugin_colorize01.ms` on the CD-ROM. If you evaluate it, it will appear as a new render effect, as seen in Figure 10.1.

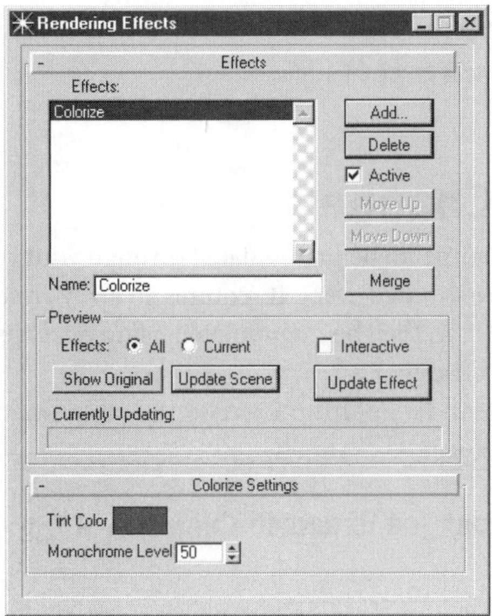

Figure 10.1 *The Colorize effect*

2. This file has the rollout and the parameter block. You will now add the *on apply bmp* event. After the rollout, enter the following code in the script:

```
on apply bmp do
(
for h=0 to bmp.height do
(
local sline = getPixels bmp [0,h] bmp.width
for w = 1 to sline.count do
(
monocolor = sline[w]*(100-strength)/100 + \
   tint_color*strength/100
sline[w] = monocolor
)
setPixels bmp [0,h] sline
)
)
```

This code steps through each pixel and adds *tint_color*, depending on the *strength* value. You can find the final code in the file `plugin_colorize02.ms` on the CD-ROM.

This script is very slow because it processes each pixel of the image. Use it on small images so that you can test the effects. The only workaround is to use C++ plug-ins.

Using Extended Channels

You can request any extended channel to be manipulated through your render effect. This is done using the *on channelsrequired* event. It requires an array containing the channels needed. These channels can then be manipulated using *getchannels* or *getchannelasmask*, as you saw in Chapter 5.

In Exercise 10.2, we'll rewrite the script from Exercise 10.1, this time adding an option to select the material or object ID channels.

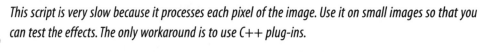

Exercise 10.2: Adding Support for Extended Channels in the Colorize Effect

1. Open the file `plugin_colorize03.ms` on the CD-ROM. This file contains new parameters and new rollout items, as seen in Figure 10.2.

Figure 10.2 *Object and material ID options*

2. Before *on apply bmp*, add the following event:

```
on channelsrequired do #(#objectid,#matid)
```

   This will require the renderer to process the object ID and material ID channels.

3. Before *monocolor* =, add the following code:

```
objchan = getchannel bmp [w,h] #objectID
matchan = getchannel bmp [w,h] #matID
if (objid and objid_no == objchan[1]) or (matid and \
matid_no == matchan[1]) or (not objid and not matid) do
(
```

4. Before *setpixels*, add a *)* (close parenthesis) to close the *If* expression.

The script now checks to see if the Object ID checkbox is turned on and processes the color only on the pixels that match the object ID. This also happens for the material ID. If both checkboxes are off, all pixels are processed.

Creating Modifier Plug-Ins

You can write simple modifiers, like `Bend`, `Twist`, and `Taper`, using MAXScript. These modifiers will change the position of vertices based on their original position, but in a parametric form. This means that you will not have access to the vertex position, but will change it using a math formula.

You will now write a modifier that will deform an object like a sine wave, so that you can define the axis, the amount of deformity, and the number of curves, as seen in Figure 10.3.

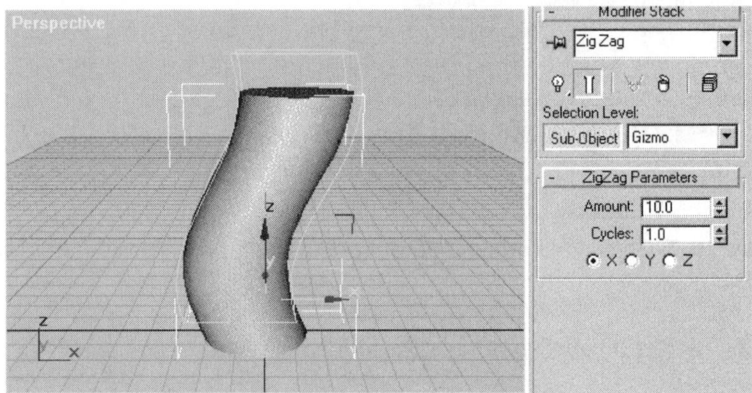

Figure 10.3 *The* ZigZag *modifier*

Start a new script and type the code in Listing 10.1 into it, or open the file named `plugin_zigzag.ms` on the CD-ROM.

LISTING 10.1: THE ZIGZAG MODIFIER PLUG-IN SCRIPT (*PLUGIN_ZIGZAG.MS*)

```
plugin simpleMod Zigzag
name:"Zig Zag"
classID:#(0xa8eba5be, 0x89ff7eab)
(
parameters main rollout:params
   (
   amount type:#worldunits ui:amtSpin default:20
   cycles type:#float ui:times default:0.5
   z_axis type:#radiobtnindex ui:zaxis default:1
   )
```

```
rollout params "ZigZag Parameters"
   (
   spinner amtSpin "Amount: " type:#float range:[-1000,1000,20]
   spinner times "Cycles: " type:#float range:[0,100,1]
   radiobuttons zaxis labels:#("X","Y","Z") coluns:3
   )
on map i p do
   (
   case z_axis of
      (
      1: p.x += amount*sin((p.z-(center.z))*pi*cycles)
      2: p.y += amount*sin((p.z-(center.z))*pi*cycles)
      3: p.z += amount*sin((sqrt(p.x^2+p.y^2)-\
               sqrt(center.x^2+center.y^2))*pi*cycles)
      )
   p
   )
)
```

As you can see, the Modifier plug-in doesn't need a tool to be created. However, it has a rollout and a parameter block like any other plug-in script.

This type of Modifier plug-in works through the *on map i p* event. This event is called for each vertex in the object and will copy its position in the `p` variable. Then, the plug-in will modify the position and will output the new `p` value.

In your script, you defined three different axes, which will be called using the *Case* expression. The position of the vertex in each axis will be modified, using a Sine expression. This expression has another parameter, *center*, which is the center position of the object. This allows you to use this value as part of the formula. In Listing 10.1, *center* defines where the deformation is zero, because when `p.z` is equal to `center.z`, sine will evaluate zero.

Notice that this modifier also has Gizmo and Center, which can be animated as any regular modifier.

Creating Geometry Plug-Ins

You can also create geometry from scratch. This is done by defining vertices and faces manually through a script. The finished script will create a parametric geometry object with vertices and faces just like any MAX object.

In Exercise 10.3, we will create a box object from scratch, adding a new option to position the pivot point on the center or on the base of the object, as seen in Figure 10.4.

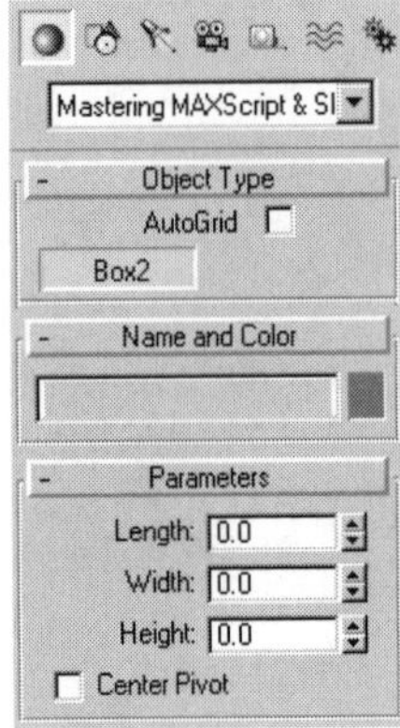

***Figure 10.4** The new Box plug-in script*

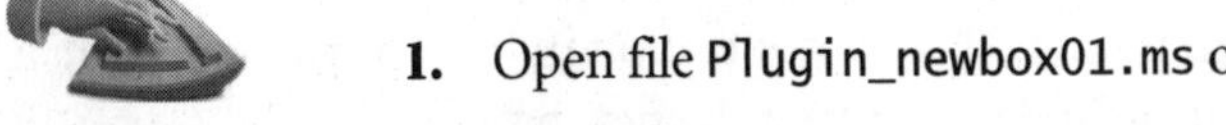

EXERCISE 10.3: CREATING A NEW BOX OBJECT

1. Open file `Plugin_newbox01.ms` on the CD-ROM.
2. This file already has the parameter block, the rollout, and the tool defined. All you need to do is create the geometry. This is done by assigning the vertices position in local X, Y, and Z coordinates, and then assigning which vertices make each face. Before the *tool*, enter the following code:

```
on buildMesh do
(
if center_pivot == true then pvt = [0,0,-height/2] else pvt = 0
v = #()
v[1] = [-length/2,-width/2,0] + pvt
v[2] = [length/2,-width/2,0] + pvt
v[3] = [-length/2,width/2,0] + pvt
v[4] = [length/2,width/2,0] + pvt
for i in 5 to 8 do v[i] = v[i-4] + [0,0,height]
f = #()
f[1] = [1,3,4]
```

```
f[2] = [4,2,1]
f[3] = [5,6,8]
f[4] = [8,7,5]
f[5] = [1,2,6]
f[6] = [6,5,1]
f[7] = [2,4,8]
f[8] = [8,6,2]
f[9] = [4,3,7]
f[10] = [7,8,4]
f[11] = [3,1,5]
f[12] = [5,7,3]
setMesh mesh verts:v faces:f
)
```

3. Evaluate this script and create a box2 in any view. Then go to the Modify tab and adjust its values. Notice that this works just like a regular object.

The *buildmesh* event is called to create the geometry and uses the *setmesh* function to do so. This function requires an array of vertices and an array of faces. The vertex array holds each vertex position in the local coordinate system. The face array holds a list of the vertices that make the face. Figure 10.5 illustrates the vertex and face numbering system.

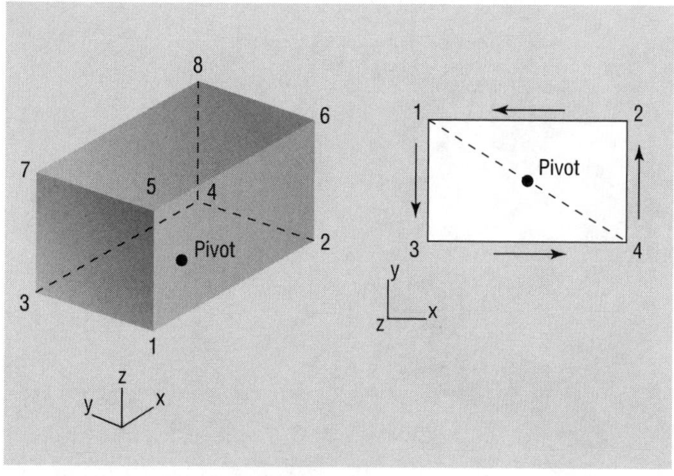

***Figure 10.5** Vertex and face numbering*

When numbering faces, the trick is to always look from the outside and then consider the points in a counter-clockwise direction, always creating one triangle at a time. If you consider the vertices in a clockwise direction, the face normal will be inverted.

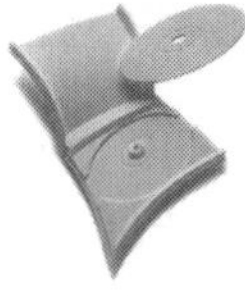

The final script file is named `plugin_newbox02.ms` and can be found on the CD-ROM.

Defining Smoothing Groups and Material IDs

You can use any regular Editable Mesh method (see Chapter 3) to adjust any parameter of the Mesh object you are creating. These methods need to be used after you create the mesh using *setmesh*, and will refer to the Mesh object.

Using these methods, you can define smoothing groups, material IDs, and other properties.

The final object in Exercise 10.3 does not look like a real cube. This is because it has no smoothing groups set, so its corners blend instead of showing a real cube edge. Figure 10.6 shows the difference between our plug-in box (left) and MAX's Box object (right).

Using `setfacesmoothgroup mesh 1 1`, we can set the first face in Exercise 10.3 to smoothing group 1.

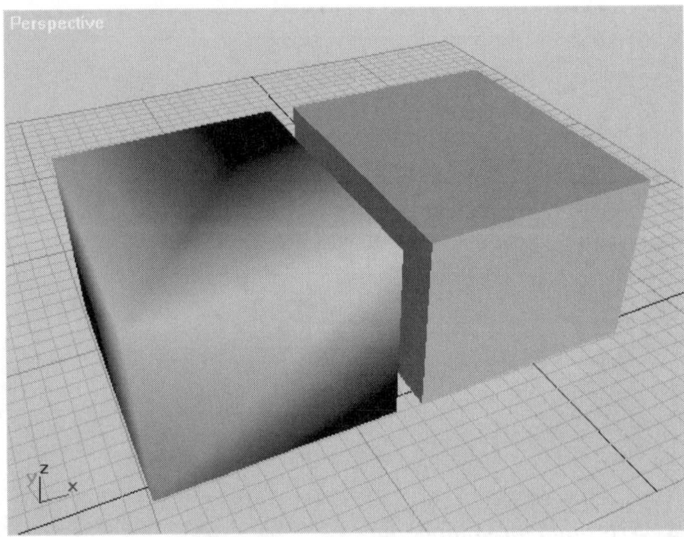

***Figure 10.6** The difference between Box2 and Box objects*

Smoothing groups are set using a 32-bit value, which defines which smoothing groups are on or off. This means that each smooth group is equal to 2^(sg−1), where sg *is the smooth group number. Using this formula, if you use* setfacesmoothgroup *with a value of 5, you are turning on smoothing groups 1 and 3 (2^0 + 2^2 = 5).*

In Exercise 10.4, let's continue Exercise 10.3 by adding the smooth groups and the material IDs to the Box2 plug-in.

Exercise 10.4: Defining Smoothing Groups and Material IDs

1. Open file `plugin_newbox02.ms` on the CD-ROM.
2. On the lines that follow *setmesh*, add the following code:

```
for i in 1 to mesh.numfaces do
(
setfacesmoothgroup mesh i (2^((i+1)/2))
setfacematid mesh i ((i+1)/2)
)
```

Make use of the incorrect round-off (truncation) in integer calculations. In step 2, you need to have each pair of faces with the same material ID and smoothing group. So, how can you do it? Using (i+1)/2 will do it for you, since you are only dealing with integers. For instance, when i = 5 or 6, the result is 3, which is mathematically incorrect but saves us the many steps it would take to get to the same result using float numbers.

3. Evaluate the script. Apply a Multi-Sub material and notice that each face will have a different material on it.

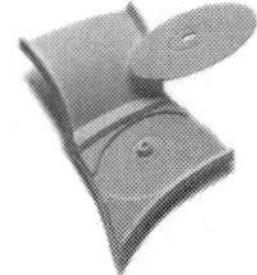

The final script can be found in `plugin_newbox03.ms` on the CD-ROM.

Adding Mapping Coordinates

An important feature of the Geometry plug-in scripts is the ability to assign mapping coordinates to the object. To do so, you'll need to use a series of functions that will specify texture vertices and texture faces.

In Exercise 10.5, we'll apply mapping coordinates to the plug-in you created in Exercises 10.3 and 10.4, so you can learn how they work.

Exercise 10.5: Adding Mapping Coordinates

1. Open file `plugin_newbox03.ms` on the CD-ROM.
2. After the code added in Exercise 10.4, add the following code:

   ```
   setnumtverts mesh 4
   buildTVFaces mesh
   ```

   These functions define the number of texture vertices and apply the mapping coordinates to the mesh.
3. Now, define the texture vertices that will be applied to the object by adding the following code:

   ```
   settvert mesh 1 [0,0,0]
   settvert mesh 2 [1,0,0]
   settvert mesh 3 [0,1,0]
   settvert mesh 4 [1,1,0]
   ```

   These commands define the mapping coordinates of a rectangle, as in Figure 10.7. The mapping coordinate origin is [0,0,0] and defines the lower-left corner of the bitmap. The top-right corner of the bitmap is defined by a mapping coordinate of [1,1,0]. In our case, a box, all faces have an entire bitmap on them, which means that the mapping coordinates are always the same for each face.

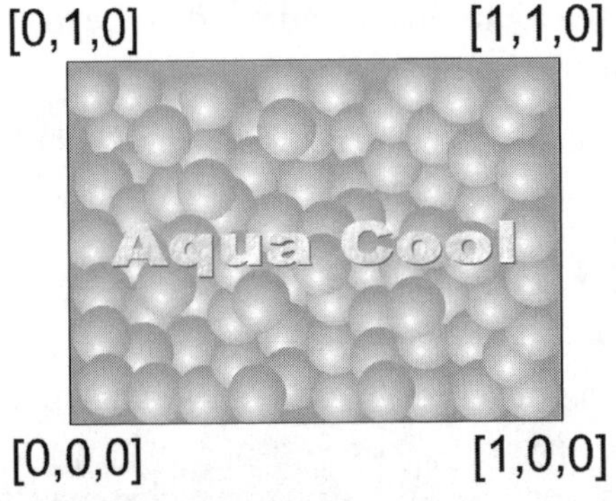

Figure 10.7 *Mapping coordinates in a bitmap*

4. Now, define each face's mapping coordinates by adding the following code to the script:

```
tf = #()
tf[1] = [3,1,2]
tf[2] = [2,4,3]
tf[3] = [1,2,4]
tf[4] = [4,3,1]
tf[5] = [1,2,4]
tf[6] = [4,3,1]
tf[7] = [1,2,4]
tf[8] = [4,3,1]
tf[9] = [1,2,4]
tf[10] = [4,3,1]
tf[11] = [1,2,4]
tf[12] = [4,3,1]
for i in 1 to 12 do settvface mesh i tf[i]
```

There's a little trick to define the order of the mapping coordinates in the faces. In Figure 10.8, there are two rectangles. The left one represents the texture mapping coordinates that you wish to apply and their respective texture vertex numbers, which you already defined in step 3. In the right rectangle, you have the face and its vertices. There's also an indication of the first vertex of face 1, which is very important. To define the face mapping of this face, you need to specify the order of the texture vertices, following the order that the face was created in. In this figure, the order would be [3,1,2]. Repeating this same concept for the remaining faces, we get the numbers you entered in step 4.

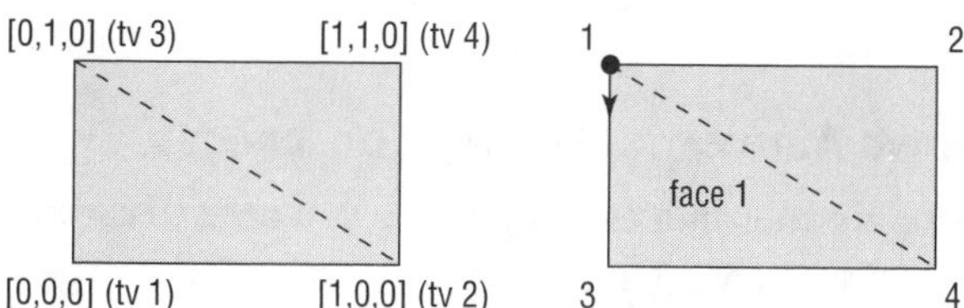

***Figure 10.8** Mapping coordinates applied to the faces*

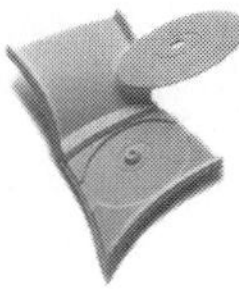

You can always rotate the texture by cycling the order of the texture vertices. The final script can be found in `plugin_newbox04.ms` on the CD-ROM.

Generating Mapping Coordinates Automatically

All primitives in MAX have a Generate Mapping Coords. checkbox (see Figure 10.9), which turns on mapping coordinates for that object. Why would you not turn them on by default? That's simple: Every vertex uses 20 bytes of RAM to store the mapping coordinates. Consider an object with a million faces, and you would have 20MB less RAM available for rendering.

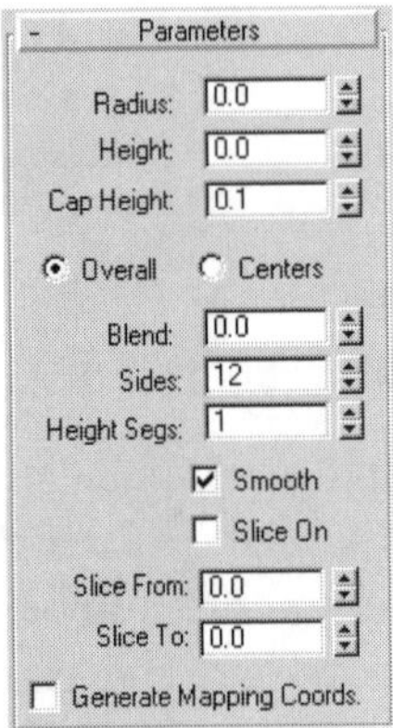

Figure 10.9 *The Oiltank Parameters rollout with a Generate Mapping Coords. checkbox*

On the other hand, to avoid warning you that an object does not have mapping coordinates, MAX generates default coordinates for primitives when they are needed. You can also do this with a plug-in script.

In Exercise 10.6, we'll add automatic mapping coordinates to the plug-in that we created in Exercise 10.5.

EXERCISE 10.6: ADDING AUTOMATIC MAPPING COORDINATES

To add automatic mapping coordinates to a plug-in, you need to use an *on setgenuvw* event. This event is called when MAX renders the object and tries to generate the mapping coordinates.

1. Open file `plugin_newbox04.ms` on the CD-ROM.
2. Create a function containing all the mapping coordinates' code, name it *fn genuvw*, and move all the code between *setnumtverts* and *for i in 1 to 12 do settvface*, including all the content on these lines too. Place this function before the rollout.

3. Create a function to remove the mapping coordinates, entering the following code after the function you created in step 2:

```
fn removeuvw = buildtvfaces mesh false
```

4. Add a new checkbox to the rollout by inserting the following code:

```
checkbox adduvw "Generate Mapping Coords." checked:false
```

5. On the line that follows *setmesh*, instruct the script to generate mapping coordinates when the checkbox is on by adding the following code:

```
if params.adduvw.checked do genuvw()
```

6. Now, add the event that will automatically generate the mapping coordinates. Add the following code after the *buildmesh* event:

```
on setgenuvw val do
(
if val then genuvw() else removeuvw()
params.adduvw.checked = true
)
```

7. Add another event that will turn on the checkbox if the object has mapping coordinates:

```
on hasuvw do params.adduvw.checked
```

8. Finally, add an event that will generate mapping coordinates when the user turns on or off the Generate Mapping Coords. checkbox. Add this event inside the rollout:

```
on adduvw changed state do
(
if mesh != undefined do if state then genuvw() else removeuvw()
)
```

9. Evaluate the script and create a new object. Drag any material that contains a bitmap and make sure that *Show Map in Viewport* is on. You will see the texture displayed, and the Generate Mapping Coords. checkbox will be automatically enabled.

The final script can be found in the file `plugin_newbox05.ms` on the CD-ROM.

The `plugin_enemybox.ms` script on the CD-ROM is another example of a plug-in script that involves a little more math because it's a cylinder with two segments with a variable top radius.

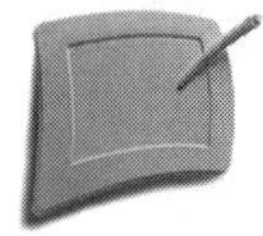

An easy way to create a plug-in script is by using the MXSExport sample script that comes with MAX. It saves an object as a plug-in script, adding all the code to define smoothing groups, material IDs, and mapping coordinates.

Summary

In this chapter, you learned how to create your own render effects and modifiers. You also learned how to create your own Geometry plug-ins, and even how to add texture maps, smoothing groups, and material IDs to enhance them.

In the next chapter, you will see how to use MAXScript Extension plug-ins and how to query for MAXScript constructors, structures, and methods.

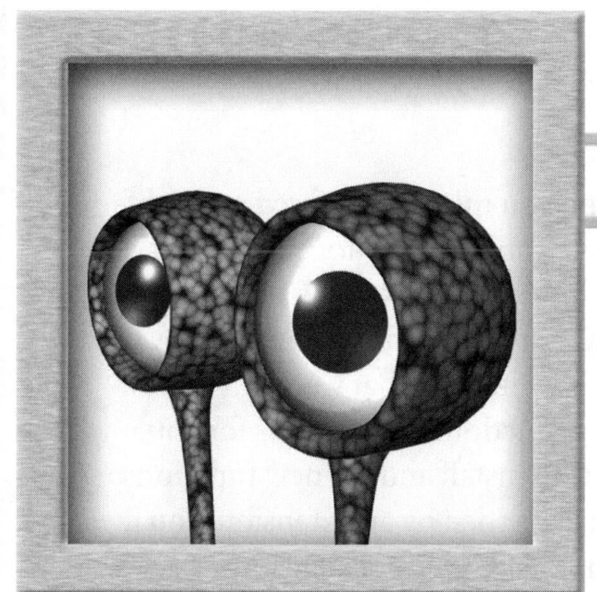

MAXScript Extensions

MAXSCRIPT

Chapter 11

When using MAXScript, you might have faced some difficulties because some features were not exposed, or maybe your life would have been easier if a certain function existed. This is where *MAXScript extensions* come in. They are plug-ins that give you access to certain tools that were not accessible, and they can also create new functions and options for you.

In this chapter, you'll see how to install and list new functions, methods, and constructors that are added by an extension. You'll also learn how to use some sample MAXScript extensions.

In this chapter, you'll learn how to:

- Use MAXScript extensions
- List constructors, methods, and functions
- List properties
- Use the Binary File Stream extension
- Use the MAXScript Control Library extension
- Use the Avguard extension

Using MAXScript Extensions

A MAXScript extension is a regular MAX plug-in, usually with the DLX extension. These plug-ins are installed in any regular MAX plug-in folder. If you want to install them in a different folder, simply make sure that this folder is added to the plug-in path by using Customize → Configure Paths... in the main menu.

Once the plug-in is installed, it will load automatically when MAX is started. Since it's a MAXScript extension, it will not appear in the user interface, but instead will give you access to new functions and constructors through MAXScript.

Listing Constructors, Methods, and Functions

MAX does not add a new interface or any information when a MAXScript extension is added. Although some plug-ins might offer you MAXScript capabilities, how do you know how to access these commands?

MAXScript has a function called *apropos*. This function lists all constructors, methods, and variables that are available in MAX. It allows you to specify wildcards to refine your search but will already assume that the specified keyword can be found anywhere in a string. For example, `apropos "chamfer"` lists everything that has *chamfer* in it, as in the result that follows:

```
ChamferBox (const MAXClass): ChamferBox
ChamferCyl (const MAXClass): ChamferCyl
meshOps.startChamfer (Primitive): startChamfer()
Fillet_Chamfer (const MAXClass): Fillet_Chamfer
splineOps.startChamfer (Primitive): startChamfer()
NURBSChamferCurve (const Class): NURBSChamferCurve
```

Another way to list new constructors is using *showclass*. *Showclass* lists all constructors that meet the specified keyword. Similarly to *apropos*, you can also use wildcards when specifying your keyword.

For example, `showclass "*chamfer*"` returns the following result:

```
Fillet_Chamfer : modifier {15033a86,10b62c69}
ChamferBox : GeometryClass {1ad73f40,48ea0f97}
ChamferCyl : GeometryClass {7b9a546e,21a446a1}
```

One of the advantages of *showclass* is that you can also list the properties of the specified class. For example, `showclass "chamfer*.*"` lists the classes starting with *chamfer* and also lists their properties. This option gives you a lot of freedom to search, allowing you to list all classes that have a similar property.

A good way to use *apropos* is by using the `aproposgui.ms` sample Macro Script that comes with MAX. It allows you to list the specified keywords and places them on the interface, making it easier for you to search and visualize the results. Its interface looks like Figure 11.1.

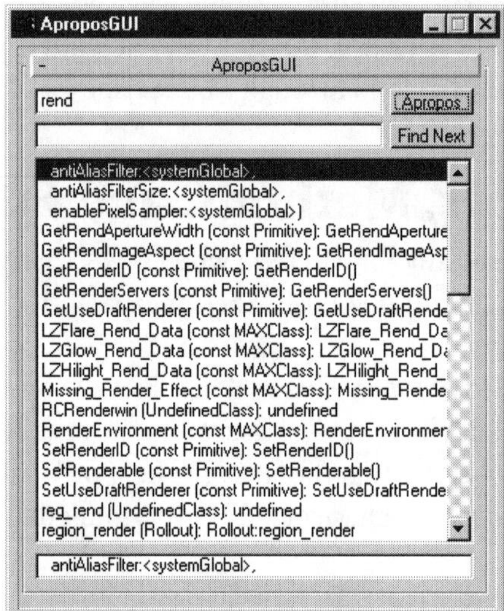

Figure 11.1 *The AproposGUI dialog box listing all constructors, methods, and variables starting with* rend

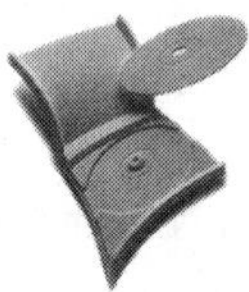

Take a look at the `showclassgui.ms` sample script on the CD-ROM. It is the exact same as the `aproposgui.ms` file, modified to use the *showclass* function.

Listing Properties

Knowing a constructor's properties is as important as knowing the constructor itself. You already learned how to use *getpropnames*, *getproperty*, *setproperty*, and *showproperties*. These functions list the properties that you can access in any constructor. Look at Chapter 1 and Chapter 3 for more information on how to use these functions.

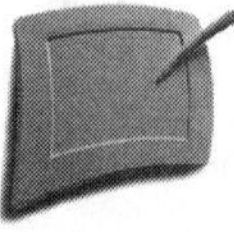

Most of the MAXScript extensions and plug-ins have a help file to teach you how to use them. Other extensions have a built-in Help command. Use `apropos "help"` *to list all functions that have the word* help *in them.*

Using Sample Extensions

After MAX 3 was released, a series of MAXScript extensions were made available for download on the Internet. We'll now see how you can use some of these extensions in your scripts. Keep in mind that these plug-ins need to be installed for the scripts to run.

All plug-ins needed in this section are supplied on the CD-ROM and will need to be installed in MAX before you can play with them.

The Binary File Stream Extension

The *Binary File Stream extension*, developed by Simon Feltman from Asylum Soft, allows you to read and write binary files. This feature isn't available in MAX, so you'll need to use this extension to have this capability.

Take a look at the section "Binary File I/O" in Chapter 6 for an explanation on how to use this extension.

The MAXScript Control Library 2.2 Extension

The *MAXScript Control Library extension* adds new interface items and methods to enhance your scripts. Besides the interface items, it allows you to control the mouse position and also features a nice help interface.

Specifying the Cursor Position and Requesting Help

You can use *getcursorpos()* to read the current cursor position on-screen, based on the upper-left corner of the screen. If you want to set the mouse position, you can use *setcursorpos*.

To access the Control Library Help, all you need to do is use the *ctrllib.help()* function. It searches for the `ctrllib.txt` file in the Help folder in MAX and displays it. Using *ctrllib.version* displays the current Control Library plug-in version. This is useful because often you need to make sure your script is compatible with a specific version of the extension, and your script might not work if a user has an older version.

Using New Interface Items

Sometimes, when building a script, we need to group items to make the interface cleaner. But there's no tool in MAXScript that allows us to create two groups side by side in a rollout, or even to create nested groups as we have in some plug-ins and rollouts in MAX. Figure 11.2 shows an example of a rollout with a single group around all interface items, and can be found on the CD-ROM as `rollout_eyes01.ms`.

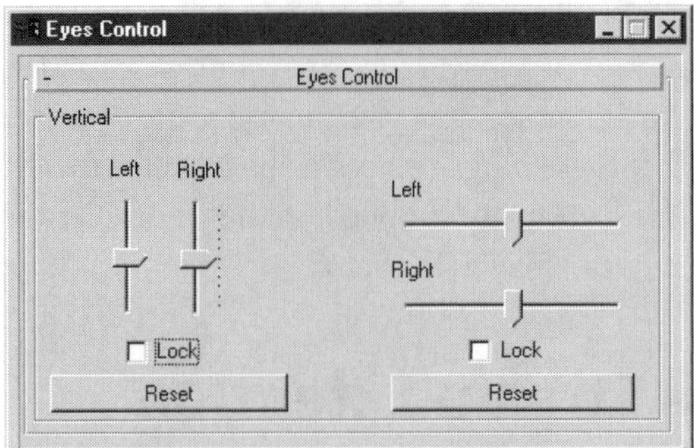

***Figure 11.2** The Eyes Control floater with a single group around all the interface items*

The MAXScript Control Library extension contains a new interface item called *groupbox*. It allows you to draw a single group line with a specific size. All you will need to specify is the width and height. The file `rollout_eyes02.ms` adds two group box items that draw the two groups seen in Figure 11.3. This file can be found on the CD-ROM as `rollout_eyes02.ms`.

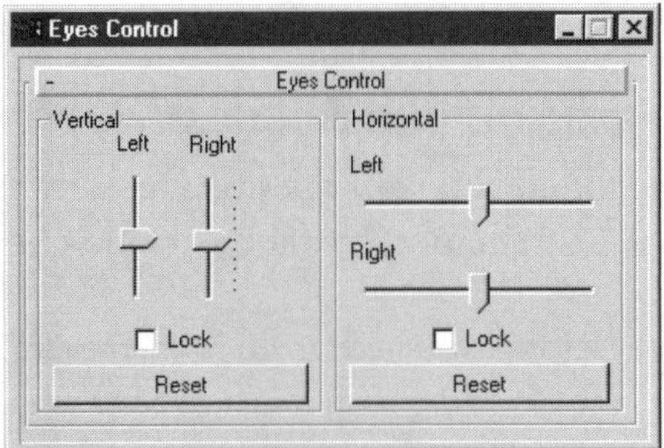

***Figure 11.3** The Eyes Control floater with two groups separating the vertical and horizontal movements*

The second interface item implemented by the Control Library is the *angle*. The angle is a circle that displays the angle in a pie format and also allows you to drag and specify a desired angle. The file `utility_angle.ms` on the CD-ROM has an example of how to use this item. You will need to copy the `angle_spiral.jpg` into your scripts folder for it to work. While dragging the angle, the selected object will be rotated accordingly, and the interface will look like Figure 11.4.

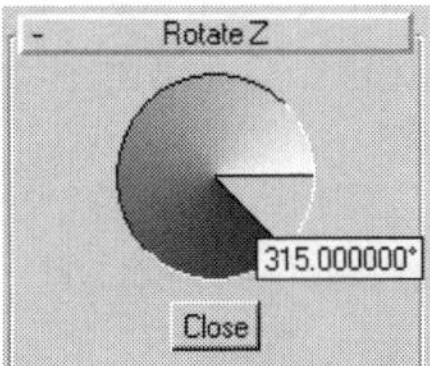

***Figure 11.4** The Angle interface item in a utility*

Another interface item that this extension implements is the *hyperlink*. It's basically a label, but it's clickable and allows you to embed a Web site link to it. It's useful for you to add information about the scripts you write, or anything else that will start another application outside of MAX. Take a look at the `rollout_eyes03.ms` file on the CD-ROM, which has a hyperlink that takes you to the Sybex Web site and looks like Figure 11.5.

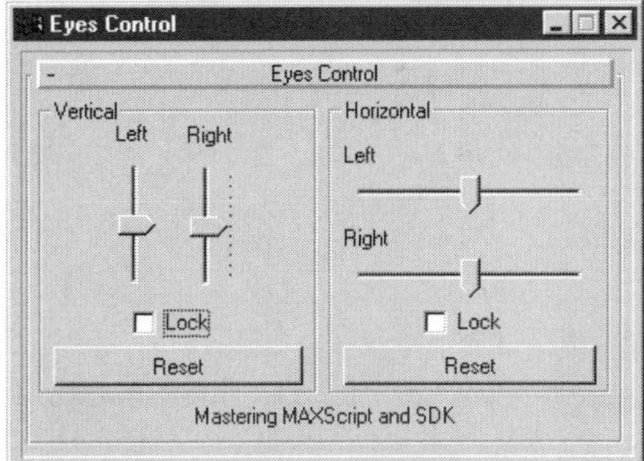

***Figure 11.5** The Eyes Control floater with a hyperlink*

The last interface item that this extension implements is the *imgtag*. An imgtag is a button that has a bitmap that can be stretched, centered, or tiled to fit the button.

Besides the regular events called, imgtag has four other events:

on mouseover Called when the mouse is over the button

on mouseout Called when the mouse leaves the button area

on mousedown Called when the mouse is clicking the button

on mouseup Called when the mouse is being lifted after clicking the button

These events make this button's implementation similar to JavaScript, Macromedia Director, and other languages. You can even swap the images during these events, as was done in the file `rollout_eyes04.ms` on the CD-ROM. The image appears as a bitmap interface item, as shown in Figure 11.6.

Make sure you copy the `button*.jpg` *files to the scripts folder before you execute the* `rollout_eyes04.ms` *file.*

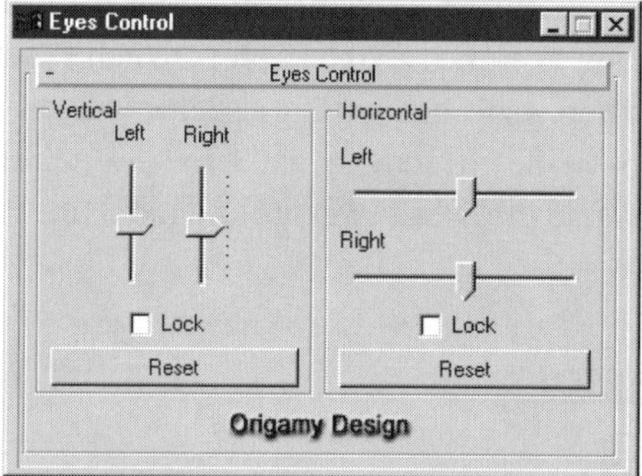

Figure 11.6 *The Eyes Control floater with an imgtab*

Creating Dialogs

When using MAXScript, you can create only utilities and floaters. Using the Control Library, you can also create dialogs.

To create a dialog, simply use *createdialog*. It loads a rollout into a dialog without the border and the rollout bar. It has a few options that allow you to specify if it's resizable, if a menu bar will be added, and a couple of other options. Check the Control Library Help for more information on these options.

Figure 11.7 shows the evaluated `rollout_eyes05.ms` file from the CD-ROM, using a dialog instead of a floater.

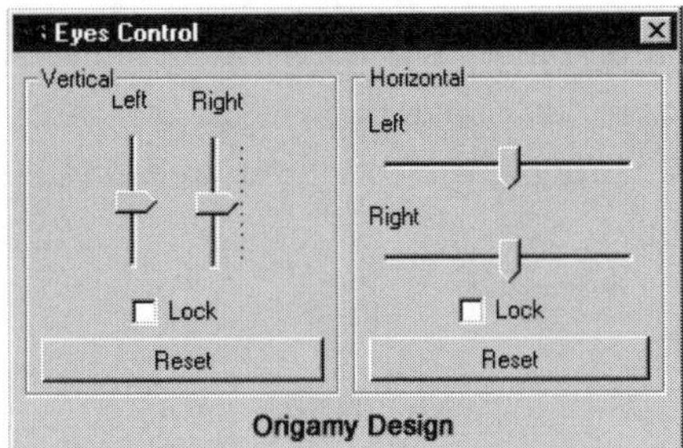

Figure 11.7 *The Eyes Control dialog box version of the Eyes Control floater*

To remove a dialog, you can use the *destroydialog* method.

Adding Pop-Up Menus

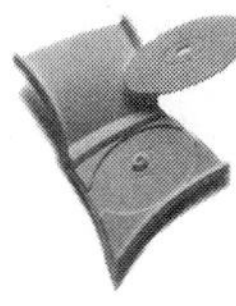

The last constructor implemented by the Control Library is a *pop-up menu.* It allows you to load an RC menu through any event so that you can create interesting options, like a drop-down list, anywhere on the screen. Take a look at the `macro_vp_layout.ms` file on the CD-ROM. It has an RC menu and a Macro Script that uses the `popupmenu` constructor to call the RC menu when the button is clicked. It will look like the menu in Figure 11.8.

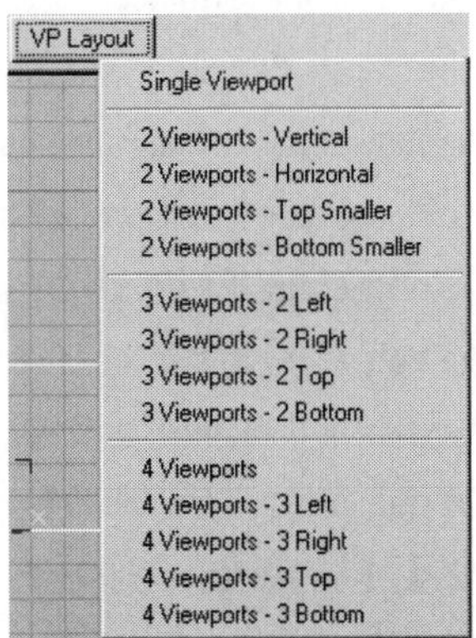

Figure 11.8 *The Viewport Layout RC menu executed from a Macro Script*

The Avguard Extension

The *Avguard extension* is so far the largest MAXScript Extension plug-in available for MAX. It has more than 100 methods and variables that expose several options that are not available in MAXScript. We'll see some of these methods and variables and learn how they can help you in MAXScript.

Setting Renderer Options

MAXScript gives access to only a few options in the Render Scene dialog box. Using the Avguard extension, you can access the remaining options in the Render Scene dialog box, and even some other options in the Preferences dialog box. Table 11.1 lists all the renderer variables accessed using the Avguard extension.

Table 11.1 Renderer variables in the Avguard Extension

VARIABLE	DESCRIPTION
Render Scene Dialog	
rendtimetype	Specifies the type of time range to be rendered.
rendstart	Specifies the range start time.
rendend	Specifies the range end time.
rendnthframe	Specifies the Every Nth Frame value.
rendfilenumberbase	Specifies the value of File Number Base.
rendpickupframes	Specifies the Frames string.
rendshowvfb	Defines the state of the Virtual Frame Buffer checkbox.
rendsavefile	Defines the state of the Save File checkbox.
rendusedevice	Defines the state of the Use Device checkbox.
rendusenet	Defines the state of the Net Render checkbox.
rendfieldrender	Defines the state of the Render to Fields checkbox.
rendcolorcheck	Defines the state of the Video Color Check checkbox.
rendsuperblack	Defines the state of the Super Black checkbox.
rendhidden	Defines the state of the Render Hidden checkbox.
rendforce2side	Defines the state of the Force 2-sided checkbox.
rendatmosphere	Defines the state of the Atmospherics checkbox.

Table 11.1 Renderer variables in the Avguard Extension (*continued*)

VARIABLE	DESCRIPTION
Rendering Preferences Dialog	
renddithertrue	Defines the state of the Dither True Color checkbox.
renddither256	Defines the state of the Dither Paletted checkbox.
rendmultithread	Defines the state of the Multithreading checkbox.
rendnthserial	Defines the state of the Nth Serial Numbering checkbox.
rendvidcorrectmethod	Defines the type of Video Color Check option.
rendfieldorder	Defines the Field Order option.
rendntsc_pal	Defines the Video Color Check color system.
rendsuperblackthresh	Defines the Superblack Threshold option.

These variables cannot be changed if the Render Scene dialog box is open.

Editable Spline Methods

The Avguard extension also supplies a couple of methods to manipulate Editable Spline objects. These methods are described in Table 11.2.

Table 11.2 Avguard Editable Spline Methods

METHOD	DESCRIPTION
getseglengths	Returns an array of segment lengths by spline fraction and length and total spline length.
subdividesegment	Divides the segment into the specified number of divisions.
interpcurve3d	Returns a coordinate on the indexed curve.
tangentcurve3d	Returns a tangent on the indexed curve.
setmaterialid	Sets the material ID of the specified spline segment.
getmaterialid	Gets the material ID of the specified spline segment.

For example, you can create a circle using `c = circle radius:30`. You need to convert it to a Spline shape using `converttosplineshape c`, and then you can query its segments lengths using `getseglengths c 1`. You can then set each segment's material ID randomly, using

```
for i in 1 to (numsegments c 1)
do setmaterialid c 1 i (random 1 255)
```

Editable Mesh Methods

MAXScript has a series of methods to work with editable meshes. Many of these methods are associated with the Edit Mesh modifier. These methods do not execute the commands, but instead they start the command and wait for user input. The Avguard extension implements a series of these methods and allows the script to execute the commands, without needing any user input. In Table 11.3, we'll see some of these methods.

Table 11.3 Avguard Editable Mesh Methods

METHOD	DESCRIPTION
meshop.weldverts	Welds the specified vertices that are within the specified distance.
meshop.autosmooth	Smooths the specified faces based on the threshold angle.
meshop.unifynormals	Unifies the normals of the specified faces.
meshop.flipnormals	Flips the normal of the specified faces.
meshop.autoedge	Sets and clears the edge visibility for the specified edges based on the threshold angle.
meshop.turnedges	Turns the specified edges.
meshop.setvertweight	Sets the weight for the specified vertices.
meshop.getfacearea	Returns the area of the specified faces.

If you want to weld a series of vertices using *meshops.weld*, you cannot set the threshold of the weld, but you can do so using the *meshop.weldverts* method.

There are plenty other *meshop* methods available that allow you to manipulate selections, texture mapping in multiple channels, and many other options. Check the Avguard Help to see how to use these methods.

Other Methods and Variables

The Avguard extension also has many other methods and variables. Table 11.4 lists some of the most useful ones, but you can check its Help to see the remaining methods.

Table 11.4 More Avguard Methods and Variables

METHOD	DESCRIPTION
avguardhelp()	Displays a simplified Help for the Avguard extension.
getnodebyname	Gets a node by specifying its name.
updatemtlinmedit	Updates the specified material in the Materials Editor.
qsort	Sorts the elements of an array.
doesfileexist	Specifies whether a file exists or not.
sysinfo.desktopsize	Returns the desktop size in pixels.
multilistbox	Creates a listbox interface item that can have more than one entry selected.

Some of these functions can be performed in MAXScript but require a series of workarounds or tricks that eventually make them a lot slower. For example, if you have an object called Mybox and you want to use it in MAXScript, you have to use `execute "mybox = $mybox"` to assign it to the `mybox` variable, instead of using `getnodebyname "mybox"`. *Doesfileexist* can be substituted with *getfiles*, but you'd need to use other expressions to verify if the file exists.

Study the remaining options in the Avguard extension carefully because they can save you time when writing scripts and can also offer you powerful options.

Other MAXScript Extensions

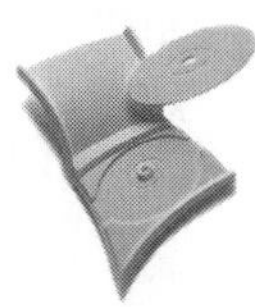

There are various other MAXScript extensions available. Each of them performs a different task or group of tasks. You will find many sample extensions on the CD-ROM along with their help files and some examples, making it easier for you to learn how to use them.

Make sure you check the developer's Web site so that you can have the newest versions available. This ensures that the extension is bug-free and will be more reliable.

Summary

In this chapter, you learned how to use MAXScript extensions. You also learned how to use the features in some of the most often used extensions.

This chapter also ends the MAXScript part of the book, in which you learned how to create, modify, and animate objects, materials, lights, and effects, as well as how to create scripts to automate your tasks.

In Part II of this book, you'll learn how to write your own plug-ins using C++ and the SDK.

Part II

Mastering the SDK

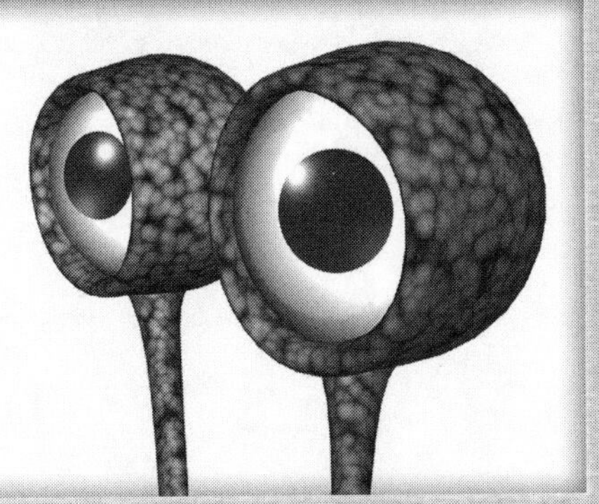

In This Part

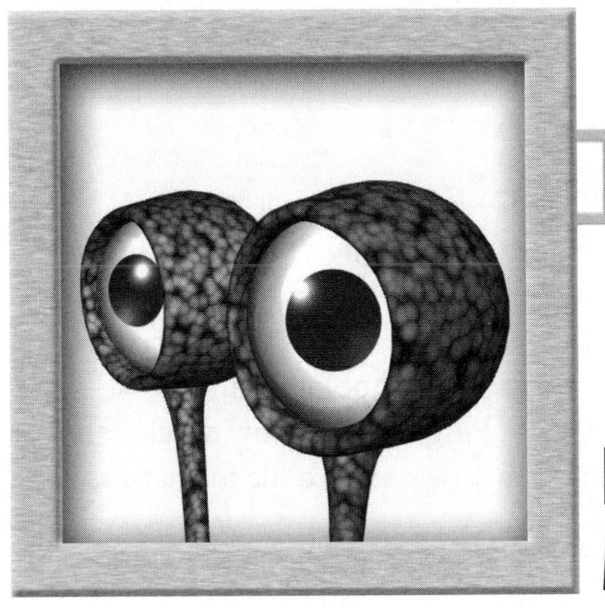

Introduction to the MAX SDK

MAXSCRIPT

Chapter 12

The 3D Studio MAX SDK is a C++-based, object-oriented software development kit for creating plug-in modules for 3D Studio MAX. *Plug-ins* dynamically add functionality to MAX. Plug-ins are what make MAX a very powerful 3D platform and allow for third parties to develop new technologies and to use MAX as a 3D application framework. Plug-ins also allow developers to import and export data from custom or standard file formats, as well as to add tools and features to MAX.

Since the MAX SDK is such a large programming library, this book does not try to fully document it, but should be used as a jump-start for getting a programmer started writing plug-ins for MAX. This book should be used in conjunction with the documentation that comes with the MAX SDK, which is a great reference for all the classes and functions.

This chapter will cover the following topics:

- Installing the 3D Studio MAX SDK
- General SDK information

Requirements

This book requires the reader to have knowledge of the following software technologies:

- 3D Studio MAX
- C++ programming
- Microsoft Win32 programming

This book requires the reader to have the following software:

- Microsoft Visual C++ 6.0
- 3D Studio MAX 3.1
- 3D Studio MAX SDK

Installing the 3D Studio MAX SDK

The 3D Studio MAX SDK comes on the standard MAX 3.1 CD-ROM. If you installed MAX without the SDK, you can install the SDK by running the standard MAX installation and choosing only the MAX SDK checkbox with all items under the MAX SDK category selected.

General SDK Information

The SDK will be installed into a subdirectory of your 3D Studio MAX directory named `<3dsmax path>\maxsdk\`. Within this directory are subdirectories that contain the SDK's header files, library files, help, and sample plug-in source code. The MAX SDK help file can be found in `<3dsmax path>\maxsdk\help\sdk.hlp`.

Much of the sample code that comes in the MAX SDK is source code to some of the standard plug-ins that come with MAX itself.

Plug-In Types

There are many plug-in types that can be used in 3D Studio MAX. This book only covers the ones that introduce new programming concepts in the MAX SDK. The plug-ins that are not covered can be created using very similar techniques to the examples in this book. The following is a list of the plug-in types that this book covers.

Utility Plug-Ins

Utility plug-ins will show up in the Utility Panel in MAX. This plug-in type is used to add generic functionality to MAX that will either extract, modify, or work on top of existing data. Chapter 13 shows how to create Utility plug-ins and introduces the geometry pipeline of MAX from a programming standpoint.

Object Plug-Ins

Object plug-ins are the foundation for creating new data objects in MAX. These plug-ins can procedurally or statically create new objects that can be accessed and modified by all of MAX. Chapter 14 shows an example of an Object plug-in that basically shows up as an orientation for game objects that can be placed in a game level. The concepts shown in this chapter can be used to create any plug-in object type.

Render Effects Plug-Ins

Render Effects plug-ins are post-process utilities that can manipulate the final rendering of an image that is output from MAX. The tutorials in Chapter 15 introduce this plug-in type and show details of the 2D side of MAX. This includes bitmap and G-Buffer access and manipulation.

Modifier Plug-Ins

Modifier plug-ins manipulate objects that exist in the scene. This plug-in type is very similar to Object plug-ins in design, but Object plug-ins create new data while Modifier plug-ins manipulate existing data.

MAXScript Extensions

MAXScript extensions are plug-ins that can add classes, functions, UI controls, and system variables to the MAXScript language.

Basic Data Types

The MAX SDK contains many classes and functions for working with basic data, such as math, color, and time. The following are some of the most used data classes in the MAX SDK.

Point3

The `Point3` class contains three floating-point data members: x, y, and z. This class represents a point in 3D space and many member functions and operators for working with a point in 3D space.

Matrix3

The `Matrix3` class is a 4 × 3 transformation matrix class used to represent translation, rotation, and scale in 3D space. Matrices are what MAX uses internally to store an object's transformation. This class contains many member functions and operators for working with 3D transformations.

Color

The `Color` class represents the red, green, and blue components of a color with floating-point numbers in the range of 0.0 to 1.0. The SDK also provides the `AColor` class, which also stores the alpha component of a color along with the red, green, and blue components.

TimeValue

A `TimeValue` is an alias for a 32-bit integer value but is used to represent time in ticks. A *tick* is 1/4800 of a second. MAX uses ticks to store all time representation internally because they are evenly divisible by the standard frame-per-second settings. The SDK provides many macros and functions for converting between time representations.

Summary

This chapter was an introduction to the 3D Studio MAX SDK and provided basic information about what plug-ins are and how the MAX SDK is structured.

The next chapter will show how to create a Utility plug-in that accesses scene data.

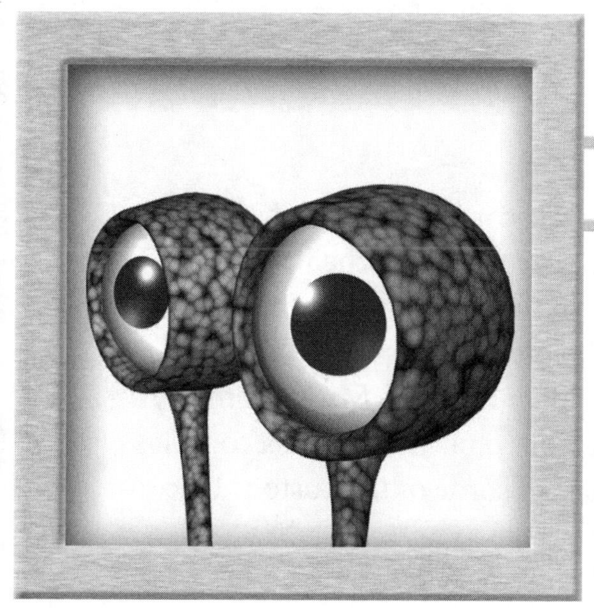

Creating a Scene Export Utility Plug-In

MAXSCRIPT

Chapter 13

This chapter explains the basic concepts behind Utility plug-ins and how scene objects are treated in the MAX SDK. You will create a Utility plug-in that generates text files with all the scene object names and their colors. You will also learn the advanced concepts of extracting data from the MAX geometry pipeline, and you will create a Utility plug-in to write a complex binary file. You will also make use of some of the custom UI controls provided with the SDK.

This chapter will cover the following topics:

- Using the 3D Studio MAX SDK App Wizard
- Creating Utility plug-ins
- Understanding the 3D Studio MAX Plug-In model
- Working with scene objects
- Understanding the geometry pipeline
- Writing a binary file

The MAX SDK App Wizard and Utility Plug-Ins

The *3D Studio MAX SDK App Wizard* is a plug-in for Microsoft Visual Studio that aids in the creation of MAX plug-ins. The wizard can create a skeleton plug-in of many of the MAX plug-in types. The App Wizard can be found on your hard drive in the `<3dsmax directory>\Maxsdk\Help\SDKAPWZ.ZIP` MAX installation directory. Just unzip the contents of this file into the `<Visual Studio directory>\Common\MSDev98\Bin\IDE` directory on your hard drive, and the wizard will show up in Visual Studio.

Utility plug-ins are found in the Utility tab of the Command Panel. A Utility plug-in is completely controlled by direct user interaction, with rollouts added to the Utility Panel or pop-up dialog boxes invoked from the Utility Panel.

Generating the Utility Plug-In Skeleton

Let's create the Utility plug-in skeleton:

1. In DevStudio, select File ➜ New from the main menu.
2. Select 3D Studio MAX Plug-in AppWizard R3.0.
3. Type in the Project name **ExpUtil**.
4. Click OK.
5. Select Utility from the list of types.
6. Click Next.
7. Enter **Plug-in Tutorials** in the Plug-In Category field. This is where the plug-in will be listed in the Configure Button Sets dialog in the Utility Panel.
8. Enter **Scene Export Utility** as the plug-in description. This will show up in Summary Info / Plug-In Info.
9. Click Next.
10. Enter your MAX SDK path. This path is specific to your machine, but it should be `<3dsmax directory>\maxsdk>`.
11. Enter your MAX plug-in path. It should be `<3dsmax directory\plugins>`.

12. Check the Add Source Code Comments checkbox.
13. Click Finish.
14. Click OK on the Information dialog box.

Take a look at the files generated from the File View; you should see the following:

`DllEntry.cpp` This contains functions that MAX will interface with to load the DLL.

`ExpUtil.cpp` Contains the core code for the plug-in.

`ExpUtil.def` A library definition file so MAX will know where to find the functions defined in `DllEntry.cpp`.

`ExpUtil.rc` Contains the resources for this plug-in.

`ExpUtil.h` Basic header file that includes the main SDK headers and declares GetString and the DLL's instance handle.

`Resource.h` Contains the resource definitions.

You now have a fully buildable Utility plug-in skeleton that contains all the code MAX needs to load and initialize your plug-in.

The 3D Studio MAX Plug-In Model

3D Studio MAX plug-ins are actually just Windows Dynamic Link Libraries (DLLs). A plug-in must contain at least the functions defined in `DllEntry.cpp` to be valid.

The first function defined in `DllEntry.cpp` is *DllMain*. This gets called when MAX loads and unloads the DLL, so it is a good place to put the initializations of the control libraries and store away the DLL's instance handle.

Let's take a look at what the App Wizard generates for us:

```
HINSTANCE hInstance;
int controlsInit = FALSE;

BOOL WINAPI DllMain(HINSTANCE hinstDLL, ULONG fdwReason,
                    LPVOID lpvReserved)
{
   // Hang on to this DLL's instance handle.
   hInstance = hinstDLL;
```

```
    if(!controlsInit)
    {
        controlsInit = TRUE;

        // Initialize MAX's custom controls
        InitCustomControls(hInstance);

        // Initialize Win95 controls
        InitCommonControls();
    }

    return (TRUE);
}
```

The functions declared after this are exported from the DLL. This means that another executable or DLL module that loads this DLL can easily locate and call these functions using the Win32 API. Also, for the exported functions, there is a corresponding definition file (`.def`). Contained in this definition file is a list of our exported functions along with numbers, or ordinal values, that tell where the function can be located in the DLL.

The following is a list of the exported functions from the DLL and their descriptions.

LibDescription The *LibDescription* function will return the description string you typed in when using the App Wizard. This is the basic code generated from the App Wizard:

```
__declspec( dllexport ) const TCHAR* LibDescription()
{
    return GetString(IDS_LIBDESCRIPTION);
}
```

LibNumberClasses A plug-in can contain more then one plug-in class (Class Descriptor). *LibNumberClasses* will return the number of Class Descriptors in this plug-in. Class Descriptors are described later. Your plug-in will only have one Class Descriptor so this will not need modification.

```
__declspec( dllexport ) int LibNumberClasses()
{
    return 1;
}
```

LibClassDesc The *LibClassDesc* function will return a Class Descriptor corresponding to the integer parameter passed.

```
__declspec( dllexport ) int LibClassDesc()
{
   return 1;
}
```

LibVersion The *LibVersion* function will return the 3DSMAX SDK version that the plug-in was compiled with. This allows 3DSMAX to filter out and not load obsolete plug-ins or plug-ins compiled with the wrong version of the SDK.

```
__declspec( dllexport ) ULONG LibVersion()
{
   return VERSION_3DSMAX;
}
```

GetString The *GetString* function is also defined in `DllEntry.cpps`. This function makes it easy to grab strings defined in your string table. All you have to do is pass it the string's ID, and it gives back the corresponding text, as shown here.

```
TCHAR *GetString(int id)
{
   static TCHAR buf[256];

   if (hInstance)
   {
      return LoadString(
         hInstance, id, buf, sizeof(buf)) ? buf : NULL;
   }
   return NULL;
}
```

A Look at *ExpUtil.cpp*

`ExpUtil.cpp` will contain the code for user interaction and do the work of exporting your scene. The second line of code in this file defines the Class ID that the plug-in will use, as shown here.

```
#define EXPUTIL_CLASS_ID   Class_ID(0x39d70798, 0x2b220e8b)
```

Class and Super Class IDs

A *Class ID* is a unique, randomly generated, eight-byte number that every plug-in class must have. Class IDs are used so that the MAX core and other plug-ins have a way (at run time) to determine what plug-in class it is working with. However, the *Super Class ID* is a predefined, eight-byte number that describes the category of the plug-in class. For example, all Utility plug-ins will have the same Super Class ID defined as UTILITY_CLASS_ID.

The next lines are the declaration of the class `ExpUtil` derived from `UtilityObj`.

```
static ExpUtil theExpUtil;
class ExpUtil : public UtilityObj
{
public:
   HWND          hPanel;
   IUtil        *iu;
   Interface    *ip;

   void RecursiveWriteNode(
      INode *pNode,
      FILE *stream,
      int tabs);

   void DoExport();

   void BeginEditParams(Interface *ip, IUtil *iu);
   void EndEditParams(Interface *ip, IUtil *iu);

   void Init(HWND hWnd);
   void Destroy(HWND hWnd);

   void DeleteThis() { }

   //Constructor/Destructor
   ExpUtil();
   ~ExpUtil();
};
```

This is the main class that the MAX core will use to interact with your plug-in. This class stores data members for the window handle that you will use for the rollout (`hPanel`). It also has data members for a pointer to the main interface class (`ip`) and a pointer to the utility interface (`iu`). Plug-in developers should implement most of their data and functions for Utility plug-ins in this class. After the class definition, there is a global declaration of an ExpUtil class (theExpUtil). This global variable will be handed to MAX in your Class Descriptor, which will be described later.

For the most part, the function definitions in the ExpUtil class are either empty or don't do much. They are explained here.

BeginEditParams This function gets called when the user open's a Utility plug-in from the Utility Panel. The BeginEditParams definition that is generated sets the iu and ip members of your class and adds a rollup page to the Command Panel, passing it your plug-in's instance handle, dialog resource, windows procedure, and the string that shows up on the rollout title, as shown here.

```
void ExpUtil::BeginEditParams(Interface *ip,IUtil *iu)
{
   this->iu = iu;
   this->ip = ip;
   hPanel = ip->AddRollupPage(
      hInstance,
      MAKEINTRESOURCE(IDD_PANEL),
      ExpUtilDlgProc,
      GetString(IDS_PARAMS),
      0);
}
```

EndEditParams *EndEditParams* is called when the user closes a plug-in from the Utility Panel. The *EndEditParams* definition that is generated will clear the iu, ip, and hPanel member variables to NULL and will delete the rollup page that was added to the Utility Panel, as shown here.

```
void ExpUtil::EndEditParams(Interface *ip,IUtil *iu)
{
   this->iu = NULL;
   this->ip = NULL;
   ip->DeleteRollupPage(hPanel);
   hPanel = NULL;
}
```

Class Descriptors

After the declaration of the ExpUtil class comes your plug-in's Class Descriptor, the ExpUtilClassDesc class. Class Descriptors are basically an interface that the MAX core will use to get information about a plug-in and create instances of it, or, in your case, return your plug-in's global instance. A Class Descriptor will return information like its Class ID, description, and name. There can be more than one class descriptor in a plug-in. The following is an example of what your class descriptor will look like:

```
class ExpUtilClassDesc : public ClassDesc2
{
public:
   int IsPublic() {
      return 1;
   }
   void* Create(BOOL loading = FALSE) {
      return &theExpUtil;
   }
   const TCHAR* ClassName() {
      return GetString(IDS_CLASS_NAME);
   }
   SClass_ID SuperClassID() {
      return UTILITY_CLASS_ID;
   }
   Class_ID ClassID() {
      return EXPUTIL_CLASS_ID;
   }
   const TCHAR* Category() {
      return GetString(IDS_CATEGORY);
   }
   const TCHAR* InternalName() {
      return _T("ExpUtil");
   }
   HINSTANCE HInstance() {
      return hInstance;
   }
};
```

The following is a list of the functions and descriptions of the class descriptor.

IsPublic The *IsPublic* function will let MAX know whether or not you want your plug-in to be visible to users. This should always return 1 or true.

Create The global instance of the plug-in's utility object (`theExpUtil`) is returned by the *Create* function. In some cases, a plug-in might want to dynamically create instances of the utility object, this is where it would be done.

ClassName *ClassName* returns what the string users will see in the Utility Panel plug-in lists.

SuperClassID *SuperClassID* is where the plug-in gives MAX the super class `UTILITY_CLASS_ID`. As described previously, MAX uses this to categorize the plug-in from a dynamic programming point of view.

ClassID Also described previously, *ClassID* is where you give MAX your unique Class ID.

Category *Category* returns the plug-in category string that you typed in when you used the App Wizard to create the plug-in skeleton.

InternalName *InternalName* is the name MAXScript will use to identify your plug-in. If you ever decide to localize your plug-in, you want to keep this out of the string table so scripts will work in all languages.

Hinstance *Hinstance* gives MAX your plug-in's instance handle.

Now, your plug-in implements a global instance of your Class Descriptor and a global function that other files can use to get a pointer to the Class Descriptor without knowing the details of your Class Descriptor, as shown here.

```
static ExpUtilClassDesc ExpUtilDesc;
ClassDesc2* GetExpUtilDesc() {return &ExpUtilDesc;}
```

Working with Scene Objects

Let's look at how to get scene data out of MAX and how your plug-in will handle user interaction.

Manipulating Strings

The MAX SDK contains a very useful class for storing and manipulating strings. Instead of using char pointers, you can simply use the macro TSTR to define your strings. This macro will change depending on whether Unicode is defined in your plug-in or not. If Unicode is not defined, the TSTR macro is replaced with `CStr`. If Unicode is defined, the TSTR macro is replaced with `WStr`. The two classes are identical in functionality, except `WStr` supports multi-byte character sets for localization. The string classes have some very useful functionality like automatic resizing, char pointer casting, char pointer assignment operators, and much more. An example is shown here.

```
TSTR str = _T("Constructor");
str += _T(" Append");
printf("%s\n", (char*)str);
```

Understanding Nodes

In the MAX SDK, scene objects are referred to as nodes. (They have a one-to-one correspondence.) Nodes contain information like the name, color, texture, and transformation of an object. Nodes are arranged in a parent-child hierarchy based on the scene root or root node. To get the root node, the `Interface` class provides the method *GetRootNode*. The class used for nodes in the SDK is named `INode` because when you work with nodes in a plug-in, you are actually just using an interface to them. The following is an example of how to get the root node from the interface:

```
// Get the root node
INode *pRootNode = ip->GetRootNode();
```

You can also test if a node is the root node by calling the *IsRootNode* member function of `INode`, as follows:

```
// Test if we have the root node
if(pNode->IsRootNode())
{
   //...
}
```

Traversing the Scene Hierarchy

You can easily traverse all nodes in the scene with a recursive function, starting by passing it the root node. The functions used to recursively traverse the scene are as follows:

INode::NumberOfChildren This member function will return the number of child nodes that a node has.

INode::GetChildNode This function is used to get child nodes from a node. You must pass this function a number from 0 to *NumberOfChildren* – 1 to successfully get a child node. The following is an example of how to use the *GetChildNode* function to recurse the node tree:

```
void Utility::RecurseScene(INode *pNode)
{
   // do something with pNode..

   // traverse child nodes
   for(int i = 0; i < pNode->NumberOfChildren(); i++)
      RecurseScene(pNode->GetChildNode(i));
}
theUtil.RecurseScene(ip->GetRootNode());
```

Filtering Nodes

If you want to filter certain scene object types, you can just test the Super ClassID of the object. To get an object's Super ClassID, you must first get an ObjectState. An *ObjectState* is the final product of evaluating the node's pipeline. For example, a sphere with modifiers will result in a geometric object with a Super ClassID of `GEOMOBJECT_CLASS_ID`. ObjectStates contain a pointer to the object that can be casted to the appropriate object class depending on its Super ClassID.

To evaluate a node's ObjectState, the node interface provides the function *EvalWorldState*. This function takes a time value as a parameter, which you will pass the current position of the time slider. You can retrieve the current time slider value by a call to *Interface::GetTime*. The following is an example of using the *GetTime* function in conjunction with evaluating an ObjectState:

```
ObjectState os = node->EvalWorldState(ip->GetTime());
```

To filter out objects by their Super ClassID, you can call the evaluated objects *SuperClassID* function as follows:

```
if(os.obj->SuperClassID() == GEOMOBJECT_CLASS_ID)
{
...
}
```

Now that you know how to traverse and filter nodes, you can start outputting the data you want to export. To keep this tutorial simple, you are only going to output a few properties of the nodes.

Adding User Interaction

3D Studio MAX was entirely created using Win32, therefore, all plug-ins must handle their user interfaces with Win32.

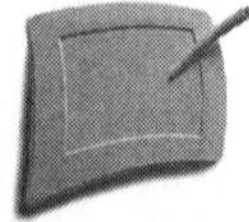

In some cases, it is possible to use MFC, but this is out of scope for this book.

In the Resource View, open up the IDD_PANEL dialog that was generated by the App Wizard and delete all the controls. Add some static text to the dialog with a description and your name. Now, add a button and change the caption to **Export** and change the ID to **IDC_DOEXPORT** (see Figure 13.1). Scale the height of your dialog to fit your controls but keep the width 108 units wide. This is the width that all rollouts used in the Command Panel should be.

Figure 13.1 *Rollout dialog resource*

In Win32, for every window, there must be a function that filters the user interaction. This is called a window or dialog procedure. This is basically just a global function that gets passed a handle to the window, the message, and two generic parameters that change depending on the message being sent. Luckily, the SDK App Wizard generated one for us named *ExpUtilDlgProc*. Inside this procedure is a big switch statement that is used to filter out messages that will be of use to us. In the case of the Utility plug-in, the only message you really care about is when the user clicks the Export button.

Windows messages that come from a control, in our case from a button, are usually sent in the form of a `WM_COMMAND` message. These messages contain the ID of the control in the low word of its `wParam` parameter. So, to know when the Export button is being pressed, you simply check if the low word is equal to `IDC_DOEXPORT` inside the `WM_COMMAND` case, as follows:

```
case WM_COMMAND:
// Filter out when the IDC_DOEXPORT button is hit.
if(LOWORD(wParam) == IDC_DOEXPORT)
{
   // Do the exporting here !
}
break;
```

From within the command filter code example shown here, you will call a member function of your `ExpUtil` class that will handle your button-pressed action (`DoExport`). In this member function, you will write code to display a Win32 Save As dialog box so the user can pick a file name to save the scene as when exporting. You will then write code to save scene data to this file. The function that does the actual work will be a recursive function similar to the *RecurseScene* function described earlier. Your recursive function will be called *RecursiveWriteNode*. It will be passed the following parameters: the standard pointer to a node, a file stream for writing, and an integer number for the recursion depth.

Listing 13.1 shows the main plug-in header file generated by the App Wizard. Take note of the headers being included in this file. You can access this code on the CD-ROM that accompanies this book in the file named ExpUtil.h.

LISTING 13.1: MAIN PLUG-IN HEADER FILE (*EXPUTIL.H*)

```
/**************************************************
 *<
   FILE: ExpUtil.h

   DESCRIPTION: Scene Export Utility

   CREATED BY: Simon Feltman

   HISTORY: Created: 3-14-2000

 *>   Copyright (c) 2000, All Rights Reserved.
 **************************************************/

#ifndef __EXPUTIL__H
#define __EXPUTIL__H

// Main include file for MAX plug-ins.
#include "Max.h"

// Contains resource defines for this dll
#include "resource.h"

// Contains the ClassDesc2 declaration
#include "iparamb2.h"

// Contains interfaces into some of the standard
//  plug-ins that ship with MAX
#include "istdplug.h"

// Utility plug-ins interface
//  (UtilityObj and IUtil classes)
#include "utilapi.h"
```

```
// Used to get resource strings from our string table
extern TCHAR *GetString(int id);

// Global instance handle of this dll
extern HINSTANCE hInstance;

#endif // __EXPUTIL__H
```

Open up the main plug-in file (`ExpUtil.cpp`), take a look at the code layout, and then make the changes shown in Listing 13.2. These code changes will use a recursive function to export the scene nodes name, the super class name, and the color.

LISTING 13.2: MAIN PLUG-IN FILE (*EXPUTIL.CPP*)

```
/**********************************************************
 *<
   FILE: ExpUtil.cpp

   DESCRIPTION: Scene Export Utility

   CREATED BY: Simon Feltman

   HISTORY: Created: 3-14-2000

 *>   Copyright (c) 2000, All Rights Reserved.
 **********************************************************/

#include "ExpUtil.h"

#define EXPUTIL_CLASS_ID Class_ID(0x39d70798, 0x2b220e8b)

// This function returns a string with num tabs
//  appended to it.
TSTR GetTabs(int num)
{
   TSTR tabs = _T("");
   for(int i = 0; i < num; i++)
      tabs += _T("\t");
   return tabs;
}
```

```
// Lookup for super class ID strings
TSTR GetSIDString(int sid)
{
   TSTR str = _T("");
   switch(sid)
   {
   case GEOMOBJECT_CLASS_ID:
      str = _T("Geometry");
      break;
   case CAMERA_CLASS_ID:
      str = _T("Camera");
      break;
   case LIGHT_CLASS_ID:
      str = _T("Light");
      break;
   case SHAPE_CLASS_ID:
      str = _T("Shape");
      break;
   case HELPER_CLASS_ID:
      str = _T("Helper");
      break;
   case SYSTEM_CLASS_ID:
      str = _T("System");
      break;
   case OSM_CLASS_ID:
      str = _T("Object Space Modifier");
      break;
   case WSM_CLASS_ID:
      str = _T("World Space Modifier");
      break;
   case WSM_OBJECT_CLASS_ID:
      str = _T("World Space Modifier Object");
      break;
   case MATERIAL_CLASS_ID:
      str = _T("Material");
      break;
   case TEXMAP_CLASS_ID:
      str = _T("Texture");
      break;
   case SOUNDOBJ_CLASS_ID:
      str = _T("Sound");
```

```
      break;
   }

   return str;
}

class ExpUtil : public UtilityObj
{
public:
   HWND         hPanel;
   IUtil       *iu;
   Interface   *ip;

   void RecursiveWriteNode(
      INode *pNode,
      FILE *stream,
      int tabs);

   void DoExport();

   void BeginEditParams(Interface *ip, IUtil *iu);
   void EndEditParams(Interface *ip, IUtil *iu);

   void Init(HWND hWnd);
   void Destroy(HWND hWnd);

   void DeleteThis() { }

   //Constructor/Destructor
   ExpUtil();
   ~ExpUtil();
};

static ExpUtil theExpUtil;

class ExpUtilClassDesc : public ClassDesc2
{
public:
   int IsPublic() {
      return 1;
   }
```

```
    void* Create(BOOL loading = FALSE) {
        return &theExpUtil;
    }
    const TCHAR* ClassName() {
        return GetString(IDS_CLASS_NAME);
    }
    SClass_ID SuperClassID() {
        return UTILITY_CLASS_ID;
    }
    Class_ID ClassID() {
        return EXPUTIL_CLASS_ID;
    }
    const TCHAR* Category() {
        return GetString(IDS_CATEGORY);
    }
    const TCHAR* InternalName() {
        return _T("ExpUtil");
    }
    HINSTANCE HInstance() {
        return hInstance;
    }
};

static ExpUtilClassDesc ExpUtilDesc;

ClassDesc2* GetExpUtilDesc() {
    return &ExpUtilDesc;
}

static BOOL CALLBACK ExpUtilDlgProc(
    HWND hWnd, UINT msg, WPARAM wParam, LPARAM lParam)
{
    switch(msg)
    {
    case WM_INITDIALOG:
        theExpUtil.Init(hWnd);
        break;

    case WM_DESTROY:
        theExpUtil.Destroy(hWnd);
        break;
```

```
   case WM_COMMAND:
      // Filter out when the IDC_DOEXPORT button is hit.
      if(LOWORD(wParam) == IDC_DOEXPORT)
         theExpUtil.DoExport();
      break;

   case WM_LBUTTONDOWN:
   case WM_LBUTTONUP:
   case WM_MOUSEMOVE:
      theExpUtil.ip->RollupMouseMessage(
         hWnd, msg, wParam, lParam);
      break;

   default:
      return FALSE;
   }
   return TRUE;
}


//--- ExpUtil ----------------------------------
ExpUtil::ExpUtil()
{
   iu = NULL;
   ip = NULL;
   hPanel = NULL;
}
ExpUtil::~ExpUtil() {}

void ExpUtil::BeginEditParams(Interface *ip,
                              IUtil *iu)
{
   this->iu = iu;
   this->ip = ip;
   hPanel = ip->AddRollupPage(
      hInstance,
      MAKEINTRESOURCE(IDD_PANEL),
      ExpUtilDlgProc,
      GetString(IDS_PARAMS),
      0);
}
```

```
void ExpUtil::EndEditParams(Interface *ip, IUtil *iu)
{
   this->iu = NULL;
   this->ip = NULL;
   ip->DeleteRollupPage(hPanel);
   hPanel = NULL;
}

void ExpUtil::Init(HWND hWnd) {}
void ExpUtil::Destroy(HWND hWnd) {}

void ExpUtil::RecursiveWriteNode(
   INode *pNode,
   FILE *stream,
   int tabs)
{
   // Build the output string as
   // "<tabs><node name> (<SuperClassID>) - <color>"
   TSTR str = GetTabs(tabs) + pNode->GetName() + _T(" (");

   // Find the super class identity
   ObjectState os = pNode->EvalWorldState(ip->GetTime());
   if(os.obj)
      str += GetSIDString(os.obj->SuperClassID());
    str += _T(")");

   COLORREF col = pNode->GetWireColor();

   fprintf(stream, "%s - R:%d G:%d B:%d\n", str.data(),
      GetRValue(col), GetGValue(col), GetBValue(col));

   // recurse children
   for(int i = 0; i < pNode->NumberOfChildren(); i++) {
      RecursiveWriteNode(
         pNode->GetChildNode(i),
         stream,
         tabs+1);
   }
}
```

```
// Function is called when the DoExport button is hit.
void ExpUtil::DoExport()
{
   // Fill an OPENFILENAME structure used to popup a
   //  SaveAs dialog
   OPENFILENAME ofn;
   TCHAR   fname[MAX_PATH] = _T("");

   memset(&ofn, 0, sizeof(OPENFILENAME));
   ofn.lStructSize = sizeof(OPENFILENAME);
   ofn.hwndOwner = ip->GetMAXHWnd();
   ofn.hInstance = hInstance;
   ofn.lpstrFile = fname;
   ofn.nMaxFile = MAX_PATH;
   ofn.lpstrFilter = _T("Text Files (*.txt)\0*.txt\0All ~CA Files
(*.*)\0*.*\0\0");
   ofn.nFilterIndex = 1;
   ofn.Flags = OFN_OVERWRITEPROMPT;

   // Popup the SaveAs dialog and get file name,
   //  return if the user cancelled
   if(!GetSaveFileName(&ofn))
      return;

   // open a file stream object for writing
   FILE *stream = fopen(fname, "wt");
   if(!stream)
   {
      MessageBox(hPanel, "Couldn't open file for writing.",
         NULL, MB_OK);
      return;
   }

   // Recursively go through all scene nodes starting at
   //  the root node, also start out at tab level of 0
   RecursiveWriteNode(ip->GetRootNode(), stream, 0);

   fclose(stream);
```

The Geometry Pipeline

Now that you have learned how to traverse the scene hierarchy and work with scene objects in their most basic representation (nodes), you will be introduced to the underlying complexity of the MAX geometry pipeline.

A Look at Objects

In the MAX SDK, *nodes* are placeholders for what the artist sees. For instance, two nodes will have a different name, color, and position, but both reference the same geometry (see Figure 13.2). This geometry is represented in the MAX SDK with the `Object` class and its derived classes. To an artist, this is what is known as an *instance*. When the artist modifies the geometry on one of the nodes, it modifies the referenced geometric object and tells all the other nodes referencing the object to update their display. This is because the node itself stores the name, color, and position and has a reference to the geometric object.

Imagine this concept as a client-server architecture, where a node is the client, and an object is the server: All important data is stored on one server and more than one client can view and modify its data. Objects in MAX contain many levels of derivation to make it easy for the programmer to work with general categories or specifics of an object type.

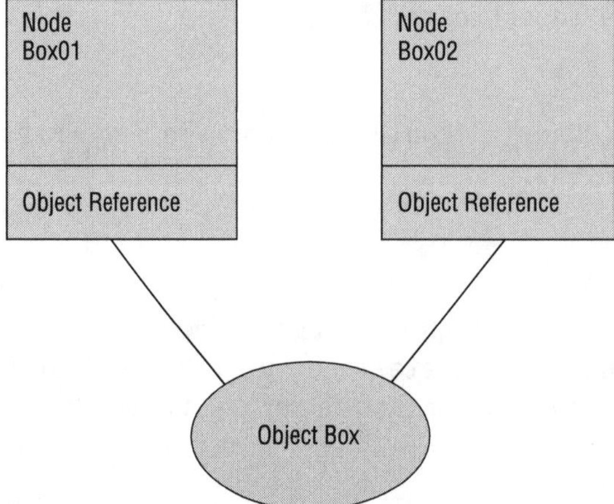

Figure 13.2 *Node object references*

In the next tutorial, you will be working with the following object classes:

Object `Object` is the base class for anything you can create via the Create Panel in MAX. The sub-classes of `Object` that you will be using are `GeomObject`, `HelperObject`, `CameraObject`, and `LightObject`.

GeomObject `GeomObject` is derived from `Object` and is the base class for any geometric object. This includes objects that get converted to triangle-based geometry, patch-based geometry, shapes, particles, and NURBS.

TriObject `TriObject` is derived from `GeomObject` and is the class that represents triangle-based geometry. For the most part, we will just retrieve the actual mesh from a `TriObject` and work with that.

HelperObject Classes derived from `HelperObject` are used for objects that help the artist work with the scene and usually don't show up in the final rendering. Examples would be compass, tape, or dummy objects.

CameraObject `CameraObject` is the base class for any camera object. This class contains many general functions for getting camera information, such as field of view.

LightObject `LightObject` is the base class for any light object and implements many general functions for any type of light.

Working with Objects

Next, you will actually get the objects from a node. In the previous chapter, you learned how to get an object state from a node. This is the basis we will use to test at run-time the type of object and to cast the object pointer to the appropriate class.

Casting Objects

As previously described, Class IDs can be used for run-time testing of object types or classes. You will now use Class IDs to test whether an object is appropriate for casting to a certain type. The `Object` class contains a function for doing this called *CanConvertToType*. You pass this function a Class ID, and it will return true if the object has the ability to be cast to the specified class. The function will return false if the object cannot be cast to the specified class. You can use the following utility function, *IsNodeValid*, for ease of testing object classes:

```
bool IsNodeValid(INode *pNode, int cid)
{
```

```
      // don't use root or hidden nodes.
      if(pNode->IsRootNode() || pNode->IsNodeHidden())
         return false;

      Object *obj = pNode->EvalWorldState(0).obj;
      if(obj && obj->CanConvertToType(Class_ID(cid, 0)))
         return true;

      return false;
   }
```

You can use the *IsNodeValid* function in a recursive scene iterator to filter out an object and cast it. After checking it with the *IsNodeValid* function, you can use the cast object, as shown here:

```
void Utility::RecurseScene(INode *pNode)
{
   if(IsNodeValid(pNode, LIGHT_CLASS_ID))
   {
      // evaluate the object then cast to a LightObject
      LightObject *light = (LightObject*)
         pNode->EvalWorldState(ip->GetTime()).obj;

      // do something with light ...
   }

   // traverse child nodes
   for(int i = 0; i < pNode->NumberOfChildren(); i++)
      RecurseScene(pNode->GetChildNode(i));
}
theUtil.RecurseScene(ip->GetRootNode());
```

Object Transformations

Object transformations are stored in the nodes. This allows reference-based systems to work because the node itself holds the transformation while it poles its geometric data from an `Object`. To get a node transformation, the `INode` class contains the function *GetObjectTM* for getting a `Matrix3` object.

Camera Objects

To retrieve a camera object, first test whether the node has the ability to cast to a camera and then cast it. We will only be using the *GetFOV* member function of `CameraObject` as follows:

```
if(IsNodeValid(node, SIMPLE_CAM_CLASS_ID))
{
   CameraObject *cam =
      (CameraObject*)node->EvalWorldState(time).obj;
   float fov = cam->GetFOV(ip->GetTime());
}
```

Light Objects

You can retrieve a light object the same way that you retrieve any other object. In this tutorial, you will use only Omni lights and will retrieve the lights' near and far attenuations along with the lights' colors. The following code example shows how to retrieve a light and get its attenuation and color values:

```
LightObject *light =
   (LightObject*)node->EvalWorldState(ip->GetTime()).obj;

// get the lights color and attenuation values
Point3 rgb = light->GetRGBColor(time);
float nearAtten = light->GetAtten(time, LIGHT_ATTEN_START);
float farAtten = light->GetAtten(time, LIGHT_ATTEN_END);

// get the position of the light
Matrix3 tm = node->GetObjectTM(time);
Point3 pos = tm.GetRow(3);
```

Triangle-Based Objects

Triangle-based objects are one of the main types of objects MAX uses to draw in the viewport and in the renderer. Triangle-based objects are represented in the MAX SDK by the class `TriObject`, which is derived from `GeomObject`. From a `TriObject`, you can retrieve a mesh, which will contain vertex, face, vertex color, texture coordinates, and so on, and is represented by the class `Mesh`. To retrieve a mesh, the `TriObject` class contains a method called *GetRenderMesh*, in which you pass a time, a node, a view, and a Boolean that lets you know if you should delete the mesh. The function is declared as follows:

```
Mesh* GetRenderMesh(
   TimeValue t,
   INode *inode,
   View &view,
   BOOL& needDelete);
```

Since you are not writing a renderer and just want the mesh, you can pass the view parameter a null view, which you can define as follows:

```
class NullView : public View
{
public:
   Point2 ViewToScreen(Point3 p) {
      return Point2(p.x,p.y);
   }
   NullView() {
      worldToView.IdentityMatrix();
      screenW = 640.0f; screenH = 480.0f;
   }
};
static NullView nullView;
```

Now that you have all the necessary parameters needed to get a mesh, let's put it all together by first testing if you have a valid `TriObject`; then casting the object; and finally, getting the mesh:

```
if(IsNodeValid(node, TRIOBJ_CLASS_ID))
{
   BOOL needDel = FALSE;
   ObjectState os = node->EvalWorldState(ip->GetTime());
   Mesh *mesh = ((TriObject*)os.obj)->GetRenderMesh(
      ip->GetTime(), node, nullView, needDel);

   // do something with the mesh ! ...

   // delete mesh if needDel is true
   if(needDel) mesh->DeleteThis();
}
```

Working with the Mesh *Class*

Now that you know how to retrieve a Mesh object, let's take a look at how meshes are represented in the MAX SDK. A mesh consists of vertices and faces along with other data such as color vertices and texture coordinates. Vertices on a mesh are defined by an array of `Point3` objects. The `Point3` class contains three float values defined as x, y, and z. The `Point3` class not only contains many of the standard math functions like addition and subtraction of points but also has many useful functions like getting the length of a vector or normalizing the vector.

You can find the number of vertices in a mesh by calling the *getNumVerts* member function or by using the `numVerts` member variable. To get an actual `Point3` from a mesh, you can use the `verts` `Point3` array data member or use the *getVert* member function and pass it the index of the vertex you want to retrieve. You can step through all the vertices in a mesh as follows:

```
for(int i = 0; i < mesh->numVerts; i++)
{
   Point3 pnt = mesh->getVert(i);
   // do something with this point...
}
```

The faces on a mesh are represented by an array of `Face` objects defined as the member variable `faces` in the `Mesh` class. The `Face` class contains a three-integer array, of which each element is an index into the `Mesh` class's array of vertices (see Figure 13.3). The number of faces on a mesh can be retrieved with the `Mesh` class's `numFaces` integer data member or from the *getNumFaces* member function. To get a face from a mesh, you can either use the `faces` data member or the *getFace* member function of the `Mesh` class.

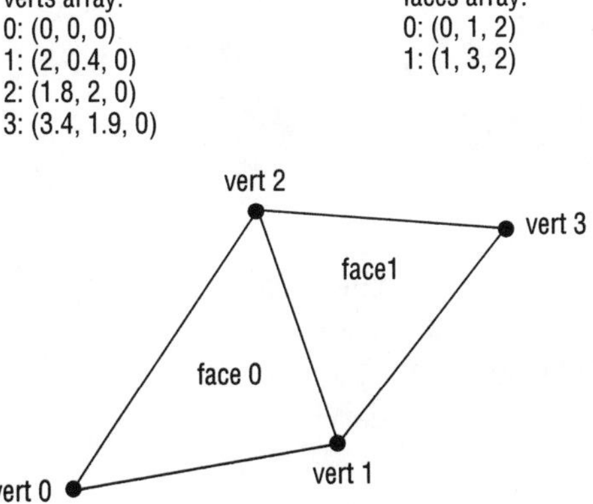

Figure 13.3 *Vertex and face representation on a mesh*

Texture coordinates are represented the exact same way as vertices and faces are. The members for texture coordinates are `numTVerts` for getting the number of texture coordinates, and the `tVerts` array stores the coordinates. The data member for texture faces is `tvFace`, which is an array that is the same size as the `mesh faces` array. However when iterating the `tvFace` array, make sure that `numTVerts` is greater than zero. If `numTVerts` is zero, the object does not have mapping information.

Writing a Binary File

For this example, you will be writing to a binary file rather than developing some complex system for writing a text file. Then, if you create a file viewer, you won't have to spend time writing a parser for the text file. For the most part, binary files are easier to read and write in an application, but you don't get the ability to view the file with a text editor.

To develop a binary file format, you first must devise a file header structure that contains a magic number and any global data. The magic number guarantees that you have opened a file of the correct type when reading it. To write data and structures to a binary file, you can simply call the ANSI C *fwrite* function and pass it a pointer to the data. The following code is an example of a header structure and writing it to a binary file:

```
// file header structure
struct FileHeader
{
   unsigned int magic;
   int numInts;
};

// create the file header
FileHeader hdr;
hdr.magic = 0xdeadbeef;
hdr.numInts = 10;
int arr[10];

// open a binary file and write the header
FILE *stream = fopen(fname, "wb");
fwrite(&hdr, sizeof(FileHeader), 1, stream);
fwrite(arr, sizeof(int), 10, stream);
fclose(stream);
```

Defining the Binary Format

Now that you know how to extract detailed object information from MAX and how binary file input and output works, let's define a file format called MSF, or Mesh Scene Format. This is a binary file that holds hard mesh information along with lights, cameras, and dummy objects. Start a new text file and type all the code shown in Listing 13.3. You can access this code on the CD-ROM that accompanies this book in the file named `MSF.h`. Then, add this file to your project by right-clicking anywhere in the text and choosing Insert File into Project ➜ ExpUtil.

Listing 13.3: Mesh Scene Format Header File (*MSF.h*)

```
// ===========================================================
// MSF.h  -  Mesh Scene Format
// Copyright ©2000, Simon Feltman
// -----------------------------------------------------------
#ifndef __MSF_H__
#define __MSF_H__

#define MSF_VERSION 1
const unsigned long msf_magic =
   (('m'<<24) | ('s'<<16) | ('f'<<8) | MSF_VERSION);

// ===========================================================
struct MSF_Header
{
   unsigned long magic;

   int meshOfs;  // offset of meshes from beginning of file
   int meshCnt;  // count of mesh objects

   int dummyOfs;  // offset of dummy objects
   int dummyCnt;  // number of dummy objects

   int lightOfs;  // offset of lights
   int lightCnt;  // number of lights

   int cameraOfs; // offset of cameras
   int cameraCnt; // number of cameras
};
```

```
/* ==========================================================
 Meshes will be stored as follows:
 - Mesh header
 - Vertices (an array vertices numVerts long)
 - Texture Verts (an array of tverts numTVerts long)
 - Normals (an array of vectors numNormals long)
 - Faces (array of faces numFaces long)
*/

typedef float Vertex[3];
typedef float Vector[3];
typedef float TexVtx[2];

struct MSF_Face
{
   int verts[3];   // indices into the list of vertices
   int tverts[3];  // indices into the list of texture verts
   int normals[3]; // indices into the list of normals
};

struct MSF_Mesh
{
   char name[32];          // node name
   char texture[256];      // texture file name
   float tm[4][4];  // matrix transformation
   unsigned long rgb;      // color

   int  numVerts;
   int  numTVerts;
   int  numNormals;
   int  numFaces;
};

// ==========================================================
struct MSF_Dummy
{
   char name[32];
   float tm[4][4];
};
```

```
// ============================================================
struct MSF_Light
{
   char name[32];
   float pos[3];
   float nearAtten;
   float farAtten;
   unsigned long rgb;
};

// ============================================================
struct MSF_Camera
{
   char name[32];
   float tm[4][4];
   float fov;
};

#endif //__MSF_H__
```

Implementing the Binary Exporter

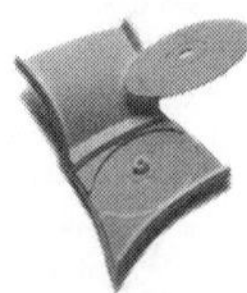

Now that you have the file format defined, you can modify the ExpUtil.cpp file and add all the code necessary to extract the correct data and write it to the binary file, as shown in Listing 13.4. You can access this code on the CD-ROM that accompanies this book in the file named ExpUtil.cpp.

Listing 13.4: Main Plug-In File (*ExpUtil.cpp*)

```
// ============================================================
// ExpUtil.cpp
// Scene Export Utility
// Copyright ©2000, Simon Feltman
// ------------------------------------------------------------
#include "ExpUtil.h"
#include "MSF.h"

#define EXPUTIL_CLASS_ID Class_ID(0x39d70798, 0x2b220e8b)

void PointToArr(const Point3 &pnt, float arr[3])
```

```
{
   arr[0] = pnt.x;
   arr[1] = pnt.y;
   arr[2] = pnt.z;
}

// =========================================================
class ExpUtil : public UtilityObj
{
public:
   HWND          hPanel;
   IUtil        *iu;
   Interface    *ip;

   int RecursiveWriteMesh(
      INode *node,
      FILE *stream,
      TimeValue time);

   int RecursiveWriteDummy(
      INode *node,
      FILE *stream,
      TimeValue time);

   int RecursiveWriteLight(
      INode *node,
      FILE *stream,
      TimeValue time);

   int RecursiveWriteCamera(
      INode *node,
      FILE *stream,
      TimeValue time);

   void DoExport();

   void BeginEditParams(Interface *ip, IUtil *iu);
   void EndEditParams(Interface *ip, IUtil *iu);

   void Init(HWND hWnd);
```

```
   void Destroy(HWND hWnd);

   void DeleteThis() { }

   //Constructor/Destructor
   ExpUtil();
   ~ExpUtil();
};

static ExpUtil theExpUtil;

// ========================================================
class ExpUtilClassDesc : public ClassDesc2
{
public:
   int IsPublic() {
      return 1;
   }
   void* Create(BOOL loading = FALSE) {
      return &theExpUtil;
   }
   const TCHAR* ClassName() {
      return GetString(IDS_CLASS_NAME);
   }
   SClass_ID SuperClassID() {
      return UTILITY_CLASS_ID;
   }
   Class_ID ClassID() {
      return EXPUTIL_CLASS_ID;
   }
   const TCHAR* Category() {
      return GetString(IDS_CATEGORY);
   }
   const TCHAR* InternalName() {
      return _T("ExpUtil");
   }
   HINSTANCE HInstance() {
      return hInstance;
   }
};
```

```
static ExpUtilClassDesc ExpUtilDesc;

ClassDesc2* GetExpUtilDesc() {
   return &ExpUtilDesc;
}

// ==========================================================
// For use with GetRenderMesh
class NullView : public View
{
public:
   Point2 ViewToScreen(Point3 p) {
      return Point2(p.x,p.y);
   }
   NullView() {
      worldToView.IdentityMatrix();
      screenW = 640.0f; screenH = 480.0f;
   }
};
static NullView nullView;

// ==========================================================
bool IsNodeValid(INode *node, int cid)
{
   // don't use root or hidden nodes.
   if(node->IsRootNode() || node->IsNodeHidden())
      return false;

   Object *obj = node->EvalWorldState(0).obj;
   if(obj && obj->CanConvertToType(Class_ID(cid, 0)))
      return true;

   return false;
}

// ==========================================================
static BOOL CALLBACK ExpUtilDlgProc(
   HWND hWnd, UINT msg, WPARAM wParam, LPARAM lParam)
{
   switch(msg)
   {
```

```
    case WM_INITDIALOG:
       theExpUtil.Init(hWnd);
       break;

    case WM_DESTROY:
       theExpUtil.Destroy(hWnd);
       break;

    case WM_COMMAND:
       // Filter out when the IDC_DOEXPORT button is hit.
       if(LOWORD(wParam) == IDC_DOEXPORT)
          theExpUtil.DoExport();
       break;

    case WM_LBUTTONDOWN:
    case WM_LBUTTONUP:
    case WM_MOUSEMOVE:
       theExpUtil.ip->RollupMouseMessage(
          hWnd, msg, wParam, lParam);
       break;

    default:
       return FALSE;
    }
    return TRUE;
}

// ============================================================
ExpUtil::ExpUtil()
{
   iu = NULL;
   ip = NULL;
   hPanel = NULL;
}
ExpUtil::~ExpUtil() {}

// ============================================================
void ExpUtil::BeginEditParams(Interface *ip,
                              IUtil *iu)
{
```

```
   this->iu = iu;
   this->ip = ip;
   hPanel = ip->AddRollupPage(
      hInstance,
      MAKEINTRESOURCE(IDD_PANEL),
      ExpUtilDlgProc,
      GetString(IDS_PARAMS),
      0);
}

// ============================================================
void ExpUtil::EndEditParams(Interface *ip, IUtil *iu)
{
   this->iu = NULL;
   this->ip = NULL;
   ip->DeleteRollupPage(hPanel);
   hPanel = NULL;
}

// ============================================================
void ExpUtil::Init(HWND hWnd) {}
void ExpUtil::Destroy(HWND hWnd) {}

// ============================================================
// Function will recurse all nodes filtering only meshes
int ExpUtil::RecursiveWriteMesh(
   INode *node,
   FILE *stream,
   TimeValue time)
{
   int count = 0;

   // Filter out geometry objects.
   if(IsNodeValid(node, TRIOBJ_CLASS_ID))
   {
     // get a snapshot of the same mesh the renderer uses
      BOOL needDel = FALSE;
      ObjectState os = node->EvalWorldState(time);
      Mesh *mesh = ((TriObject*)os.obj)->GetRenderMesh(
         time, node, nullView, needDel);
```

```
MSF_Mesh msfMesh;
memset(&msfMesh, 0, sizeof(MSF_Mesh));

strncpy(msfMesh.name, node->GetName(), sizeof(msfMesh.name));
msfMesh.rgb = node->GetWireColor();

msfMesh.numVerts = mesh->getNumVerts();
msfMesh.numTVerts = mesh->getNumTVerts();
msfMesh.numFaces = mesh->getNumFaces();

// write the mesh header
fwrite(&msfMesh, sizeof(MSF_Mesh), 1, stream);

// write vertices
for(int i = 0; i < msfMesh.numVerts; i++)
{
   Vertex vtx;
   Point3 pnt = mesh->getVert(i);
   vtx[0] = pnt.x; vtx[1] = pnt.y; vtx[2] = pnt.z;
   fwrite(vtx, sizeof(Vertex), 1, stream);
}

// write texture vertices
for(i = 0; i < msfMesh.numTVerts; i++)
{
   TexVtx tv;
   UVVert uvw = mesh->getTVert(i);
   tv[0] = uvw.x; tv[1] = uvw.y;
   fwrite(tv, sizeof(TexVtx), 1, stream);
}

// write faces
for(i = 0; i < msfMesh.numFaces; i++)
{
   MSF_Face msfFace;
   memset(&msfFace, 0, sizeof(MSF_Face));

   msfFace.verts[0] = mesh->faces[i].v[0];
   msfFace.verts[1] = mesh->faces[i].v[1];
   msfFace.verts[2] = mesh->faces[i].v[2];
```

```
            if(msfMesh.numTVerts > 0)
            {
               msfFace.tverts[0] = mesh->tvFace[i].t[0];
               msfFace.tverts[1] = mesh->tvFace[i].t[1];
               msfFace.tverts[2] = mesh->tvFace[i].t[2];
            }

            fwrite(&msfFace, sizeof(MSF_Face), 1, stream);
         }

         count = 1;
      }

      // recurse children
      for(int i = 0; i < node->NumberOfChildren(); i++)
      {
         count += RecursiveWriteMesh(
            node->GetChildNode(i),
            stream, time);
      }

      return count;
   }

   // ===========================================================
   int ExpUtil::RecursiveWriteDummy(
      INode *node,
      FILE *stream,
      TimeValue time)
   {
      int count = 0;

      // Filter out dummy objects
      if(IsNodeValid(node, DUMMY_CLASS_ID))
      {
         MSF_Dummy msfDummy;
         memset(&msfDummy, 0, sizeof(MSF_Light));

         strncpy(msfDummy.name,
            node->GetName(),
```

```
         sizeof(msfDummy.name));

      Matrix3 tm = node->GetObjectTM(time);
      MatrixToArr(tm, msfDummy.tm);

      fwrite(&msfDummy, sizeof(MSF_Dummy), 1, stream);
      count = 1;
   }

   // recurse children
   for(int i = 0; i < node->NumberOfChildren(); i++)
   {
      count += RecursiveWriteDummy(
         node->GetChildNode(i),
         stream, time);
   }

   return count;
}

// ============================================================
int ExpUtil::RecursiveWriteLight(
   INode *node,
   FILE *stream,
   TimeValue time)
{
   int count = 0;

   // Filter out light objects
   if(IsNodeValid(node, OMNI_LIGHT_CLASS_ID))
   {
      MSF_Light msfLight;
      memset(&msfLight, 0, sizeof(MSF_Light));
      strncpy(msfLight.name,
         node->GetName(),
         sizeof(msfLight.name));

      LightObject *light =
         (LightObject*)node->EvalWorldState(time).obj;
```

```
        Point3 pnt = light->GetRGBColor(time);
        msfLight.rgb = RGB(pnt.x, pnt.y, pnt.z);
        msfLight.nearAtten =
            light->GetAtten(time, LIGHT_ATTEN_START);
        msfLight.farAtten  =
            light->GetAtten(time, LIGHT_ATTEN_END);

        // convert vertex from 3dsmax format.
        Matrix3 tm = node->GetObjectTM(time);
        PointToArr(tm.GetRow(3), msfLight.pos);

        fwrite(&msfLight, sizeof(MSF_Light), 1, stream);
        count = 1;
    }

    // recurse children
    for(int i = 0; i < node->NumberOfChildren(); i++)
    {
        count += RecursiveWriteLight(
            node->GetChildNode(i),
            stream, time);
    }

    return count;
}

// ==========================================================
int ExpUtil::RecursiveWriteCamera(
    INode *node,
    FILE *stream,
    TimeValue time)
{
    int count = 0;

    // Filter out camera objects
    if(IsNodeValid(node, SIMPLE_CAM_CLASS_ID))
    {
        MSF_Camera msfCam;
        memset(&msfCam, 0, sizeof(MSF_Camera));
        strncpy(msfCam.name, node->GetName(), sizeof(msfCam.name));
```

```
      CameraObject *cam = (CameraObject*)node->EvalWorldState
(time).obj;
      msfCam.fov = cam->GetFOV(time);

      // convert vertex from 3dsmax format.
      Matrix3 tm = node->GetObjectTM(time);
      MatrixToArr(tm, msfCam.tm);

      fwrite(&msfCam, sizeof(MSF_Camera), 1, stream);
      count = 1;
   }

   // recurse children
   for(int i = 0; i < node->NumberOfChildren(); i++)
   {
      count += RecursiveWriteCamera(
         node->GetChildNode(i),
         stream, time);
   }

   return count;
}

// ===========================================================
// Function is called when the DoExport button is hit.
void ExpUtil::DoExport()
{
   // Fill an OPENFILENAME structure used to popup a
   //  SaveAs dialog
   OPENFILENAME ofn;
   TCHAR   fname[MAX_PATH] = _T("");

   memset(&ofn, 0, sizeof(OPENFILENAME));
   ofn.lStructSize = sizeof(OPENFILENAME);
   ofn.hwndOwner = ip->GetMAXHWnd();
   ofn.hInstance = hInstance;
   ofn.lpstrFile = fname;
   ofn.nMaxFile = MAX_PATH;
   ofn.lpstrFilter = _T("Mesh Scene Format (*.msf)\0*.msf\0All
Files (*.*)\0*.*\0\0");
```

```
ofn.nFilterIndex = 1;
ofn.Flags = OFN_OVERWRITEPROMPT;

// Popup the SaveAs dialog and get file name,
//  return if the user cancelled
if(!GetSaveFileName(&ofn))
   return;

// open a file stream object for writing
FILE *stream = fopen(fname, "wb");
if(!stream)
{
   MessageBox(hPanel, "Couldn't open file for writing.",
      NULL, MB_OK);
   return;
}

MSF_Header hdr;
memset(&hdr, 0, sizeof(MSF_Header));
hdr.magic = msf_magic;

// Move file pointer passed header.
fseek(stream, sizeof(MSF_Header), SEEK_SET);

// Store the mesh offset and write meshes.
hdr.meshOfs = ftell(stream);
hdr.meshCnt = RecursiveWriteMesh(
   ip->GetRootNode(), stream, ip->GetTime());

// Store the dummy offset and write dummies.
hdr.dummyOfs = ftell(stream);
hdr.dummyCnt = RecursiveWriteDummy(
   ip->GetRootNode(), stream, ip->GetTime());

// Store the light offset and write lights.
hdr.lightOfs = ftell(stream);
hdr.lightCnt = RecursiveWriteLight(
   ip->GetRootNode(), stream, ip->GetTime());

// Store the camera offset and write cameras.
```

```
    hdr.cameraOfs = ftell(stream);
    hdr.cameraCnt = RecursiveWriteCamera(
       ip->GetRootNode(), stream, ip->GetTime());

    // Move file pointer back to the beginning of file
    // and write the header.
    fseek(stream, 0, SEEK_SET);
    fwrite(&hdr, sizeof(MSF_Header), 1, stream);

    fclose(stream);
}
```

Summary

In this chapter, you learned some of the details about how objects are represented in the MAX SDK. You also learned how to type check objects and cast them to their appropriate type. You then moved on to working with cameras, lights, and helper objects. You were also introduced to the details of the `Mesh` class.

We focused on an introductory use of 3D Studio MAX SDK by creating a simple export Utility plug-in. Thanks to the SDK App Wizard, you were able to jump right into the programming without going through the pains of creating a plug-in project from scratch. From the generated skeleton, you were able to learn the basics of the main classes used in a Utility plug-in.

After understanding the basics of your Utility plug-in foundation, you jumped right into using the SDK to manipulate strings, retrieve scene information, and add user interaction to your utility.

In the next chapter, you will move on to learning about the architecture of MAX by creating an actual Geometry Object plug-in.

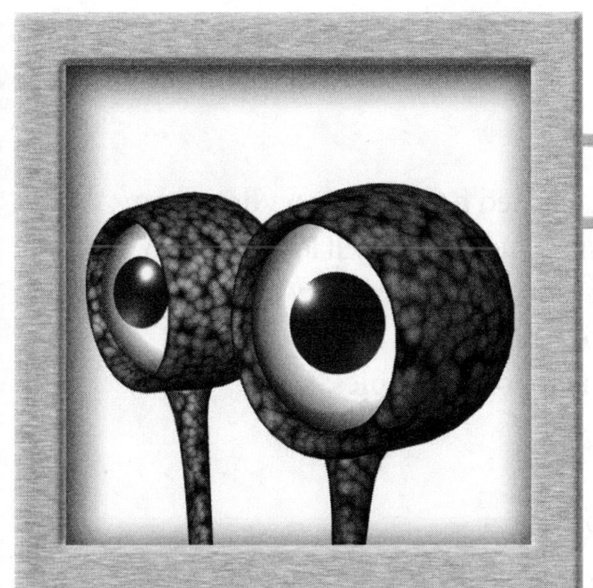

Object Plug-Ins

MAXSCRIPT

Chapter 14

In the previous chapter, you learned how to extract data from existing MAX objects. In this chapter, you will learn how to implement new object classes that add geometry to the pipeline and get saved along with the MAX scene files.

In this chapter, we'll cover the following topics:

- Creating parameter blocks
- Using the parameter map system
- Implementing helper objects

Parameter Blocks

Parameter blocks are a fundamental concept in the object plug-in paradigm. A *parameter block* is basically a storage class for an object's parameters. These blocks of data can hold multiple animatable parameters that automatically get loaded and saved in MAX scene files. The parameters are accessible through a metadata (generic data) style of API that will allow for automatic exposure to other parts of MAX, such as Track View, Schematic View, and MAXScript. This document only describes the second version of parameter blocks (ParamBlock2).

Creating a Parameter Block

To create a parameter block, you must first create a *parameter block descriptor*, which describes all the parameters you will use. A parameter block descriptor can be created with the `ParamBlockDesc2` class. The constructor for this class has the ability to take a variable number of arguments, allowing multiple parameters to be described using only one constructor. The `ParamBlockDesc2` constructor is defined as follows:

```
ParamBlockDesc2(
   BlockID ID,
   TCHAR* int_name,
   int local_name,
   ClassDesc2* cd,
   BYTE flags,
   ...);
```

ParamBlockDesc2 *Constructor Parameters*

The following are the required parameters that you must pass to the `ParamBlockDesc2` constructor.

BlockID ID This is an integer ID used to distinguish parameter blocks for a plug-in that uses more than one block. This should usually be 0 for your first block, 1 for your second, and so on.

TCHAR* int_name This is the non-localized string name for the parameter block, usually something like "params".

Int local_name This parameter should be passed a string resource ID that is the localized name of the parameter block.

*ClassDesc2 *cd* The `ClassDesc2` class maintains a list of parameter block descriptors. This is the class descriptor that our parameter block descriptor will be added to.

BYTE flags Place a combination of any flag you wish to use for the parameter block here. There are flags for things like letting the parameter block know that you will be using an automatic user interface management. Please see the official MAX SDK documentation for a complete list of flags.

Optional Arguments

The optional arguments allow you to add as many parameters to the block descriptor as you wish. The required parameter ordering for optional arguments are defined as follows.

ParamID id This is a position independent integer identifier for the parameter.

TCHAR* internal_name This is the non-localized name of this parameter. You will use this name to access this parameter through MAXScript.

ParamType type This is the data types that this parameter will store. There are many data types that you can use for parameters, including types like integers, real numbers, strings, points, colors, and many more. For a complete list of parameter types, please see the MAX SDK documentation.

[**int table_size**] If the parameter type is defined as an array, you need to use this specific parameter as the initial size of the array.

Int flags Specify flags here to tell the parameter how you want it to behave. There are flags that can do anything through MAXScript from making the parameter animatable to making the parameter read-only. For a complete list of parameter flags, please see the MAX SDK documentation.

int local_name_res_ID This parameter should be passed a string resource ID that is the localized name of the parameter.

Using the ParamBlockDesc2 *Constructor*

To use the `ParamBlockDesc2` constructor, you must at least pass the required parameters and optionally add parameter definitions. After the definition of a parameter in the constructor and at the end of the variable arguments list, you must supply the key word *end* as a constructor parameter. The following is an example of how you would create a parameter block descriptor:

```
enum { object_params; }
enum { object_size; }
```

```
ParamBlockDesc2 param_block_desc(
   // required parameters
   object_params, "params", IDS_PARAMS, &objectDesc, 0,

   // optional parameter definitions
   object_size, "size", TYPE_FLOAT, 0, IDS_SIZE,
      p_default, 10.f,   // optional default value
      p_range,   0.1f, FLT_MAX, // optional range
   end,  // end of parameter definition

end);  // end of parameter desc
```

There are two methods to create the parameter block. The first method is by calling the static member function of the `ClassDesc2` class, called *CreateParameterBlock2*. Pass this function a `ParamBlockDesc2` and a reference to the owner of the parameter block. The second method is described in the "Parameter Maps" section. The following shows an example of creating an instance of parameter block using the first method:

```
IParamBlock2 *pblock = ClassDesc2::CreateParameterBlock2(
   &param_block_desc,
   pObject);
```

Parameter Maps

Parameter maps are a way to automatically link parameter block parameters to user interface items. For instance, you can link a Spinner control to an integer or float parameter, and all user interface specific code is handled automatically by the parameter map system. This eases programming and can greatly simplify your plug-in code base.

Installing Parameter Mapping

Parameter mapping can be easily installed by specifying optional flags and parameters to the `ParamBlockDesc2` constructor. To install parameter mapping in your parameter block, add the P_AUTO_UI flag to the flags argument of the required parameters in the constructor. If this flag is specified, you are required to specify additional parameters after the required constructor parameters to let the system know information about the user interface that you are mapping the parameter block to.

Required ParamBlockDesc2 *Arguments*

The following is a list of parameters specific to the user interface that you are mapping the parameter block to. These parameters must go directly after the required constructor parameters and before any parameter definitions. It is required to implement them if the P_AUTO_UI flag is set.

int dialog_template_ID This is the ID of the dialog template used for your user interface.

int dialog_template_res_ID This is the string table resource ID used for the title of the dialog.

int flag_mask This lets *ClassDesc2::BeginEditParams* and *ClassDesc2::EndEditParams* know if the ParamMap2 should be created and deleted in these function calls.

int rollup_flags This argument can be the flags used for rollup creation. Currently, there is only one flag that can be used here, APPENDROLL_CLOSED. This flag tells the rollup to be initially closed.

ParamMap2UserDlgProc* proc You can use this to specify a dialog procedure to handle controls that cannot be linked to parameters, or you can use this for special window processing. This is described later.

Implementing the Parameter Map System

After adding the correct flags and arguments to the `ParamBlockDesc2` constructor, call your class descriptor's *MakeAutoParamBlocks* function. This function replaces the *CreateParameterBlock2* function that was described earlier. To use the *MakeAutoParamBlocks* function, you also need to add the additional flag P_AUTO_CONSTRUCT to the `ParamBlockDesc2` required flag's argument. Adding the P_AUTO_CONSTRUCT flag lets the parameter block know that it is being created with the *MakeAutoParamBlocks* function. If this flag is specified, you are also required to add an additional argument that lets the parameter block know what the reference index of this parameter block is. The following code illustrates the parameter mapping system used with parameter blocks:

```
#define PBLOCK_REF  0
enum { object_params; }
enum { object_size; }
```

```
ParamBlockDesc2 param_block_desc(
   // required parameters
   object_params, "params", IDS_PARAMS, &objectDesc,
   P_AUTO_CONSTRUCT + P_AUTO_UI,

   // required since P_AUTO_CONSTRUCT is in the flags
   PBLOCK_REF,

   // required since P_AUTO_UI is in the flags
   IDD_PANEL, IDS_PARAMS, 0, 0, NULL,

   // optional parameter definitions
   object_size, "size", TYPE_FLOAT, 0, IDS_SIZE,

      // optional default value
      p_default, 10.f,

      // optional range
      p_range,   0.1f, FLT_MAX,

      // link this parameter to spinner/edit control
      p_ui, TYPE_SPINNER, EDITTYPE_UNIVERSE,
         IDC_EDIT_SIZE, IDC_SPIN_SIZE, SPIN_AUTOSCALE,

   end,  // end of parameter definition

end);  // end of parameter desc

// build the parameter block and link to ui in the
// constructor
Object::Object()
{
   // auto build the param block and param map
   objectDesc.MakeAutoParamBlocks(this);
}

// forward BeginEditParams to the class desc
void Object::BeginEditParams(
   IObjParam *ip,
```

```
    ULONG flags,
    Animatable *prev)
{
    this->ip = ip;
    objectDesc.BeginEditParams(ip, this, flags, prev);
}

// forward EndEditParams to the class desc
void Object::EndEditParams(
    IObjParam *ip,
    ULONG flags,
    Animatable *next)
{
    ojectDesc.EndEditParams(ip, this, flags, next);
    this->ip = NULL;
}
```

Custom Dialog Procedures

When using parameter maps, you have no control over filtering your rollout's window messages. There is a custom class for hooking into a parameter maps window procedure, called `ParamMap2UserDlgProc`. This is a pure virtual class that you must derive your own custom class from and implement some of its functions.

The following code shows how to implement the custom dialog procedure and install it in the parameter map:

```
class CustObjectDlgProc : public ParamMap2UserDlgProc
{
public:
    CustObject *obj;

    CustObjectDlgProc(CustObject *obj) {
        this->obj = obj;
    }

    BOOL DlgProc(
        TimeValue t,
        IParamMap2 *map,
        HWND hWnd,
```

```
      UINT msg,
      WPARAM wParam,
      LPARAM lParam);

   void DeleteThis() { delete this; }
};

// dialog procedure
BOOL CustObjectDlgProc::DlgProc(
   TimeValue t, IParamMap2 *map, HWND hWnd,
   UINT msg, WPARAM wParam, LPARAM lParam)
{
   switch(msg)
   {
   case WM_INITDIALOG:
      // place dialog initialization code here
      break;
   case WM_COMMAND:
      // handle non-param map supported controls here
      break;
   }
   return FALSE;
}

// setup the dialog procedure in BeginEditParams
void CustObject::BeginEditParams(
   IObjParam *ip,
   ULONG flags,
   Animatable *prev)
{
   this->ip = ip;
   objectDesc.BeginEditParams(ip, this, flags, prev);

   // this creats a new dialog procedure and hooks it
   // into the parameter map
   object_param_blk.SetUserDlgProc(
      new CustObjectDlgProc(this));
}
```

Implementing a Helper Object

As described in previous chapters, helper objects assist the artist in constructing the scene and can also work as placeholders for more complex objects that show up in external viewers or game engines. This tutorial will teach you how to implement a placeholder type of helper for game engines. The class being implemented is called `GameObject` and is directly derived from the `HelperObject` class.

To begin, create a skeleton plug-in with the plug-in App Wizard and give it the project name GameObj . The plug-in type should be `Helper Objects` with a class name of `GameObject` derived from `HelperObject`.

Adding the User Interface

The user interface for this object will contain a size edit and Spinner control, a drop-down list for the game item type, and four checkboxes to select the skill level that the designer wants the object to show up in (see Figure 14.1).

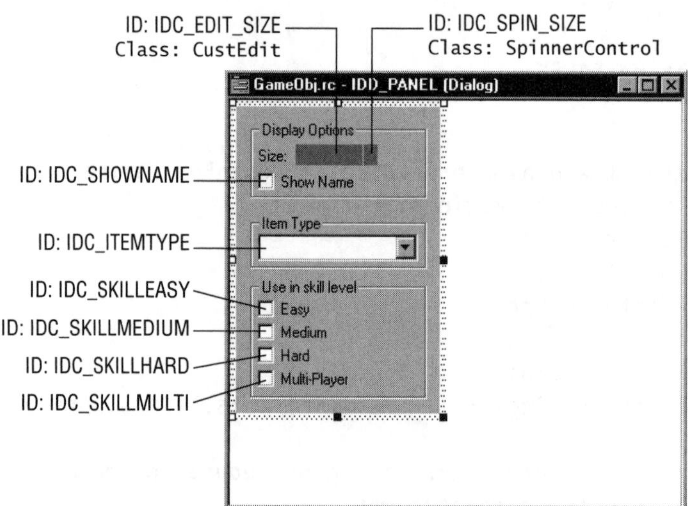

Figure 14.1 GameObject *user interface*

Implementing the Parameter Block and Map

The parameter block will use the automatic user interface support with parameter maps. The parameter block will contain the following parameters: one float parameter for the object size, one integer parameter for the drop-down list index, one string for the current item name, and four Boolean parameters for the skill checkboxes. You will also need to implement a custom dialog procedure to handle the drop-down list messages and manually update the parameter block data when the selection changes.

Viewport Mouse Callbacks

Any class deriving from `BaseObject` needs to implement the *GetCreateMouseCallBack* pure virtual member function and return a pointer to a `CreateMouseCallBack` derived class. From this, MAX will know how to handle the mouse clicking and dragging to create your object.

The CreateMouseCallback *Class*

The `CreateMouseCallback` class is a pure virtual class that requires the implementation of its *proc* member function. This member function is passed information about the state of the mouse. It returns the state of the creation process. You can implement a custom mouse callback class as follows:

```
class GameObjectMouseCallBack : public CreateMouseCallBack
{
protected:
   GameObject *gameObj;

public:
   int proc(
      ViewExp *vpt,
      int msg,
      int point,
      int flags,
      IPoint2 m,
      Matrix3 &mat);
   void SetObject(GameObject *obj) { gameObj = obj; }
};
```

The Mouse Procedure

The mouse procedure is passed the following arguments:

ViewExp *vpt The viewport this mouse procedure is running in.

int msg This is the mouse message getting sent to the procedure. Table 14.1 shows a list of the most commonly used messages.

Table 14.1 Common Messages

MOUSE MESSAGE	DESCRIPTION
MOUSE_ABORT	Sent when the user aborts
MOUSE_POINT	Sent when the user clicks the left button
MOUSE_MOVE	Sent when the mouse button is down and the user moves the mouse
MOUSE_DBLCLICK	Sent when the user double-clicks the left button
MOUSE_FREEMOVE	Sent when the mouse is moving without the left button down

int point This is the click number. The first time the left mouse button is pressed, this number is 0 when the mouse is down and increments whenever the mouse button is depressed after this. The following is a list of point values when a user is clicking:

```
Point:0 - left button is pressed down
Point:1 - left button is pressed and let up
Point:2 - left button is pressed and let up
Point:3 - left button is pressed and let up
...
```

int flags Describes what mouse buttons are down and if the Shift, Alt, or Ctrl keys are down. This can be any combination of the flags shown in Table 14.2.

Table 14.2 Flag Descriptions

FLAG	DESCRIPTION
MOUSE_SHIFT	Shift key is pressed.
MOUSE_CTRL	Ctrl key is pressed.
MOUSE_ALT	Alt key is pressed.

Table 14.2 Flag Descriptions (*continued*)

FLAG	DESCRIPTION
MOUSE_LBUTTON	Left mouse button is pressed.
MOUSE_MBUTTON	Middle mouse button is pressed.
MOUSE_RBUTTON	Right mouse button is pressed.

IPoint2 m This is the 2D viewport coordinate of the mouse position.

Matrix3 &mat This is the transformation of the object relative to the construction plane.

Return Values

Table 14.3 shows the valid values you can return from a mouse procedure.

Table 14.3 Mouse Procedure Return Values

RETURN VALUE	DESCRIPTION
CREATE_CONTINUE	Continue with the object creation.
CREATE_STOP	The creation process has completed normally.
CREATE_ABORT	The creation process has been aborted, and the object will be deleted.

Implementing the Mouse Procedure

The following code shows a fairly standard implementation of a mouse creation procedure. This procedure will handle a mouse down, mouse drag, and mouse up, and will then stop the creation process successfully.

```
int GameObjectMouseCallBack::proc(
   ViewExp *vpt,
   int msg,
   int point,
   int flags,
   IPoint2 m,
```

```
    Matrix3 &mat)
{
    Point3 p1;

    switch(msg)
    {
    case MOUSE_POINT:
    case MOUSE_MOVE:
        switch(point)
        {
        case 0:
            sp0 = m;
            p0 = vpt->SnapPoint(m, m, NULL, SNAP_IN_PLANE);
            mat.SetTrans(p0);
            break;
        case 1:
            mat.IdentityMatrix();
            p1 = vpt->SnapPoint(m, m, NULL, SNAP_IN_PLANE);
            mat.SetTrans(p0);
            float radius = Length(p1-p0);

            // set object size to drag size
            gameObj->pblock->SetValue(
                gameobject_size,
                gameObj->ip->GetTime(),
                radius);
            gameobject_param_blk.InvalidateUI();

            if(flags & MOUSE_CTRL)
            {
                float ang = (float)atan2(p1.y-p0.y, p1.x-p0.x);
                mat.PreRotateZ(gameObj->ip->SnapAngle(ang));
            }

            if(msg == MOUSE_POINT)
                return (Length(m-sp0) < 1 ?
                    CREATE_ABORT : CREATE_STOP);
            break;
        }
        break;
```

```
        case MOUSE_ABORT:
            return CREATE_ABORT;
        }
        return CREATE_CONTINUE;
    }
```

Building the Mesh

To build the actual mesh that is displayed in the viewports, you first need to create the mesh in MAX and then export the mesh data to a C++ file. Create a box and collapse it to an editable mesh, then manipulate the vertices as follows. There should be one vertex pointing down the y axis at [0, 1, 0], one pointing up the z axis at [0, 0, 0.5], and the other two mirrored on the y axis at [0.5,0,0] and [–0.5,0,0]. Delete all other vertices and faces, then add faces manually to optimize the mesh (see Figure 14.2).

Use the script shown in Listing 14.1 to export the mesh as a C++ header file. Export the file as `ObjDef.h` into the GameObj directory and include the file in the workspace.

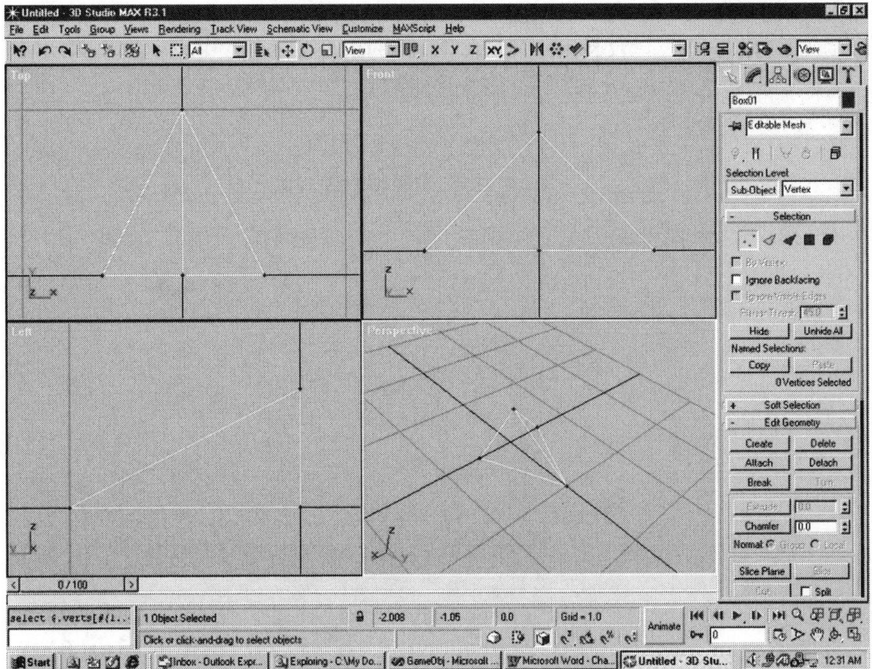

Figure 14.2 The GameObject *mesh*

LISTING 14.1: MESH TO C++ HEADER FILE SCRIPT (*MESH2CPP.MS*)

```
-------------------------------------------------------------
-- mesh2cpp.ms
-- By Simon Feltman   simon@asylum-soft.com
-------------------------------------------------------------
macroScript Mesh2CPP
   category:"SDK Tools"
   tooltip:"Mesh to CPP"
(
   fn ExportCPP obj stream =
   (
      format "\tmesh.setNumVerts(%);\n" \
         obj.numverts to:stream

      format "\tmesh.setNumFaces(%);\n" \
         obj.numfaces to:stream

      for i = 1 to obj.numverts do
      (
         pnt = getvert obj i
         format "\tmesh.setVert(%,size*Point3(%,%,%));\n" \
            (i-1) pnt.x pnt.y pnt.z to:stream
      )

      for i = 1 to obj.numfaces do
      (
         pnt = getface obj i
         format "\tmesh.faces[%].setVerts(%, %, %);\n" \
            (i-1) \
            (pnt.x as integer - 1) \
            (pnt.y as integer - 1) \
            (pnt.z as integer - 1) \
            to:stream

         format \
            "\tmesh.faces[%].setEdgeVisFlags(%,%,%);\n" \
            (i-1) \
            (if (getedgevis obj i 1) then 1 else 0) \
            (if (getedgevis obj i 2) then 1 else 0) \
            (if (getedgevis obj i 3) then 1 else 0) \
            to:stream
```

```
            format "\tmesh.faces[%].setSmGroup(%);\n" \
               (i-1) (getfacesmoothgroup obj i) to:stream
         )
      )

      if selection[1] != undefined and
         (classof selection[1]) == Editable_mesh then
      (
         local fname = \
            getsavefilename types:"Header Files (*.h)|*.h|"
         local stream = createfile fname
         if stream != undefined then
         (
            ExportCPP (selection[1]) stream
            close stream
         )
         else
            messagebox ("Error opening file \"" + fname + "\"")
      )
      else
         messagebox "You must select an editable mesh."
   )
```

After running this script on the mesh that you've created, you should get an output file that looks something like Listing 14.2.

LISTING 14.2: THE OUTPUT OF MESH2CPP (*OBJDEF.H*)

```
mesh.setNumVerts(4);
mesh.setNumFaces(4);
mesh.setVert(0, size * Point3(0.0, 1.0, 0.0));
mesh.setVert(1, size * Point3(0.0, 0.0, 0.5));
mesh.setVert(2, size * Point3(0.5, 0.0, 0.0));
mesh.setVert(3, size * Point3(-0.5, 0.0, 0.0));
mesh.faces[0].setVerts(0, 1, 2);
mesh.faces[0].setEdgeVisFlags(1, 1, 1);
mesh.faces[0].setSmGroup(0);
mesh.faces[1].setVerts(0, 3, 1);
mesh.faces[1].setEdgeVisFlags(1, 1, 1);
mesh.faces[1].setSmGroup(0);
mesh.faces[2].setVerts(0, 2, 3);
```

```
    mesh.faces[2].setEdgeVisFlags(1, 1, 1);
    mesh.faces[2].setSmGroup(0);
    mesh.faces[3].setVerts(3, 2, 1);
    mesh.faces[3].setEdgeVisFlags(1, 1, 1);
    mesh.faces[3].setSmGroup(0);
```

The BuildMesh *Function*

To implement a utility function for building your mesh, simply add a member variable of type `Mesh` to the `GameObject` class. Then implement a member function *BuildMesh* and pass it a *TimeValue* function. Include `ObjDef.h` in the function definition to fill in all the correct mesh data as follows:

```
class GameObject : public HelperObject
{
public:
    Mesh mesh;
    void BuildMesh(TimeValue t);
    ...
}

void GameObject::BuildMesh(TimeValue t)
{
    // get the size of your object from the parameter block
    float size = pblock->GetFloat(PB_SIZE, t);

#include "ObjDef.h"
}
```

Drawing the Mesh

Now that you have the mesh object of the plug-in completed and filled in, you can learn how the actual drawing of the mesh is handled in viewports. The 3D Studio MAX SDK contains classes and functions that allow plug-ins to draw directly into the viewports.

The Display *Function*

The MAX core calls the plug-in implemented function *Display* when it is time for an object to be drawn. This function is passed a time, a node, a viewport interface, and some flags. In this function, you need to implement any drawing code necessary to correctly display the mesh. The function is defined as follows:

```
int BaseObject::Display(
   TimeValue t,
   INode *node,
   ViewExp *vpt,
   int flags);
```

The ViewExp class contains high-level functions for snapping points, manipulating the view matrix, and other view related operations.

The GraphicsWindow *Class*

Also from the ViewExp class, your can retrieve a pointer to a GraphicsWindow class. The GraphicsWindow class contains low-level viewport drawing functions for drawing lines, triangles, and text. To get a GraphicsWindow pointer, you can simply make a call to *ViewExp::getGW*, which will return it. To draw the mesh, you can call the *render* member function of the Mesh class and pass it a pointer to a Material class and a pointer to a GraphicsWindow class. The following code shows how to draw a mesh and some text using the GraphicsWindow pointer:

```
// get the GraphicsWindow
GraphicsWindow *gw = vpt->getGW();

// get the material
Material *mtl = gw->getMaterial();

// render your mesh using the GraphicsWindow
mesh.render(gw, mtl, NULL, COMP_ALL);

// now draw some text in the viewport
gw->text(&Point3(0,0,0), "Test Text");
```

You will also want to draw the mesh in wire frame regardless of what the user's viewport settings are. This can be achieved by setting the rendering limits of the viewport by calling the *GraphicsWindow::setRndLimits* function as follows:

```
// store current rendering limits
DWORD limits = gw->getRndLimits();

// set custom rendering limits to wireframe and
// backface culling
```

```
gw->setRndLimits(GW_WIREFRAME | GW_BACKCULL);

// draw stuff ...

// restore old rendering limits when done drawing
gw->setRndLimits(limits);
```

You will also want to change the color setting depending on whether the object is selected or frozen. This can be done by calling *GraphicsWindow::setColor*. Pass this function the drawing color type and a color as follows:

```
// if the node is selected set both line and text colors
// to white
if(node->Selected()) {
   gw->setColor(TEXT_COLOR, 1.f, 1.f, 1.f);
   gw->setColor(LINE_COLOR, 1.f, 1.f, 1.f);
}

// otherwise if the node isn't frozen, set the colors
// to light blue
else if(!node->IsFrozen()) {
   gw->setColor(TEXT_COLOR, 0.5f, 0.5f, 1.f);
   gw->setColor(LINE_COLOR, 0.5f, 0.5f, 1.f);
}
```

Implementing the GameObject Plug-In

Now that you know all the details about implementing a helper object plug-in, modify `GameObj.cpp` and add all the code necessary to correctly implement the `GameObject` object, as shown in Listing 14.3. You can access this code on the CD-ROM that accompanies this book in the file named `GameObj.cpp`.

LISTING 14.3: THE MAIN PLUG-IN SOURCE FILE (*GAMEOBJ.CPP*)

```
// ============================================================
// GameObj.cpp
// Copyright ©2000, Simon Feltman
// ------------------------------------------------------------
#include "GameObj.h"

#define GAMEOBJECT_CLASS_ID  Class_ID(0xf24b941, 0x4ba8bd4)
```

```
#define PBLOCK_REF  0

// ============================================================
// main plug-in object class
class GameObject : public HelperObject
{
public:
   Mesh mesh;
   IObjParam    *ip;
   IParamBlock2 *pblock;

   GameObject();
   ~GameObject();

   TCHAR* GetObjectName() { return _T("GameObject"); }
   void InitNodeName(TSTR& s) { s = _T("GameObject"); }

   void DeleteThis() { delete this; }
   Class_ID ClassID() {return GAMEOBJECT_CLASS_ID;}
   void GetClassName(TSTR& s) {
      s = GetString(IDS_CLASS_NAME);
   }

   RefTargetHandle Clone(RemapDir &remap);
   RefResult NotifyRefChanged(
      Interval changeInt,
      RefTargetHandle hTarget,
      PartID& partID,
      RefMessage message) { return REF_SUCCEED; }

   int NumRefs() { return 1; }
   RefTargetHandle GetReference(int i) { return pblock; }
   void SetReference(int i, RefTargetHandle rtarg) {
      pblock = (IParamBlock2*)rtarg;
   }

   // allow retreival of our paramblock from other plug-ins
   // and the max core
   int NumParamBlocks() { return 1; }
   IParamBlock2* GetParamBlock(int i) { return pblock; }
```

```
IParamBlock2* GetParamBlockByID(BlockID id) {
   return (pblock->ID() == id) ? pblock : NULL;
}

// plug-in mouse creation callback
CreateMouseCallBack* GetCreateMouseCallBack();

// called when the rollout UI needs to be created
void BeginEditParams(
   IObjParam *ip,
   ULONG flags,
   Animatable *prev);

// called when the rollout UI need to be destroyed
void EndEditParams(
   IObjParam *ip,
   ULONG flags,
   Animatable *next);

// main function the will build our mesh
void BuildMesh(TimeValue t);
void FreeCaches();

// retreives bounding box in object space
void GetLocalBoundBox(
   TimeValue t,
   INode *node,
   ViewExp *vpt,
   Box3 &box);

// retreives bounding box in world space
void GetWorldBoundBox(
   TimeValue t,
   INode *node,
   ViewExp *vpt,
   Box3 &box);

// main display function for this object
int Display(
   TimeValue t,
```

```
      INode *node,
      ViewExp *vpt,
      int flags);

   // hit testing of this object
   int HitTest(
      TimeValue t,
      INode *node,
      int type,
      int crossing,
      int flags,
      IPoint2 *p,
      ViewExp *vpt);

   // Called to retreive the state of this object at the
   // specified time.
   ObjectState Eval(TimeValue t);
};

// ============================================================
// Our plug-ins class descriptor
class GameObjectClassDesc : public ClassDesc2
{
public:
   int            IsPublic() { return 1; }
   void*          Create(BOOL loading = FALSE) {
      return new GameObject();
   }
   const TCHAR*   ClassName() {
      return GetString(IDS_CLASS_NAME);
   }
   SClass_ID      SuperClassID() { return HELPER_CLASS_ID; }
   Class_ID       ClassID() { return GAMEOBJECT_CLASS_ID; }
   const TCHAR*   Category() {
      return GetString(IDS_CATEGORY);
   }
   const TCHAR*   InternalName() { return _T("GameObject"); }
   HINSTANCE      HInstance() { return hInstance; }
};
```

```
static GameObjectClassDesc gameObjectDesc;
ClassDesc2* GetGameObjectDesc() { return &gameObjectDesc; }

// ============================================================
enum { gameobject_params, };

// parameter id's / indices
enum {
   gameobject_size = 0,
   gameobject_showname,
   gameobject_itemname,
   gameobject_itemindex,
   gameobject_skilleasy,
   gameobject_skillmedium,
   gameobject_skillhard,
   gameobject_skillmulti,
};

// ============================================================
// Parameter block definition
static ParamBlockDesc2 gameobject_param_blk(
   gameobject_params, _T("params"),  0, &gameObjectDesc,
   P_AUTO_CONSTRUCT + P_AUTO_UI, PBLOCK_REF,

   //rollout
   IDD_PANEL, IDS_PARAMS, 0, 0, NULL,

   // parameters
   gameobject_size,  _T("size"), TYPE_FLOAT, 0, IDS_SIZE,
      p_default,  10.f,
      p_range,    0.1f, FLT_MAX,
      p_ui,       TYPE_SPINNER, EDITTYPE_UNIVERSE,
         IDC_EDIT_SIZE, IDC_SPIN_SIZE, SPIN_AUTOSCALE,
      end,

   gameobject_showname,  _T("showName"), TYPE_BOOL,
         P_RESET_DEFAULT, IDS_SHOWNAME,
      p_default, TRUE,
      p_ui,      TYPE_SINGLECHEKBOX, IDC_SHOWNAME,
      end,
```

```
    gameobject_itemname,  _T("itemName"), TYPE_STRING,
          P_RESET_DEFAULT | P_READ_ONLY, IDS_ITEMTYPE,
       p_default,  "",
       end,

    gameobject_itemindex,  _T("itemIndex"), TYPE_INT,
          P_RESET_DEFAULT | P_READ_ONLY, IDS_ITEMTYPE,
       p_default,  0,
       end,

    gameobject_skilleasy,  _T("skillEasy"), TYPE_BOOL,
          P_RESET_DEFAULT, IDS_SKILLEASY,
       p_default, TRUE,
       p_ui,      TYPE_SINGLECHEKBOX, IDC_SKILLEASY,
       end,

    gameobject_skillmedium,  _T("skillMedium"), TYPE_BOOL,
          P_RESET_DEFAULT, IDS_SKILLMEDIUM,
       p_default, TRUE,
       p_ui,      TYPE_SINGLECHEKBOX, IDC_SKILLMEDIUM,
       end,

    gameobject_skillhard,  _T("skillHard"), TYPE_BOOL,
          P_RESET_DEFAULT, IDS_SKILLHARD,
       p_default, TRUE,
       p_ui,      TYPE_SINGLECHEKBOX, IDC_SKILLHARD,
       end,

    gameobject_skillmulti, _T("skillMultiPlayer"), TYPE_BOOL,
          P_RESET_DEFAULT, IDS_SKILLMULTI,
       p_default, TRUE,
       p_ui,      TYPE_SINGLECHEKBOX, IDC_SKILLMULTI,
       end,
    end
);

// =========================================================
// Custom dialog procedure class for automatic param maps
class GameObjectDlgProc : public ParamMap2UserDlgProc
{
```

```
public:
   GameObject *gameObj;

   GameObjectDlgProc(GameObject *gameObj) {
      this->gameObj = gameObj;
   }

   BOOL DlgProc(
      TimeValue t,
      IParamMap2 *map,
      HWND hWnd,
      UINT msg,
      WPARAM wParam,
      LPARAM lParam);

   void DeleteThis() { delete this; }
};

// ==============================================================
// Custom dialog procedure for automatic param maps.
BOOL GameObjectDlgProc::DlgProc(
   TimeValue t, IParamMap2 *map, HWND hWnd,
   UINT msg, WPARAM wParam, LPARAM lParam)
{
   char str[128];

   switch(msg)
   {
   case WM_INITDIALOG:
      {
         // Open up GameObjects.txt in the plugcfg directory
         TSTR fname = TSTR(gameObj->ip->GetDir(
            APP_PLUGCFG_DIR)) + "\\GameObjects.txt";

         FILE *stream = fopen((char*)fname, "rt");
         if(stream != NULL)
         {
            // Read each line of GameObjects.txt add to
            // the list box
            while(fgets(str, sizeof(str), stream))
            {
```

```
            char *nl = strrchr(str, '\n');
            if(nl) *nl = '\0';
            SendDlgItemMessage(hWnd, IDC_ITEMTYPE,
               CB_ADDSTRING, 0, (LPARAM)str);
         }

         fclose(stream);
      }
      else
      {
         // give error if we cant open GameObjects.txt
         SendDlgItemMessage(hWnd, IDC_ITEMTYPE,
            CB_ADDSTRING, 0, (LPARAM)"-- none --");

         MessageBox(hWnd, "Can't load GameObjects.txt",
            NULL, MB_OK);
      }

      // Get the current index from the param block and
      // update the listbox.
      int idx = gameObj->pblock->GetInt(
         gameobject_itemindex, t);

      SendDlgItemMessage(hWnd, IDC_ITEMTYPE,
         CB_SETCURSEL, (WPARAM)idx, 0);
   }
   break;

case WM_COMMAND:
   if(LOWORD(wParam) == IDC_ITEMTYPE &&
      HIWORD(wParam) == CBN_SELCHANGE)
   {
      // Drop down selection changed,
      // get the new index and string at that index
      // and store in parameter block
      int idx = SendDlgItemMessage(
         hWnd, IDC_ITEMTYPE, CB_GETCURSEL, 0, 0);

      gameObj->pblock->SetValue(
         gameobject_itemindex,
```

```
                gameObj->ip->GetTime(),
                idx);

            SendDlgItemMessage(hWnd, IDC_ITEMTYPE,
                CB_GETLBTEXT, idx, (LPARAM)str);

            gameObj->pblock->SetValue(
                gameobject_itemname,
                gameObj->ip->GetTime(),
                str);
        }
        break;
    }

    return FALSE;
}


// ==========================================================
// Mouse creation callback class for this plug-in
class GameObjectMouseCallBack : public CreateMouseCallBack
{
protected:
    IPoint2 sp0;
    Point3 p0;
    GameObject *gameObj;

public:
    int proc(
        ViewExp *vpt,
        int msg,
        int point,
        int flags,
        IPoint2 m,
        Matrix3 &mat);
    void SetObject(GameObject *obj) { gameObj = obj; }
};
GameObjectMouseCallBack mouseCallback;
```

```
// ============================================================
// Mouse creation callback procedure
int GameObjectMouseCallBack::proc(
   ViewExp *vpt,
   int msg,
   int point,
   int flags,
   IPoint2 m,
   Matrix3 &mat)
{
   Point3 p1;

   switch(msg)
   {
   case MOUSE_POINT:
   case MOUSE_MOVE:
      switch(point)
      {
      case 0:
         sp0 = m;
         p0 = vpt->SnapPoint(m, m, NULL, SNAP_IN_PLANE);
         mat.SetTrans(p0);
         break;
      case 1:
         // calc the drag size
         mat.IdentityMatrix();
         p1 = vpt->SnapPoint(m, m, NULL, SNAP_IN_PLANE);
         mat.SetTrans(p0);
         float radius = Length(p1-p0);

         // set object size to drag size
         gameObj->pblock->SetValue(
            gameobject_size,
            gameObj->ip->GetTime(),
            radius);
         gameobject_param_blk.InvalidateUI();

         if(flags & MOUSE_CTRL)
         {
            float ang = (float)atan2(p1.y-p0.y, p1.x-p0.x);
```

```
            mat.PreRotateZ(gameObj->ip->SnapAngle(ang));
         }

         if(msg == MOUSE_POINT)
            return (Length(m-sp0) < 1 ?
               CREATE_ABORT : CREATE_STOP);
         break;
      }
      break;
   case MOUSE_ABORT:
      return CREATE_ABORT;
   }
   return CREATE_CONTINUE;
}

// ============================================================
GameObject::GameObject()
{
   ip = NULL;
   pblock = NULL;

   // auto build the param block and param map
   gameObjectDesc.MakeAutoParamBlocks(this);
}

// ============================================================
GameObject::~GameObject()
{
   DeleteAllRefsFromMe();
}

// ============================================================
CreateMouseCallBack* GameObject::GetCreateMouseCallBack()
{
   mouseCallback.SetObject(this);
   return &mouseCallback;
}

// ============================================================
void GameObject::BeginEditParams(
   IObjParam *ip,
```

```
   ULONG flags,
   Animatable *prev)
{
   this->ip = ip;
   gameObjectDesc.BeginEditParams(ip, this, flags, prev);

   // setup our custom dialog procedure
   gameobject_param_blk.SetUserDlgProc(
      new GameObjectDlgProc(this));
}

// ============================================================
void GameObject::EndEditParams(
   IObjParam *ip,
   ULONG flags,
   Animatable *next)
{
   gameObjectDesc.EndEditParams(ip, this, flags, next);
   this->ip = NULL;
}

// ============================================================
RefTargetHandle GameObject::Clone(RemapDir &remap)
{
   GameObject *obj = new GameObject();
   obj->ReplaceReference(0, pblock->Clone(remap));
   return obj;
}

// ============================================================
void GameObject::BuildMesh(TimeValue t)
{
   float size = pblock->GetFloat(gameobject_size, t);

   // build the mesh
#include "ObjDef.h"

   mesh.InvalidateGeomCache();
}
```

```
// ============================================================
void GameObject::FreeCaches()
{
   mesh.FreeAll();
}

// ============================================================
void GameObject::GetLocalBoundBox(
   TimeValue t, INode *node,
   ViewExp *vpt, Box3 &box)
{
   BuildMesh(t);
   box = mesh.getBoundingBox();
}

// ============================================================
void GameObject::GetWorldBoundBox(
   TimeValue t, INode *node,
   ViewExp *vpt, Box3 &box)
{
   BuildMesh(t);
   Matrix3 tm = node->GetObjectTM(t);
   box = mesh.getBoundingBox() * tm;
}


// ============================================================
int GameObject::Display(
   TimeValue t, INode *node,
   ViewExp *vpt, int flags)
{
   BuildMesh(t);

   // get the graphics window API and setup for drawing
   GraphicsWindow *gw = vpt->getGW();
   Material *mtl = gw->getMaterial();
   DWORD limits = gw->getRndLimits();
   gw->setRndLimits(GW_WIREFRAME | GW_BACKCULL);

   // setup colors
```

```
    if(node->Selected()) {
        gw->setColor(TEXT_COLOR, 1.f, 1.f, 1.f);
        gw->setColor(LINE_COLOR, 1.f, 1.f, 1.f);
    }
    else if(!node->IsFrozen()) {
        gw->setColor(TEXT_COLOR, 0.5f, 0.5f, 1.f);
        gw->setColor(LINE_COLOR, 0.5f, 0.5f, 1.f);
    }

    // setup window transformation
    Matrix3 tm(1);
    tm = node->GetObjectTM(t);
    gw->setTransform(tm);

    // draw item type text
    if(pblock->GetInt(gameobject_showname, t))
    {
        float size = pblock->GetFloat(gameobject_size, t);
        TCHAR *str = pblock->GetStr(gameobject_itemname, t);
        gw->text(&Point3(0.f, size*0.3f, size*0.1f), str);
    }

    // finally draw the mesh itself
    mesh.render(gw, mtl, NULL, COMP_ALL);

    gw->setRndLimits(limits);
    return 0;
}

// =============================================================
int GameObject::HitTest(
    TimeValue t, INode *node, int type, int crossing,
    int flags, IPoint2 *p, ViewExp *vpt)
{
    HitRegion hitRegion;
    Point2 pt((float)p[0].x, (float)p[0].y);
    GraphicsWindow *gw = vpt->getGW();

    BuildMesh(t);
    gw->setTransform(node->GetObjectTM(t));
```

```
   MakeHitRegion(hitRegion, type, crossing, 4, p);

   return mesh.select(
      gw,
      node->Mtls(),
      &hitRegion,
      flags & HIT_ABORTONHIT,
      node->NumMtls());
}

// ===========================================================
ObjectState GameObject::Eval(TimeValue t)
{
   return ObjectState(this);
}
```

Summary

In this chapter, you learned some of the advanced concepts used in the 3D Studio MAX SDK, such as parameter blocks and parameter maps. These concepts are widely used across all classes of plug-ins, not just with helper objects. Implementing other types of object plug-ins is very similar to the helper object paradigm in that you have parameter storage, creation using the mouse, mesh generation, and mesh display.

In the next chapter, you will learn about the 2D portion of the MAX SDK. This will include rendering effects and bitmaps.

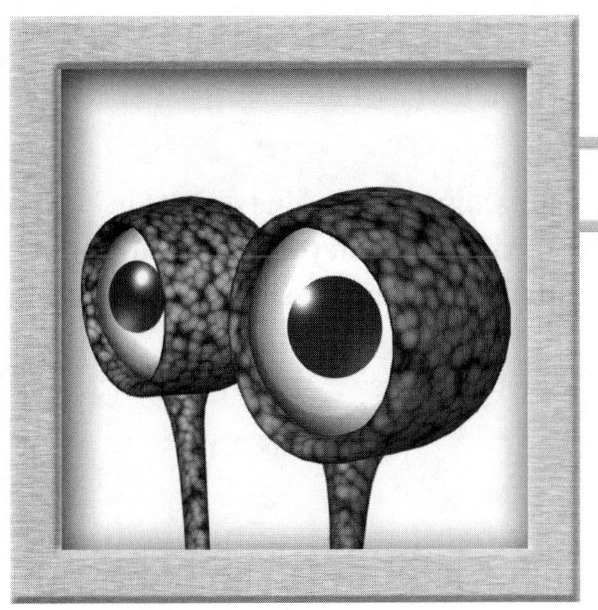

Bitmaps, the G-Buffer, and Render Effects Plug-Ins

MAXSCRIPT

Chapter 15

You now know how to create geometric pipeline objects in MAX and how to extract their data. Next, you will learn how MAX handles bitmaps and post-process effects, called render effects.

This chapter will cover the following topics:

- Bitmaps
- Render effects plug-ins
- The G-Buffer

Bitmaps

The 3D Studio MAX SDK contains a rich set of classes and functions for working with bitmap images. Bitmap images in MAX can be device and format independent, making it easy to work with any file format in a very general way.

Managing Bitmaps

Managing bitmaps is done through the `BitmapManager` class, which provides an interface for creating new bitmaps and loading existing bitmap files. There is a global instance of this class named `TheManager`, which is what you should use. Most functions of the `BitmapManager` class work with the `BitmapInfo` class.

The BitmapInfo *Class*

The `BitmapInfo` class stores properties of a bitmap like width, height, and aspect, but no data. This class is used as info for creating new bitmaps and retrieving existing bitmap information. Table 15.1 shows the `BitmapInfo` member variable defaults with the default constructor.

Table 15.1 *BitmapInfo* Defaults

PROPERTY	DEFAULT
Width	640
Height	480
Custom width	320
Custom height	240
Custom flags	`BMM_CUSTOM_RESFIT | BMM_CUSTOM_FILEGAMMA`
Custom gamma	1.0
Frame number	0
Aspect ratio	1.0
Gamma setting	1.0
Name	`NULL`
Device name	`NULL`
Looping flag	`BMM_SEQ_WRAP`

The BitmapInfo class provides member functions for getting and setting the properties. Please see the MAX SDK help file or look at the BitmapInfo class declaration for a list of member functions.

The Bitmap *Class*

The Bitmap class is the storage class for the actual image data. This class provides functions for display functions, as well as for getting image properties, manipulating the image data, and manipulating the G-Buffer. Please see the MAX SDK help or the Bitmap class declaration for a complete list of member functions.

The following code shows how to create a new Bitmap object named MyBitmap with a color depth of 64 bit and a size of 1024×768.

```
// Setup a BitmapInfo class
BitmapInfo bi("MyBitmap");
bi.SetType(BMM_TRUE_64);
bi.SetWidth(1024);
bi.SetHeight(768);

// Create the bitmap image
Bitmap *bm = TheManager->Create(&bi);
// ...
```

The *SetType* member function of the BitmapInfo class sets the color depth of the image. Table 15.2 shows a list of valid color depths used for creating bitmaps.

Table 15.2 Bitmap Color Depths

Bitmap Type	Color Depth
BMM_LINE_ART	1-bit monochrome image
BMM_PALETTED	8-bit paletted image
BMM_GRAY_8	8-bit grayscale bitmap
BMM_GRAY_16	16-bit grayscale bitmap
BMM_TRUE_16	16-bit true color image
BMM_TRUE_32	32-bit color
BMM_TRUE_64	64-bit color

Working with Bitmaps

You can get and set pixels of a bitmap in a format independent manner using 64-bit color depth. The structure for 64-bit pixels is `BMM_Color_64`, which contains four 16-bit values named `r`, `g`, `b`, and `a`. To manipulate a bitmap image, use the *PutPixels* and *GetPixels* member functions of the `Bitmap` class.

The following code illustrates how to create a black image, draw red borders, and display the result in a VFB (Virtual Frame Buffer).

```
int width = 640;
int height = 480;

// Setup a BitmapInfo class
BitmapInfo bi("MyBitmap");
bi.SetType(BMM_TRUE_64);
bi.SetWidth(width);
bi.SetHeight(height);

// Create the bitmap image
Bitmap *bm = TheManager->Create(&bi);

// Setup pixel color
BMM_Color_64 pxl;
pxl.r = 0xFFFF;
pxl.g = pxl.b = pxl.a = 0;

// Draw top and bottom borders
for(int i = 0; i < width; i++)
{
   bm->PutPixels(i, 0, 1, &pxl);
   bm->PutPixels(i, height-1, 1, &pxl);
}

// Draw left and right borders
for(i = 0; i < height; i++)
{
   bm->PutPixels(0, i, 1, &pxl);
   bm->PutPixels(width-1, i, 1, &pxl);
}

// Display the bitmap
bm->Display();
```

Render Effects Plug-Ins

Render effects plug-ins are post-image manipulation tools that allow for changes after the scene is rendered. These plug-ins show up in the Render Effects dialog box, which can be accessed from the Rendering ➜ Effects... menu. Render effects plug-ins are derived from the `Effect` class. You basically just have to implement the *Apply* member function, which gets called when the image needs to be updated.

The following example simply rotates pixels based on a user-defined rotation value and the pixel's distance from the center of the bitmap. This creates a swirl effect of the image. To create the plug-in, use the 3D Studio MAX Plug-in App Wizard and create a render effects plug-in named SwirlFX. Then modify `SwirlFX.cpp` and add all the code necessary to correctly implement the `SwirlFX` class, as shown in Listing 15.1. You can access this code on the CD-ROM that accompanies this book in the file named `SwirlFX.cpp`.

LISTING 15.1: THE SWIRLFX PLUG-IN MAIN SOURCE FILE (*SWIRLFX.CPP*)

```
// ============================================================
// SwirlFX.cpp
// Copyright ©2000, Simon Feltman
// ------------------------------------------------------------
#include "SwirlFX.h"

#define SWIRLFX_CLASS_ID  Class_ID(0x23963031, 0x43e8ca14)
#define PBLOCK_REF  0


// =============================================================
class SwirlFX : public Effect
{
public:
   IParamBlock2 *pblock;

   SwirlFX();
   ~SwirlFX();
   void DeleteThis() { delete this; }

   // Custom function to create our swirl lookup table.
   IPoint2* CreateLookup(Bitmap *bm, float rot);

   // Effect class methods
   TSTR GetName() { return GetString(IDS_CLASS_NAME); }
   EffectParamDlg* CreateParamDialog(IRendParams *pParams);
```

```
    // This is the main function that gets called to
    // manipulate the image on a per-frame basis.
    void Apply(
        TimeValue t,
        Bitmap *pBM,
        RenderGlobalContext *pGC,
        CheckAbortCallback *checkAbort);

    // From Animatable
    Class_ID ClassID() { return SWIRLFX_CLASS_ID; }
    SClass_ID SuperClassID() {
        return RENDER_EFFECT_CLASS_ID;
    }
    void GetClassName(TSTR& s) {
        s = GetString(IDS_CLASS_NAME);
    }

    RefTargetHandle Clone(RemapDir &remap);
    RefResult NotifyRefChanged(
        Interval changeInt, RefTargetHandle hTarget,
        PartID& partID,  RefMessage message);

    // Sub-anim and reference functions
    int NumSubs() { return 1; }
    TSTR SubAnimName(int i) { return GetString(IDS_PARAMS);}
    Animatable* SubAnim(int i) { return pblock; }
    int NumRefs() { return 1; }
    RefTargetHandle GetReference(int i) { return pblock; }
    void SetReference(int i, RefTargetHandle rtarg) {
        pblock = (IParamBlock2*)rtarg;
    }

    // Parameter block functions
    int NumParamBlocks() { return 1; }
    IParamBlock2* GetParamBlock(int i) { return pblock; }
    IParamBlock2* GetParamBlockByID(BlockID id) {
        return (pblock->ID() == id) ? pblock : NULL;
    }
};

// =========================================================
```

```
class SwirlFXClassDesc : public ClassDesc2
{
public:
   int IsPublic() { return 1; }

   void* Create(BOOL loading = FALSE) {
      return new SwirlFX();
   }

   const TCHAR* ClassName() {
      return GetString(IDS_CLASS_NAME);
   }

   SClass_ID SuperClassID() {
      return RENDER_EFFECT_CLASS_ID;
   }

   Class_ID ClassID() { return SWIRLFX_CLASS_ID; }

   const TCHAR* Category() {
      return GetString(IDS_CATEGORY);
   }

   const TCHAR* InternalName() { return _T("SwirlFX"); }

   HINSTANCE HInstance() { return hInstance; }
};

static SwirlFXClassDesc swirlFXDesc;
ClassDesc2* GetSwirlFXDesc() { return &swirlFXDesc; }

// ============================================================
enum { swirlfx_params };
enum { pb_amount, };

static ParamBlockDesc2 swirlfx_param_blk(
   swirlfx_params, _T("params"),  0, &swirlFXDesc,
   P_AUTO_CONSTRUCT + P_AUTO_UI, PBLOCK_REF,

   //rollout
   IDD_PANEL, IDS_PARAMS, 0, 0, NULL,
```

```
   // params
   pb_amount,           _T("amount"),
        TYPE_FLOAT,     P_ANIMATABLE,     IDS_AMOUNT,
      p_default,        0.1f,
      p_range,        0.0f,1000.0f,
      p_ui,           TYPE_SPINNER,
         EDITTYPE_FLOAT, IDC_EDIT_AMOUNT,
         IDC_SPIN_AMOUNT, 0.01f,
      end,
   end
);


// ============================================================
SwirlFX::SwirlFX()
{
   swirlFXDesc.MakeAutoParamBlocks(this);
   assert(pblock);
}

// ============================================================
SwirlFX::~SwirlFX() {}


// ============================================================
RefTargetHandle SwirlFX::Clone( RemapDir &remap )
{
   SwirlFX* newObj = new SwirlFX();
   newObj->ReplaceReference(0,remap.CloneRef(pblock));
   return (RefTargetHandle)newObj;
}

// ============================================================
EffectParamDlg *SwirlFX::CreateParamDialog(IRendParams *ip)
{
   return swirlFXDesc.CreateParamDialogs(ip, this);
}

// ============================================================
RefResult SwirlFX::NotifyRefChanged(
   Interval changeInt, RefTargetHandle hTarget,
```

```
   PartID& partID,  RefMessage message)
{
   switch(message)
   {
   case REFMSG_CHANGE:
      swirlfx_param_blk.InvalidateUI();
      break;
   }
   return REF_SUCCEED;
}

// ============================================================
IPoint2* SwirlFX::CreateLookup(Bitmap *bm, float rot)
{
   IPoint2 *lookup = NULL;

   int width = bm->Width();
   int height = bm->Height();

   int halfWidth = width >> 1;
   int halfHeight = height >> 1;

   int mSquared = halfWidth*halfWidth +
                  halfHeight*halfHeight;

   lookup = new IPoint2[width*height];

   for(int y = 0, cy = -halfHeight; y < height; y++, cy++)
   {
      int sy = cy * cy;
      for(int x = 0, cx = -halfWidth; x < width; x++, cx++)
      {
         int sx = cx * cx;
         int s = sy + sx;
         float r = rot - (rot * s / mSquared);
         float sinR = sin(r);
         float cosR = cos(r);

         lookup[y*width+x].x =
            halfWidth + (cx * cosR + cy * sinR);
```

```
            lookup[y*width+x].y =
               halfHeight + (cy * cosR - cx * sinR);
         }
      }

      return lookup;
   }

   // ============================================================
   void SwirlFX::Apply(
      TimeValue t,
      Bitmap *bm,
      RenderGlobalContext *gc,
      CheckAbortCallback *checkAbort)
   {
      Bitmap *copyBM = TheManager->Create(&bm->Storage()->bi);
      copyBM->CopyImage(bm, COPY_IMAGE_RESIZE_HI_QUALITY, 0);

      float rot = pblock->GetFloat(pb_amount, t);
      IPoint2 *lookup = CreateLookup(bm, rot);

      BMM_Color_64 pxl;
      for(int y = 0; y < bm->Height(); y++)
      {
         for(int x = 0; x < bm->Width(); x++)
         {
            IPoint2 *pnt = &lookup[y*bm->Width()+x];
            copyBM->GetPixels(pnt->x, pnt->y, 1, &pxl);
            bm->PutPixels(x, y, 1, &pxl);
         }
      }

      copyBM->DeleteThis();
      delete[] lookup;
   }
```

The following images show the image before the SwirlFX plug-in was applied (see Figure 15.1) and after it was applied (see Figure 15.2). Both images are courtesy of Brandon Jones.

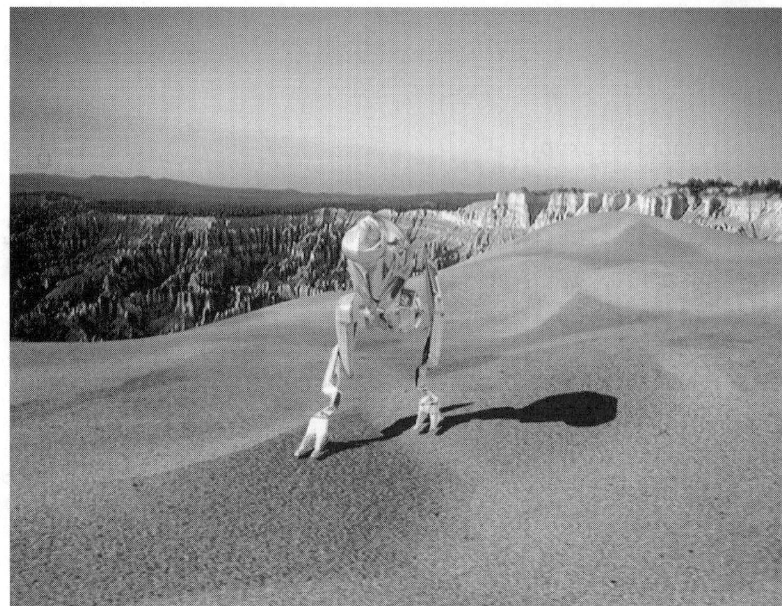

Figure 15.1 *Before SwirlFX was applied*

Figure 15.2 *After SwirlFX was applied*

The G-Buffer

Bitmap images not only store color but can also store geometric scene information per pixel. The *G-Buffer* is a method of storing extra scene information per pixel in a rendered image. G-Buffer data is stored in channels, which are composed of different layers. Each G-Buffer channel can store very useful information about each pixel, such as Z depth, pixel velocity, material IDs, and so on. With this rich set of pixel information, you can do some very powerful post render effects like Motion Blur or lighting effects.

The `Bitmap` class supplies utility functions for working directly with G-Buffer channels, as well as for getting the actual G-Buffer storage class. The main class used for the G-Buffer storage is called `GBuffer`. This class allows complete access to all G-Buffer channels and layers.

G-Buffer Channels

To get a G-Buffer channel from a bitmap, the `Bitmap` class supplies the function *GetChannel*, which takes the channel ID as a parameter and returns a pointer to the channel's buffer and a size of how big each pixel is. The function is defined as follows:

```
void* GetChannel(ULONG channelID, ULONG& chanType);
```

where `channelID` can be one of the types found in Table 15.3.

Table 15.3 *ChannelID* Return Types

Channel ID	Return Type
BMM_CHAN_Z	float*
BMM_CHAN_MTL_ID	BYTE*
BMM_CHAN_NODE_ID	WORD*
BMM_CHAN_UV	Point2*
BMM_CHAN_NORMAL	Point3*
BMM_CHAN_REALPIX	RealPixel*
BMM_CHAN_COVERAGE	UBYTE*
BMM_CHAN_BG	Color24*
BMM_CHAN_NODE_RENDER_ID	UWORD*
BMM_CHAN_COLOR	Color24*
BMM_CHAN_TRANSP	Color24*
BMM_CHAN_VELOC	Point2*
BMM_CHAN_WEIGHT	Color24*

The *GetChannel* function will fill in chanType with one of the values in Table 15.4.

Table 15.4 Values for *chanType*

CHANNEL TYPE	PIXEL SIZE
BMM_CHAN_TYPE_1	1 bit per pixel
BMM_CHAN_TYPE_8	1 byte per pixel
BMM_CHAN_TYPE_16	1 word per pixel
BMM_CHAN_TYPE_32	2 words per pixel
BMM_CHAN_TYPE_48	3 words per pixel
BMM_CHAN_TYPE_64	4 words per pixel
BMM_CHAN_TYPE_96	6 words per pixel

You can use the Bitmap class's *ChannelsPresent* function to determine if a bitmap has a G-Buffer channel. The following code tests if a bitmap has Z and Velocity buffer channels and then gets the channel:

```
ULONG chanType, channels;
Channels = bm->ChannelsPresent();

// get the Z channel if present
if(channels & BMM_CHAN_Z)
{
   float *zBuf = (float*)bm->GetChannel(
      BMM_CHAN_Z, chanType);
   // chanType should be BMM_CHAN_TYPE_32
}

// get the velocity channel if present
if(channels & BMM_CHAN_VELOC)
{
   Point2 *velBuf = (Point2*)bm->GetChannel(
      BMM_CHAN_VELOC, chanType);
   // chanType should be BMM_CHAN_TYPE_64
}
```

This method of working with the G-Buffer channels only works with the first layer. This means that if you want to do anti-aliasing or handle transparency, you can access extra information on object edges that partially occlude other objects or objects that are translucent. Also, if an object has the *Render Occluded Object* property set, another layer will be added for the object that it occludes. In the case of accessing multiple layers, you must use the `GBuffer` class.

The *GBuffer* Class

The `GBuffer` class contains all the functionality that the `Bitmap` class's G-Buffer utility functions do, as well as allowing access to different layers. You can get a bitmap's G-Buffer with the `Bitmap` member function *GetGBuffer*. The `GBuffer` class uses reader and writer classes to access different channels and layers.

Reading GBuffer *Pixels*

To read pixel information from the G-Buffer, there is a class called `GBufReader`. You can create an instance to this class with the *CreateReader* member function of the `GBuffer` class. The following example shows how to read all the layers for the Z and Velocity buffer channels using the `GBufReader` class:

```
float z;
Point2 vel;

// get the G-Buffer and create a reader
GBuffer *gbuf = bm->GetGBuffer();
GBufReader *rdr = gbuf->CreateReader();

for(int y = 0; y < bm->Height(); y++)
{
   // set current scanline
   rdr->StartLine(y);

   for(int x = 0; x < bm->Width(); x++)
   {
      // set current pixel
      rdr->StartPixel(x);

      // read first layer then loop if there are more
      do {
         rdr->ReadChannelData(GB_Z, (void*)&z);
         rdr->ReadChannelData(GB_VELOC, (void*)&vel);
```

```
        } while(rdr->StartNextLayer());
    }
}

// delete the reader
gbuf->DestroyReader(rdr);
```

The reader functions used in the previous code segment are defined as follows:

GBufReader::StartLine(int y) This function sets the current scan-line (y coordinate) for the G-Buffer reader. This function is also in the `GBufWriter` class.

GBufReader::StartPixel(int x) This function sets the current pixel (x coordinate) of the G-Buffer reader. This function is also in the `GBufWriter` class.

GBufReader::ReadChannelData(int chan, void *data) Use this function to get the actual pixel data at the current layer. The types you can use for `chan` are defined in Table 15.5 and correspond to the `BMM_CHAN_*` channel IDs that were previously described.

GBufReader::StartNextLayer() After you have read a pixel from the first layer *ReadChannelData*, use this function to set the G-Buffer for reading the underlying layers. If this function returns false, there are no more layers. This function is also defined in the `GBufWriter` class, but in this case, it needs to get called before a pixel is written to the first layer.

Table 15.5 *chan* Types

CHANNEL	DESCRIPTION
GB_Z	Z-Buffer depth
GB_MTL_ID	Material ID assigned from the Material Editor
GB_NODE_ID	Node ID assigned from the Properties dialog
GB_UV	UV coordinates
GB_NORMAL	Normal vector in view space
GB_REALPIX	Non-clamped colors in `RealPixel` format
GB_COVERAGE	Pixel coverage of the front surface
GB_BG	Background RGB color
GB_NODE_RENDER_ID	System node number (valid during a render)

Table 15.5 *chan* Types (continued)

CHANNEL	DESCRIPTION
GB_COLOR	The color returned by the material shader for the fragment
GB_TRANSP	The transparency returned by the material shader for the fragment
GB_VELOC	Velocity vector of the fragment relative to the screen
GB_WEIGHT	Weight of layers contribution to pixel color

Writing G-Buffer *Pixels*

Writing to the G-Buffer is done in a very similar manner as reading. Writing is done via the `GBufWriter` class. You can create an instance of this class with the *CreateWriter* member function of the `GBuffer` class. The following example shows how to create G-Buffer channels and layers in a bitmap and how to write to these channels using the `GBufWriter` class:

```
// Get the G-Buffer with Z and Velocity channels
// then create a writer.
GBuffer *gbuf = bm->GetGBuffer();
gbuf->CreateChannels(BMM_CHAN_Z | BMM_CHAN_VELOC);
GBufWriter *wtr = gbuf->CreateWriter();

for(int y = 0; y < bm->Height(); y++)
{
   // set current scanline
   wtr->StartLine(y);

   for(int x = 0; x < bm->Width(); x++)
   {
      // set current pixel
      wtr->StartPixel(x);

      // Create the first layer, any additional layers
      // can be created the same way after writing data.
      wtr->StartNewLayer();

      // write data
```

```
            float z = 5. f * float(x) * float(y);
            wtr->WriteChannelData(GB_Z, (void*)&z);
            wtr->WriteChannelData(GB_VELOC, (void*)&Point2(x,y));
        }

        // finish the line
        wtr->EndLine();
    }

    // delete the writer
    gbuf->DestroyWriter(wtr);
```

Render Effects using the G-Buffer

Now that you know how to work with bitmaps and G-Buffer, you can use this in a render effect plug-in to create powerful post effects. The only thing you will need to add in your plug-in class to get G-Buffer access in a render effect plug-in is the *GBuffer-ChannelsRequired* function. From this function, you should return the channels you want to use bitwise or with each other. The next example creates a new bitmap and copies the Z and Velocity buffer channels into it. It then displays the new bitmap in a separate VFB.

To create the plug-in, use the 3D Studio MAX Plug-in App Wizard and create a render effects plug-in named GBufCopy. Then, modify `GBufCopy.cpp` and add all the code necessary to correctly implement the `GBufCopy` class, as shown in Listing 15.2. You can access this code on the CD-ROM that accompanies this book in the file named `GBufCopy.cpp`.

LISTING 15.2: THE GBUFCOPY PLUG-IN MAIN SOURCE FILE (*GBUFCOPY.CPP*)

```
// ============================================================
// GBufCopy.cpp
// Render Effect that copies Z and Velocity channels to a
//  seperate VFB.
// Copyright ©2000, Simon Feltman
// ------------------------------------------------------------
#include "GBufCopy.h"

#define GBUFCOPY_CLASS_ID  Class_ID(0x3c247ab4, 0x290b2c25)
```

```
// ==========================================================
class GBufCopy : public Effect
{
public:
   TSTR GetName() { return GetString(IDS_CLASS_NAME); }

   DWORD GBufferChannelsRequired(TimeValue t) {
      return (BMM_CHAN_Z | BMM_CHAN_VELOC);
   }

   void Apply(
      TimeValue t,
      Bitmap *pBM,
      RenderGlobalContext *pGC,
      CheckAbortCallback *checkAbort);

   Class_ID ClassID() { return GBUFCOPY_CLASS_ID; }
   SClass_ID SuperClassID() {
      return RENDER_EFFECT_CLASS_ID;
   }
   void GetClassName(TSTR& s) {
      s = GetString(IDS_CLASS_NAME);
   }
   void DeleteThis() { delete this; }
};

// ==========================================================
class GBufCopyClassDesc : public ClassDesc2
{
public:
   int  IsPublic() { return 1; }
   void* Create(BOOL loading = FALSE) {
      return new GBufCopy();
   }
   const TCHAR* ClassName() {
      return GetString(IDS_CLASS_NAME);
   }
   SClass_ID SuperClassID() {
      return RENDER_EFFECT_CLASS_ID;
   }
   Class_ID ClassID() {
```

```
        return GBUFCOPY_CLASS_ID;
    }
    const TCHAR* Category() {
        return GetString(IDS_CATEGORY);
    }
    const TCHAR* InternalName() { return _T("GBufTest"); }
    HINSTANCE HInstance() { return hInstance; }
};

static GBufCopyClassDesc GBufCopyDesc;
ClassDesc2* GetGBufCopyDesc() {return &GBufCopyDesc;}

// ===============================================================
void GBufCopy::Apply(
    TimeValue t,
    Bitmap *bm,
    RenderGlobalContext *gc,
    CheckAbortCallback *checkAbort)
{
    // Get the G-Buffer and a reader
    GBuffer *gb = bm->GetGBuffer();
    GBufReader *rdr = gb->CreateReader();

    // Create a new bitmap and channels
    Bitmap *newBM = TheManager->Create(&bm->Storage()->bi);
    newBM->CreateChannels(BMM_CHAN_Z | BMM_CHAN_VELOC);
    GBuffer *newGB = newBM->GetGBuffer();
    GBufWriter *wrt = newGB->CreateWriter();

    for(int y = 0; y < bm->Height(); y++)
    {
        // set current scan line
        rdr->StartLine(y);
        wrt->StartLine(y);

        for(int x = 0; x < bm->Width(); x++)
        {
            // set current pixel
            rdr->StartPixel(x);
            wrt->StartPixel(x);
```

```
            do {
               // create a new destination layer
               wrt->StartNextLayer();

               // read and write Z data
               float z;
               rdr->ReadChannelData(GB_Z, (void*)&z);
               wrt->WriteChannelData(GB_Z, (void*)&z);

               // read and write velocity data
               Point2 pnt;
               rdr->ReadChannelData(GB_VELOC, (void*)&pnt);
               wrt->WriteChannelData(GB_VELOC, (void*)&pnt);

            } while(rdr->StartNextLayer());
         }
         wrt->EndLine();
      }

      // cleanup
      gb->DestroyReader(rdr);
      newGB->DestroyWriter(wrt);
      newGB->UpdateChannelMinMax();

      // display our new VFB
      newBM->Display();
   }
```

Summary

Having the ability to create plug-in rendering pipeline hooks makes MAX very powerful for tailoring scene renderings to look the way you want.

This chapter covered some of the fundamental 2D concepts used in 3D Studio MAX, such as bitmaps, the G-Buffer, and render effects. However, there are still many more rendering plug-ins that this chapter did not cover, such as plug-in shaders and texture maps.

In the next chapter, you will jump back into the geometry pipeline by writing modifier plug-ins.

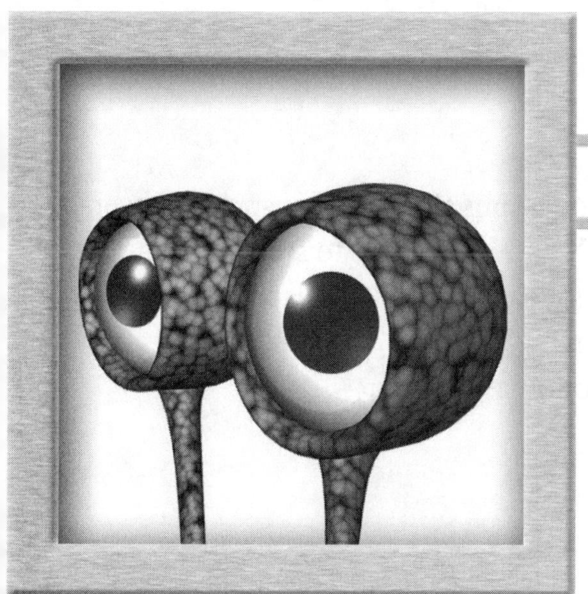

Modifier Plug-Ins

MAXSCRIPT

Chapter 16

Modifiers are one of the reasons that MAX is such a powerful 3D platform. MAX allows the user to stack object modifications on top of each other with each one maintaining its own state information.

This chapter will cover the following topics:

- Simple modifiers
- The deformer
- Advanced modifiers
- Geometry pipeline channels

Simple Modifiers

Simple modifiers are a type of modifier that can only change the geometry of an object. Using simple modifiers can greatly reduce the amount of code needed to implement a modifier that just manipulates vertices.

Simple modifiers use something called a *deformer* to do the actual vertex manipulation. Pulling the manipulation code away from the main plug-in class makes it easy to implement both an object space and a world space modifier using the same deformer code.

Simple Modifier plug-in classes should be derived from the `SimpleMod2` class. This is the second version of the `SimpleMod` class that supports the parameter block 2 system. This is a pure virtual class that requires the implementation of the *GetDeformer* function, which is defined as follows:

```
Deformer& MyMod::GetDeformer(
   TimeValue t,
   ModContext &mc,
   Matrix3& mat,
   Matrix3& invmat);
```

The parameters passed to this function are described as follows.

TimeValue t This is the time that the modifier is to be evaluated. Animated parameters of the modifier will use this time to get the correct value.

ModContext &mc A `ModContext` is a simple class that stores information about the transform space that the modifier was applied in. The class also stores the bounding box of the object.

Matrix3 &mat This matrix is the transform space you are supposed to apply the vertex modification in. Multiply any vertices you get by this, then do the modification.

Matrix3 &invmat This is the inverse of the `mat` parameter. You are supposed to apply this transform to vertices after the modification has occurred.

The Deformer

Deformers are represented by the pure virtual class named `Deformer`. This is basically a callback class, which only has one function that you are required to implement, called *Map*. The following is an example of a custom `deformer` class:

```
class MyDef : public Deformer
{
   Point3 Map(int i, Point3 p);
};
```

The Map *Function*

The *Map* function of the deformer class gets called for each vertex in the object. This function is passed the index of the vertex, the vertex itself, and must return the modified vertex. The following example code shows the *Map* function for scaling an object's vertices by two:

```
Point3 MyDef::Map(int i, Point3 p)
{
   // scale the point by 2
   p = p * 2.f;
   return p;
}
```

Validity Intervals

Another function of the SimpleMod2 class that you are going to want to implement is the *GetValidity* function. This function takes a TimeValue parameter and returns an Interval. An Interval is a class that contains two TimeValue member variables (start and end) used to represent a range of time. The *GetValidity* function gives MAX a time range that the object will be valid through so that it doesn't have to rebuild the object cache every frame. If the time that MAX is evaluating is within the returned interval, the object cache is still valid and does not need to be rebuilt. To correctly implement the *GetValidity* function, you combine the intervals of all animatable parameters of your modifier. The following is an example of the *GetValidity* function:

```
// ==========================================================
Interval MyMod::GetValidity(TimeValue t)
{
   float f;

   // First set the validity from negative infinity to
   // positive infinity.
   Interval valid = FOREVER;

   // Now build up the correct validity from each
   // animatable parameter.
   pblock2->GetValue(pb_width, t, f, valid);
   pblock2->GetValue(pb_height, t, f, valid);

   return valid;
}
```

Using this function, let's pretend that it is passed a TimeValue of 25. The width parameter has a validity interval of 20 to 30 at time 25. The height parameter has a validity interval of 22 to 35 at time 25. First, the valid variable will be in the range of negative infinity to positive infinity. When the *GetValue* function is called for the width parameter, it will shorten the valid variable to 20 to 30. Then, when the *GetValue* function is called for the height parameter, the valid variable is shortened even more to 22 to 30. Now, if the TimeValue is within this combined validity interval, the object cache is still valid and won't need to be rebuilt.

Implementing a *SimpleMod2*

Now that you know the main functions for implementing a simple modifier, let's move on to a plug-in example. This example will scale an object's vertices in an axial direction specified by the user.

Using the SDK App Wizard, create a new plug-in called ScaleMod of type Modifier based on the SimpleMod class. This will generate a lot of extra code that is not needed in a simple Modifier plug-in. The code shown in Listing 16.1 is a stripped down version of the code generated from the App Wizard with the scaling code in the deformer class. Since the SimpleMod2 class is not directly supported by the App Wizard, you will also need to manually change the class that your plug-in is derived from, from SimpleMod to SimpleMod2. You will also need to manually implement three functions from the SimpleMod2 class since they are not contained in the SDK libraries. These functions are *GetReference*, *SetReference*, and *SubAnim*.

For the user to specify the axial direction for scaling, let's use a group of three radio buttons specifying each axis (x, y, and z). Modify the IDD_PANEL dialog resource to look like Figure 16.1.

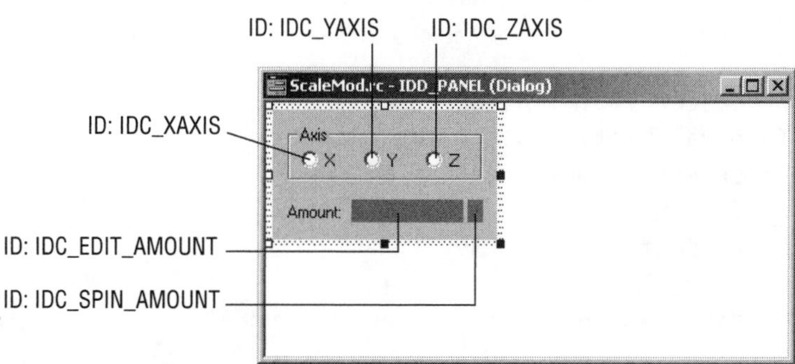

Figure 16.1 ScaleMod *dialog resource*

Now, modify ScaleMod.cpp and add all code necessary to correctly implement the ScaleMod class, as shown in Listing 16.1. You can access this code on the CD-ROM that accompanies this book in the file named ScaleMod.cpp.

LISTING 16.1: MAIN PLUG-IN SOURCE (*SCALEMOD.CPP*)

```
// ==============================================================
// ScaleMod.cpp
// Copyright ©2000, Simon Feltman
// --------------------------------------------------------------
#include "ScaleMod.h"

#define SCALEMOD_CLASS_ID  Class_ID(0x1d49e280, 0x5354699e)


// ==============================================================
class ScaleMod : public SimpleMod2
{
public:
   static IObjParam *ip;

   ScaleMod();
   void DeleteThis() { delete this; }

   // plug-in identification
   Class_ID ClassID() { return SCALEMOD_CLASS_ID; }
   void GetClassName(TSTR& s) {
      s = GetString(IDS_CLASS_NAME);
   }
   TCHAR* GetObjectName() {
      return GetString(IDS_CLASS_NAME);
   }

   // object modification functions
   Interval  GetValidity(TimeValue t);
   Deformer& GetDeformer(
      TimeValue t,
      ModContext &mc,
      Matrix3& mat,
      Matrix3& invmat);
```

```
    // open / close of ui rollouts
    void BeginEditParams(
       IObjParam *ip,
       ULONG flags,
       Animatable *prev);
    void EndEditParams(
       IObjParam *ip,
       ULONG flags,
       Animatable *next);

    // parameter block access
    int NumParamBlocks() { return 1; }
    IParamBlock2* GetParamBlock(int i) { return pblock2; }
    IParamBlock2* GetParamBlockByID(BlockID id) {
       return (pblock2->ID() == id) ? pblock2 : NULL;
    }

    RefTargetHandle Clone(RemapDir &remap);
    void InvalidateUI();
};

IObjParam *ScaleMod::ip = NULL;

// =============================================================
class ScaleModClassDesc : public ClassDesc2
{
public:
    int IsPublic() { return 1; }
    void* Create(BOOL loading = FALSE) {
       return new ScaleMod();
    }
    const TCHAR* ClassName() {
       return GetString(IDS_CLASS_NAME);
    }
    SClass_ID    SuperClassID() {return OSM_CLASS_ID;}
    Class_ID     ClassID() {return SCALEMOD_CLASS_ID;}
    const TCHAR* Category(){return GetString(IDS_CATEGORY);}
    const TCHAR* InternalName() { return _T("ScaleMod"); }
    HINSTANCE    HInstance() { return hInstance; }
};
```

```
static ScaleModClassDesc scaleModDesc;
ClassDesc2* GetScaleModDesc() { return &scaleModDesc; }

// ==========================================================
enum { scalemod_params };
enum {
   pb_axis,
   pb_amount,
};

static ParamBlockDesc2 scalemod_param_blk(
   scalemod_params, _T("params"), 0, &scaleModDesc,
   P_AUTO_CONSTRUCT + P_AUTO_UI, SIMPMOD_PBLOCKREF,
   IDD_PANEL, IDS_PARAMS, 0, 0, NULL,

   pb_axis, _T("axis"), TYPE_INT,
         P_RESET_DEFAULT, IDS_AXIS,
      p_default, 0,
      p_ui,      TYPE_RADIO, 3,
         IDC_XAXIS, IDC_YAXIS, IDC_ZAXIS,
      end,

   pb_amount, _T("amount"), TYPE_FLOAT,
         P_ANIMATABLE|P_RESET_DEFAULT, IDS_AMOUNT,
      p_default, 0.f,
      p_range,   -FLT_MAX, FLT_MAX,
      p_ui,      TYPE_SPINNER, EDITTYPE_FLOAT,
         IDC_EDIT_AMOUNT, IDC_SPIN_AMOUNT, SPIN_AUTOSCALE,
      end,
   end
);


// ==========================================================
// Deformer class that does the actual object modification
// on a point by point basis.
class ScaleModDeformer: public Deformer
{
public:
   int axis;
```

```
   float amount;
   Box3 *bbox;

   ScaleModDeformer();
   ScaleModDeformer(int axis, float amount, Box3 *bbox);
   Point3 Map(int i, Point3 p);
};

// ============================================================
ScaleModDeformer::ScaleModDeformer()
{
   amount = 0.f;
   axis = 0;
   bbox = NULL;
}

// ============================================================
ScaleModDeformer::ScaleModDeformer(
   int axis, float amount, Box3 *bbox)
{
   if(axis < 0)
      axis = 0;
   else if(axis > 2)
      axis = 2;

   this->axis = axis;
   this->amount = amount;
   this->bbox = bbox;
}

// ============================================================
Point3 ScaleModDeformer::Map(int i, Point3 p)
{
   Point3 width = bbox->Width();
   Point3 center = bbox->Center();
   float scale = (p[axis]-center[axis]) / width[axis];
   p[axis] += scale * amount;

   return p;
}
```

```
// ==========================================================
ScaleMod::ScaleMod()
{
   scaleModDesc.MakeAutoParamBlocks(this);
   assert(pblock2);
}

// ==========================================================
RefTargetHandle ScaleMod::Clone(RemapDir& remap)
{
   ScaleMod* newmod = new ScaleMod();
   newmod->ReplaceReference(
      SIMPMOD_PBLOCKREF, pblock2->Clone(remap));
   newmod->SimpleModClone(this);
   return(newmod);
}

// ==========================================================
void ScaleMod::BeginEditParams(
   IObjParam *ip,
   ULONG flags,
   Animatable *prev)
{
   this->ip = ip;
   SimpleMod::BeginEditParams(ip, flags, prev);
   scaleModDesc.BeginEditParams(ip, this, flags, prev);
}

// ==========================================================
void ScaleMod::EndEditParams(
   IObjParam *ip,
   ULONG flags,
   Animatable *next)
{
   SimpleMod::EndEditParams(ip, flags, next);
   scaleModDesc.EndEditParams(ip, this, flags, next);
   this->ip = NULL;
}
```

```
// ============================================================
Interval ScaleMod::GetValidity(TimeValue t)
{
   float f;
   Interval valid = FOREVER;
   pblock2->GetValue(pb_amount, t, f, valid);
   return valid;
}

// ============================================================
Deformer& ScaleMod::GetDeformer(
   TimeValue t,
   ModContext &mc,
   Matrix3& mat,
   Matrix3& invmat)
{
   static ScaleModDeformer deformer;

   deformer = ScaleModDeformer(
      pblock2->GetInt(pb_axis, t),
      pblock2->GetFloat(pb_amount, t),
      mc.box);

   return deformer;
}

// ============================================================
void ScaleMod::InvalidateUI()
{
   scalemod_param_blk.InvalidateUI(
      pblock2->LastNotifyParamID());
}


// ============================================================
// The following functions were taken from simpmod.cpp
// located int maxsdk\samples\HowTo\Misc\.
RefTargetHandle SimpleMod2::GetReference(int i)
{
```

```
    switch(i)
    {
    case 0: return tmControl;
    case 1: return posControl;
    case 2: return pblock2;
    default: return NULL;
    }
}

// ============================================================
void SimpleMod2::SetReference(int i, RefTargetHandle rtarg)
{
    switch(i)
    {
    case 0: tmControl = (Control*)rtarg; break;
    case 1: posControl = (Control*)rtarg; break;
    case 2: pblock2 = (IParamBlock2*)rtarg; break;
    }
}

// ============================================================
Animatable* SimpleMod2::SubAnim(int i)
{
    switch(i)
    {
    case 0: return posControl;
    case 1: return tmControl;
    case 2: return pblock2;
    default: return NULL;
    }
}
```

Advanced Modifiers

Advanced modifiers in MAX have the ability to modify all portions of the geometry for an object, not just the vertices. These portions of an object are called *geometry pipeline channels.*

Geometry Pipeline Channels

Modifiers use different channels to represent portions of an object. This allows objects flowing through the pipeline to get built faster because the pipeline can filter out the exact portions of an object that need to be rebuilt without rebuilding the entire object. Channels are represented by integer flags that can be combined with each other to represent more than one channel.

Channel Flags

Table 16.1 lists the channels used in the pipeline along with the corresponding channel flag that Modifier plug-ins will work with.

Table 16.1 Channel Flags

CHANNEL FLAG	DESCRIPTION
GEOM_CHANNEL	Vertices
TOPO_CHANNEL	Topology (faces, polygons, edge visibility, smoothing groups, texture IDs)
TEXMAP_CHANNEL	Texture vertices and mapping
MTL_CHANNEL	Material on per-face basis
SELECT_CHANNEL	Selection bits
SUBSEL_TYPE_CHANNEL	Vertex / Face / Edge
DISP_ATTRIB_CHANNEL	Display attributes
VERTCOLOR_CHANNEL	Color per vertex
GFX_DATA_CHANNEL	Stripping, edge list, etc.
DISP_APPROX_CHANNEL	Displacement approximation

The *Modifier* Class

The `Modifier` class represents advanced modifiers in the MAX SDK. This class is very similar to all other plug-in classes since it is directly derived from the `BaseObject` class and inherits the standard functions from the `Animatable` and `ReferenceTarget` classes. The `SimpleMod` class used earlier is actually derived from `Modifier` and behaves very similarly, except you do not use a deformer. To implement a `Modifier`-based plug-in, you will need to override the following functions, which are specific to the `Modifier` class.

ChannelMask ChannelsUsed() This function should return a combination of the channel flags corresponding to the channels your Modifier plug-in will use. For instance, if your plug-in needs vertices, faces, and vertex colors, you would return `(GEOM_CHANNEL | TOPO_CHANNEL | VERTCOLOR_CHANNEL)`. The following code shows an example of the *ChannelsUsed* function:

```
ChannelMask MyMod::ChannelsUsed() {
   return (VERTCOLOR_CHANNEL|GEOM_CHANNEL|TOPO_CHANNEL);
}
```

ChannelMask ChannelsChanged() This function should return a combination of the channel flags corresponding to the channels that your plug-in will modify. For instance, if your plug-in modifies vertices and texture coordinates, you would return `(GEOM_CHANNEL | TEXMAP_CHANNEL)`. The following code shows an example of the *ChannelsChanged* function:

```
ChannelMask MyMod::ChannelsChanged() {
   return (GEOM_CHANNEL | TEXMAP_CHANNEL);
}
```

Class_ID InputType() This is where you let MAX know the type of object that this plug-in can work with. This function should return the Class ID of the object type supported by this modifier. For the most part, you will just return the globally defined `triObjectClassID` variable for triangle-based geometry. The following code shows an example of the *InputType* function:

```
Class_ID MyMod::InputType() { return triObjectClassID; }
```

BOOL ChangeTopology() This function lets MAX know if your plug-in changes the topology of the object. It returns true if your plug-in does; otherwise, it returns false. You will need to override this function if your plug-in does not change the topology since the default implementation returns true.

ModifyObject(TimeValue t, ModContext &mc, ObjectState *os, INode *node) This is the main function MAX calls to do the actual modification of the object. This is called to rebuild the pipeline object cache when the time is no longer within the validity interval. This function is passed the time when the modification is to take place, where `ModContext` lets you know what space the modifier was applied in, `ObjectState` is what you'll be doing the modification on, and `INode` will always be `NULL` for object space modifiers. The following code shows an example of the *ModifyObject* function that just scales all vertices by two. Since your *InputType* function returned `triObjectClassID`, you don't need to worry about the type of object you're working with because it is guaranteed to be a `TriObject`.

```
void MyMod::ModifyObject(
   TimeValue t, ModContext &mc,
   ObjectState *os, INode *node)
{
   // get the mesh
   TriObject *triObj = (TriObject*)os->obj;
   Mesh &mesh = triObj->GetMesh();

   // run through each vertex and scale by 2
   for(int i = 0; i < mesh.numVerts; i++)
   {
      Point3 &vtx = mesh.getVert(i);
      vtx *= 2.f;
   }
}
```

Interval LocalValidity(TimeValue t) This function should return the validity interval of all animatable properties combined. This will let MAX know when it needs to rebuild the cache for the object. `LocalValidity` is very similar to the *GetValidity* function used for simple modifiers. The following code shows an example of the *LocalValidity* function:

```
Interval MeshPull::LocalValidity(TimeValue t)
{
   float f;
   Interval valid = FOREVER;

   // Build up the validity interval from all the
   // animatable parameters.
   pblock->GetValue(pb_length, t, f, valid);
   pblock->GetValue(pb_width, t, f, valid);

   return valid;
}
```

Implementing a Modifier

Now that you know the functions needed to implement a modifier, let's move on to an example. This example shows how to create a Modifier plug-in that uses the geometry and vertex color channels and modifies the geometry channel. The plug-in will pull a mesh's vertices in a vertex's normal direction by a user-specified amount using the vertex color as a weight value.

Use the SDK App Wizard to create a plug-in named MeshPull of type `Modifiers` derived from the `Modifier` class. Change the `IDD_PANEL` dialog resource to look like Figure 16.2.

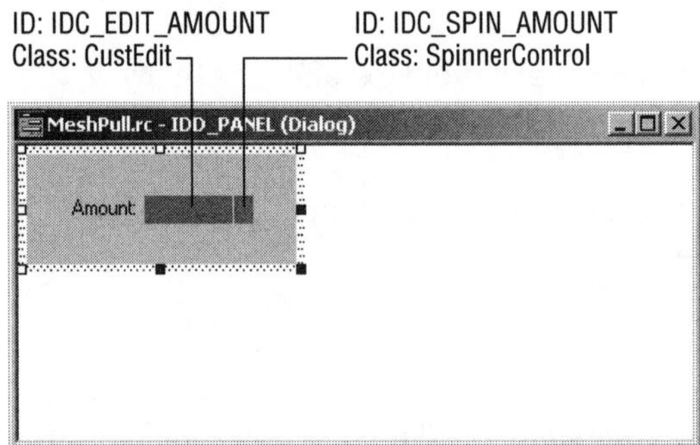

Figure 16.2 *The MeshPull dialog resource*

Now, modify `MeshPull.cpp` and add all the code necessary to correctly implement the `MeshPull` class, as shown in Listing 16.2. You can access this code on the CD-ROM in the file named `MeshPull.cpp`.

LISTING 16.2: THE MAIN PLUG-IN SOURCE (*MESHPULL.CPP*)

```
// ==============================================================
// MeshPull.cpp
// Copyright ©2000, Simon Feltman
// --------------------------------------------------------------
#include "MeshPull.h"

#define MESHPULL_CLASS_ID  Class_ID(0x4ed6bff3, 0x278b47cf)
#define PBLOCK_REF   0
```

```
// ===========================================================
class MeshPull : public Modifier
{
public:
   IParamBlock2 *pblock;
   static IObjParam *ip;

   MeshPull();
   ~MeshPull();
   void DeleteThis() { delete this; }

   // Class identification
   void GetClassName(TSTR& s) {
      s = GetString(IDS_CLASS_NAME);
   }
   TCHAR *GetObjectName() {
      return GetString(IDS_CLASS_NAME);
   }
   Class_ID ClassID() {
      return MESHPULL_CLASS_ID;
   }

   // Return what parts of an object this modifier needs
   ChannelMask ChannelsUsed() {
      return (VERTCOLOR_CHANNEL|GEOM_CHANNEL|TOPO_CHANNEL);
   }

   // Return what parts of an object this modifier changes
   ChannelMask ChannelsChanged() { return GEOM_CHANNEL; }

   // Type of object this modifier can modify
   Class_ID InputType() { return triObjectClassID; }

   // True if this modifier changes the topology
   BOOL ChangeTopology() { return FALSE; }

   // This function does the actual object modification
   void ModifyObject(
      TimeValue t,
      ModContext &mc,
```

```
        ObjectState *os,
        INode *node);

    // Time range that the parameters are valid
    Interval LocalValidity(TimeValue t);

    // Reference support
    int NumRefs() { return 1; }
    RefTargetHandle GetReference(int i) { return pblock; }
    void SetReference(int i, RefTargetHandle rtarg) {
        pblock=(IParamBlock2*)rtarg; }
    RefTargetHandle Clone( RemapDir &remap );
    RefResult NotifyRefChanged(
        Interval changeInt, RefTargetHandle hTarget,
        PartID& partID,  RefMessage message);

    // Subanim support
    int NumSubs() { return 1; }
    TSTR SubAnimName(int i) { return GetString(IDS_PARAMS); }
    Animatable* SubAnim(int i) { return pblock; }

    // Parameter block functions
    int   NumParamBlocks() { return 1; }
    IParamBlock2* GetParamBlock(int i) { return pblock; }
    IParamBlock2* GetParamBlockByID(BlockID id) {
        return (pblock->ID() == id) ? pblock : NULL;
    }
    int GetParamBlockIndex(int id) { return id; }

    CreateMouseCallBack* GetCreateMouseCallBack() {
        return NULL;
    }
    void BeginEditParams(IObjParam *ip,
        ULONG flags, Animatable *prev);
    void EndEditParams(IObjParam *ip,
        ULONG flags, Animatable *next);
};

IObjParam *MeshPull::ip = NULL;
```

```
// ================================================================
class MeshPullClassDesc : public ClassDesc2
{
public:
   int IsPublic() { return 1; }
   void* Create(BOOL loading = FALSE) {
      return new MeshPull();
   }
   const TCHAR* ClassName() {
      return GetString(IDS_CLASS_NAME);
   }
   SClass_ID SuperClassID() { return OSM_CLASS_ID; }
   Class_ID  ClassID() { return MESHPULL_CLASS_ID; }
   const TCHAR* Category() {return GetString(IDS_CATEGORY);}
   const TCHAR* InternalName() { return _T("MeshPull"); }
   HINSTANCE HInstance() { return hInstance; }
};

static MeshPullClassDesc MeshPullDesc;
ClassDesc2* GetMeshPullDesc() {return &MeshPullDesc;}


// ================================================================
enum { meshpull_params };
enum {
   pb_amount = 0,
};

// ================================================================
static ParamBlockDesc2 meshpull_param_blk(
   meshpull_params, _T("params"),  0, &MeshPullDesc,
   P_AUTO_CONSTRUCT + P_AUTO_UI, PBLOCK_REF,
   IDD_PANEL, IDS_PARAMS, 0, 0, NULL,

   pb_amount,      _T("amount"), TYPE_FLOAT,
                   P_ANIMATABLE | P_RESET_DEFAULT,
                   IDS_AMOUNT,
      p_default,   10.f,
      p_range,     -FLT_MAX, FLT_MAX,
```

```
      p_ui,        TYPE_SPINNER, EDITTYPE_FLOAT,
                   IDC_EDIT_AMOUNT, IDC_SPIN_AMOUNT,
                   SPIN_AUTOSCALE,
      end,
   end
);


// ============================================================
MeshPull::MeshPull()
{
   MeshPullDesc.MakeAutoParamBlocks(this);
}
MeshPull::~MeshPull() {}

// ============================================================
Interval MeshPull::LocalValidity(TimeValue t)
{
   float f;
   Interval valid = FOREVER;
   pblock->GetValue(pb_amount, t, f, valid);
   return valid;
}

// ============================================================
RefTargetHandle MeshPull::Clone(RemapDir& remap)
{
   MeshPull* newmod = new MeshPull();
   newmod->ReplaceReference(0, pblock->Clone(remap));
   return(newmod);
}

// ============================================================
void MeshPull::BeginEditParams(
   IObjParam *ip, ULONG flags,Animatable *prev )
{
   this->ip = ip;
   MeshPullDesc.BeginEditParams(ip, this, flags, prev);
}
```

```
// ==========================================================
void MeshPull::EndEditParams(
   IObjParam *ip, ULONG flags,Animatable *next)
{
   MeshPullDesc.EndEditParams(ip, this, flags, next);
   this->ip = NULL;
}

// ==========================================================
RefResult MeshPull::NotifyRefChanged(
      Interval changeInt, RefTargetHandle hTarget,
      PartID& partID,  RefMessage message)
{
   switch(message)
   {
   case REFMSG_CHANGE:
      meshpull_param_blk.InvalidateUI();
      break;
   }
   return REF_SUCCEED;
}

// ==========================================================
void MeshPull::ModifyObject(TimeValue t, ModContext &mc,
                            ObjectState * os, INode *node)
{
   // get the mesh
   TriObject *triObj = (TriObject*)os->obj;
   Mesh &mesh = triObj->GetMesh();

   // get the amount parameter
   float amount = pblock->GetFloat(pb_amount, t);

   // check if the mesh has vertex colors defined
   if(mesh.mapSupport(0) == FALSE)
      return;

   // create arrays to calculate the weights
   float *weights = new float[mesh.numVerts];
```

```
    int   *colCnt  = new int[mesh.numVerts];

    memset(weights, 0, sizeof(float) * mesh.numVerts);
    memset(colCnt, 0, sizeof(int) * mesh.numVerts);

    Point3 *vcVerts = mesh.mapVerts(0);
    TVFace *vcFace = mesh.mapFaces(0);
    Face   *face   = mesh.faces;

    // run through all vertex color faces and add up
    // colors that overlap, then average them later
    for(int i = 0; i < mesh.numFaces; i++, vcFace++, face++)
    {
       for(int j = 0; j < 3; j++)
       {
          Point3 *col = &vcVerts[vcFace->t[j]];
          weights[face->v[j]] +=
             1.f - (col->x + col->y + col->z) / 3.f;
          colCnt[face->v[j]] += 1;
       }
    }

    // extrude each vertex based on its normal based on
    // weights already calculated
    mesh.checkNormals(TRUE);
    for(i = 0; i < mesh.numVerts; i++)
    {
       Point3 &vtx = mesh.getVert(i);
       Point3 &norm = mesh.getNormal(i);

       weights[i] /= colCnt[i];
       float weight = amount * weights[i];

       vtx += norm * weight;
    }

    delete[] weights;
    delete[] colCnt;
}
```

Using the MeshPull *Modifier*

Now that you have a cool modifier implemented, let's put it to use. First, create a quad patch and apply the `Vertex Paint` modifier to it. Now, paint a landscape. Remember that black vertices are going to be pulled 100%; white vertices will be pulled 0%; and all colors will be averaged in between. After painting, apply the `MeshPull` modifier and play with the `amount` parameter. Figure 16.3 shows an example of what you can do with the `MeshPull` modifier.

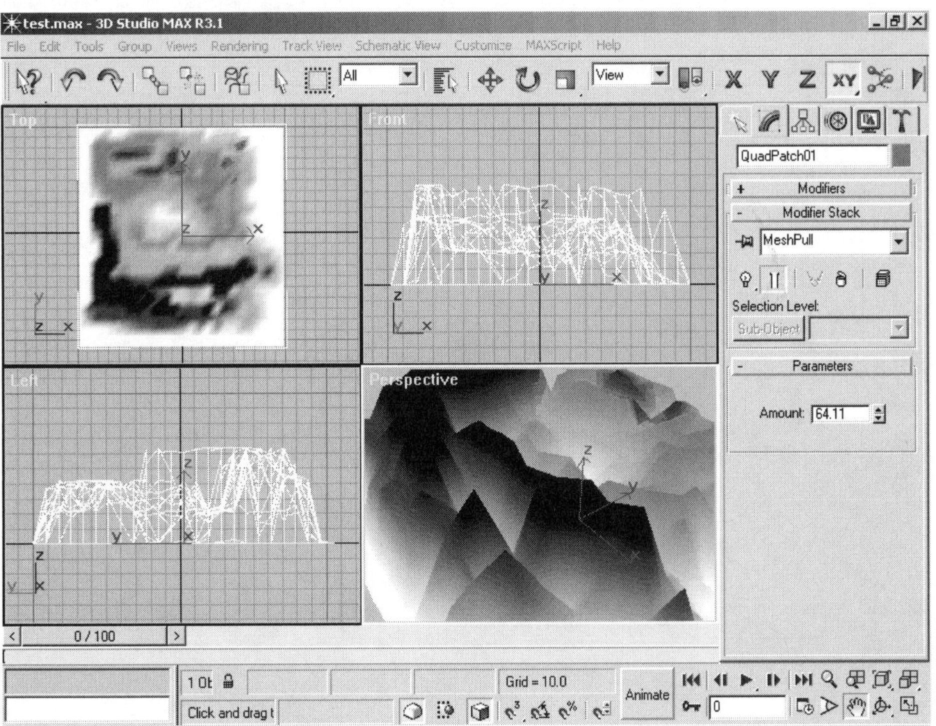

Figure 16.3 Using the MeshPull *modifier*

Summary

In this chapter, you learned some of the advanced concepts used in the 3D Studio MAX SDK, such as geometry pipeline channels, deformers, and validity intervals. Using these concepts, you can implement some very powerful object modifiers.

This ability to create complex Modifier plug-ins that are either utilities for modeling or are totally new modeling concepts can greatly enhance what artists have to work with and allows almost anyone to try new modeling techniques.

In the next chapter, you will move on to learning about some of the more subtle plug-ins that you can create in MAX, such as exporters, importers, and global utilities.

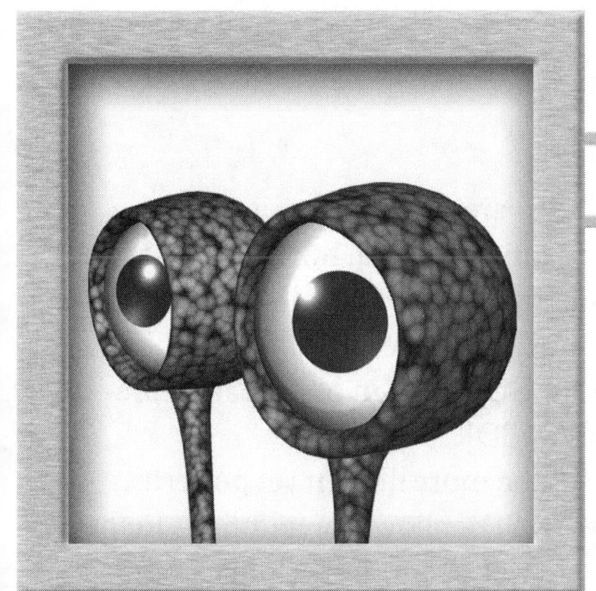

Global Utility Plug-Ins

MAXSCRIPT

Chapter 17

G*lobal Utility plug-ins* (GUPs) are plug-ins that are run at MAX startup time and can add global functionality to MAX. These plug-ins are probably the simplest of plug-in types for MAX but still provide much power, especially for adding and changing the way MAX works. GUP plug-in objects are represented with the class `GUP` in the MAX SDK.

This chapter will cover some of the more hidden yet powerful aspects of the MAX SDK. The MAX SDK allows for additions to the Right-Click menu, for system event notification, and for custom scene and object data. The following is a list of SDK features that this chapter will cover:

- Global Utility plug-ins
- Custom user properties
- Custom Right-Click menus
- Custom notification callbacks

Creating a Global Utility Plug-In

To create a Global Utility plug-in (GUP), use the SDK App Wizard to create a skeleton of type `Global Utility Plug-ins` that is named GameUtil.

GUP Implementation

For GUP derived classes, you are required to implement two functions. These functions are described as follows:

Start() The *Start* member function is called when MAX starts up. All initialization code and custom MAX functionality should be implemented in this function. You must return a code from this function to let MAX know how this utility should be handled. The following table describes the valid return codes you can return from the *Start* function.

Return Code	Description
GUPRESULT_KEEP	Returns this value to have the plug-in remain loaded
GUPRESULT_NOKEEP	Returns this value to discard
GUPRESULT_ABORT	Return this value to shut down MAX

Stop() The *Stop* member function is called by the system when MAX is shutting down. You can do any cleanup and proper de-registration of objects in this function. You can also optionally implement the saving and loading of custom data, along with a function named *Control*, which allows other plug-ins to access the Global Utility plug-in. The *Control* function is described as follows:

Control(DWORD parameter) The *Control* member function can be implemented to perform operations on the Global Utility plug-in, depending on the parameter passed. The following is an example of a Global Utility plug-in's implementation:

```
#define GU_OP1 0x01
#define GU_OP2 0x02

class GameUtil : public GUP
{
public:
```

```
    DWORD   Start();
    void    Stop();
    DWORD   Control(DWORD parameter);
    DWORD   Op1() { return 1; }
    DWORD   Op2() { return 2; }
};

DWORD GameUtil::Start()
{
    return GUPRESULT_KEEP;
}

void GameUtil::Stop() {}

DWORD GameUtil::Control(DWORD parameter)
{
    switch(parameter)
    {
    case GU_OP1:
        return Op1();
    case GU_OP2:
        return Op2();
    };

    return 0;
}
```

Custom User Properties

The scene and individual nodes have the ability to store custom user data that gets saved and loaded from MAX scene files.

Custom Node Properties

The `INode` class contains functions for getting and setting custom properties. These functions allow you to get and set string, boolean, float, and integer value's. The following code shows an example of setting and getting a custom string property on a given node:

```
TSTR str("c:\\temp");
node->SetUserPropString(TSTR("TEMPDIR"), str);
node->GetUserPropString(TSTR("TEMPDIR"), str);
```

Custom Scene Properties

Custom properties and data that is global to the scene can be stored through the app data mechanism. *App data* stores buffers of data at unique IDs for a given `Animatable`-derived class. This means you can also use app data for nodes. To get a pointer to the global scene, the `Interface` class contains the *GetScenePointer* function. The following code sample shows how to add custom data to the scene and how to retrieve it:

```
// Get a pointer to the scene
ReferenceTarget *pScene = ip->GetScenePointer();

char str = "Test String";

// Add an app data chunk
pScene->AddAppDataChunk(
   GAMEUTIL_CLASS_ID,
   GUP_CLASS_ID,
   ID_STRING,
   (DWORD)sizeof(str)+1, str);

// Get the app data chunk
AppDataChunk *adc = pScene->GetAppDataChunk(
   GAMEUTIL_CLASS_ID, GUP_CLASS_ID, ID_STRING);

// adc will now contain a pointer to the buffer and
// its length
```

Custom Right-Click Menus

It is possible to append custom menus to the Right-Click menu in MAX viewports. This can be achieved by registering an instance of a custom menu class derived from the `RightClickMenu` class. Registration of Right-Click menus is done through the

`RightClickMenuManager` class. An instance to the manager can be retrieved from MAX with the *GetRightClickMenuManager* function of the `Interface` class.

The *RightClickMenuManager* Class

The `RightClickMenuManager` class also contains a function for adding menu items called *AddMenu*. This function has the ability to add general menu item commands and separators. The *AddMenu* function is defined as follows:

```
int AddMenu(
    RightClickMenu *menu,
    UINT flags,
    UINT id,
    LPCTSTR data);
```

This function takes an instance of the `RightClickMenu` class, flags, a unique ID, and a string for the text that will show up on the menu. The `RightClickMenu` class is described later. The flags can be one or more of the following flags described in Table 17.1.

Table 17.1 Flag Options

FLAGS	DESCRIPTION
MF_CHECKED	The menu item will be checked.
MF_UNCHECKED	The menu item will be unchecked.
MF_STRING	The menu item is a string.
MF_DISABLED	The menu item is disabled.
MF_GRAYED	The menu item is grayed.
MF_SEPARATOR	The menu item is a seperator.

The *RightClickMenu* Class

The `RightClickMenu` class is a base class for custom menu classes that implement additions to the Right-Click menu. To properly register a Right-Click menu, you must use the `RightClickMenuManager` class's *Register* function, passing it an instance to the `RightClickMenu` class. This instance is also passed to the `RightClickMenuManager`'s *AddMenu* function.

Classes derived from `RightClickMenu` are required to implement two functions. These functions are described as follows:

Init The *Init* function is called whenever the menu needs to be opened. This allows you to filter additions to the Right-Click menu based on the state that MAX is in. For instance, you can add a menu item only if an editable mesh is selected. From within this function, you should directly add menu items via the `RightClickMenuManager`'s *AddMenu* function.

Selected The *Selected* function is called when an item is clicked in the menu. This function is passed the ID of the item that is clicked. The ID passed to this function is the same ID used in the *AddMenu* function.

Adding a Right-Click Menu

Using the classes and functions described, it is possible to add Right-Click menu items, as follows:

```
#define ID_TEST 1

// custom right click menu class
class CustRCMenu : public RightClickMenu
{
public:
   void Init(RightClickMenuManager *manager,
             HWND hWnd, IPoint2 m);
   void Selected(UINT id);
};
CustRCMenu custMenu;  // global instance of the rcmenu

// Get a pointer to a manager and register our menu
RightClickMenuManager *rcmm =
   ip->GetRightClickMenuManager();
rcmm->Register(&custMenu);

// Function called to add menu items
void CustRCMenu::Init(
   RightClickMenuManager *manager, HWND hWnd, IPoint2 m)
{
   manager->AddMenu(this, MF_SEPARATOR, 0, NULL);
   manager->AddMenu(this, MF_STRING, ID_TEST, _T("Test"));
}
```

```
// ==============================================================
void CustRCMenu::Selected(UINT id)
{
   if(id == ID_TEST)
      MessageBox(NULL, "Test!", NULL, MB_OK);
}
```

Custom Notification Callbacks

The MAX SDK allows programmers the ability to implement notification callback functions that MAX will call when certain events occur. These callback functions are implemented as global functions and must be registered with MAX for them to work. General callback functions are defined as follows:

```
void NotificationCallback(void *param, NotifyInfo *info);
```

The notification callback functions are passed a pointer to custom user data and a pointer to a `NotifyInfo` class. To register the callback function, the MAX SDK provides the *RegisterNotification* and *UnRegisterNotification* functions. You pass both of these functions the callback function, custom data, and the notification code. There are many notification codes, please see the SDK help file for a complete listing.

The following code shows how to implement and register a notification callback that pops up a message box after a file has been opened:

```
// define the callback function
static void FilePostOpen(void *param, NotifyInfo *info)
{
   MessageBox(NULL, "FilePostOpen", NULL, MB_OK);
}

// register the callback function
RegisterNotification(
   FilePostOpen, 0, NOTIFY_FILE_POST_OPEN);
```

Implementing a Custom Properties GUP

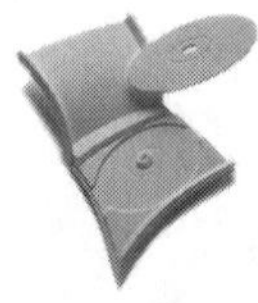

Now that you have the file format defined, you can modify the `GameUtil.cpp` file and add all the code necessary to implement custom world and entity properties, as shown in Listing 17.1. You can access this code on the CD-ROM in the file named `GameUtil.cpp`.

Figures 17.1 and 17.2 show what the Properties dialog box resources should look like.

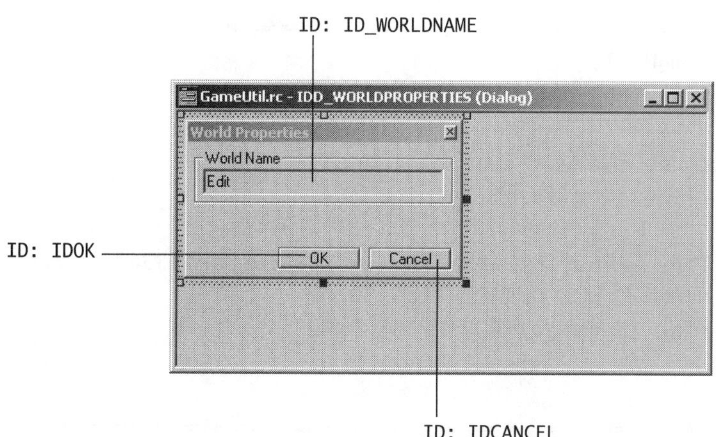

Figure 17.1 *The World Properties dialog box user interface*

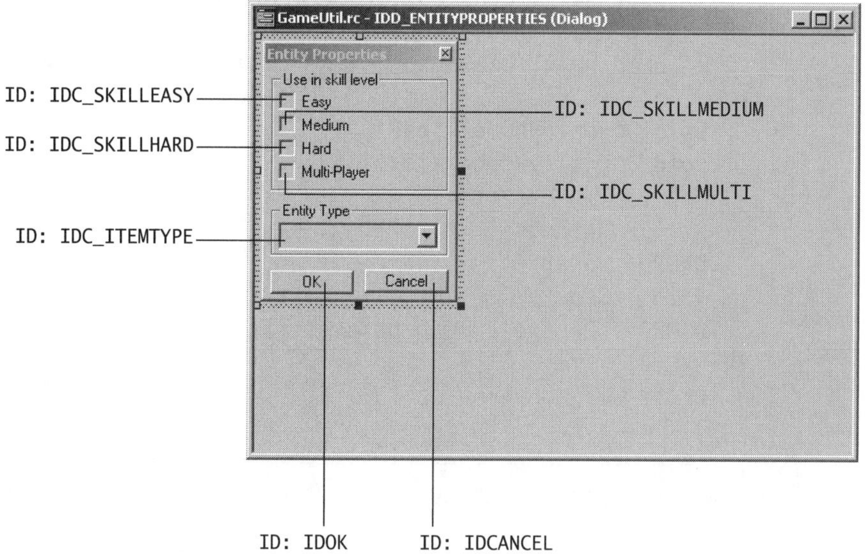

Figure 17.2 *The Entity Properties user interface*

Listing 17.1: The Main Plug-in File (*GameUtil.cpp*)

```
// ===========================================================
// GameUtil.cpp
// Copyright ©2000, Simon Feltman
// -----------------------------------------------------------
#include "GameUtil.h"
#include "Notify.h"

#define GAMEUTIL_CLASS_ID   Class_ID(0x61133631, 0xaac13eb)
#define ID_WORLDPROPERTIES  0x01
#define ID_ENTITYPROPERTIES 0x02


// ===========================================================
class GameUtil : public GUP
{
public:
   static BOOL WorldPropDlgProc(
      HWND hDlg, UINT msg, WPARAM wParam, LPARAM lParam);
   static BOOL EntityPropDlgProc(
      HWND hDlg, UINT msg, WPARAM wParam, LPARAM lParam);

   void DoWorldPropertiesDlg();
   void DoEntityPropertiesDlg();

   // GUP Methods
   DWORD   Start();
   void   Stop();
   DWORD   Control(DWORD parameter);
};


// ===========================================================
class GameUtilClassDesc : public ClassDesc2
{
public:
   int IsPublic() { return 1; }
   void* Create(BOOL loading = FALSE) {
      return new GameUtil();
   }
   const TCHAR* ClassName() {
```

```
      return GetString(IDS_CLASS_NAME);
   }
   SClass_ID SuperClassID() { return GUP_CLASS_ID; }
   Class_ID ClassID() { return GAMEUTIL_CLASS_ID; }
   const TCHAR* Category() {
      return GetString(IDS_CATEGORY);
   }
   const TCHAR* InternalName() { return _T("GameUtil"); }
   HINSTANCE HInstance() { return hInstance; }
};

static GameUtilClassDesc GameUtilDesc;
ClassDesc2* GetGameUtilDesc() {return &GameUtilDesc;}


// ==========================================================
class CustRCMenu : public RightClickMenu
{
protected:
   GUP *gup;

public:
   void SetGUP(GUP *gup) { this->gup = gup; }
   void Init(RightClickMenuManager *manager,
             HWND hWnd, IPoint2 m);
   void Selected(UINT id);
};
CustRCMenu custMenu;

// ==========================================================
static void SystemPostNew(void *param, NotifyInfo *info)
{
   GUP *gup = (GUP*)param;
   gup->Control(ID_WORLDPROPERTIES);
}

// ==========================================================
BOOL GameUtil::WorldPropDlgProc(
   HWND hDlg, UINT msg, WPARAM wParam, LPARAM lParam)
{
```

```
GUP *gup = (GUP*)GetWindowLong(hDlg, DWL_USER);

switch(msg)
{
case WM_INITDIALOG:
   {
      gup = (GUP*)lParam;
      SetWindowLong(hDlg, DWL_USER, lParam);

      // Center this dialog
      CenterWindow(hDlg, gup->MaxWnd());

      // Get the app data, if it exists use it otherwise
      // use default
      ReferenceTarget *pScene =
         gup->Max()->GetScenePointer();
      AppDataChunk *adc = pScene->GetAppDataChunk(
        GAMEUTIL_CLASS_ID, GUP_CLASS_ID, IDC_WORLDNAME);

      if(adc)
      {
         SetDlgItemText(
            hDlg, IDC_WORLDNAME, (TCHAR*)adc->data);
      }
      else
      {
         SetDlgItemText(
            hDlg, IDC_WORLDNAME, "My World");
      }
      return TRUE;
   }

case WM_COMMAND:
   switch(LOWORD(wParam))
   {
   case IDOK:
      {
         // Allocate a text buffer for the world
         // name and get it
         int len = GetWindowTextLength(
            GetDlgItem(hDlg, IDC_WORLDNAME)) + 1;
```

```
            char *buf = (char*)malloc(len);
            GetWindowText(
               GetDlgItem(hDlg, IDC_WORLDNAME), buf, len);
            buf[len-1] = '\0';

            // Remove the app data chunk if it exists then
            // add it back.
            ReferenceTarget *pScene =
               gup->Max()->GetScenePointer();

            pScene->RemoveAppDataChunk(
               GAMEUTIL_CLASS_ID,
               GUP_CLASS_ID,
               IDC_WORLDNAME);

            pScene->AddAppDataChunk(
               GAMEUTIL_CLASS_ID,
               GUP_CLASS_ID,
               IDC_WORLDNAME,
               (DWORD)len, buf);

            EndDialog(hDlg, 0);
            return TRUE;
         }

      case IDCANCEL:
         EndDialog(hDlg, 0);
         return TRUE;
      };
   };
   return FALSE;
}

// ===========================================================
BOOL GameUtil::EntityPropDlgProc(
   HWND hDlg, UINT msg, WPARAM wParam, LPARAM lParam)
{
   char str[128];
   GUP *gup = (GUP*)GetWindowLong(hDlg, DWL_USER);
```

```
switch(msg)
{
case WM_INITDIALOG:
   {
      gup = (GUP*)lParam;
      SetWindowLong(hDlg, DWL_USER, lParam);

      // Center this dialog
      CenterWindow(hDlg, gup->MaxWnd());

      //Open up GameObjects.txt in the plugcfg directory
      TSTR fname = TSTR(gup->Max()->GetDir(
         APP_PLUGCFG_DIR)) + "\\GameObjects.txt";

      FILE *stream = fopen((char*)fname, "rt");
      if(stream != NULL)
      {
         // Read each line of GameObjects.txt add to
         // the list box
         while(fgets(str, sizeof(str), stream))
         {
            char *nl = strrchr(str, '\n');
            if(nl) *nl = '\0';
            SendDlgItemMessage(hDlg, IDC_ITEMTYPE,
               CB_ADDSTRING, 0, (LPARAM)str);
         }

         fclose(stream);
      }
      else
      {
         // give error if we cant open GameObjects.txt
         SendDlgItemMessage(hDlg, IDC_ITEMTYPE,
            CB_ADDSTRING, 0, (LPARAM)"-- none --");

         MessageBox(hDlg, "Can't load GameObjects.txt",
            NULL, MB_OK);
      }

      int idx = 0;
```

```
        BOOL bSkillEasy = TRUE;
        BOOL bSkillMedium = TRUE;
        BOOL bSkillHard = TRUE;
        BOOL bSkillMulti = TRUE;

        // Try getting the user properties if they exist
        INode *node = gup->Max()->GetSelNode(0);
        node->GetUserPropInt("ItemType", idx);
        node->GetUserPropBool("SkillEasy", bSkillEasy);
        node->GetUserPropBool("SkillMedium",bSkillMedium);
        node->GetUserPropBool("SkillHard", bSkillHard);
        node->GetUserPropBool("SkillMulti", bSkillMulti);

        // Update the dialog controls.
        SendDlgItemMessage(hDlg, IDC_ITEMTYPE,
           CB_SETCURSEL, (WPARAM)idx, 0);
        SendDlgItemMessage(hDlg, IDC_SKILLEASY,
           BM_SETCHECK,
           (bSkillEasy ? BST_CHECKED : BST_UNCHECKED),0);
        SendDlgItemMessage(hDlg, IDC_SKILLMEDIUM,
           BM_SETCHECK,
           (bSkillMedium ? BST_CHECKED:BST_UNCHECKED),0);
        SendDlgItemMessage(hDlg, IDC_SKILLHARD,
           BM_SETCHECK,
           (bSkillHard ? BST_CHECKED : BST_UNCHECKED), 0);
        SendDlgItemMessage(hDlg, IDC_SKILLMULTI,
           BM_SETCHECK,
           (bSkillMulti ? BST_CHECKED : BST_UNCHECKED),0);
     }
     return TRUE;

  case WM_COMMAND:
     switch(LOWORD(wParam))
     {
     case IDOK:
        {
           // Get all the controls values
           int idx = SendDlgItemMessage(
              hDlg, IDC_ITEMTYPE, CB_GETCURSEL, 0, 0);
           BOOL bSkillEasy = SendDlgItemMessage(
```

```
                hDlg, IDC_SKILLEASY, BM_GETCHECK, 0, 0);
             BOOL bSkillMedium = SendDlgItemMessage(
                hDlg, IDC_SKILLMEDIUM, BM_GETCHECK, 0, 0);
             BOOL bSkillHard = SendDlgItemMessage(
                hDlg, IDC_SKILLHARD, BM_GETCHECK, 0, 0);
             BOOL bSkillMulti = SendDlgItemMessage(
                hDlg, IDC_SKILLMULTI, BM_GETCHECK, 0, 0);

             // Set the nodes custom properties
             INode *node = gup->Max()->GetSelNode(0);
             node->SetUserPropInt(
                "ItemType", idx);
             node->SetUserPropBool(
                "SkillEasy", bSkillEasy);
             node->SetUserPropBool(
                "SkillMedium", bSkillMedium);
             node->SetUserPropBool(
                "SkillHard", bSkillHard);
             node->SetUserPropBool(
                "SkillMulti", bSkillMulti);

             EndDialog(hDlg, 0);
             return TRUE;
          }

       case IDCANCEL:
          EndDialog(hDlg, 0);
          return TRUE;
       };
       break;
    }

    return FALSE;
}

// ==============================================================
DWORD GameUtil::Start()
{
   // Setup and register our right click menu
   custMenu.SetGUP(this);
   RightClickMenuManager *rcmm =
```

```
      Max()->GetRightClickMenuManager();
   rcmm->Register(&custMenu);

   // Register the notification callback
   RegisterNotification(
      SystemPostNew, this, NOTIFY_SYSTEM_POST_NEW);

   return GUPRESULT_KEEP;
}

// ===========================================================
void GameUtil::Stop()
{
   // unregister the right click menu
   RightClickMenuManager *rcmm =
      Max()->GetRightClickMenuManager();
   rcmm->Unregister(&custMenu);

   // Unregister the notification callback
   UnRegisterNotification(
      SystemPostNew, this, NOTIFY_SYSTEM_POST_NEW);
}

// ===========================================================
DWORD GameUtil::Control(DWORD parameter)
{
   // This function allows for other plug-ins to display
   // the dialogs.
   switch(parameter)
   {
   case ID_WORLDPROPERTIES:
      DoWorldPropertiesDlg();
      break;

   case ID_ENTITYPROPERTIES:
      DoEntityPropertiesDlg();
      break;
   };
   return 0;
}
```

```
// ============================================================
void GameUtil::DoWorldPropertiesDlg()
{
      DialogBoxParam(
         hInstance,
         MAKEINTRESOURCE(IDD_WORLDPROPERTIES),
         MaxWnd(),
         (DLGPROC)GameUtil::WorldPropDlgProc,
         (LONG)this);
}

// ============================================================
void GameUtil::DoEntityPropertiesDlg()
{
      DialogBoxParam(
         hInstance,
         MAKEINTRESOURCE(IDD_ENTITYPROPERTIES),
         MaxWnd(),
         (DLGPROC)GameUtil::EntityPropDlgProc,
         (LONG)this);
}

// ============================================================
void CustRCMenu::Init(
   RightClickMenuManager *manager, HWND hWnd, IPoint2 m)
{
   manager->AddMenu(this, MF_SEPARATOR, 0, NULL);
   if(gup->Max()->GetSelNodeCount() > 0)
   {
      manager->AddMenu(this, MF_STRING,ID_ENTITYPROPERTIES,
         _T("Entity Properties..."));
   }
   manager->AddMenu(this, MF_STRING, ID_WORLDPROPERTIES,
      _T("World Properties..."));
}

// ============================================================
void CustRCMenu::Selected(UINT id)
{
   gup->Control(id);
}
```

Summary

This chapter focused on Global Utility plug-ins along with some really cool MAX SDK features, like custom Right-Click menus, custom node and scene data, and callback notifications. With this set of programming tools, it is possible to create very powerful editing and customization plug-ins.

In the next chapter, we will explore MAXScript extensions and how they can extend the MAXScript scripting language.

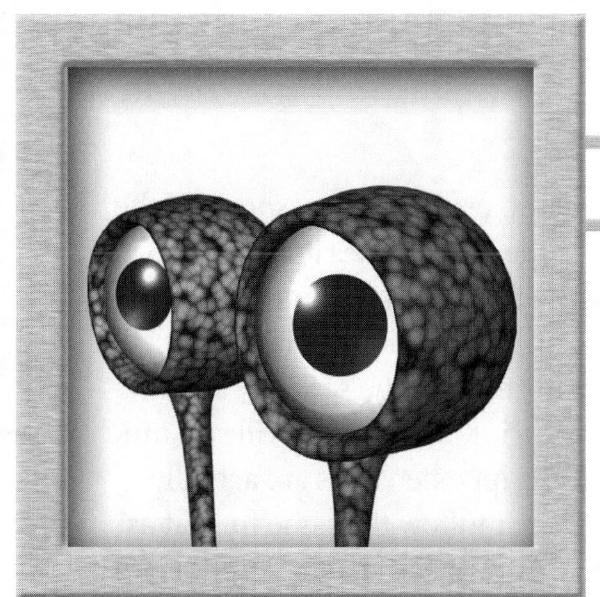

MAXScript Extensions

MAXSCRIPT

Chapter 18

The MAX SDK has the ability to extend many aspects of the MAXScript scripting language. This makes it possible to expose portions of the MAX SDK to the scripter that are not currently exposed; to implement utility functions, classes, and UI controls in C++ and to access them through the scripter; and to implement core functionality of a script in C++ that will run much faster for time-critical tasks. MAXScript extensions are actually plug-ins to the MAXScript and do not follow the same format as standard MAX plug-ins. The SDK App Wizard has no support for MAXScript extensions, so this chapter will go over details of creating an extension project for Developer Studio.

This chapter will cover the following topics:

- Creating a MAXScript extension
- The MAXScript SDK
- Exposing functions
- Exposing system variables

Creating a MAXScript Extension

MAXScript extensions are standard Win32 DLLs with a few functions exported so that the MAXScript core can check the version of the extension and call the extension's initialization function. MAXScript extensions use the file extension of `.DLX` and are placed in the `<3dsmax path>\plugins` directory, just as standard plug-ins are.

Building an Extension Skeleton

Use the following steps to create a MAXScript Extension project in Developer Studio:

1. In Developer Studio, select File ➔ New from the main menu.
2. Select Win32 Dynamic-Link Library from the Projects tab.
3. Type in the Project name **MxsUtils** and click OK.
4. Select "An empty DLL project" from the DLL choices and click Finish.
5. Click OK in the dialog that pops up.

Changing the Project Settings

Now that you have created a project, let's set up the paths and libraries that you will need to link to, to successfully create a MAXScript extension.

1. Select Project ➔ Settings... from the main menu.
2. Change the Settings For drop-down list to All Configurations.
3. Select Category General from the Debug tab and set the Executable for the debug session to `<3dsmax path>\3dsmax.exe`.
4. Select the Category Preprocessor from the C/C++ tab. Set the Additional include directories to `<3dsmax path>\maxsdk\include`.
5. Select Category General from the Link tab. Set the Output filename to `<3dsmax path>\plugins\MxsUtils.dlx`. Also, add the following libraries to the Object/library modules: `core.lib`, `geom.lib`, `gfx.lib`, `mesh.lib`, `maxutil.lib`, `maxscrpt.lib`, and `paramblk2.lib`.
6. In the Input Category of the Link tab, set the Additional library path to `<3dsmax path>\maxsdk\lib`.

Implementing the Export Functions

You should now have a Developer Studio project with all the correct settings to build the Extension DLL. Let's export the functions that the MAXScript core needs to correctly load the DLL as an extension.

The first function you will need to implement is the DLL's standard *DllMain* function. With this, you will grab onto the DLL's instance handle for later use. The function is declared as follows:

```
BOOL WINAPI DllMain(
   HINSTANCE hinstDLL,
   DWORD fdwReason,
   LPVOID lpvReserved);
```

There are three functions that need to be exported for MAXScript extensions:

void LibInit() This function is called right after loading the extension and should do any first time initialization that the plug-in needs.

const TCHAR* LibDescription() You should implement this function to return a description of what the extension does.

ULONG LibVersion() This function should return the MAX SDK version, just as a regular MAX plug-in does.

Creating DllEntry.cpp

To implement these functions in your extension project, create a new text file while your project is open by using File ➜ New ➜ Text File, or through the New Text File button on the toolbar. Save the file as `DllEntry.cpp`. Add the file to your project by using Project ➜ Add To Project ➜ Files. Implement the functions as described.

Your DllEntry file should look like Listing 18.1. You can access this code on the CD-ROM that accompanies this book in the file named `DllEntry.cpp`.

LISTING 18.1: EXPORT FUNCTIONS FOR MAXSCRIPT EXTENSIONS (*DLLENTRY.CPP*)

```
// =============================================================
// DllEntry.cpp
// Copyright ©2000, Simon Feltman
// -------------------------------------------------------------
```

```
#include "MAXScrpt/MAXScrpt.h"

HINSTANCE hInstance;

// ============================================================
// Grab onto this DLL's instance handle.
BOOL WINAPI DllMain(
   HINSTANCE hinstDLL,
   DWORD fdwReason,
   LPVOID lpvReserved)
 {
   switch(fdwReason)
   {
   case DLL_PROCESS_ATTACH:
      hInstance = hinstDLL;
      break;
   }
   return TRUE;
}

// ============================================================
// Put any initialization code needed for the extension
// in here.
__declspec(dllexport) void LibInit() {}

// ============================================================
// This should return a string describing what this
// extension does.
__declspec(dllexport) const TCHAR* LibDescription()
{
   return _T("MAXScript Utility Library");
}

// ============================================================
// Return the MAX SDK version.
__declspec(dllexport) ULONG LibVersion()
{
   return VERSION_3DSMAX;
}
```

Creating Exports.def

You will also need to create a module definition file (`.def`), which is similar to standard MAX plug-ins that will correctly export these functions from the DLL. Create a new text file named `MxsUtils.def` and add this to the project. This `.def` file should look like Listing 18.2. You can access this code on the CD-ROM in the file named `MxsUtils.def`.

LISTING 18.2: MODULE DEFINITION FILE (*MXSUTILS.DEF*)

```
LIBRARY MxsUtils
EXPORTS
   LibDescription      @1
   LibInit             @2
   LibVersion          @3
SECTIONS
   .data READ WRITE
```

With this `.def` file, your project should compile correctly into a MAXScript extension. You are now ready to add some functionality to MAXScript using this as your base.

The MAXScript SDK

The *MAXScript SDK* is a subset of the MAX SDK that provides many classes and macros for wrapping C++ functions and classes. These wrappers make C++ functions and classes visible to the MAXScript language. These macros help hide details of how code gets exposed and make programming a lot easier.

Data classes in the MAXScript SDK are derived from the generic class `Value`. This allows for MAXScript to work with generic `Value` objects that store type information. This allows for `Value`-derived objects to be passed around in MAXScript and for run-time–type checking to be used in both MAXScript and the MAXScript SDK.

Global Value Instances

The MAXScript SDK contains a few global instances of `Value`-based classes that only need one instance. Table 18.1 is a list of global instanced `Value`-based classes.

Table 18.1 Global Instanced *Value*-Based Classes

Global Instance	Description
`undefined`	This is a global instance of the `Undefined` class, which is usually assigned to values that have not yet been initialized.
`ok`	The `ok` global is an instance of the `Ok` class, which is used for a return value for functions that don't return a useful value.
`unsupplied`	The `unsupplied` global is an instance of the `Unsupplied` class, which can be used to pass to functions that don't require a parameter.
`true_value`	`True_value` is an instance of the `Boolean` class that can be used directly to test if values of the `Boolean` type are true by comparing the value's pointer with the address of `true_value`.
`false_value`	`False_value` is an instance of the `Boolean` class that can be used directly to test if values of the `Boolean` type are false by comparing the value's pointer with the address of `false_value`.

Type Checking Values

The `Value` class contains functions for type checking `Value` class pointers. The `Value` class also contains a public data member named `tag`, which is a pointer to the type that the class is. With the `tag` member, you can directly identify what type the `Value` class is. The following is a list of functions and macros that can be used to test a value's type.

class_tag This is a macro that returns a class tag from a class name. You can use this to directly test the tag member of a `Value` class instance as follows:

```
Value *val = &undefined;
if(val->tag == class_tag(Undefined))
{
   // the class is of Undefined type
}
```

type_check This is a macro that throws a type error exception if the `Value` passed does not have the same type tag as the class passed. The following is an example of using this macro:

```
Value *val = &true_value;
type_check(val, Boolean, "<function is failed in>: ");
```

is_kind_of This is a virtual member function of the `Value` class, which tests all class tags of underlying parent classes. The following is an example of using the *is_kind_of* virtual member function:

```
Value *val = &unsupplied;
if(val->is_kind_of(class_tag(Unsupplied)))
{
   // val can either directly be of type Unsupplied or
   // derived from Unsupplied.
}
```

Wrappers for C++ Types and Classes

The MAXScript SDK contains many classes that wrap C++ data types and MAX SDK classes. These wrappers have a direct correspondence to the data types available in MAXScript. Table 18.2 is a list of data types and classes with the corresponding MAXScript SDK wrapper. All wrappers are in some way derived from `Value`.

Table 18.2 Data Types and MAXScript Wrappers

C++ Type or Class	MAXScript Wrapper Class
float	Float
TCHAR*	String
int	Integer
BOOL	Boolean
BitArray	BitArrayValue
Point3	Point3Value
Point2	Point2Value
AColor	ColorValue
COLORREF	ColorValue
INode	MAXNode
Object	MAXObject
Ray	RayValue
Interval	MSInterval
Quat	QuatValue

Table 18.2 Data Types and MAXScript Wrappers (*continued*)

C++ Type or Class	MAXScript Wrapper Class
AngAxis	AngAxisValue
Matrix3	Matrix3Value
Bitmap	MAXBitMap
Modifier	MAXModifier
TimeValue	MSTime
Control	MAXControl
ReferenceTarget	MAXRefTarg
Mesh	MeshValue

Constructing MAXScript Values

Use the following list of constructors to create Value-based data type wrappers that will be visible in MAXScript:

- `Value* Float::intern(float init_val)`
- `Value* Integer::intern(int init_val)`
- `Value* Name::intern(char* str)`
- `Value* Name::find_intern(char* str)`
- `Value* MSTime::intern(TimeValue t)`
- `AngAxisValue(const AngAxis& iaa)`
- `AngAxisValue(const Matrix3& m)`
- `AngAxisValue(const Quat& q)`
- `AngAxisValue(float angle, Point3 axis)`
- `AngAxisValue(float* angles)`
- `AngAxisValue(Value* angle, Value* axis)`

- AngAxisValue(Value*)
- Array(int init_size)
- ColorValue(AColor col)
- ColorValue(BMM_Color_64& col)
- ColorValue(Color col)
- ColorValue(COLORREF col)
- ColorValue(float r, float g, float b, float a = 1.0f)
- ColorValue (Point3 col)
- ColorValue(Point3Value* col)
- EulerAnglesValue(const AngAxis&)
- EulerAnglesValue(const Matrix3&)
- EulerAnglesValue(const Quat&)
- EulerAnglesValue(float ax, float ay, float az)
- Matrix3Value(const AngAxis& aa)
- Matrix3Value(const Matrix3& im)
- Matrix3Value(const Point3& row0, const Point3& row1 , const Point3& row2, Point3& row3)
- Matrix3Value(const Quat& q)
- Matrix3Value(float* angles)
- Matrix3Value(int i)
- MSInterval(Interval i)
- MSInterval(TimeValue s, TimeValue e)
- Point2Value(float x, float y)
- Point2Value(POINT ipoint)
- Point2Value(Point2 ipoint)

- `Point2Value(Value* x, Value* y)`
- `Point3Value(float x, float y, float z)`
- `Point3Value(Point3 init_point)`
- `Point3Value(Value* x, Value* y, Value* z)`
- `QuatValue(AngAxis& aa)`
- `QuatValue(const Quat& init_quat)`
- `QuatValue(float w, float x, float y, float z)`
- `QuatValue(float* angles)`
- `QuatValue(Matrix3& m)`
- `QuatValue(Value* val)`
- `QuatValue(Value* w, Value* x, Value* y, Value* z)`
- `RayValue(Point3 init_origin, Point3 init_dir)`
- `RayValue(Ray init_ray)`

Casting Values

Casting a `Value` pointer is as simple as just casting the pointer to the appropriate type. First, type check the pointer, then cast it to the type that you checked. The following is an example of how you can do this:

```
Value *val = new Point3Value(1.f, 1.f, 1.f);
if(val->tag == class_tag(Point3Value))
{
   Point3Value *pnt3val = (Point3Value*)val;
}
```

Converting from MAXScript Data Types to C++ Data Types

The `Value` class contains many virtual functions for converting a MAXScript `Value`-based class to a C++ type or class. Table 18.3 is a list of conversion member functions of the `Value` class.

Table 18.3 *Value* Class Conversion Member Functions

C++ Return Type	*Value* Class Member Function
`float`	*to_float()*
`TCHAR*`	*to_string()*
`int`	*to_int()*
`BOOL`	*to_bool()*
`BitArray&`	*to_bitarray()*
`Point3`	*to_point3()*
`Point2`	*to_point2()*
`AColor`	*to_acolor()*
`COLORREF`	*to_colorref()*
`INode*`	*to_node()*
`Ray`	*to_ray()*
`Interval`	*to_interval()*
`Quat`	*to_quat()*
`AngAxis`	*to_angaxis()*
`Matrix3&`	*to_matrix3()*
`float*`	*to_eulerangles()*
`Mtl*`	*to_mtl()*
`Texmap*`	*to_texmap()*
`MtlBase*`	*to_mtlbase()*
`Modifier*`	*to_modifier()*
`TimeValue`	*to_timevalue()*
`Control*`	*to_controller()*
`Atmospheric*`	*to_atmospheric()*
`Effect*`	*to_effect()*
`ShadowType*`	*to_shadowtype()*
`FilterKernel*`	*to_filter()*
`INode*`	*to_rootnode()*
`ITrackViewNode*`	*to_trackviewnode()*
`ReferenceTarget*`	*to_reftarg()*
`Mesh*`	*to_mesh()*

These conversion functions check the `Value` class's tag to make sure that it is of the appropriate type. They then return the corresponding C++ type or class. If the `Value` class being converted is not of an appropriate type, MAXScript will throw a conversion error exception. The following code shows some examples of converting a MAXScript wrapped data type to a direct C++ data type:

```
// Create an integer Value and convert back to a C++ int
Value *iVal = Integer::intern(256);
int i = ival->to_int();

// Create a Point3Value and convert back to a C++ Point3
Value *pntVal = new Point3Value(0.f, 0.f, 0.f);
Point3 pnt = pntVal->to_point3();
```

Exposing Functions

Functions are exposed to MAXScript by creating an instance of the `Function` class, which is a direct descendant of the `Value` class. In the `Function` classes constructor, you pass a pointer to a C++ function and a string name that will be used as the scripter-visible function name. The C++ function that you want exposed will get passed an array of `Value` pointers and a number, which tells how many elements are in the array. This method is very similar to the way the *main* function works in ANSI C, except that the C++ function is passed an array of `Values` rather than an array of strings. C++ functions that get exposed to MAXScript are usually declared as follows:

```
Value* function(Value **arg_list, int count);
```

The `Function` class's constructor registers the function pointer and scripter-visible name that you pass to the MAXScript core. There are many macros that can automatically create an instance of a `Function` class and its descendants.

Function Registration Macros

The following is a list of macros that are used for registering C++ functions to be visible in the MAXScript language.

def_visible_primitive(<C++ function name>, <scripter-visible string>) The `def_visible_primitive` macro declares the C++ global function and passes it the Function class's constructor. You are then required to implement this C++ function, which is declared as follows:

```
Value* <C++ function name>_cf(Value **arg_list, int count);
```

def_struct_primitive(<C++ function name>, <scripter struct>, <scripter-visible name>) The def_stuct_primitive macro is very similar to the def_visible_primitive macro, except that the scripter-visible name is categorized into a global structure in MAXScript. The C++ function declared by this macro works in exactly the same way that the def_visible_primitive macro declares C++ functions.

def_mapped_primitive(<C++ function pointer>, <scripter-visible string>) A mapped primitive is a function that automatically iterates over a collection of values passed to the function in MAXScript. The C++ function declared by this macro works in exactly the same way that the def_visible_primitive macro declares C++ functions.

Checking Parameter Counts

Within the C++ function definition, it is a good idea to check the parameter count that is passed so that you can guarantee that you are getting the correct number of arguments. Since MAXScript itself does not know the proper argument count that your function requires, you must do it manually. There are a few macros that can help with this and give an error message if the argument count is not correct. The following is a list of macros used for checking argument counts.

check_arg_count(<C++ function name>, <required argument count>, <argument count>) The check_arg_count macro tests the required argument count against the argument count that your function was passed and throws an argument count error exception if they are not the same. The following is an example of using the check_arg_count macro:

```
Value* my_func_cf(Value **arg_list, int count)
{
   check_arg_count(my_func, 2, count);

   // use the arguments..
   arg_list[0]->to_string();
   arg_list[1]->to_boolean();

   return &ok;
}
```

check_arg_count_with_keys(<C++ function name>, <required argument count>, <argument count>) In MAXScript, it is possible to pass optional key arguments to functions. The `check_arg_count_with_keys` macro checks the required argument count and leaves out the optional arguments in the check.

Working with Optional Arguments

To allow functions to work with optional arguments, first check the required argument count with `check_arg_count_with_keys`, then get the optional key argument using the `key_arg` or `key_arg_or_default` macro.

Before using key arguments, you must first define the key names that will be used with the function. Keys are defined by type `Name`, which is derived from `Value` and is used to represent non-string names. Keys are declared globally and initialized in the *LibInit* exported function. Keys are declared and assigned using the `def_name` macro. This macro gives the key a unique `Value` depending on what header file is included before using the `def_name` macro. The following is an example of creating keys and using them in a function that uses optional key arguments:

```
// This will define the correct macro to declare
// globals for option1 and option2.
#include "MAXScrpt/lclinsfn.h"
def_name(option1);
def_name(option2);

void LibInit()
{
   // This will define the correct macro to assign
   // the globals a
   #include "MAXScrpt/lclimpfn.h"
   def_name(option1);
   def_name(option2);
}

Value* my_func_cf(Value **arg_list, int count)
{
   check_arg_count_with_keys(my_func, 1, count);
   INode *node = arg_list[0]->to_node();
   Value *opt1 = key_arg(option1);
   Value *opt2 = key_arg(option2);
   return &ok;
}
```

The key_arg macro will return unsupplied if the argument is not specified when the function is called in MAXScript. To deal with unsupplied arguments, you can either test what is returned from key_arg against the address of the unsupplied global variable or use the key_arg_with_default macro.

Exposing System Variables

System variables in MAXScript are global variables that you can get and set the value of. When setting or getting a system variable, the MAXScript core will call C++ *get* and *set* functions that you define.

Get and *Set* Functions

The C++ functions used with system variables are defined by *get* and *set* functions. These functions must be declared as follows:

```
Value* <get_function_name>();
Value* <set_function_name>(Value *val);
```

Registering System Variables

To register system variables, the MAXScript SDK has two global functions for doing this. Both functions need to be called when the *LibInit* export function of your extension is called. The functions are defined as follows:

define_system_global(TCHAR* name, Value* (*getter)(), Value* (*setter)(Value*))
Call this function to register a general system global. Pass this function the string name, *get* function, and *set* function. You can also pass this function NULL for either the *getter* or *setter* to make the global read or write only, or both. The following is an example of using the *define_system_global* function:

```
BOOL bGlobal = FALSE;

Value* get_val()
{
   return (bGlobal ? &true_value : &false_value);
}

Value* set_val(Value *val)
```

```
{
   bGlobal = val->to_boolean();
   return &ok;
}

void Init()
{
   define_system_global("bGlobal", get_val, set_val);
}
```

define_struct_global(TCHAR* name, TCHAR* struct_name, Value* (*getter)(), Value* (*setter)(Value*)) The *define_struct_global* function is very similar to the *define_system_global* function except that the variable will show up in the global structure that is specified.

Completing the MxsUtils Extension

Now that you know how to expose functions and system globals to MAXScript, let's add some to the MxsUtils project that you started earlier.

First, you will need to create an empty file, save it as `ClassCfg.h`, and add it to the project. This file is required in your project if you are defining new keys, but it doesn't necessarily have to have anything in it. After this, create a new file named `MxsUtils.cpp` and add it to the project. This will be the main file that you implement your functions and system globals in. Listing 18.3 is a full working example of exposing a function to MAXScript. Use this as a base and add any other functions or system globals to this file.

LISTING 18.3: MAIN PLUG-IN FILE FOR THE MXSUTILS PROJECT (*MXSUTILS.CPP*)

```
// ==========================================================
// MxsUtils.cpp
// Copyright ©2000, Simon Feltman
// ----------------------------------------------------------
#include "MAXScrpt/MAXScrpt.h"
#include "MAXScrpt/3DMath.h"
#include "MAXScrpt/Name.h"

// Declare C++ function and register it with MAXScript
#include "MAXScrpt/definsfn.h"
   def_visible_primitive(GetCursorPos, "GetCursorPos");
```

```
// Declare key names
#include "MAXScrpt/lclinsfn.h"
   def_name(relative);

// ===========================================================
void MxsUtilsInit()
{
// Initialize key names
#include "MAXScrpt/lclimpfn.h"
   def_name(relative);
}

// ===========================================================
Value* GetCursorPos_cf(Value **arg_list, int count)
{
   check_arg_count_with_keys(GetCursorPos, 0, count);

   // Get the cursor position from windows
   POINT pnt;
   GetCursorPos(&pnt);

   // If the optional key argument was specified
   BOOL bRelative = key_arg_or_default(relative,
      &false_value)->to_bool();

   if(bRelative)
   {
      // Calculate cursor position relative from
      // underlying window
      HWND hWnd = WindowFromPoint(pnt);
      if(hWnd != NULL)
      {
         RECT rect;
         GetWindowRect(hWnd, &rect);
         pnt.x -= rect.left;
         pnt.y -= rect.top;
      }
   }

   // Return a new Point2 that is visible to MAXScript
   return new Point2Value(pnt.x, pnt.y);
}
```

Summary

In this chapter, you learned how to expose C++ functions and globals to the MAXScript language using the MAXScript extension SDK. This can be very useful for customizing the current scripter and making it more powerful.

This chapter did not, however, cover exposing classes and UI controls to MAXScript. You can accomplish this by using the knowledge from this chapter in combination with the examples that come with the MAX SDK.

Index

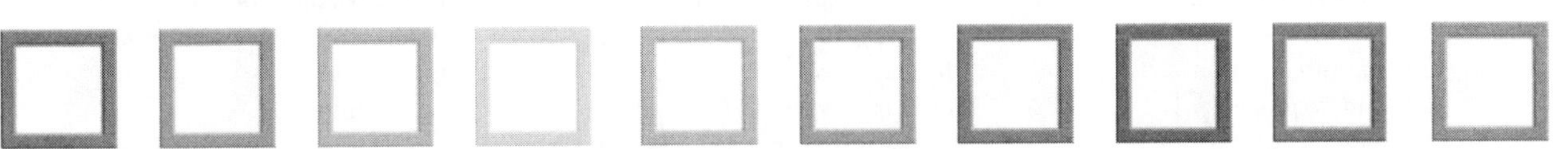

Note to the Reader: Throughout this index **boldfaced** page numbers indicate primary discussions of a topic. *Italicized* page numbers indicate illustrations.

A

D

F

G

H

N

Q

R

T

V

W

X

Y

Z

What's on the CD-ROM

This CD-ROM is packed with scripts and plug-ins to help you work through the tutorials in this book. You can check them out as you read the chapters and play around with them as you experiment on your own. We included Adobe Acrobat and Internet Explorer 5 to read HTML and PDF files.

The CD-ROM also contains MAXScript extensions and scripts from expert programmers and 3D artists, as well as their Web site addresses so you can stay up-to-date.

The CD-ROM includes useful plug-ins, such as

- **MAXScript Control Library 2.2** By Simon Feltman, this is a suite of UI controls and methods to make sharp interfaces for MAXScript.
- **Binary File Stream MAXScript Extension** By Simon Feltman, this plug-in allows you to read and write binary data in 8-, 16-, and 32-bit formats along with strings.
- **Mulitple Mapping Channel MAXScript Extension** By Simon Feltman, this plug-in accesses all 99 mapping channels available through the scripter!
- **Skeletal Animation Viewer and Export Plug-in for 3D Studio MAX Application and Plug-in** By Simon Feltman, this application exports meshes and animations from MAX and views them in the real-time viewer. Supports Character Studio and the MAX Skin modifier.
- **Avguard MAXScript Extensions** By Chris Dragon, this plug-in adds MAXScript functionality to your scripts.
- **MAXScript Shortcuts Manager** By Chris Dragon, this plug-in allows you to assign keyboard shortcuts to scripts.
- **Mousetrack Extension** By John Wainwright, this plug-in allows you to attach a function driven by the mouse movement on-screen.